D0897714

Theocritus's Urban Mimes

HELLENISTIC CULTURE AND SOCIETY
General Editors: Anthony W. Bulloch, Erich S. Gruen,
A. A. Long, and Andrew F. Stewart

Theocritus's Urban Mimes

Mobility, Gender, and Patronage

Joan B. Burton

UNIVERSITY OF CALIFORNIA PRESS

Berkeley / Los Angeles / London

University of California Press
Berkeley and Los Angeles, California

University of California Press, Ltd.
London, England

© 1995 by the Regents of the University of California

Library of Congress Cataloging-in-Publication Data

Burton, Joan B., 1951–
    Theocritus's urban mimes : mobility, gender, and patronage /
Joan B. Burton.
      p.   cm. — (Hellenistic culture and society ; 19)
    Includes bibliographical references and index.
    ISBN 0-520-08858-1 (alk. paper)
    1. Theocritus — Political and social views. 2. Greek poetry,
Hellenistic — Egypt — Alexandria — History and criticism. 3. Literature and society — Egypt — Alexandria — History. 4. Women
and literature — Egypt — Alexandria — History. 5. Authors and
patrons — Egypt — Alexandria — History. 6. Art and state —
Egypt — Alexandria — History. 7. Social mobility in literature.
8. Sex role in literature. I. Title. II. Series.
PA4444.B87 1995
884'.01 — dc20   94-28938
                                                          CIP

Printed in the United States of America
9 8 7 6 5 4 3 2 1

The paper used in this publication meets the minimum requirements of
American National Standard for Information Sciences — Permanence of
Paper for Printed Library Materials, ANSI Z39.48-1984.

Contents

Acknowledgments

My greatest debt is to my teacher and friend, Anthony Bulloch, who started me reading Hellenistic poetry and whose example of scholarly excellence has been an inspiration ever since. I would also like to thank my many other teachers at the University of California, Berkeley. I am particularly grateful to Florence Verducci for her early confidence and support. Amelia Van Vleck read portions of an early version of this book and gave helpful advice. David Stinchcomb read the entire manuscript with great care and provided a general reader for me to address. I am thankful for the interest and support of my colleagues at Trinity University during the period of my writing this book, particularly Colin Wells and James Pearce. Trinity University awarded me the John Rogers Faculty Fellowship, which provided support for three summers to work on the book. I also thank my students, particularly the members of my courses on gender and identity, for their willingness to listen to fledgling ideas. While formulating these ideas, I delivered several papers at academic conferences, and I would like to thank the audiences for their comments. I am very grateful to the anonymous readers of the University of California Press for their careful attention and valuable comments, which helped improve the book significantly, to Anthony Bulloch and Erich Gruen for their helpful suggestions as series editors, and to Mary Lamprech, Tony Hicks, Alice Falk, Diana Murin, and Roberta Engleman for their generous support and assistance in preparing the manuscript for the Press. I would also like to thank my family and friends for their steady faith in my work and ideas.

Portions of the discussions of the symposium in chapter 1 and of Ptolemy in chapter 4 previously appeared in "The Function of the Symposium Theme in Theocritus' *Idyll* 14," *Greek, Roman, and Byzantine Studies* 33 (1992), 227–45.

A Note on Texts, Translations, and Abbreviations

All citations of Theocritus's Greek text are taken from A. S. F. Gow, *Theocritus*, 2d ed., 2 vols. (Cambridge: Cambridge University Press, 1952), vol. 1. All citations of Herodas's Greek text are taken from I. C. Cunningham, *Herodae Mimiambi cum Appendice Fragmentorum Mimorum Papyraceorum* (Leipzig: B. G. Teubner, 1987). All citations of Callimachus's Greek text are taken from Rudolf Pfeiffer, *Callimachus*, 2 vols. (Oxford: Clarendon Press, 1949–53), unless marked otherwise. The sources of other texts are identified as they appear. All translations are my own unless marked otherwise. Ancient writers and works are abbreviated as in *The Oxford Classical Dictionary,* 2d ed., ed. N. G. L. Hammond and H. H. Scullard (Oxford: Clarendon Press, 1970).

Introduction

Because of current attention to the effects of ethnicity, class, and gender,[1] as well as colonialism and patronage,[2] on audience reception of works of art and on the creative imagination,[3] readers today are in a position to pose new questions of Hellenistic poetry which were relevant to its contemporary audience but perhaps not as accessible to formulation by past generations of scholars. Thus a crucial debate has arisen concerning the principal forces that define the Alexandrian poetic sensibility. The forces traditionally assumed are elitism, aestheticism (the credo of "art for art's sake"), and irony; realism and romanticism are sometimes rejected, sometimes suggested as central. The exclusive museum community at Alexandria and the library's emphasis on textual scholarship support the association of Alexandrian poetry with elitism and encourage the linkage of Hellenistic poetry with aestheticism.[4] Yet the nature of our understanding of elitism and aestheticism must change in conjunction with an increased awareness of the social and cultural forces at work during the Hellenistic period, and scholars are beginning to pay more attention to how questions of gender can affect our view of Hellenistic poetry[5] and to explore Hellenistic poetry's engagement with issues linked to mobility, colonialism, and immigration.[6] Theocritus's urban mimes — *Idylls* 2, 14, and 15 — are central examples of the value of these considerations in approaching Hellenistic poetry, for their representations of the experiences of urban Greeks in a mobile Hellenistic world highlight issues of gender relations, colonialism, immigration, and cultural dislocation.

This study focuses on how Theocritus's urban mimes explore issues of contemporary importance in the Hellenistic age: the impact of mobility on social and cultural life, the role of gender in power relations, the function of aesthetic experience in life, and the influence of court patronage on the poetic imagination. Theocritus's urban mimes *Idylls* 2 and 15 are often cited in discussions of Hellenistic religion and magic (e.g., Arnold, Atallah, Green, Winkler, Kraemer),[7] Alexandrian life (e.g., Fraser, Green, Smith),[8] Hellenistic women (e.g., Seltman, Schneider, Pomeroy, Griffiths),[9] and Hellenistic aesthetics (e.g., Hagstrum, Zanker, Green).[10] Further, *Idyll* 15 is routinely cited as evidence of the Adonis festival and Arsinoe's patronage.[11] *Idyll* 14 seems to have been overlooked by cultural historians, but as this book shows, its representation of a nonelite symposium, mercenary soldiery, and friendship among mobile Hellenistic males can also contribute significantly toward our picture of Hellenistic life.[12] Most recent studies of Theocritus concentrate on his bucolic poems.[13] But in view of the importance of Theocritus's urban mimes to the cultural and literary history of the Hellenistic world, and especially Ptolemaic Alexandria, a unified study of these mimes, with attention to social, cultural, and literary issues, is long overdue.

The text is organized as follows. Chapter 1 focuses on themes of mobility, immigration, and social assimilation, and includes the topics of friendship and the symposium. Chapter 2 explores gender issues that arise in the urban mimes. Chapter 3 examines the motif of rhetorical description of visual art, with a focus on representations of women viewing works of art. Chapter 4 explores themes of patronage and politics that arise in Theocritus's urban mimes, with particular attention to Queen Arsinoe's powerful role in the cultural life of Ptolemaic Alexandria.

In the Hellenistic age, the trend of migration toward cultural and economic centers caused an increasing cosmopolitanism and internationalism of these centers. Theocritus's urban mimes explore the conditions of life in such centers, the possible feelings of isolation and powerlessness, the need of dislocated persons to reestablish self-identity. Like many other poets and intellectual figures of his day, Theocritus's travels eventually led him to the great cultural center of Alexandria. Although Theocritus's urban mimes center on the experiences of ordinary men and women, poetic explorations of issues of displacement and cultural alienation could appeal to Alexandrian court intellectuals, themselves mostly immigrants. The encomium of Ptolemy in Theocritus's *Idyll* 14 and the celebration of Arsinoe's Adonis festival in *Idyll* 15 make the Ptolemaic court an obvious audience of these two urban mimes.

Arsinoe herself was not unfamiliar with life as a displaced person.[14] Ptolemy I sent her abroad at age sixteen to marry Thrace's elderly king, Lysimachus;[15] nineteen years and three sons later, she lost her husband in a battle against Seleucus and her half-brother Ceraunus (281 B.C.). She fled from Arsinoeia (Ephesus) in disguise, retreating to Lysimachus's Macedonian stronghold Cassandreia. Meanwhile the ambitious Ceraunus, heading north with Seleucus to conquer Macedonia, killed his benefactor as he stepped from a boat at Lysimacheia (App. *Syr.* 63). Ceraunus's recent act of treachery made him amorous: he stopped at Cassandreia to ask the widowed Arsinoe to marry him.[16] Hoping to ensure her security Arsinoe agreed, but cautiously demanded an oath from Ceraunus, as well as a wedding ceremony witnessed by the military force. These juridical measures did not deflect Ceraunus's murderous ambition, however. Shortly after the wedding, assassins killed her two younger sons and Arsinoe fled again, this time to Samothrace, an international cult center. Thence, after twenty years away, she returned to Egypt, a widow with child, stripped of queenship and unsure of the future. Certainly the topics of mobility, gender, and power in Theocritus's urban mimes would have struck a responsive chord in Arsinoe.

The Ptolemaic family's enterprising manipulations of Greek cultural norms, as exemplified by Arsinoe's strikingly successful dynastic career in Egypt,[17] would have presented many challenges to artistic imagination and tact. When she returned from abroad, her prospects for queenship in Egypt did not appear favorable: her full brother Ptolemy II had recently ascended to the throne and already had a queen, Arsinoe's own stepdaughter by Lysimachus. Yet a creative solution was available, if one disregarded the incest taboo, the unconventional difference in age (Arsinoe was eight years older), and Ptolemy's marital status. We can only guess what machinations led to the banishment of Ptolemy II's first wife to Coptus for treason,[18] but the result was that Arsinoe married her full brother Ptolemy II and again became a queen.[19] Although inventive marriage maneuvers were the norm among Alexander's successors and their progeny, still the incestuous irregularity of Ptolemy and Arsinoe's marriage challenged normative Greek social and hegemonic expectations.[20] The royal house was defiantly assertive about the relationship, with Arsinoe adopting the title *Philadelphos*, "brother-lover." Fraser suggests that Arsinoe's epithet *Philadelphos* "had a positive moral significance, 'fraternal' in the best sense, 'full of brotherly love,' and this helped both to soften the incestuous nature of the relationship and to emphasize the community of rule between brother and sister."[21] Whatever the epithet's intention, by the end of Arsinoe's reign, the iconography of

Ptolemaic coinage represented a sovereignty shared by husband and wife: some coins emphasize the royal partnership by showing the queen in jugate with (and looking remarkably like) the king, and others show the queen alone.[22] Thus, Arsinoe and Ptolemy's dynamic career transformed the Greek view of monarchy and contributed to a hegemonic myth which poets could reflect, explore, reinforce, and test by such devices as seemingly gratuitous references to Zeus and Hera's union.[23] Indiscreet remarks could be risky, however: Sotades' scurrilous verses on Ptolemy's marriage to Arsinoe sent him to prison, and he ended his bold career in a lead casket at the bottom of the sea.[24] Yet to talk about a dominant regime does not necessarily mean one defends it: a poet can explore it because it is worthy of being explored — its exploration helps make sense of the world in which a poet finds him- or herself.

For poets grounded in Alexandria during the period of Arsinoe's queenship, and thus witness to the changes in gender roles and hegemony exemplified by Arsinoe's extraordinary career, relationships between men and women could become a natural forum for addressing issues of hierarchy, change, and power. Factors of importance for the creative enterprise in the Hellenistic age included an increase in women's visibility and an emphasis on heterosexuality and the sensual female, as shown by, e.g., the dramatic rise in lush nude female statuary emulating fourth-century Praxiteles' Knidian Aphrodite.[25] The expansion of women's economic and social rights since the fifth century included the use of marriage contracts in Egypt,[26] the expansion of education for females and the limited introduction of coeducational schools,[27] the admission of women (and slaves) to the philosophical cults of the Epicureans and the Cynics,[28] and the increased opportunities for women to attain civic honors for philanthropic activity and to win prizes in poetry and athletic contests.[29]

With women's greater visibility in the public domain comes a greater awareness among men of a female presence in audiences as well. Theocritus's urban mimes, by exploring interactions of males and females at home, at a symposium, on the public streets, and in a festival audience, provide representations of the effects of an increasing female presence. Two of Theocritus's three urban mimes are presented through women characters. *Idyll* 2, Simaetha's monologue, focuses on an urban woman's response to being mistreated by a man, and *Idyll* 15, a mime in dialogue form, focuses on a friendship between two housewives, Praxinoa and Gorgo.[30] The third urban mime, *Idyll* 14, explores the effects of a woman's disruption of a male-defined symposium. An older, sentimental view of Theocritus as "an intelligent and sensitive feminist"[31] has now been essentially dismissed by scholars.[32] Instead, assumptions of elitism underlie a pervasive scholarly judgment that such poems as *Idyll* 15 are designed to mock their fictive women. A recent, sophisticated evaluation of *Idyll* 15 locates this mockery of the female characters in a class- and culture-based collusion between poet and royal patron against "the masses."[33] But this study shows that the choice about *Idyll* 15's representations of fictive women is not limited to naive sentimentality, dismissive mockery, or a sophisticated reconstruction of elitist mockery.

An important factor in a consideration of Hellenistic poetry is the dependence of the arts and sciences on court patronage. Griffiths's important monograph, *Theocritus at Court,* examines the influence of patronage on Theocritus's poetry. But this salutary move away from overemphasis on Hellenistic "aestheticism" can lead a reader to oversimplify the relation between court and poet and to conclude that poetry oriented toward the court must parrot the dominant regime's ideology: so Griffiths himself, in a later discussion of *Idyll* 15, asserts that "the women are better able to bear their oppressive home lives because of periodic enjoyment of such escapist fantasies, while their pronounced limitations as people confirm the essential justice of the social stratification."[34] Schwinge's monograph, on the other hand, draws much-needed attention to politically oppositional aspects of Alexandrian poetry,[35] but in making his case, Schwinge sometimes overplays elements of negativism in courtly poetry.[36] Most scholars basically follow Griffiths's lead, however. Thus one scholar recently described *Idylls* 14, 15, and 17 as "grandiose propaganda for Ptolemy's monarchy."[37] Yet what might appear to be prevailing orthodoxies of the period within poetic fictions need not be interpreted as a defense of the ideologies, but an occasion to acknowledge and to probe them. The Alexandrian poets were writing during a period of major social and hegemonic change. Alexander the Great's conquests had transformed the political geography of the Greek world irretrievably: the old city-state world had been replaced by large commercial bureaucratic kingdoms, and this hegemonic change affected all aspects of life, public and private.

A risk in privileging any artificial construct such as a static *Zeitgeist* (e.g., elitism) is that readers may become inappropriately complacent through models that do not help them recognize the distinctive pleasures of the various poems. For example, a focus on elitism in Hellenistic poetry can result in the perennial equation of the fictive women represented in Theocritus's *Idyll* 15 and Herodas's *Mime* 4: "We eavesdrop on a group of women, as featherbrained and talkative as Theocritus's Syracusan matrons, making *ex voto* offerings in the temple of Asclepius, and praising, like so many Aunt Ednas, the realism of the artwork on display."[38]

Further, in the course of writing on Theocritus's pastoral poetry, scholars often merge the social responses evoked by Theocritus's urban mimes and his pastoral poetry.[39] Yet the factor of gender complicates any attempt to equalize social responses toward the fictive characters of Theocritus's pastoral and urban poems. Theocritus's pastoral poems explore the function of song and friendship by focusing on the male experience, with women entering the poems mostly as the "other," who can reject or threaten a male's sense of autonomy and integrity, and thus paradoxically reinforce male friendships and solidarity. All of Theocritus's urban mimes, on the other hand, represent women in more central and powerful roles, and two are presented through female characters and represent the subjective experiences of women.[40]

In summary, mobility was an important factor in the experience of persons living in the Hellenistic world. For many Greek men, there was a diminishment of public political power linked with the rise of autocratic hegemonies. But for women, life's opportunities in many ways expanded due to the rise in mobility. All these factors affected the ways men and women perceived themselves, the world, and each other. Also, Hellenistic poets were writing in a world where royal sponsorship dominated cultural life and audiences for modern works of art seemed limited. Theocritus's urban mimes reflect these changing conditions and explore the effects of these changes on the production of art, the lives of ordinary persons, and relations with the royal court. This study shows the value of approaching Theocritus's urban mimes by suspending preconceived notions about elitism or aestheticism and instead interposing questions about such issues as mobility and ethnicity, immigration and assimilation, gender and power, audience reception and the academy, and patronage and the creative project.

CHAPTER I

Mobility and Immigration

The Hellenistic age was a time of great mobility for Greeks. Alexander's conquest of the Persian Empire had resulted in tremendous expansion of the Greek world, with the spread of Greek settlements from Egypt to India.[1] Cities founded or restructured by Alexander and his successors privileged Greek settlers and provided generous employment opportunities for such itinerants as mercenary soldiers, traders, physicians, temple builders, scholars, actors, and prostitutes.[2] The dominance of autocratic hegemonies and the decline of city-state autonomy helped loosen local ties for many Greeks, while the glittering wealth of such new centers of culture and power as Alexandria offered significant attractions. A social order favoring Greeks helped offset Greek anxieties about moving into places where Greeks were a minority, but many social and political problems faced immigrant and itinerant Greeks, not least the problem of maintaining a sense of Greek identity when separated from the traditions of home and surrounded by an alien culture.[3]

Many forces can encourage mobility: poverty, war, famine, political upheaval, commerce, occupational opportunities, tourism, etc. Mobility and colonization were nothing new to the Greek world. The archaic age was also a period of great colonization and expansion.[4] Greek tyrants traditionally offered employment to such itinerants as poets, artists, builders, and mercenary soldiers. The Ionian revolt and the Persian wars caused many Greeks of Asia Minor to move West. Individuals — even entire city populations — relocated, sometimes voluntarily, sometimes not.[5] After the Peloponnesian war, during the fourth century, the mo-

bility of individuals seeking a better life for themselves was again a significant factor in the Greek world, due partly to diminished conditions
in the old Greek world (e.g., Athens, no longer the center of an empire;
Corinth, no longer a major power) and due also to a general increase in
numbers of political exiles.[6]

Theocritus's Syracusan background[7] gave him a special vantage on
problems of relocation and immigration. Sicily itself had been a site of
much migration and colonization from the old Greek world. In 734/733
B.C., Syracuse was founded by Corinthians, who expelled and enslaved
native Sicels (Hdt. 7.155; Thuc. 6.3.2).[8] In 485 B.C., Gelon, Gela's tyrant,
made Syracuse his capital and forcibly relocated half of Gela's population
to Syracuse (Hdt. 7.156). Gelon also conquered and destroyed cities,
whose populations he moved to Syracuse.[9] Hieron, Gelon's brother, suc-
ceeded him and also pursued a policy of mass relocations.[10] Soon after
Hieron's death, the Syracusans established a democracy, expelled the tyrants' mercenary soldiers, and encouraged relocated populations to return to their home cities and exiled Syracusans to return to Syracuse
(Diod. Sic. 11.76). All this shifting of populations created much confusion over land rights.[11] But when Dionysius I established tyranny again
at Syracuse, he reinstated the policy of forced, mass relocations.[12] Later,
after a period of diminished population and resources at Syracuse, Corinth's Timoleon restored order, which resulted in a general call for Syracusan exiles and other Greek immigrants and mercenaries to repopulate
Syracuse and resettle abandoned Sicilian cities.[13]

In Theocritus's time, Syracuse, like Alexandria, was a very large city
of ethnically mixed, mostly immigrant population. Agathocles, formerly
a mercenary soldier, had seized power in Syracuse and extended his rule
over most of Sicily.[14] He claimed the title of king in 304 B.C.,[15] shortly
before Theocritus was born. A period of anarchy followed Agathocles'
death in 289 B.C. Finally Hieron, one of Pyrrhus's Syracusan lieutenants,
came to power (275/274 B.C.).[16] Soon thereafter, Theocritus may have
attempted to obtain poetic patronage from Hieron and, having failed,
left Syracuse.[17] Alexandria, with its thriving cultural community supported by the Ptolemaic hegemony, would have looked attractive to a
young Syracusan poet set loose in the world. Further, its stability of politics promised the continuance of royal patronage for the arts.

Theocritus's urban mimes reflect his Syracusan literary background.[18]
Greek Sicily was closely associated with a preliterary genre of mime, a
dramatic performance of a comical scene of everyday life.[19] From popular mime, typically perhaps a form of buffoonery, Sophron, a fifth-

century Syracusan writer, had developed a form of literary prose mime much admired among the ancients.[20] According to the scholiasts, Theocritus's *Idylls* 2 and 15 show special indebtedness to the mimes of Sophron.[21] By writing his mimes not in prose but in dactylic hexameter, a meter commonly associated with the elevated ethos of epic,[22] Theocritus expands the literary mime's versatility of tone.[23] In Alexandria, his mimes would have seemed exotic insofar as they recalled Syracuse in genre and perhaps also in dialect (Doric). But their hexameter meter accommodated the taste for Homer prevalent at this time.[24] Further, the mime, which typically featured the voices of ordinary persons (e.g., housewives, pimps, mercenaries), offered a special forum for exploring the effects of mobility and immigration on everyday urban life in an expanded, international world. The mixed, open texture of Theocritus's urban mimes (which could include, e.g., song, hymn, and street talk) was especially well-suited for representing a heterogeneous world, with its mix of old and new, native and immigrant, ordinary and privileged, everyday and fantastic.

Theocritus's urban mimes raise numerous issues related to mobility, ethnicity, and immigration, and offer clear examples of the engagement of Theocritus's poetry with issues of contemporary importance in his world.[25] The following section of this chapter shows some of the ways Theocritus's urban mimes highlight themes of mobility and internationalism. The next section shows how the symposium theme featured in *Idylls* 2 and 14 provides a special forum for exploring issues of mobility and marginality in the Hellenistic world. This section also examines other Hellenistic poems in which the symposium theme is linked with issues related to mobility. The last section shows how Theocritus's urban mimes highlight friendship's role in a world where persons frequently become separated from kinship ties and their former traditions.

Themes of Mobility and Internationalism

The Hellenistic period was an age of immense, cosmopolitan cities (e.g., Alexandria, Antioch, Pergamon), crowded with immigrants, citizens, natives, itinerants, and slaves, representing a multiplicity of races, ethnicities, and languages. Although huge metropolises had a long history elsewhere (e.g., Babylon), for most Greeks the dominance of such cities in the political and cultural landscape was a new phenomenon. One of Theocritus's three urban mimes, *Idyll* 15, offers a vivid portrait of the huge, heterogeneous city of Ptolemaic Alexandria.[26] In the course of the poem, two fictive Syracusan women go on an excursion through the congested streets of Alexandria. The poem underscores Alexandria's internationalism by highlighting its variety of ethnicities: Syracusans, native Egyptians, various non-Dorian Greeks, an Argive woman's daughter.

Themes of mobility and internationalism are clearly integral to all of Theocritus's urban mimes: *Idyll* 15 focuses on Syracusan immigrants who have settled in Alexandria, *Idyll* 2 explores the results of a failed love affair between a Myndian outlander and a local woman, and *Idyll* 14 includes the story of a symposium with ethnically diverse guests (including an Argive and a Thessalian) and ends with one friend advising another to migrate to Egypt and become a mercenary soldier. Of these poems, *Idyll* 15, with its central motif of movement through city streets, offers the most elaborate exploration of the mobility theme.

In the course of *Idyll* 15, the reader moves with Gorgo and Praxinoa, in a continuum of time and space, from the safe mimetic space of Praxinoa's remote house through the dangerous realm of Alexandria's streets to the palace grounds for the Adonis festival.[27] In representing Praxinoa's and Gorgo's excursion, the poet explores the difficulties of crossing boundaries: between outskirts and city center, city and court, outlander and citizen, man and woman, child and adult, subject and ruler, mortal and immortal, lover and beloved. The Adonia is itself a festival that celebrates transitions, changes. Insofar as chance meetings on a road can offer opportunities to learn to adjust to the requirements of new social arenas, by representing such encounters the poet can explore social rituals, rites of passage for moving from one space to another.[28] Movement through poetic space can also be a metaphor for passage between spiritual states. In a rapidly changing Hellenistic world, by representing the movement of outlanders from the outskirts to the heart of Alexandria, Theocritus can explore what Alexandria can offer the spirit and what it means to move from abroad to Alexandria.

As Bakhtin emphasizes, the road motif, with its associated motif of encounters on the road,[29] provides a valuable forum for exploring collisions of ethnicities, modes of speech, cultural expectations:

On the road . . . the spatial and temporal paths of the most varied people — representatives of all social classes, estates, religions, nationalities, ages — intersect at one spatial and temporal point. People who are normally kept separate by social and spatial distance can accidentally meet; any contrast may crop up, the most various fates may collide and interweave with one another.[30]

The Syracusan women's initial response to Alexandria's crowded urban streets is alienation. Through their encounters with persons of different ethnicity, gender, age, and class, Theocritus raises social issues related to the themes of immigration and cultural difference — e.g., the difficulties involved in establishing or maintaining identity, finding a place in the world, dealing with the rejection of others.

Closely associated with the motif of the road is the motif of the threshold.[31] In a mobile world, thresholds are especially frequent and momentous: the moment of decision to leave home, the place of departure, the shore on which a traveler first lands in a new world, the entrance to a new home. But thresholds pervade everyday life as well: the moment of rising from bed, the doorway opening to the outside world, the entrance to a friend's house.

Idyll 15 begins with Gorgo's arrival at Praxinoa's house at the outskirts of Alexandria. Through Gorgo's description of her experiences on the road, the poet explores a privatized person's sense of alienation and disorientation in a crowded, public setting:

ὦ τᾶς ἀλεμάτω ψυχᾶς· μόλις ὕμμιν ἐσώθην,
Πραξινόα, πολλῷ μὲν ὄχλῳ, πολλῶν δὲ τεθρίππων·
παντᾷ κρηπῖδες, παντᾷ χλαμυδηφόροι ἄνδρες·
ἁ δ' ὁδὸς ἄτρυτος· τὺ δ' ἑκαστέρω αἰὲν ἀποικεῖς.

(4–7)

How distraught I've been; it was difficult to reach your house safely,
Praxinoa: the crowd was so big, the chariots so numerous;
everywhere boots, everywhere men wearing cloaks.
The road is endless; you live farther away all the time.

The impulse of scholars to try to identify the "boots" and "men wearing cloaks" seems misplaced.[32] The text's indeterminacy reflects Gorgo's alienation in the public space: through metonymy the poet can recreate Gorgo's experience of defamiliarization for the reader as well. Gorgo feels threatened regardless of whether "boots" and "men wearing cloaks" denote soldiers or men on holiday.[33]

Praxinoa's first response to the crowd on the streets as she leaves her house also underscores alienation from the public arena:

ὦ θεοί, ὅσσος ὄχλος. πῶς καὶ πόκα τοῦτο περᾶσαι
χρὴ τὸ κακόν; μύρμακες ἀνάριθμοι καὶ ἄμετροι.

(44–45)

Oh gods, what a huge crowd. How and when are we to get through
this dreadful mob? Like ants, innumerable and incalculable.

By projecting feelings of estrangement onto Syracusan housewives, the
poet explores an aspect of the Alexandrian experience not unfamiliar to
his contemporary readers, many of whom may have come from abroad
(e.g., members of the academy). By dehumanizing the urban mob and
emphasizing its "otherness," the poem shows how immigrant women
can try to authorize themselves as the norm rather than the "other" (the
immigrant, the woman). Similarly later in the poem, by having Praxinoa, uneasy on the city streets, bolster her self-identity as a Greek by
denigrating Egyptians (as others), the poet again draws attention to how
boundaries of otherness can shift in a mobile world. But also, by having
Praxinoa describe the crowds she meets on the road as ants (45) and
Gorgo describe the men she met on the way to Praxinoa's house as boots
(6), the poet can explore how verbally dehumanizing others can diminish fear and strengthen group identity.[34]

The motif of a walk through crowded city streets is not new with
Theocritus, of course. Homer's *Odyssey* offers an early example when
Odysseus, clothed in a mist, walks through the city of the Phaeacians
(7.39–45). But before Theocritus, the walker's response was characteristically wonderment rather than alienation. Theocritus's *Idyll* 15, however,
shows the power of the motif of movement on a road for representing
large, cosmopolitan cities and the moods of alienation and anonymity
they can evoke. After Theocritus, the mood of alienation became more
common in representations of fictive walks through crowded cities, although a mood of wonderment seems to have remained typical (e.g.,
the response of Vergil's Aeneas to Dido's city, *Aen.* 1.421–40). Juvenal's
Satire 3, in using the motif of movement through crowded streets
(232–314) to establish a mood of alienation in a cosmopolitan city
(Rome), comes perhaps closest to Theocritus's use of the road motif in
Idyll 15.[35]

Like Theocritus's Syracusan women, Juvenal's Umbricius deplores
the anonymous violence of city streets (e.g., *Sat.* 3.243–61). Like Gorgo,
Umbricius uses the special motif of disembodied boot parts to dramatize
the menace and anonymity of Rome's crowded streets:

pinguia crura luto, planta mox undique magna
calcor, et in digito clauus mihi militis haeret.

(*Sat.* 3.247–48 *O.C.T.*)

My legs are coated with mud, from all sides I am trampled
by big soles, and in my toe sticks the nail of a soldier's shoe.

Like Praxinoa, Umbricius establishes his identity in contrast to foreigners and "others":

non est Romano cuiquam locus hic, ubi regnat
Protogenes aliquis uel Diphilus aut Hermarchus.

(119–20 *O.C.T.*)

There's no room here for any Roman; the city is ruled by
some Protógenes or other, some Díphilus or Hermarchus.

(trans. Rudd, *Juvenal*, 18)

Although the political worlds of the poems are far different,[36] Juvenal's use of the motif of movement on a road to evoke a mood of urban alienation illustrates the continued vitality of poetic strategies developed by Theocritus in *Idyll* 15.

Alexandria, a cosmopolitan city where many different dialects and languages were spoken and where the new international Greek (Koinè) was gaining acceptance, offered Theocritus a fictional setting in which to explore the cultural clashes that criticisms of speech characteristics can represent. A key encounter at the center of *Idyll* 15 explicitly raises the issue of ethnic prejudice in a heterogeneous city. As the Syracusan women enter the precinct of the Adonia, a hostile bystander ridicules their manner of speech, the broad vowels characteristic of their native Doric dialect:

παύσασθ᾽, ὦ δύστανοι, ἀνάνυτα κωτίλλοισαι,
τρυγόνες· ἐκκναισεῦντι πλατειάσδοισαι ἄπαντα.

(87–88)

You wretched women, stop that endless twittering —
like turtle doves they'll grate on you, with all their broad vowels.

Praxinoa responds by asserting her right to speak in her native dialect. She refuses to be silenced. She frustrates the attempt to dismiss her as a nonperson:

μᾶ, πόθεν ὤνθρωπος; τί δὲ τίν, εἰ κωτίλαι εἰμές;
πασάμενος ἐπίτασσε· Συρακοσίαις ἐπιτάσσεις.
ὡς εἰδῇς καὶ τοῦτο, Κορίνθιαι εἰμὲς ἄνωθεν,
ὡς καὶ ὁ Βελλεροφῶν. Πελοποννασιστὶ λαλεῦμες,
Δωρίσδειν δ᾽ ἔξεστι, δοκῶ, τοῖς Δωριέεσσι.

(89–93)

Mother, where does this man come from? What's it to you if we twitter?
If you have slaves, order them around. You're giving orders to
    Syracusans.
And let me assure you: we are Corinthians by descent,
like Bellerophon. We "babble" in the Peloponnesian manner;
Dorians are permitted, I think, to speak Doric.

In the impersonal city of Alexandria, individuals could try to relieve their
isolation by joining self-serving groups that privileged local origin, sex,
occupation, etc. By showing how the bystander's insults force Praxinoa
and Gorgo to think about their self-identity as Doric-speakers from Syracuse, the poet raises the issue of cultural alienation.[37]

Another incident reflects a tension between native peoples (Egyptians) and "colonialist" Greeks in the heterogeneous Alexandrian
world.[38] Feeling uneasy on Alexandria's public streets, Praxinoa praises
Ptolemy's law-and-order campaign by denigrating the Egyptian ruffians
who used to harass pedestrians:[39]

πολλά τοι, ὦ Πτολεμαῖε, πεποίηται καλὰ ἔργα,
ἐξ ὦ ἐν ἀθανάτοις ὁ τεκών· οὐδεὶς κακοεργός
δαλεῖται τὸν ἰόντα παρέρπων Αἰγυπτιστί,
οἷα πρὶν ἐξ ἀπάτας κεκροτημένοι ἄνδρες ἔπαισδον,
ἀλλάλοις ὁμαλοί, κακὰ παίχνια, πάντες ἀραῖοι.

(46–50)

You have accomplished many good deeds, Ptolemy,
since your father took his place among the immortals; no evildoer
sneaks up to someone on the street, Egyptian style, and hurts him,
doing tricks that men forged from deceit used to play,
each rascal as bad as the other, wicked pranksters, curse them all.

This passage shows how immigrant Greek women can (temporarily)
suppress feelings of alienation and insignificance by elevating themselves
as "colonials" over natives.

Alexandria, as a Hellenistic center of Greek culture and power, had
no traditions and history before Alexander. A nostalgia for the old Greek
world among Greeks who relocated to Alexandria may have helped encourage the popularity of aetiological topics (causes and origins) among
Alexandrian writers, notably Callimachus.[40] Theocritus's *Idyll* 15 shows
how the motif of the road also offers an economical forum for exploring
linkages and disjunctions between the old world and the new, particularly insofar as a road can encompass both real (spatial) and mythic
(spiritual) dimensions. The Syracusan women's journey from the out-

skirts of Alexandria to the court takes them from the everyday world to the spiritual realm of the Adonia.

A key incident in *Idyll* 15 shows how Theocritus's use of the dactylic hexameter (a meter readily evocative of Homer) in presenting sketches of daily life can facilitate a complex and nuanced interplay between the old world and the new, the mythic and the "real." As the Syracusan women near the palace, they encounter a peculiar old woman. When they consult her about entering the palace grounds, she replies with an analogy drawn from epic tales of the conquest of Troy:

ἐς Τροίαν πειρώμενοι ἦνθον Ἀχαιοί,
κάλλισται παίδων· πείρᾳ θην πάντα τελεῖται.

(61–62)

The Achaeans got into Troy by trying,
my young beauties; all things are accomplished by trying.

In the midst of the polyglot, cosmopolitan world of Alexandria, in an alien land, immigrant Greeks encounter an old woman who speaks the language of Homer.[41]

Relatively little attention has been paid to the mythic and epic nuance of *Idyll* 15's encounter between two Syracusan women and an old woman on a crowded road in Alexandria.[42] Yet this encounter explicitly raises the issue of the place of the old Homeric ethos in the new, cosmopolitan world of Alexandria (an issue perhaps already implicit in Theocritus's use of dactylic hexameter). Discussions of *Idyll* 15 have traditionally focused on Theocritus's use of irony in characterizing the fictive women: how he uses Homerisms to underscore how unheroic and even silly these women are.[43] Yet although there may be elements of irony present here, irony is only one of a multiplicity of perspectives that readers should bring to the poem. By evoking the Homeric world in a homely context, the poet underscores the gap between the mythic and contemporary world. In underscoring this gap, the poet introduces a reminder of Greek identity, of a focal point of traditional Greek culture, in cosmopolitan Alexandria.

The literary motif of a road typically involves type-scenes — e.g., receptions, departures, encounters, returns — that can be traced back to the mythic world and Homer's epics.[44] In epic journeys, needy travelers often meet helpers midway on their journeys or when approaching their destinations.[45] Similarly, in *Idyll* 15, when Praxinoa and Gorgo find themselves engulfed by the crowd (59), an old woman appears coming from the palace. Thus the circumstances of the old woman's appearance, as well as her Homeric language and explicit reference to Troy's capture, encourage the perception of her role as mythic helper. By linking contemporary events to a mythic past, the poet can also raise the problematic issue of the relevance of the old world to modern poetry (and life).

Other Homeric motifs also contribute to the interplay of epic and mime, old world and new, in *Idyll* 15. Epic representations of receptions conventionally include two or more of the following elements: exchange of greetings, seating of visitor, comments on infrequency of visits,[46] and sometimes also comments on difficulty of travel.[47] The reception scene starting *Idyll* 15 (1–10) includes all these elements. Praxinoa's scene of bathing and dressing for departure (29–40) is another type-scene linking *Idyll* 15's morning outing with mythic (epic) journeys. Perhaps too the son and dog left at home on departure (41–43), like the *Odyssey*'s Telemachus and Argus,[48] add a thematic grace note reinforcing the epic resonance that already comes with Theocritus's choice of hexameter meter, epic motifs, and Homeric vocabulary and phraseology.[49] By including these traces of familiar Homeric motifs in *Idyll* 15's structuring of chance encounters and events (and by writing an urban mime in dactylic hexameter), Theocritus can offer an element of familiarity to common readers who might otherwise find modernist poetry too strange, establish linkages to a mythic tradition that he can exploit in the poem, and challenge the hierarchical literary tradition that devalues small projects featuring "common" subjects.

Gorgo's and Praxinoa's ironic responses to the old woman's mythic analogy underscore the gap between the everyday world and the epic, between high culture and low, for if the old woman's persona recalls an archetypal epic helper, Gorgo and Praxinoa dismiss her as an old crone, peculiar and misplaced, an intrusion from an outmoded mythic tale:

ΓΟ. χρησμὼς ἀ πρεσβῦτις ἀπῴχετο θεσπίξασα.
ΠΡ. πάντα γυναῖκες ἴσαντι, καὶ ὡς Ζεὺς ἀγάγεθ' Ἥραν.

(63–64)

GO: The old woman has gone off, having spoken her oracles.
PR: Women know all things, even how Zeus married Hera.

Yet although the skeptical tone of Praxinoa's evaluation continues the ironic strain in Gorgo's remark, Gorgo's remark on the old woman's prophetic function also further establishes the old woman's role as mythic helper.[50]

The events that immediately follow the encounter with the old woman reinforce her role as mythic helper, for the entrance that Gorgo and Praxinoa seek appears (the unclear path becomes clear: they find the doors to the palace grounds):

ΓΟ. θᾶσαι, Πραξινόα, περὶ τὰς θύρας ὅσσος ὅμιλος.
ΠΡ. θεσπέσιος.

(65–66)

GO: Look, Praxinoa, what a huge crowd is around the doors.
PR: An awe-inspiring crowd.

Gorgo's and Praxinoa's shift to the Homeric register when describing the crowd around the doors heightens the epic resonance of their encounter with the old woman: the Homeric noun ὅμιλος appears only here in the poem (the un Homeric ὄχλος appears elsewhere), and the Homeric adjective θεσπέσιος immediately follows.[51] Further, just as traditionally mythic helpers come in pairs, often with the female preceding the male,[52] so too in *Idyll* 15 the encounter with a "prophetic" old woman precedes an encounter with a helpful man (70–75).

The shaping of the Syracusan women's chance encounter with an old woman exemplifies Theocritus's interest in how epic allusion and thematic motif can help stabilize chance events by grounding the everyday (contemporary, urban) world in the mythic, thus making these worlds seem contiguous. Further, the spiritual dimension to the road becomes more intense as Gorgo and Praxinoa approach the palace, for the appearance of the old woman helps draw the women into the mythic world represented by the Adonia.

In *Idyll* 15's representation of a journey from everyday life to a spiritual (and courtly) realm, the shaping and coloration of one threshold in particular offer a dramatic exemplar of the value of paying close attention to the motif of the threshold in Theocritus's poetry. Outside the doors to the palace grounds are urban mobs and chaotic streets; inside, an Adonis festival. Between these two mimetic realms stands a threshold and within this liminal space a work of art — a tapestry decorated with moving figures — represents a passageway for the women to move from secular to ceremonial space (78–79).[53]

The liminality of the moment of entry into the palace grounds is underscored by the repetition of adverbs denoting spatial transitions. The adverb ἔνδοι marks Gorgo's entry into the safety of Praxinoa's house (1), the adverb ἔσω and the verb ἀποκλάω mark the locking up of the household as the women leave Praxinoa's house to enter the dangerous environment of Alexandria's streets (43), and the adverb ἔνδοι and the verb ἀποκλάω mark entry through doors into the safety of the palace grounds:

κάλλιστ'· 'ἔνδοι πᾶσαι', ὁ τὰν νυὸν εἶπ' ἀποκλάξας.

(77)

Perfectly done. "All women inside," said the man, locking the door on
    the bride.

The repetition of the verb for locking up and its transference to a sexual context highlight the women's passage into the sensual realm of the Adonia.[54] By appropriating the bridegroom's power, Praxinoa asserts power in the liminal situation of the entry to the Adonia. She is comfortable here: a special place that welcomes women is available in the heart of the alien urban environment. The fact that the singer (an Argive woman's daughter) has Doric connections also can help make Doric-speaking immigrant women feel more welcome in the mimetic space of the festival.

But the passage into the festival space is not made easy; on the threshold stands a monster and they must break through to participate in the ceremony. The women have just entered through doors: they are in a liminal area, where crises naturally occur. The issue is power here; the poem hesitates. In the intense space of the sanctuary, a bystander challenges them and presents a crisis of identity. The bystander exercises his right to make fun and to refuse to listen. Like a "fool," he refuses to understand the women's speech about art. Thus, the bystander's interruption highlights the metalinguistic qualities of the moment of passage:[55] the Syracusan women respond to the art, the bystander responds to the Doric-speaking women, and the real audience responds to the poem (written in Doric by a man from Syracuse).

In *Idyll* 15, the use of the motif of movement on a road facilitates linkages between commonplace and mythic, epic and mime, everyday life and the heightened ceremonial realm of an Adonia. The Syracusan women's initial responses to the crowded streets of Alexandria evoke a mood of alienation; their various encounters involve persons of different ethnicities, sexes, social classes, languages. In such a context, the Homerisms and mythic patterning of the poem, by animating (however ironically) the latent epic dimension inherent when dactylic hexameter is used for describing everyday life, help create a bridge between the old world and the new. Thus by evoking the mythic tradition in the lowly context of congested urban streets, *Idyll* 15 could offer culturally dislocated

Greeks in the expanded Hellenistic world ways to remember and revalue the past.

Idyll 2, although not as directly focused on issues of immigration or mobility as *Idyll* 15, also highlights the internationalism of its fictive world. Simaetha falls in love with Delphis, an outlander from Myndus (in Caria), attends a festival with a Thracian nurse,[56] and learns about drugs from an Assyrian expert. Further, the town's location near the sea would encourage mobility. Additional details in the poem may suggest that it is set in Cos, an international center for the study of medicine[57] and at one time Ptolemy's headquarters in the Aegean:[58] Delphis mentions outrunning Philinus, perhaps a reference to the famous runner Philinus of Cos,[59] and Simaetha swears by the fates, perhaps a typically Coan oath.[60]

Idyll 2 draws attention to complications that can arise in relationships between persons of different ethnicity and class. Theocritus highlights the issue of eros and ethnicity by having Simaetha refer to Delphis as simply "the Myndian" when explaining her situation to her maid: πᾶσαν ἔχει με τάλαιναν ὁ Μύνδιος ("The Myndian possesses me totally," 96). Also, the emphasis on the social gap between Simaetha, whose nonelite friends include a Thracian nurse and a flute girl's mother, and Delphis, a member of the upper-class gymnastic and sympotic set, brings the issue of class difference to the center of *Idyll* 2's poetic project. Further, by representing Simaetha as making choices and taking action without family supervision, Theocritus approaches the issue of mobility's effects on traditional family structures and values.

The road motif, with its associated motif of the encounter, also appears in *Idyll* 2, although not as elaborately as in *Idyll* 15. In *Idyll* 2, as in *Idyll* 15, a festival provides a motivation for women to be on public streets: it was on a walk to a festival of Artemis that Simaetha first saw Delphis. Also in *Idyll* 2, as in *Idyll* 15, midpoint and threshold motifs shape the story of Simaetha's relations with Delphis:

ἤδη δ' εὖσα μέσαν κατ' ἀμαξιτόν, ᾇ τὰ Λύκωνος,
εἶδον Δέλφιν ὁμοῦ τε καὶ Εὐδάμιππον ἰόντας.

(76–77)

And I was already midway on the road, at Lycon's place,
when I saw Delphis walking with Eudamippus.

Further, Theocritus highlights the moment of Delphis's first coming to Simaetha by having Simaetha describe him as stepping across the threshold of her door:

ἐγὼ δέ νιν ὡς ἐνόησα
ἄρτι θύρας ὑπὲρ οὐδὸν ἀμειβόμενον ποδὶ κούφῳ.

(103–4)

And as soon as I saw him
stepping over my threshold with light foot.

This moment represents a crucial threshold in Simaetha's life as well: the transition from childhood to adulthood (106–10).[61]

Theocritus's *Idyll* 14 is also set in an international and mobile world. The occasion is a chance meeting between two male friends, Aeschinas and Thyonichus. The cosmopolitan orientation of their conversation reflects the mobility of the Hellenistic world: Thyonichus compares Aeschinas's disheveled appearance to an Athenian Pythagorist's, and Aeschinas explains by describing a drinking party he hosted, whose guests included an Argive, a Thessalian horse trainer, and a soldier. At the poem's end, Aeschinas is contemplating going abroad and becoming a mercenary soldier (in order to forget his faithless girlfriend). Thyonichus advises him to go to Egypt and join Ptolemy's mercenaries. A more detailed discussion of *Idyll* 14's mobility themes is found in the following section ("Symposia").

Herodas's *Mimes* 1 and 2 also approach the mobility theme in the context of presenting dramatic sketches of urban life. Like Theocritus, Herodas writes literary mimes in verse.[62] Meter and dialect help set their mimes apart: Herodas adopts the meter and dialect of Hipponax, a sixth-century writer of invective poetry,[63] while Theocritus writes in hexameter.[64] Although Herodas's dates and origins are uncertain, it is generally conjectured that he too was writing in the third century B.C. (*Mime* 1.30 lists as an attraction of Alexandria the sanctuary of the brother-sister gods, Ptolemy II and Arsinoe II).[65]

In Herodas's *Mime* 1, Metriche's husband left for Egypt ten months ago and has not communicated with her since.[66] Gyllis, an old bawd, now comes to her with an athletic suitor's proposition and reminds her that her husband is unlikely to stay faithful in Egypt where there are, she claims, more charming women than stars in the sky:

γυναῖκες, ὁκόσους οὐ μὰ τὴν Ἀιδεω Κούρην
ἀστέρας ἐνεγκεῖν οὐραν[ὸ]ς κεκαύχηται,
τὴν δ' ὄψιν οἷαι πρὸς Πάριν κοτ' ὥρμησαν
.].[κρ]ιθῆναι καλλονήν — λάθοιμ' αὐτάς.

(32–35)

Women more in number — I swear by Kore wife of Hades —
than the sky boasts of stars,

and in charms like the goddesses who went on a time to Paris
to have their beauty judged — I pray they may not hear me.

(trans. Knox, in Headlam and Knox, Herodas, 5)

The bawd's list of Egypt's attractions makes it abundantly clear why
Hellenistic Greeks might want to migrate to Alexandria:[67]

τὰ γὰρ πάντα,
ὅσσ᾽ ἔστι κου καὶ γένετ᾽, ἔστ᾽ ἐν Αἰγύπτωι·
πλοῦτος, παλαίστρη, δύναμις, εὐδίη, δόξα,
θέαι, φιλόσοφοι, χρυσίον, νεηνίσκοι,
θεῶν ἀδελφῶν τέμενος, ὁ βασιλεὺς χρηστός,
Μουσῆιον, οἶνος, ἀγαθὰ πάντ᾽ ὅσ᾽ ἂν χρήιζηι.

(26–31)

For all
that exists and is produced in the world is in Egypt:
wealth, wrestling grounds, might, peace, renown,
shows, philosophers, money, young men,
the domain of the Θεοὶ ἀδελφοί [Ptolemy and Arsinoe], the king a
   good one,
the museum, wine, all good things one can desire.

(trans. Knox, in Headlam and Knox, Herodas, 5)

In tempting a seemingly respectable married woman to commit adultery, the bawd's voice resists the normative social order and underscores its fragility in a mobile world.

Like Theocritus, Herodas sometimes complicates the worlds of his mimes by including motifs that can recall the worlds of myth and legend. For example, *Mime* 1, like *Idyll* 15, opens with a standard reception scene: Gyllis's arrival at Metriche's house prompts an exchange of traditional remarks about infrequent visits and difficult journeys. Through the hostess Metriche's ironic greeting to Gyllis, the poet underscores how even the low, fictive arrival of an old bawd can be shaped to evoke a mythic world in which mortals and immortals could mingle:[68] τίς σε μοῖρ᾽ ἔπεισ᾽ ἐλθεῖν, / Γυλλίς, πρὸς ἡμέας; τί σὺ θεὸς πρὸς ἀνθρώπους; ("What fate has sent you here to us, Gyllis? / Why have you come like a god unto mortals?"; trans. Knox, in Headlam and Knox, *Herodas,* 3; 8–9). In a poem that extols the attractions of Alexandria, whose hegemonic rulers seemed increasingly to be emulating gods, Herodas shows the boundary between gods and mortals fluctuating (momentarily) to include an old bawd as well.

Herodas's *Mime* 2, set on the international island of Cos, also centers on the theme of mobility's disruptive effects on civic life and social boundaries. Battaros, a poor metic pander, is suing Thales, a rich Phrygian merchant, for personal injury and property damage. His strategy is to appropriate the Greek social prejudices that marginalize himself and to redirect them against his opponent. Thus Battaros discredits Thales by appealing to a Greek's anxiety about the decline of city-state values in the Hellenistic world and a resident's distrust of itinerants:

σὺ δ' οὐκ οἶσθας
οὔτε πόλιν οὔτε πῶς πόλις διοικεῖται,
οἰκεῖς δὲ σήμερον μὲν ἐν Βρικινδήροις
ἐχθὲς δ' ἐν Ἀβδήροισιν, αὔριον δ' ἤν σοι
ναῦλον διδοῖ τις, ἐς Φασηλίδα πλώσηι.

(55–59)

You [Thales] know not
of a city nor how a city is governed,
but live to-day at Brikindera
and yesterday at Abdera, and to-morrow, if one
give you your fare you will sail to Phaselis.

(trans. Knox, in Headlam and Knox, *Herodas*, 65–67)

Through the comic voice of a poor pimp, *Mime* 2 makes public the prejudices of provincial (citizen) Greeks against rich outsiders who might threaten the established social community. Marshalling arguments from within the power structure, Battaros claims that Thales' crimes show disdain for the established social hierarchy which elevates the lowest citizen over a foreigner (25–30). Rich Greek metics too had a long, problematic history of participation and exclusion in Greek society, as shown by, e.g., the vicissitudes in the lives of Cephalus and his sons Lysias and Polemarchus.[69]

By emphasizing Thales' alien status as a Phrygian (and as a scorner of civic authority), Battaros deconstructs the elite social identity Thales has been carefully forging (by, e.g., adopting a Greek name):[70]

ἀλλ' ὁ Φρὺξ οὗτος,
ὁ νῦν Θαλῆς ἐών, πρόσθε δ', ἄνδρες, Ἀρτίμμης,
ἄπαντα ταῦτ' ἔπρηξε κοὐκ ἐπῃδέσθη
οὔτε νόμον οὔτε προστάτην οὔτ' ἄρχοντα.

(37–40)

But this Phrygian,
who now calls himself Thales, but was once, gentlemen, Artimmes,
has done all these things without shame
of law, governor, or ruler.

(trans. Knox, in Headlam and Knox, *Herodas*, 65)

Battaros, a noncitizen and possibly a non-Greek, poor and a pimp, is low man in a social order privileging citizens, Greeks, and the rich, but he shows command of the power structure's strategies of exclusion and reorders them to include himself and exclude a rich merchant.

In the Hellenistic age, the loss of autonomous city-state life for Greeks had intensified the blurring of social categories and distinctions between citizens and others (both Greek and non-Greek).[71] Herodas's poetry focuses on points of weakness and instability in the social structure: unrefined housewives, bawds, non-Greeks, dildo makers. But can a poor, foreign pander's attempt to include himself among the privileged succeed? By choosing the lowest test case, a pimp, and having him reassign social categories to privilege himself, Herodas highlights the instability of distinctions of insider and outsider in the Hellenistic world and thus approaches a central anxiety of his age: can the categories shift to exclude me? Battaros ends his speech by reidentifying his cause with resident aliens (against Phrygian itinerants; 92–102).

Symposia

In periods of expansion and mobility, traditional social forums such as symposia and gymnasia could provide displaced Greeks — e.g., colonists, itinerants, immigrants, exiles — settings in which to assert their self-identity and regain a sense of community. Scholars have established that in Hellenistic urban settlements, traveling freeborn Greek males could find gymnasia, settings in which to reestablish membership in a privileged class.[72] But the topic of how symposia enabled mobile Hellenistic Greek males to regain a sense of self, privilege, and social connectedness has been largely overlooked in literary and historical studies.

Greek symposia traditionally helped reinforce the class solidarity of male aristocrats, both within a local community and also on an international scale, by providing private settings in which to claim social privilege and establish solidarity with other elitist Greek males.[73] Painted sympotic vessels and lyric poetry on sympotic themes attest to the tremendous popularity of the symposium in the seventh and sixth centuries. Linked closely with the propertied and leisured class, archaic symposia offered settings in which aristocrats could associate privately, first as members of the ruling class, then as subversive groups opposed to what they perceived as a usurpation of power by tyrants and statesmen with more broadly based support. Symposia were often followed by high-spirited drunken revelry (*komos*), during which aristocrats would further display their class difference from nonaristocrats by publicly assaulting them (*hybris*). Despite the passage of legislation against public acts of drunken violence, aristocrats continued to defy the cooperative norms of behavior encouraged in Greek city-states by engaging in komastic acts.[74]

By the fifth century, due in part to the rise of participatory democracy (particularly in Athens), the elitist symposium, along with lyric poetry and sympotic vases, had declined in popularity, though its oppositional force continued.[75] During the fourth century, however, as the mobile population increased, due in part to the large number of political exiles, symposia seemed to regain centrality in the cultural discourse: elitist fourth-century philosophers produced treatises dealing with questions of social conduct,[76] and poets began to compose sympotic epigrams. In the Hellenistic age, the dominance of autocratic hegemonies further contributed to a mood of skepticism about public life, and the increased money made available to Greeks through Alexander the Great's looting of the East may have encouraged the popularity of such expensive leisure-time activities as courtship and symposia. Further, Alexander's special taste for drunken revelry and the Hellenistic kings' proclivity for lavish display[77] may have helped spread elitist sympotic practices throughout the Greek-dominated parts of the Hellenistic world.

When scholars refer to the symposium theme in Hellenistic literature, they are generally thinking of Hellenistic epigrams which belong "to a world divorced from public life" and pay "no attention to war or politics, and no attention to patronage or inequality within the poetic group."[78] Yet a consideration of several longer Hellenistic poems will show how the symposium theme offered Hellenistic poets a forum for approaching social and political issues of contemporary importance. Theocritus's urban mime *Idyll* 14 offers perhaps Hellenistic poetry's richest exploration of the symposium's role in Hellenistic life.[79] But other poems too — notably Herodas's *Mime* 2, Callimachus's *Aetia*, fr. 178–85 (*Icos*), and Theocritus's urban mime *Idyll* 2 — feature the symposium theme.

Idyll 14's symposium reflects an expanded and mobile world in the geographical diversity and occupational mobility of its male guests: an Argive, a Thessalian horse trainer, and a soldier (12–13).[80] The symposium's placement in an unspecified countryside (14) further underscores the guests' status as men set loose in the world. Insofar as symposia and gymnasia traditionally reinforced Greek male solidarity and fellowship, dislocated Greek males could try to restore their sense of self-identity and community by participating in such institutions. But *Idyll* 14's symposium, rather than affirming its host's sense of self and community, leaves Aeschinas feeling isolated and depressed.

In brief, *Idyll* 14 represents a conversation between two friends, Aeschinas and Thyonichus, who have not seen one another for some time. Thyonichus notes Aeschinas's neglected appearance, and Aeschinas explains by telling the story of how he had a fight with his girlfriend Cynisca at a symposium two months ago. Aeschinas was hosting an intimate drinking party: three male friends and Cynisca. The basic components of the symposium were conventional, if unpretentious: plentiful food and drink (two chickens, a sucking pig, Bibline wine, and onions and snails, 14–17) and traditional party activities (toasts, riddles, and song, 19–31). By popular decision everyone was to toast his or her favorite, but Cynisca refused. Cynisca's reaction to the other guests' jocular behavior showed Aeschinas why: she preferred Lycus, a neighbor's boy, to him. In anger Aeschinas struck her with his fist. Cynisca fled the symposium and since then has been consorting with his rival. Now the lovelorn Aeschinas, grown shaggy, thin, and pale, is considering enlisting abroad as a mercenary. Thyonichus sympathizes and recommends going to Egypt to join Ptolemy's soldiers. In the Greek patriarchal world, men expected women who attended symposia (typically *hetairai*, other entertainers, and slaves) to satisfy their desires and comply with their demands. *Idyll* 14 explores how a woman's challenge to this hierarchical code destabilizes a fictive sympotic community.

Idyll 14's focus on a nonelite symposium draws attention to the issue of mobility's effects on social relations and modes of behavior. The rise in availability of mercenary soldiers that began in the fourth century B.C., due in part to the increased number of political exiles, was linked with the decline of the citizen-soldier and the autonomous city-state. Mercenaries and horse trainers, such as those attending Aeschinas's symposium, were generally itinerant, and their economic status varied with employment opportunities.[81] *Idyll* 14 suggests that in the Hellenistic period Greek symposia extended beyond the elite to include nonelite persons as well.[82]

Although Gow cites Cynisca's presence at a symposium as evidence of her status as a *hetaira* (see Dem. 59.24 [*Neaira*]), Dover rightly remarks that "the social class to which Aischinas belongs did not necessarily observe bourgeois proprieties."[83] Further, in the Hellenistic world, some women were experiencing a rise in personal freedom, as shown by the use of marriage contracts in Egypt and the increased opportunities to attain civic honors.[84] This freedom might well have extended in some cases (especially in the absence of close kin) to increased mobility in the public realm. In addition, respectable women were not unknown at symposia.[85] I suggest that *Idyll* 14's Cynisca is probably not a hired girl (or slave) since her actions do not reflect fear of an employer's (or owner's) wrath.[86] In any case, by leaving Cynisca's social status unspecified, by focusing on a nonelite symposium, and by including characters of various ethnicities and occupations, the poet establishes in *Idyll* 14 a fictive environment that reflects the instability of social categories (and boundaries of behavior) in an expanded and increasingly heterogeneous Hellenistic world.[87]

Through sympotic activity such as making toasts, posing riddles, and singing, symposiasts could display self-identity and establish group unity. Further, through acts that transgressed the normative social code (e.g., the *komos*), symposiasts could show solidarity against others.[88] Abuse of women, especially, could function to unite symposiasts by (re)affirming a male sexual hegemony. But in *Idyll* 14, when a symposiast teased Cynisca with a song, the physical violence that followed was not a group act but a solitary one that isolated the host from the male sympotic community.

Aeschinas's redescriptions of the symposium reflect his current isolation from customary sympotic practices. Aeschinas links the sympotic incidents that led to him beating Cynisca (34–35) with high levels of wine consumption: the making of love-toasts with unmixed wine (18–21)[89] and the performance of the song "My Wolf" when "we four were already deep in our drinking" (29).[90] The emphasis on wine here reflects a traditional motif among those seeking to reform the symposium or reject its values: the association of wine (and the symposium) with violence. Thus, in Aristophanes' *Wasps*, Philocleon cites potential violence as a reason for not attending a symposium:

κακὸν τὸ πίνειν· ἀπὸ γὰρ οἴνου γίγνεται
καὶ θυροκοπῆσαι καὶ πατάξαι καὶ βαλεῖν,
κἄπειτ' ἀποτίνειν ἀργύριον ἐκ κραιπάλης.
(1253–55 O.C.T.)

Drinking is no good: it leads to
breaking down doors, assault and battery—
and then a headache and a fine to pay.
(trans. based on Rogers, *Aristophanes,* 1:527)

Plato's kinsman Critias condemns the toasting ritual in particular for inviting excessive wine consumption.[91] Aeschinas can describe the symposium before the toasting ritual as πότος ἀδύς (a pleasant drinking party, 17), but not afterwards.

At the poem's start, by having Thyonichus compare Aeschinas to a Pythagorist, the poet underscores Aeschinas's current alienation from sympotic culture. Ascetic philosophers were often set in opposition to the normative (sympotic) male community, as Plato's *Theaetetus* shows: "To take any interest in the rivalries of political cliques, in meetings, dinners, and merrymakings with flute-girls, never occurs to them [ascetic philosophers] even in dreams" (173d, trans. Cornford, *Theaetetus*, 84–85). In *Idyll* 14, the Pythagorist's lack of footwear (ἀνυπόδητος, 6) highlights his unsuitability for symposia, for even Socrates dons slippers before attending Agathon's victory party (Pl. *Symp.* 174a). Aeschinas's contrast of his own socially isolated, near-mad condition to Thyonichus's tendency to jest, a skill prized in sympotic communities, further emphasizes his distance from the sympotic model of manhood:

> παίσδεις, 'ωγάθ', ἔχων· ἐμὲ δ' ἀ χαρίεσσα Κυνίσκα
> ὑβρίσδει· λασῶ δὲ μανείς ποκα, θρὶξ ἀνὰ μέσσον.
>
> (8–9)

You're always joking, my friend. But as for me, the lovely Cynisca maltreats me, and I'll go suddenly mad one day—I'm just a hair's breadth away.

An option available to social misfits is to start a new life elsewhere. But doing what? Aeschinas resolves to become a mercenary soldier. An army can offer Aeschinas a way out of isolation, a new sense of male comradery, a community. Drama and poetry had long featured professional soldiers, e.g., the poet-soldier Archilochus, the self-glorifying Lamachos of Aristophanes' *Acharnians*, the hesitant lover Thrasonides in Menander's *Misoumenos* (e.g., 262–68). Theocritus's *Idyll* 14 focuses on the anxieties and alienation that could lead to such a vocational choice in a privatized world.

Thyonichus offers Aeschinas a sturdy soldier to emulate:

> ὥστ' εἴ τοι κατὰ δεξιὸν ὦμον ἀρέσκει
> λῶπος ἄκρον περονᾶσθαι, ἐπ' ἀμφοτέροις δὲ βεβακώς
> τολμασεῖς ἐπιόντα μένειν θρασὺν ἀσπιδιώταν,
> ᾇ τάχος εἰς Αἴγυπτον.
>
> (65–68)

So if pinning your cloak on your right shoulder
suits you, and if you can stand firm on your feet

and bravely meet a bold soldier's assault,
go straightway to Egypt.

By having Thyonichus's description of a soldier echo Tyrtaeus's and Archilochus's,[92] the poet can recall the archaic ideal of an egalitarian fellowship of sturdy soldiers, and also the archaic sympotic culture that fostered lyric representations of the soldierly and sympotic life.[93] Insofar as Alexander's conquests in the fourth century initiated a new age of expansion and colonization, which recalled the great age of colonization that preceded the rise of fifth-century democracies, Hellenistic poets naturally looked back to archaic Greek lyric poets and the sympotic themes they emphasized.[94]

By ending *Idyll* 14 with the carpe diem theme, Theocritus emphasizes the linkage between soldiery and the sympotic life and also underscores the thematic centrality of the symposium to the poem:[95]

> ἀπὸ κροτάφων πελόμεσθα
> πάντες γηραλέοι, καὶ ἐπισχερὼ ἐς γένυν ἕρπει
> λευκαίνων ὁ χρόνος· ποιεῖν τι δεῖ ἇς γόνυ χλωρόν.
>
> (68–70)
>
> We're all growing old
> from the temple, and whitening time creeps hair by hair
> toward the cheek. One must act while the knee's still supple.

Traditional social institutions must often change in response to the changing needs of a changing society. By representing *Idyll* 14's symposium in a context of (itinerant) mercenary soldiery,[96] Theocritus evokes a mobile world in which symposia can provide forums not only for elite celebrants but also for celebrants outside the elite class to establish solidarity and exclusivity (against non-Greeks, nonsoldiers, nonphilosophers, etc.).[97]

Unlike Theocritus's *Idyll* 14, which approaches the male-dominated world of symposia from the insider perspective of celebrants, Theocritus's *Idyll* 2, Simaetha's monologue, offers a (mediated) view of sympotic activities from an outsider's vantage.[98] By having the fictive Simaetha stress Delphis's symposium and gymnasium activities, the poet underscores the distance between Simaetha's and Delphis's cultural horizons and also approaches the issue of the role of social institutions in a mobile world. Although Delphis is an outlander from Myndus (in Caria), as Simaetha repeatedly emphasizes (29, 96), by having Delphis spend most of his time at the gymnasium (80, 97–98) and in sympotic

activities (149–53), the poet highlights his membership in the local leisured community. Further, when admitted to Simaetha's chamber, Delphis displays his elite status to her by showing off in detail his knowledge
of the dress code and courtship maneuvers typical of a *komos* (118–28).
The poet heightens the contrast between Delphis's insider and Simaetha's outsider status by having Delphis claim not merely membership in
the sympotic and gymnastic communities but star status: he recently
outran Philinus (115), and he is known as ἐλαφρός / καὶ καλὸς πάντεσσι
μετ᾽ ἠιθέοισι ("agile and fair among all the young men," 124–25).[99]

Theocritus emphasizes Simaetha's marginal status in society by setting her loose from discernable family ties. Although she has some female friends, she mostly makes her own way in the world. As a woman,
Simaetha does not have access to the insider power and status that such
central Greek male institutions as gymnasia and symposia made available
even to outlanders. She must look for power outside the patriarchy:
among old crones, moon goddesses, an Assyrian drug expert.[100]

The symposium theme also emerges elsewhere in Theocritus's poetry,
outside the urban mimes. Brief summaries will help indicate the range
of Theocritus's handling of the symposium theme. *Idyll* 29, a lover's exhortation featuring the carpe diem theme, ends with the threat that if
the beloved boy does not stop his promiscuous behavior, the narrator
will stop coming to his house door in courtship (*komos*). In *Idyll* 3, by
representing a rustic clumsily aping an urban sophisticate's *komos* maneuvers, Theocritus gently mocks elitist social pretensions and also
approaches the issue of class difference (even if just in the goatherd's
elevated opinion of his beloved).[101] Similarly in *Idyll* 6, Damoetas's
Polyphemus, a one-eyed herdsman, fantasizes about barring his door
against Galatea's "komastic" courtship (32). *Idyll* 7, Theocritus's most
programmatic poem, features several sympotic themes: Simichidas and
friends have left the city to attend a harvest festival in the country, Lycidas's song anticipates a drinking celebration featuring singing herdsmen, and Simichidas's song features a fictive Simichidas urbanely urging
Aratus to stop his futile komastic courtship of Philinus (123–25).[102] By
locating urbanized symposia and *komoi* in countrysides, the poet probes
sympotic manners by defamiliarizing them. Theocritus's representations
of rustic *komoi* may also playfully raise the issue of the possible appropriation of elitist Greek customs by others in a heterogeneous Hellenistic
world.[103]

Other Hellenistic poets also approach social issues related to mobility
through the themes of symposia and *komoi*.[104] While Herodas's *Mime* 2

does not directly feature a symposium, it does feature *komos* activities.[105]
Battaros, the metic pander, is charging Thales, the Phrygian merchant,
with attempting to abduct one of his women by breaking and burning
the establishment's door, tearing her clothes, and beating both her and
Battaros (60–71; these are typical *komos* activities of a shut-out lover). In
the earlier discussion of *Mime* 2, we saw how Battaros reinforces normative Greek prejudices against rich outsiders to try to win his case
against Thales. The focus of discussion here is how Battaros uses the
komos theme, in particular, to discredit Thales. Battaros associates his
own panderly interests with the respectable community's traditional disapproval of the arrogant assumption that wealth can bring exemption
from the community's social norms:

> εἰ δ' οὕνεκεν πλεῖ τὴν θάλασσαν ἢ χλαῖναν
> ἔχει τριῶν μνέων Ἀττικῶν, ἐγὼ δ' οἰκέω
> ἐν γῆι τρίβωνα καὶ ἀσκέρας σαπρὰς ἕλκων,
> βίηι τιν' ἄξει τῶν ἐμῶν ἔμ' οὐ πείσας,
> καὶ ταῦτα νυκτός, οἴχετ' ἡμιν ἡ ἀλεωρή
> τῆς πόλιος, ἄνδρες, κἀπ' ὅτ⟨ε⟩ωι σεμνύνεσθε,
> τὴν αὐτονομίην ὑμέων Θαλῆς λύσει.

(21–27)

But if he intends, just because he sails the sea or has
a cloak worth three Attic minae, while I live
on shore wearing a thin coat and trodden-down sandals — if for these
    reasons
he intends to take away one of my girls by force, without my consent,
at night, of all times, why, then, the safety of the city
is ruined, and your chief pride,
your autonomy, will be undone by Thales.

(trans. Knox, in Headlam and Knox, *Herodas*, 63–65)

Battaros flatters his Coan judges here by highlighting Cos's autonomy,[106]
an elusive quality among city-states in a world dominated by large,
autocratic kingdoms.[107] Battaros then supports his condemnation of
Thales by explicitly appealing to bourgeois prejudice against allowing
elitist, often violent komastic activities in a cooperative city-state society:

> κἠμὲ τὸν ξεῖνον
> οὐδεις πολίτης ἠλόησεν οὐδ' ἦλθεν
> πρὸς τὰς θύρας μευ νυκτὸς οὐδ' ἔχων δᾶιδας
> τὴν οἰκίην ὑφῆψεν οὐδὲ τῶν πορνέων
> βίηι λαβὼν οἴχωκεν.

(33–37)

no citizen
has ever thrashed me, or come
to my doors o' nights, or fired my house
torch in hand, or taken one of my girls
by force away with him.

> (trans. Knox, in Headlam and Knox,
> *Herodas*, 65)

In a mobile world, in which boundaries between social categories can fluctuate, Battaros specifies a negative distinction between citizen and noncitizen: citizens do not engage in elitist *komos* activities. But by having a metic pander voice these normative bourgeois Greek prejudices against the *komos*, Herodas acknowledges these prejudices, while making them comically alien and public.

Another example of a Hellenistic poem approaching issues related to mobility through the symposium theme is Callimachus's *Aetia*, frs. 178–85, commonly called *Icos*, which involves a striking representation of a drinking party. The diverse identities of the celebrants at the symposium represented in this passage reflect the mobility and internationalism of the Hellenistic world. The host, an Athenian who has settled in Alexandria, is entertaining guests who include Theogenes, a stranger from Icos in Alexandria on business, and the fictive Callimachus, a settler from Cyrene. The poet further underscores the theme of mobility by having Theogenes begin his reply to the fictive Callimachus's queries by lamenting that he is constantly traveling, more at sea than a sea gull (fr. 178.33–34). In contrast to *Idyll* 14's symposium, which features mostly lower-class celebrants, the *Icos* represents a more elite symposium, whose celebrants include an Athenian settler and a poet-scholar with ties to the Ptolemaic court.

As is typical of the Alexandrian poets, Callimachus seeks to reinforce the fellowship of Hellenistic Greeks set loose in the world and representing different ethnicities, by showing their collective difference from non-Greeks. Thus the fictive Callimachus congratulates himself and the stranger from Icos for like-minded restraint in drinking, and he denigrates draining one's cup as a Thracian custom:

> ᾧ ξυνὴν εἶχον ἐγὼ κλισίην
> οὐκ ἐπιτάξ, ἀλλ᾽ αἶνος Ὁμηρικός, αἰὲν ὁμοῖον
> ὡς θεός, οὐ ψευδής, ἐς τὸν ὁμοῖον ἄγει.
> καὶ γὰρ ὁ Θρηϊκίην μὲν ἀπέστυγε χανδὸν ἄμυστιν
> οἰνοποτεῖν, ὀλίγῳ δ᾽ ἥδετο κισσυβίῳ.

> (*Aet.*, fr. 178.8–12)

I shared a couch with him—
not by design, but the saying of Homer is not false,
    that god ever brings like to like.
For he too hated the greedy Thracian draught
    of wine, and liked a small cup.

(trans. Trypanis, "Callimachus," 95)

Symposia traditionally offered displaced persons settings in which to remember the past and thus reinforce self-identity, as shown by a symposium poem by another displaced poet, Xenophanes, who when the Persians came left his home of Colophon and lived the rest of his life as a wandering exile:

πὰρ πυρὶ χρὴ τοιαῦτα λέγειν χειμῶνος ἐν ὥρηι
ἐν κλίνηι μαλακῆι κατακείμενον, ἔμπλεον ὄντα,
πίνοντα γλυκὺν οἶνον, ὑποτρώγοντ' ἐρεβίνθους·
'τίς πόθεν εἶς ἀνδρῶν; πόσα τοι ἔτε' ἐστί, φέριστε;
πηλίκος ἦσθ', ὅθ' ὁ Μῆδος ἀφίκετο;'

(fr. 18 Diehl)

Such things should be said by the fire, in the winter season,
when resting on a soft couch after a meal,
sipping sweet wine and munching chick-peas:
"Who are you, and whence do you come? How old are you, my friend?
How old were you then, when the Mede came?"

Thus in the *Icos,* Callimachus further reinforces a sense of Greek self-identity against the barbarian other by having the fictive Callimachus ask the Ician about his cultural practices:

Μυρμιδόνων ἐσσῆνα τ[ί πάτριον ὔ]μμι σέβεσθαι
  Πηλέα, κῶς ῏Ικῳ ξυν[ὰ τὰ Θεσσαλι]κά.

(*Aet.*, fr. 178.23–24)

Why is it the tradition of your country to worship Peleus,
    king of the Myrmidons? What has Thessaly to do with Icos?

(trans. Trypanis, "Callimachus," 97)

Insofar as Callimachus's *Aetia*, a four-book elegiac poem presenting aetiologies, functions as a remembrance of the old country and old customs for its readers, its *Icos* passage offers a fictive portrait of the creative artist at work gathering aetiologies. The Ptolemies would have welcomed poetic projects like Callimachus's *Aetia*, for the court's generous patronage of creative artists stemmed in part from the newness of Alexandria, the imperial center. Founded by Alexander in the recent past, the city Alexandria did not have a Greek literary and mythological past of its own, and the Ptolemies looked to the poets to provide one.

In the *Icos*, the context of the symposium is a party in honor of the Anthesteria, a three-day festival traditionally celebrated in Athens in honor of Dionysus and the new wine vintage. Thus the poem establishes a mood of nostalgia: the host, an Athenian settler, is renewing a traditional Greek ritual (e.g., the symposium) and a festival from home.[108] The first day of the Anthesteria featured the bringing of earthenware jars filled with wine from the country into Athens. The influx of country folk (e.g., small farmers, day laborers, slaves) joining with Athenian urbanites in a carnivalesque celebration[109] reinforced Attic unity and the sense of a continuum from city to country which Cleisthenes had facilitated for fifth-century Athens when he made citizenship dependent on registering in country townships.[110] The Anthesteria's second day featured a drinking contest won by the first person to drain a three-quart jug of wine. The third day featured rituals of recovery and purification. Since in the *Icos*, the symposium is taking place on the third day (fr. 178.3–4), the restraint of the fictive Callimachus and his couch partner in drinking wine coincides with the formal shape of the traditional Athenian celebration.[111] For his Alexandrian audience, separated by a court culture from the surrounding countryside, Callimachus's fictive recreation of an Athenian settler's celebration of the Anthesteria could call up a nostalgic memory of a democratized continuum of city and country.

The fictive Callimachus's conversation with the Ician is in a tradition of intellectual, restrained symposia, well-established by the fourth century and endorsed by Xenophanes earlier: thus Callimachus and the Ician add talk to the mix of wine and water in the cup (fr. 178.15–21). But by having the fictive Callimachus turn aside from the drinking party to engage his neighbor in a private intellectual discussion, the poet creates an additional enclave within the symposium. Exclusivity based on compatibility was natural to Callimachus, a prolific poet-scholar who had come to Alexandria from Cyrene, North Africa, and settled in an enclave of intellectual Greek outlanders centered around the museum, patronized by the Ptolemaic court. Alexandria's museum community offered a setting in which strangers set loose in the world could find common ground, an intellectual fellowship that transcended international boundaries and also separated them from the surrounding city.[112]

Values of exclusivity, a preference for a small cup and private conversation, are characteristic of Callimachus's poetics — e.g., θηρὶ μὲν οὐατόεντι πανείκελον ὀγκήσαιτο / ἄλλος, ἐγ]ὼ δ᾽ εἴην οὐλ[α]χύς, ὁ πτερόεις ("Like the long-eared beast others may bray, I would be the slight, the winged one"; trans. Bulloch, "Hellenistic Poetry," 559; *Aet.* 1, fr. 1.31–32). Although elsewhere the Feast of Pitchers could be more lavish, at Athens the traditional prize was a flat-cake (Ath. 10.437b–d). Insofar as Callimachus's *Icos* recalls the spare Athenian Anthesteria, in contrast to the typically extravagant, crown-sponsored Alexandrian festivals,[113] its values correspond to the polemical value Callimachus puts on a fine and pure style, in contrast to a bombastic, impure style (e.g., *Hymn* 2.105–12, *Ep.* 30).

In conclusion, for displaced Hellenistic Greeks, the recreation of traditional social institutions (e.g., symposia, gymnasia, and festivals), both in poetry and reality, could renew a nostalgic memory of home and also encourage a sense of spiritual continuity transcending physical separation. But as we have seen, through the symposium theme poets could raise other issues related to mobility and immigration as well—such as the role of social institutions in establishing and maintaining class distinctions and mobility's destabilizing effect on social boundaries.

Friendship

In an expanded and mobile Hellenistic world, the role of kinship in determining status and identity was necessarily diminished, and friendship instead would sometimes serve traditional functions of kinship.[114] Friends might even replace family in critical instances; for example, marriage contracts could specify that friends rather than family would defend the interests of the couple in future disputes.[115] Also, enclaved groups based on common interests, class, ethnicity, and gender provided settings in which itinerant and immigrant persons could find self-affirmation and support.[116] So too memberships in professional groups, such as the Dionysiac guilds,[117] became important for maintaining status, privileges, and a full social life in urban environments.

Philosophical interest in the topic of friendship increased during the fourth and third centuries B.C.: Aristotle raised friendship to a position of centrality in his ethical system (see especially *Eth. Nic.*, books 8 and 9), and Epicurus considered friendship crucial to happiness (e.g., *K.D.* 27).[118] But unlike Aristotle, Epicurus looks beyond the Greek city-state to an expanded Hellenistic world:

ἡ φιλία περιχορεύει τὴν οἰκουμένην κηρύττουσα δὴ πᾶσιν ἡμῖν ἐγείρεσθαι ἐπὶ τὸν μακαρισμόν. (*Sent. Vat.* 52 Long and Sedley)

Friendship dances round the world, proclaiming to us all to wake for happiness. (trans. Long, "Post-Aristotelian Philosophy," 628)

Theocritus created a diverse poetic world in which friendship is a central and unifying theme. Through talking with one another and telling stories, his fictive characters, whether urban, rustic, or heroic, establish self-identity and affirm values.

Theocritus's urban mimes all feature social outsiders, needy for friendship in an unstable, mobile world: *Idyll* 2's Simaetha, abandoned by her lover, set loose from her family;[119] *Idyll* 14's Aeschinas, ex-symposiast, rejected lover; *Idyll* 15's immigrant housewives, separated from Syracusan kin, isolated in Alexandria. *Idylls* 14 and 15, urban mimes in dialogue form, highlight the role of interactive friendship in establishing and remaking personal identities. *Idyll* 2, a mime in monologue form, represents a woman alone, redescribing her experiences to find their significance by herself.

Idyll 14 contrasts two friendship forums: ritualized sympotic activity and a chance encounter. Sympotic activities traditionally affirmed male friendship and solidarity. But at Aeschinas's symposium, sympotic activities instead separated Aeschinas from his fellow symposiasts. Further, the loss of his girlfriend at the symposium left him disoriented: he needs to reclaim himself and his manhood. A chance encounter with an old friend, Thyonichus, provides impetus for recovery: through talking with Thyonichus, through renewing their friendship, Aeschinas begins the process of reestablishing self-identity (and refinding community).

By having Thyonichus redescribe Aeschinas by comparing him to a Pythagorist, the poet approaches the issue of physical appearance and reality (a topic of contemporary interest, as shown by Theophrastus's fourth-century sketches of human types):

> ταῦτ' ἄρα λεπτός,
> χὠ μύσταξ πολὺς οὗτος, αὐσταλέοι δὲ κίκιννοι.
> τοιοῦτος πρώαν τις ἀφίκετο Πυθαγορικτάς,
> ὠχρὸς κἀνυπόδητος· Ἀθαναῖος δ' ἔφατ' ἦμεν.
>
> (3–6)

> That explains your thinness, then,
> and your shaggy mustache and squalid locks.
> You look like a Pythagorean who came by the other day,
> pale and unshod, claiming to be an Athenian.

Thyonichus's redescription of Aeschinas as a Pythagorist shows how the same outer appearance can signify more than one possible reality (or self). The Pythagorist's vain longing for "baked bread" (7) can coincide with Aeschinas's hapless desire for Cynisca (to consume her?):

ΑΙ. ἤρατο μὰν καὶ τῆνος;
ΘΥ.   ἐμὶν δοκεῖ, ὀπτῶ ἀλεύρω.

(7)

AE. Was that fellow in love too?
TH.   I think so—with baked bread.

Thyonichus's amalgamation of a lover's classical physical symptoms and a philosopher's startles Aeschinas into approaching the topic of his inner condition.[120] Through this wry comparison, Thyonichus begins Aeschinas's reorientation process by suggesting the possibility of a different plot, another self. The freedom to remake oneself, to relocate, to take a new name (e.g., Herod. 2's Thales, formerly Artimmes, a Phrygian), was an advantage of an expanded and mobile Hellenistic world.

But the fictive Aeschinas distances himself from Thyonichus's levity:

παίσδεις, ὠγάθ', ἔχων· ἐμὲ δ' ἀ χαρίεσσα Κυνίσκα
ὑβρίσδει· λασῶ δὲ μανείς πυκα, θρὶξ ἀνὰ μέσσον.

(8–9)

You're always joking, my friend. But as for me, the lovely Cynisca
maltreats me, and I'll go suddenly mad one day — I'm just a hair's
    breadth away.

Aeschinas's hyperbolic prediction underscores his commitment to a closed self, limited to the single plane of lover: he sees no alternative but insanity.

Thyonichus's affectionate, familiar response, characteristic of a close friend, reminds Aeschinas of his constancy of style, a disposition independent of Cynisca:

τοιοῦτος μὲν ἀεὶ τύ, φίλ' Αἰσχίνα, ἀσυχᾶ ὀξύς,
πάντ' ἐθέλων κατὰ καιρόν· ὅμως δ' εἶπον τί τὸ καινόν.

(10–11)

You're always like this, Aeschinas, a bit impulsive,
wanting everything just so. Still, tell me what's new.

By reminding Aeschinas of a time before Cynisca, Thyonichus underscores the persistence of character through many roles. Aeschinas does not need to prolong the unhappy "Cynisca and Aeschinas" story; the world offers other possibilities. Through friendship, Thyonichus provides Aeschinas with a stronger self-identity and thus pulls him back from a near loss of self (9).

The symposium, traditionally a source of egalitarian male identity and unity, failed in Aeschinas's case. Yet soldiery, also a traditional source

of male fellowship and solidarity, offers an alternative: with Thyonichus's support, Aeschinas resolves to move abroad and become a mercenary soldier. By having Aeschinas pick an occupation in which violence is licensed (soldiery), the poet underscores how a character trait
like violence can provide a functional continuity of self for Aeschinas.

A series of disjunctions and negative superlatives emphasizes Aeschinas's loss of a sense of connectedness and self-worth after Cynisca left
him (and he separated from the sympotic community):

ἄμμες δ᾽ οὔτε λόγω τινὸς ἄξιοι οὔτ᾽ ἀριθμητοί,
δύστανοι Μεγαρῆες ἀτιμοτάτᾳ ἐνὶ μοίρᾳ.

(48–49)

But as for me, I am not worth notice or account,
like the miserable Megarians, in last place.

By having Aeschinas use a similar series of disjunctive and negative superlatives in describing a soldier, the poet highlights the dynamics involved in Aeschinas's reconstitution, the value he is trying to set on being average, part of a group again, not separated by obsessive love:

οὔτε κάκιστος
οὔτε πρᾶτος ἴσως, ὁμαλὸς δέ τις ὁ στρατιώτας.

(55–56)

a soldier's not the worst
nor the first, perhaps, but an ordinary sort.

Idyll 14 explores the issue of the destabilizing effect of mobility and
privatization on personal identity among men set loose in the world. In
the course of the poem, in the company of a friend, Aeschinas encounters various models of manhood and modes of sociability: an ascetic
philosopher, an immoderate lover, a sympathetic friend, jocular symposiasts, mercenaries, a dynast. At the poem's end, Thyonichus offers
Aeschinas a sturdy soldier to emulate and tells him how to dress to fit
the role: he offers him the prospect of reconstituting self-identity, of actively making choices rather than passively suffering. Thus in *Idyll* 14,
through Aeschinas's conversation with Thyonichus, the poet approaches
the theme of friendship's role in finding personal identity and in providing continuity of self for mobile persons.

Theocritus wrote many poems featuring the casual talk of men
among themselves, but only *Idyll* 15 features the casual talk of women
among themselves.[121] In *Idyll* 15, Gorgo and Praxinoa, as Syracusan settlers in Alexandria, are separated from kinship ties and old traditions.

But they have each other to provide validations of the past, of their memories of another world, of constancies of self that can transcend changes of time and space. Their reunion provides a forum for exploring ways outsiders (e.g., immigrants, herdsmen, poets, women) can ease their alienation by talking with one another: about loneliness, errant husbands, the cost of wool and clothing.[122] The motif of a natural linkage between women and aliens is not new to the Hellenistic age. Perhaps the most explicit earlier expression of this motif occurs when Euripides' Medea, an outlander from Colchis, tries to elicit sympathy from Corinthian women by describing marriage as a form of immigration, requiring similar skills of adaptation:

ἐς καινὰ δ' ἤθη καὶ νόμους ἀφιγμένην
δεῖ μάντιν εἶναι, μὴ μαθοῦσαν οἴκοθεν
ὅτῳ μάλιστα χρήσεται ξυνευνέτῃ.

(238–40 O.C.T.)

She arrives among new modes of behavior and manners,
And needs prophetic power, unless she has learned at home,
How best to manage him who shares the bed with her.

(trans. Warner, *Medea*, 67)

In *Idyll* 15, Gorgo and Praxinoa reestablish an alliance based on their common background, interests, and shared complaints:

ΠΡ. ἀπφῦς μὰν τῆνός γα πρόαν—λέγομες δὲ πρόαν θην
'πάππα, νίτρον καὶ φῦκος ἀπὸ σκανᾶς ἀγοράσδειν'—
ἷκτο φέρων ἅλας ἄμμιν, ἀνὴρ τρισκαιδεκάπαχυς.
ΓΟ. χὤμὸς ταυτᾷ ἔχει· φθόρος ἀργυρίω Διοκλείδας·
ἑπταδράχμως κυνάδας, γραιᾶν ἀποτίλματα πηρᾶν,
πέντε πόκως ἔλαβ' ἐχθές, ἅπαν ῥύπον, ἔργον ἐπ' ἔργῳ.

(15–20)

PR: Well, that papa, just the other day we said to him—just the other day
then: "papa, buy soda and red dye from the store."
He came back with salt for us, our thirteen-cubit hero.
GO: My husband likewise: Diokleidas, waster of silver.
Five fleeces he bought yesterday, seven drachmas worth of dog hairs,
the pluckings of old wallets, all filthy, nothing but work.

Further, through the fiction of eavesdropping on housewives' confidential discussion of their husbands' shortcomings, the poet can approach the issues of gender and power by showing how private talk (and poetry) can explore and test social limitations and hegemonic (patriarchal) myths. The gratuitous nature of Praxinoa's ironic remark later in the poem, "Women know all things, even how Zeus married Hera" (64), underscores the power and freedom of private talk to appropriate even the gods' incestuous marriages as material for storytelling.

Praxinoa's hyperbolic response to Gorgo's complaint highlights her isolation, as well as her estrangement from her husband:

ταῦθ' ὁ πάραρος τῆνος· ἐπ' ἔσχατα γᾶς ἔλαβ' ἐνθών
ἰλεόν, οὐκ οἴκησιν, ὅπως μὴ γείτονες ὦμες
ἀλλάλαις, ποτ' ἔριν, φθονερὸν κακόν, αἰὲν ὁμοῖος.

(8–10)

It's that absurd husband of mine — he went to the ends of the world
and bought a hutch not a home, to keep us from being neighbors to one
    another,
and he did it for spite, the jealous scoundrel, always the same.

Later, by having Praxinoa echo Gorgo's reaction to the crowded streets (ὅσσος ὄχλος, "what a huge crowd," 44; cf. πολλῶ μὲν ὄχλω, "the crowd was so big," 5), the poet approaches the theme of how common danger and shared speech can promote a sense of unity. A thematic concern of Theocritus's poems is the function of private talk in human affairs. In *Idyll* 15, by focusing on the experiences of settlers in a big city, the poet explores how talk can affirm friendships and help establish alternative communities.[123]

The social dynamics of Gorgo and Praxinoa's dialogue can be further illuminated through a brief comparison to Herodas's *Mime* 1, which also begins with a woman's arrival at an acquaintance's house and her complaints about the hardships of the road:

μακρὴν ἀποικέω, τέκνον, ἐν δὲ τῆις λαύρηις
ὁ πηλὸς ἄχρις ἰγνύων προσέστηκεν,
ἐγὼ δὲ δραίνω μυῖ' ὅσον· τὸ γὰρ γῆρας
ἡμέ]ας καθέλκει κἠ σκιὴ παρέστηκεν.

(13–16)

I live a long way off, child, and the mud
in the lanes reaches up to my knees,
and my strength is as a fly's, for old age
weighs me down and the Shadow stands by me.

(trans. Knox, in Headlam and Knox, *Herodas,* 3)

In *Idyll* 15, the women's initial exchange of greetings creates common ground and leads to Praxinoa's acceptance of Gorgo's proposal to attend a festival. *Mime* 1's initial exchange, on the other hand, underscores age differences between guest and hostess and leads to the young hostess's rejection of her guest's proposal:

σὺ δ᾽ αὖτις ἔς με μηδὲ ἔν⟨α⟩, φίλη, τοῖον
φέρουσα χώρει μῦθον· ὃν δὲ γρήιηισι
πρέπει γυναιξὶ τῆις νέηις ἀπάγγελλε.

(73–75)

Don't come to me again, my friend, with a tale
like this! Tell your young [women] a tale befitting
old crones.

(trans. B. H. Fowler, *Hellenistic Poetry,* 237)

In *Idyll* 15 each woman presents complaints about her own husband and feels solidarity in the sharing of complaints. In *Mime* 1 the old woman's attacks on Metriche's husband instead alienate Metriche and prompt her to defend him herself: οὐ γὰρ ἐγγελᾶι τις εἰς Μάνδριν ("No one mocks my Mandris"; trans. B. H. Fowler, *Hellenistic Poetry,* 237; 77).

In *Idylls* 14 and 15, the reappearance of an old friend offering a mode of constancy in a changing world begins a dialogic revitalization process. But in *Idyll* 2 Simaetha's process of self-realization does not emerge in the presence of an old friend: instead, she narrates her story to the moon. Although her story reveals a rich community of friends, she confronts her obsession with Delphis by herself. The Hellenistic world offered a man many opportunities to distance himself spatially from the beloved: he could become a trader, a bureaucrat, a mercenary soldier (as *Idyll* 14's Aeschinas), etc. For a woman, on the other hand, options to relocate were severely limited (and generally outside normative society). But in staying where she is, Simaetha must confront the Delphis situation. She resolves to bring him back to her or disentangle their stories by killing him before he destroys her. Her actions of courtship and revenge, unconventional and unsanctioned, place her outside the norms of society and friendship. By presenting *Idyll* 2 in monologue form rather than dialogue, Theocritus avoids subjecting Simaetha's actions to judgments of approval or disapproval within the poem and thus perhaps encourages the reader to suspend moral judgment for the poem's duration as well. By not giving Simaetha a friend with whom to talk, the poet also can emphasize a negative side of the Hellenistic world's mobility: the loneliness and powerlessness that can come (especially to women) from the absence of kinship ties within a community.

CHAPTER 2

Gender and Power

The ascendancy of autocratic hegemonies, the rise in mobility, and the reliance on mercenary forces had strong effects on gendered social identities for Greeks in the Hellenistic age. Masculine power in the old Greek world was closely linked with the ideal of a citizen-soldier.[1] But in a mobile Hellenistic world, citizenship was losing its appeal as a measure of masculine power. Further, the rise in state wealth, resulting in part from Alexander's conquests in the East, enabled reliance on mercenaries in armed forces. Thus Hellenistic Greek males, for the most part, had to seek personal identities outside the role of citizen-soldiers and the realm of public political life.[2] As male political life faded, the scope of female public life expanded.[3] Strong queens, such as Olympas and Arsinoe II, were setting new levels of visibility for Greek women, and the horizon of possible social roles was expanding for less elite Greek women as well. Evidence of women receiving civic honors for poetic achievements and public benefactions attests to the growing visibility (and economic power) of women.[4] Further, marriage contracts developed which, by protecting a woman's interests in the absence of family, allowed her more independence and mobility.[5]

A basic premise of social and political order in the ancient Greek world was the subordination of female to male. Although the Hellenistic Greek world was still basically a patriarchy, and women's lives remained more circumscribed than men's, normative boundaries between public and private, male and female, domestic and political were becoming more fluid. Further, in Ptolemaic Egypt, as Ahmed has recently stressed,

Egyptian laws and customs provided an important model of sexual egalitarianism for Greeks,[6] and Pomeroy confirms that "in the economic
sphere, as in the political and social realms, there was less distinction
between the genders in Ptolemaic Egypt than there was, for example, in
Athens, or in Greek society in general of an earlier period."[7] Since Ptolemaic Alexandria was a center for advanced poetic projects, it is not sur-
prising that the subject of gender roles and relations became a central
thematic concern among Hellenistic poets.

With the loss of the autonomous city-state as an arena for Greek
males to establish self-identity, private spheres of self-realization, particularly the erotic, ascended in cultural importance. Much of Theocritus's poetry is engaged with issues of how passionate love detaches
individuals from normative life and how in song or talk, through redescription of selves and others, men and women try to remake their
gendered identities. Theocritus's urban mimes, with their attention to
interactive relations of men and women within a civic frame, best reflect
how changing social and political conditions can destabilize gendered
identities.

The first section of this chapter shows how representations of male-
female encounters in Theocritus's urban mimes reflect concerns about
changing gender roles in the Hellenistic age. An examination of Theocritus's shaping of these male-female encounters also underscores his
close attention to gender differences in both discourse and behavior. The
second section looks more closely at issues of women and power in the
urban mimes. A common source of power for women in the urban
mimes is religion and religious rituals (including witchcraft). Theocritus's poetry also contains numerous examples of powerful women linked
with subordinate males. In addition, this section compares Theocritus's
approach to the issue of gendered power with approaches of other Hellenistic poets. The third section examines the issue of sexual ambiguity
in Theocritus's poetry, with some comparative attention to other Hellenistic poetry as well. This includes a discussion of Theocritus's presentation of Adonis in *Idyll* 15, a crucial topic in a study of the theme of
gender identity in Theocritus's poetry.

Male-Female Relations

Male-female relations are central to all three urban mimes.
Idyll 2 is basically the story of Simaetha and Delphis's relationship.

Idyll 14 includes the story of the breakup of Aeschinas and Cynisca's relationship. *Idyll* 15 presents a number of complex male-female interactions in the public space. A matching of *Idylls* 2 and 14 underscores Theocritus's interest in how gender can shape experience. Both poems feature the topic of a failed heterosexual love affair, but *Idyll* 2 approaches it from the vantage of the rejected woman; *Idyll* 14, from the vantage of the rejected man.

Two other similarities link *Idylls* 2 and 14. First, in both poems, a symposium serves as a focal point in the love affair's dissolution. In *Idyll* 2, Simaetha, excluded from the sympotic community, describes how she learned from a flute player's mother that Delphis had abandoned her and returned to his former erotic recreations in the sympotic world.[8] In *Idyll* 14, Aeschinas, a sympotic insider, describes how Cynisca left him by fleeing his symposium. Second, in both poems, fictive persons adopt new gendered personae when their lovers abandon them. In *Idyll* 2, Simaetha responds to Delphis's desertion by moving outside the patriarchal state and assuming the countercultural role of a witch. In *Idyll* 14, Aeschinas responds to Cynisca's desertion first by adopting a classic lovelorn pose and then by resolving to go abroad and become a mercenary soldier.

In the first chapter, the discussion of *Idyll* 2 focuses on how Theocritus's representation of Delphis as an elite but displaced Greek raises issues of mobility and assimilation and also heightens Delphis's distance from Simaetha's social world. This chapter looks more directly at the central topic of gendered power relations in *Idyll* 2.[9] The metaphorical linkage between male domination and colonization[10] may help illuminate *Idyll* 2's power dynamics: Delphis, the privileged male colonizer, an elite Greek foreigner from Myndus, assumes erotic privilege in a patriarchal system, and Simaetha, the subordinated female, finds recourse in an alternative realm of magic, nature, earth.[11] Further, *Idyll* 2, Simaetha's monologue, has a special self-reflective edge insofar as Theocritus, a privileged Greek male, is presenting a subordinated Greek female, whose self-narrative in turn presents a privileged Greek male.

In *Idyll* 2, Theocritus situates Simaetha, without kin in evidence to uphold her, on the margins of Greek society where slaves and free persons mingle, and he shows her even so refusing to be silenced and disregarded. Instead she assumes the traditionally male initiative in courtship: she sees Delphis, an elite Greek male, experiences love symptoms, and sends her maid to summon him. Simaetha's description of falling in love underscores her appropriation of male privilege in making Delphis and his friend objects of her erotic gaze:

ἤδη δ᾽ εὖσα μέσαν κατ᾽ ἀμαξιτόν, ᾇ τὰ Λύκωνος,
εἶδον Δέλφιν ὁμοῦ τε καὶ Εὐδάμιππον ἰόντας·
τοῖς δ᾽ ἦς ξανθοτέρα μὲν ἑλιχρύσοιο γενειάς,
στήθεα δὲ στίλβοντα πολὺ πλέον ἢ τύ, Σελάνα,
ὡς ἀπὸ γυμνασίοιο καλὸν πόνον ἄρτι λιπόντων.

(76–80)

And I was already midway on the road, at Lycon's place,
when I saw Delphis walking with Eudamippus.
And their beards were more golden than helichryse,
and their breasts were far more shining than you, Selene,
for they had freshly left the gymnasium's fair exercise.

By having Simaetha emphasize her role as spectator (rather than spectacle), the poet unsettles patriarchal assumptions about the relations of men and women in a public space. Simaetha's comparison of Delphis and Eudamippus to the moon goddess reinforces their feminized position. Polarities such as male and female, public and private, help uphold hierarchical positions of privilege. *Idyll* 2 explores what happens when an unruly "other" challenges such gendered polarities by behaving inappropriately, breaking the rules. But the objectification of Delphis and Eudamippus, combined with the linkage of their glistening male beauty with the wrestling-school (a usual site of homosexual voyeurism)[12] also heightens the homoerotic pleasure made available through Simaetha's gaze.[13]

Delphis's response to Simaetha's unconventional summons shows ways a person unsettled by alien modes of behavior might try to reestablish a familiar pattern of power relations. By verbally enacting a courtship routine (*komos*) through which elitist Greek males traditionally asserted social dominance, Delphis maneuvers himself back into the conventional male position of subject not object in the seduction scene. But Delphis's seduction speech ends with a reversed-sex analogy that refeminizes his own position as love's victim, even while it suggests a repositioning of Simaetha too (as a female victim rather than initiator of love):

σὺν δὲ κακαῖς μανίαις καὶ παρθένον ἐκ θαλάμοιο
καὶ νύμφαν ἐφόβησ᾽ ἔτι δέμνια θερμὰ λιποῖσαν
ἀνέρος.

(136–38)

And with bad madness he rouses a maid from her chamber
and a bride to leave her husband's bed, still warm.

The ambiguity in Delphis's use of analogy here exemplifies the fluidity of gendered positions of power in *Idyll* 2 and underscores Theocritus's interest in how sexual self-perception can defy the rigidity of gendered polarities. Further, Delphis's use of this analogy, which shows Eros exercising power indiscriminately (without making distinctions between maiden and bride), encourages the suspicion that Delphis too did not see Simaetha as an individual but rather as a generic woman; he too would not consider the particularities of her social situation. Simaetha vividly recreates Delphis: his golden beard (78), his glow like the moon goddess's (79), his exact words of courtship. But Simaetha's redescription of Delphis's courtship never shows him particularizing her. Instead, Delphis's courtship speech focused on himself: how he would have looked and felt had he performed a *komos*. The poem itself, Simaetha's monologue, embodies the highly individualized, whole woman Delphis cannot see.

Simaetha's remembrance of the way Delphis bestowed adjectives underscores his male narcissism. He described Philinus as χαρίεις ("graceful," 115) and himself as ἐλαφρός / καὶ καλός ("agile and fair," 124–25). In both cases the epithets apply to the whole person. But the epithet he uses to describe Simaetha (καλόν, "lovely," 126) is applied to only one body part (στόμα, "mouth," 126), treated solely as an object of his personal, sexual pleasure: εὗδόν τ', εἴ κε μόνον τὸ καλὸν στόμα τεῦς ἐφίλησα ("I would have slept, if I only had kissed your lovely mouth"; 126).

In the culturally approved life of respectable Greek women, sex meant marriage and family. But Delphis comes from the sympotic/gymnastic world of easy extramarital love, with either sex (44, 150). The repetition of the adjective ἐλαφρός (light) underscores the distance between Delphis's and Simaetha's approaches to love. Delphis's reputation for being handsome and ἐλαφρός ("light in moving," 124) made him confident that lovemaking with him would be pleasing. For Simaetha, on the other hand, to experience love, to seek its cure, is οὐδὲν ἐλαφρόν ("no light matter," 92). Delphis's abandonment of Simaetha reveals to her what ἐλαφρός means in his case: that he is light-minded,[14] or as Simaetha confirms at the poem's start, that Delphis has ταχινὰς φρένας ("a fickle heart," 7). How could she expect to keep a Delphis who outran even charming Philinus? A repetition of the participle φεύγων (fleeing) also highlights the distance between them in matters of love. Delphis acts in haste, hurrying from a symposium to wreathe a doorway: ᾤχετο φεύγων ("He ran off," 152). But for Simaetha falling in love is a monumental life event, involving a rite of separation from her previous life. She suffered fever ten days, consulted old women skilled in charms: ὁ δὲ χρόνος ἄνυτο φεύγων ("time was flying by," 92), but Simaetha did not rush into love.[15]

Threshold and road motifs reinforce *Idyll* 2's shaping of Simaetha's interaction with Delphis as a female rite of passage.[16] Simaetha first saw Delphis at a midway point, on a walk to a festival of Artemis (a goddess of female initiation rituals).[17] She saw Delphis for the second time as he stepped with a light foot over her threshold (104). Simaetha's self-description underscores the liminality of this moment: suspended between childhood and adulthood, she was less articulate than babes calling to their mother and her body was as stiff as the doll she was putting aside to become a woman (108–9).[18] Simaetha infuses with epic grandeur another liminal moment, this morning's dawn, when a gossip came and told her that Delphis loved another (145–49). In an unstable environment, without visible family connections, Simaetha had created an idyllic world of love for herself. But Delphis's departure destroyed that world and Simaetha's self-identity as well.

A brief return to our comparison with *Idyll* 14 helps clarify Theocritus's handling of gender issues in *Idyll* 2. In both *Idylls* 2 and 14, the defection of a loved one destroyed the lover's sense of self-worth. In *Idyll* 14, Aeschinas describes himself as worthless: ἄμμες δ' οὔτε λόγω τινὸς ἄξιοι οὔτ' ἀριθμητοί, / δύστανοι Μεγαρῆες ἀτιμοτάτᾳ ἐνὶ μοίρᾳ ("As for me, I'm not worth notice or account, / like the miserable Megarians, in last place"; 48–49).[19] Similarly in *Idyll* 2, Simaetha describes how Delphis left her without an identity: ἀντὶ γυναικὸς ἔθηκε κακὰν καὶ ἀπάρθενον ἦμεν ("He has made me, instead of a wife, a bad woman, and a maid no more"; 41).[20] From the abyss, both Simaetha and Aeschinas have to recreate themselves. For *Idyll* 14's Aeschinas, a Greek male in a mobile, urban world, options are open: he resolves to go abroad and become a mercenary soldier. But for *Idyll* 2's Simaetha, a Greek female without husband or virginity in a patriarchal world, options are limited. Before Delphis left her, Simaetha had already made herself a monster in society through her violation of sexual and social rules. But Delphis's betrayal moves Simaetha further outside normative, patriarchal society into an alternative realm of magic and witchcraft, where the terms of the struggle between male autonomy and female self-empowerment can shift. Later in the chapter I discuss how Theocritus's shaping of Simaetha's magic rites highlights the theme of gender and power. But now let us consider in more detail how *Idyll* 14, like *Idyll* 2, raises the issue of the fragility of gendered identities in a changing world.

In the age of autocratic Hellenistic kingdoms, Greek men as well as women were looking outside public political life for privatized realms in which to rediscover self-worth. The erotic realm, with its own practices of dominance and subordination, offered a forum for establishing personal identity. *Idyll* 14 explores problems that can arise for a Greek man in a world of changing gendered identities if he lets heterosexual love become the focus of his identity. Also, in a time when Greek women were attaining increased levels of visibility and economic power, *Idyll* 14 presents an example of what could happen if a spirit of female independence invaded the men's-club atmosphere of the symposium. Although in the ancient Greek world compliance was an expected part of a woman's role (especially at symposia), in *Idyll* 14 Cynisca did not comply with Aeschinas, the symposium host, in his expectation that she would toast him as her lover. Her behavior revealed instead that she was in love with Lycus, his neighbor's son. Thus Cynisca defied Aeschinas's authority by exercising choice in whom she loved and by leaving the symposium.

Cynisca's actions upset Aeschinas's assumptions about the social order,[21] and he is still suffering an identity crisis two months later (48–49): Cynisca has brought him near madness (9). Part of Aeschinas's anxiety is due to uncertainty about gender roles. By using the term *hybris* (characteristically linked with *komos* activities), Aeschinas redescribes Cynisca's behavior as a usurpation of male sympotic privilege (the maltreatment of others): ἐμὲ δ' ἀ χαρίεσσα Κυνίσκα / ὑβρίσδει ("But as for me, the lovely Cynisca / maltreats me"; 8–9).

The obsessive quality of Aeschinas's passion for Cynisca has moved him outside normative male life. By having Aeschinas repeat the name of Cynisca's new lover Lycus both times he mentions him (47's anaphora, cf. 24's anastrophe), Theocritus emphasizes Aeschinas's jealousy at being replaced: Λύκος νῦν πάντα, Λύκῳ καὶ νυκτὸς ἀνῷκται ("Now Lycus is everything; her door's open to Lycus even at night"; 47). The mention of Lycus moves Aeschinas to project himself into Cynisca's passion and even into her bedroom,[22] and this vision propels Aeschinas into an abyss of self-pity:

ἄμμες δ' οὔτε λόγω τινὸς ἄξιοι οὔτ' ἀριθμητοί,
δύστανοι Μεγαρῆες ἀτιμοτάτᾳ ἐνὶ μοίρᾳ.
κεἰ μὲν ἀποστέρξαιμι, τὰ πάντα κεν ἐς δέον ἔρποι.
νῦν δὲ πόθεν; μῦς, φαντί, Θυώνιχε, γεύμεθα πίσσας.
χὤτι τὸ φάρμακόν ἐστιν ἀμηχανέοντος ἔρωτος,
οὐκ οἶδα.

(48–53)

But as for me, I'm not worth notice or account,
like the miserable Megarians, in last place.
If only I'd stop loving her, everything would come out right.

But as it is, how can it? I'm like the mouse caught in pitch, as they say,
    Thyonichus.
And what is the cure for helpless love,
I don't know.

Aeschinas had centered his identity on his success as a lover, and when Cynisca leaves him, his self-image plummets. The poet underscores Aeschinas's compulsive linkage of Cynisca's passion with his own by having Aeschinas use the noun *eros* only twice in *Idyll* 14, both times placed last in the line: first Cynisca's *eros* (26), and second Aeschinas's *eros* (52). Cynisca's κλύμενος ("famous," 26) love for Lycus makes Aeschinas's love for her ἀμηχανέων ("helpless," 52), but Aeschinas's passionate love for Cynisca empowers her, for she can reject him.

Aeschinas's redescriptions of Cynisca's behavior at the fateful symposium reflect male anxieties about female autonomy. Aeschinas's identity crisis began when Cynisca refused to participate in the toasting ritual:

ἀμὲς μὲν φωνεῦντες ἐπίνομες, ὡς ἐδέδοκτο·
ἃ δ᾽ οὐδὲν παρεόντος ἐμεῦ.

(20–21)

So while we were drinking and calling out names, as agreed,
she said nothing, though I was right there!

The phonetic parallelism and matching positions of the phrases ἀμὲς μέν ("while we," 20) and ἃ δ᾽ οὐδέν ("she [said] nothing," 21), by opposing male and female, group and individual, underscore Cynisca's defiance of male solidarity and control. Cynisca speaks only once and blushes. Her blush, like her silence earlier, is a powerful signifier of her separation from the male ideology which privileges talk in a sympotic context:

'οὐ φθεγξῇ; λύκον εἶδες;' ἔπαιξέ τις. 'ὡς σοφός' εἶπεν,
κἠφλέγετ᾽· εὐμαρέως κεν ἀπ᾽ αὐτᾶς καὶ λύχνον ἇψας.

(22–23)

"Won't you speak? Have you seen a wolf?" someone teased. "How
    clever," she said,
and her cheeks blazed; you could have lit a lamp from her easily.

The phonetic similarities and matching placement of the descriptions of speaking and blushing (οὐ φθεγξῇ, 22; κἠφλέγετ᾽, 23) and the echo of the noun λύκον ("wolf," 22) in λύχνον ("lamp," 23) highlight Aeschinas's sudden realization of Cynisca's sexual betrayal: the "wolf" emerges in her blush, which speaks as strongly as words of her passion for Lycus (Wolf).

Cynisca's defiant behavior at the symposium frustrated Aeschinas's assumptions of sexual hegemony. Now, in retrospect, Aeschinas uses three images to describe her conduct. First he describes her tears as worse than a little girl's: ἔκλαεν ἐξαπίνας θαλερώτερον ἢ παρὰ ματρί / παρθένος ἑξαετὴς κόλπω ἐπιθυμήσασα ("She suddenly started crying, worse than a six-year-old / who longs for her mother's lap"; 32–33). Then he compares her speed in running away to a mother swallow's: μάστακα δοῖσα τέκνοισιν ὑπωροφίοισι χελιδών / ἄψορρον ταχινὰ πέτεται βίον ἄλλον ἀγείρειν ("A swallow gives morsels to her nestlings under the eaves / and flies swiftly off again to fetch more food," 39–40). Finally he signifies her disappearance with a reference to a famous bull fable: ἔβα ποκὰ ταῦρος ἀν' ὕλαν ("A bull once went through the woods," 43). The incongruity of these images has long disturbed readers.[23] Recent scholars have approached these images principally as devices through which the poet can characterize the fictive speaker as inept.[24]

I would like to suggest that through Aeschinas's use of these incongruous images, Theocritus represents the psychological process of Aeschinas coming to terms with his recent past. The use of imagery here, as elsewhere in Theocritus, requires the poem's audience to be active, to project into the character's emotional state. Aeschinas's descriptions of Cynisca move from helpless to powerful, female to male, domestic to wild: a crying girl-child; a mother swallow; a bull. They start by domesticating Cynisca, but end by betraying Aeschinas's realization that she has broken free of him. By redescribing Cynisca first as a child with her mother and then as a mother with her offspring, Aeschinas tries to assert dominance by fixing her, containing her within the domestic sphere, subsuming her under subordinated categories, relegating her to biology. But his imagery breaks away from the female realm: instead, his description of her behavior at the party ends with the tale of a bull. Insofar as Cynisca behaved in an autonomous and disruptive manner, Aeschinas ultimately reads her actions as male.[25]

Aeschinas's redescriptions of himself reflect how Cynisca's independent behavior causes him to perceive himself as worthless and hopeless: a starving Megarian (49), a mouse caught in pitch (51).[26] Insofar as a bull and a mouse represent opposite poles of power in the animal kingdom, Aeschinas's imagery reflects male anxieties about gender privilege. He sees Cynisca finally as a bull running free to the woods and himself as a mouse caught in pitch: her, dominant and autonomous; himself, subordinate and constrained. Aeschinas's use of imagery suggesting gender reversal reflects how Cynisca's unconventional behavior has destabilized his sense of self-identity.

The image of Cynisca running from the symposium as a bull runs into the woods can enrich the poem's gender dynamics in other ways as well. Just as in Sophocles' *Oedipus the King,* the chorus use the bull fable to emphasize the savage otherness of Laius's unknown murderer (477), so too in *Idyll* 14, through the bull imagery, Aeschinas underscores Cynisca's savage otherness.[27] Further, in Greek myth and literature, woods traditionally represent escape from normative society and sexuality;[28] and the metamorphosis of woman into wild beast can also represent release from conventionally gendered identities (e.g., Atalanta the virgin huntress, later a lion, and Callisto the virgin huntress, later a bear).[29] Also, by having Cynisca mate with a wolf (Lycus), Theocritus highlights the opposition of Cynisca's wildness and Aeschinas's cultivated sympotic life.[30] Finally, a wolf, like a boar, can represent a test of manhood. But rather than challenge the wolf (Lycus, his rival), Aeschinas beats the girl: he is a bully, and all he can do to mitigate his brutish violence is refer to her as a bull.

The Greek patriarchal world separated conceptually women who attended symposia from mothers and children. But Aeschinas does not distance himself from Cynisca by underscoring her social inferiority as a woman who attends symposia. Instead, "romantically" he tries to redescribe her into the world of the family, which he has rejected by devoting himself to her. Aeschinas's use of domestic imagery for Cynisca suggests the male fantasy of domesticating the prostitute (although she may not have been, strictly speaking, a prostitute — see the discussion of Cynisca's status in chapter 1). The related theme of prostituting the housewife is central to Herodas's *Mime* 1, and Greek drinking cups conflating the images of a prostitute with a housewife show an enduring interest in these male fantasies.[31] Female social categories become even more fuzzy in the Roman world (both in life and in art) with the influx of Greek courtesans and the presence of respectable Roman women at symposia,[32] and the representation of mistress as loving wife becomes a central thematic motif in Latin elegiac poetry (e.g., Cat. 68, Tib. 1.5.21–34).[33]

Gow, in commenting on the word ἐπιθυμήσασα ("longing for [her mother's lap]," 33) in Aeschinas's description of Cynisca's tears as like a six-year-old's, refers to Achilles' description of Patroclus's tears in the *Iliad* as "T's original":[34]

τίπτε δεδάκρυσαι, Πατρόκλεες, ἠΰτε κούρη
νηπίη, ἥ θ᾽ ἅμα μητρὶ θέουσ᾽ ἀνελέσθαι ἀνώγει,
εἱανοῦ ἁπτομένη, καί τ᾽ ἐσσυμένην κατερύκει,
δακρυόεσσα δέ μιν ποτιδέρκεται, ὄφρ᾽ ἀνέληται.
(Hom. *Il.* 16.7–10 O.C.T.)

> Why then are you crying like some poor little girl, Patroklos,
> who runs after her mother and begs to be picked up and carried,
> and clings to her dress, and holds her back when she tries to hurry,
> and gazes tearfully into her face, until she is picked up?
>
> (trans. Lattimore, *Iliad,* 330)

Most commentators on *Idyll* 14 have disregarded Theocritus's echo of Homer here. Yet Theocritus uses textual echoes throughout his poetry, and it is worth exploring how such echoes can enrich the dynamics of the poems.[35] I would like to make a few suggestions concerning why the poet, in representing Aeschinas's response to Cynisca's tears, might recall Achilles' response to Patroclus's tears. First, an evocation of the valorized world of Homeric warriors heightens by contrast the comic modernity and instability of Aeschinas's mobile world of mercenaries and party girls. The heroic world has come to this: privatized, everyday triumphs and defeats in the agonistic arena of love and the symposium. The pathos of Achilles' heroic loss resonates in Aeschinas's redescription of Cynisca as a little girl and ironizes his self-representation of loss. Second, through this allusion Theocritus also highlights *Idyll* 14's plot and theme development. Just as Patroclus's tears mark a turning point in the *Iliad's* plot and lead to Achilles losing Patroclus, so Cynisca's tears mark a turning point in *Idyll* 14's plot and lead to Aeschinas losing Cynisca.[36] Further, just as Patroclus's loss causes Achilles to feel isolated and alienated from his fellow soldiers (his physical symptoms include tearfulness and inability to sleep or eat), so too Cynisca's loss causes Aeschinas to feel isolated and alienated from his fellow symposiasts (his physical symptoms include unkempt hair, thinness, and paleness). Thus, by evoking the most famous example of enclaved male bonding during wartime in the Homeric world, Theocritus can underscore the male-bonded community Aeschinas has abandoned for Cynisca. Further, the echo of a Homeric misreading of gender (Patroclus as a young girl) draws attention to Aeschinas's own trouble assigning gender to the roles of his girlfriend and himself.

Aeschinas initially limits himself to a closed identity as Cynisca's lover: when she abandons him, he puts on the "symptoms of love" mask (3–6). Aeschinas's tendency to categorize reductively both himself and others is also shown by his redescriptions of Cynisca as mother and child. But just as the roles of mother and child cannot define Cynisca (instead she becomes a bull, 43), so too the role of lover should not exhaust Aeschinas's potential. Aeschinas resolves to exchange his persona as rejected lover for the persona of soldier, a choice well-suited to his persistently violent character, as shown by his description of his mistreatment of Cynisca: τᾶμος ἐγώ, τὸν ἴσαις τύ, Θυώνιχε, πὺξ ἐπὶ κόρρας / ἤλασα, κἄλλαν αὖθις ("Then I — you know me, Thyonichus — I struck her with my fist / on the temple, and then I struck her again"; 34–35).

Through enlisting as a soldier, Aeschinas can regain the male comradery he has lost by abandoning the sympotic community and can also channel his violence. Aeschinas suggests a role model in the mercenary Simus, a man of equal age who also went abroad to forget (54). Aeschinas describes Simus's motivation with the ambiguous phrase ὁ τᾶς ἐπιχάλκω ἐρασθείς (53). Since ἡ ἐπίχαλκος can be slang for a shield ("bronze"), the scholia understand the phrase to mean "the man who fell in love with soldiery." More recent readers understand the phrase to mean instead the man "who fell in love with the brazen girl." [37] Yet both meanings can resonate in this phrase since for Aeschinas, as for Simus, the choice is between a brazen girl and a bronze shield. Aeschinas characteristically views such choices as exclusive. Thus by choosing soldiery, a masculinized profession, Aeschinas can underscore his separation from women: he can reject life-giving femaleness (exemplified in his use of child-rearing images for Cynisca) by exercising the male prerogative of becoming a death-dealing soldier.[38] In chapter 4 we return to *Idyll* 14 and this topic when we consider the place of Ptolemy's encomium in Aeschinas's story.

I would like to add a final note on the possible gender significance in the name of Aeschinas's girlfriend: Κυνίσκα ("little bitch"). Gow remarks that the name Κυνίσκος is not unusual and notes that Hesychius links the name Κύννα with prostitution.[39] Yet the name Κυνίσκα can also imply "little female Cynic."[40] The Cynics, a recent philosophical cult, admitted women. Further, according to anecdotal report, the wife of the Cynic Crates regularly attended symposia with him and also disrupted them with her clever and defiant speech (Diog. Laert. 6.96–98). *Idyll* 14's Cynisca displays Cynic-like integrity when she maintains her right to love whom she pleases, despite the symposiasts' mocking and Aeschinas's violence. Also, in fleeing the symposium, Cynisca, in Cynic-fashion, repudiates a dominant social institution of the polis-culture. Thus, the use of the name Κυνίσκα in *Idyll* 14 might underscore the poem's thematic concern with a woman's place in a changing world.

In the previous chapter I discussed *Idyll* 15's use of the motif of the road and its relation to the mobility theme. The motif of the road also pertains to this chapter's discussion of *Idyll* 15, for the movement of *Idyll* 15's women from the private realm to the public, from the outskirts of Alexandria to the center, from a domestic space to Arsinoe's Adonia, raises the issue of gender relations and a woman's place in the world. For the Syracusan women, moving into the public domain involves encounters with men.

When the women first enter the streets, Praxinoa's appeal to a man not to trample her with horses (ἄνερ φίλε, μή με πατήσῃς; "Dear man, don't trample me"; 52) receives no reply, no male acknowledgment. Her seeming invisibility intensifies her feeling of alienation from the public streets (ὠνάθην μεγάλως ὅτι μοι τὸ βρέφος μένει ἔνδον, "I am very glad that I left my baby at home," 55), and she feels childlike in her helplessness (ἵππον καὶ τὸν ψυχρὸν ὄφιν τὰ μάλιστα δεδοίκω / ἐκ παιδός; "From childhood on I've been most fearful of horses and cold snakes"; 58–59). Thus this male-female interaction illustrates how males can not only control a female's public image, but also affect her private self-image.

Praxinoa's fear of horses and snakes (58) also reinforces the poem's sexual symbolism insofar as horses can represent sexuality in both males and females (e.g., see Alkman), and snakes can in addition represent the crossing of sexual boundaries (e.g., the snake couplings involved in Teiresias's sex-changes).[41] In *Idyll* 15, Praxinoa must move beyond her sexual anxieties and the gender norms controlling access to the public streets before she can reach the Adonia. She must assert herself more successfully in interactions with men she encounters on the streets. Chance road encounters, by providing different kinds of public notice, can test and affect a person's self-identity: in *Idyll* 15, a man ignores Praxinoa's appeal, an old woman gives advice, a polite man clears the way, and a rude man insults Praxinoa and Gorgo's manner of speech. Chapter 1 discusses the encounter with the old woman. In this chapter, I examine *Idyll* 15's presentation of male-female interactions in public space and show how through these interactions the poet addresses issues of gendered power and responsibility, alienation and assimilation.

In showing different male characters eliciting different reactions from Praxinoa, Theocritus explores ways the Syracusan women (as outsiders) try to gain control of their public image and find a place for themselves in the public arena. As the women approach the doors to the ceremonial grounds, the crowd jostles Praxinoa and she brusquely exhorts a man nearby to watch out for her cloak:

ποττῶ Διός, εἴ τι γένοιο
εὐδαίμων, ἄνθρωπε, φυλάσσεο τὠμπέχονόν μευ.
(70–71)

> By Zeus, if you would hope
> for good fortune, man, watch out for my wrap.

Earlier, Praxinoa urged a man not to trample her by using the address
ἄνερ φίλε ("dear man," 52), and he did not respond. This time, Praxinoa
addresses a male stranger by using a vocative typically reserved for slaves:
ἄνθρωπε ("man," 71). But her presuppositions about men's behavior in
a crowd and how she would be treated (reinforced by her earlier encounter with a man who ignored her appeal) are false in this case, for this
stranger treats her with unexpected kindness and concern: οὐκ ἐπ᾽ ἐμὶν
μέν, ὅμως δὲ φυλάξομαι ("It is not in my power; all the same, I will
take care"; 72). His polite response and admission of powerlessness
shame Praxinoa. Disarmed by the male stranger's courteous behavior,
she redirects her hostility impersonally against the crowd: ὄχλος
ἀλαθέως· / ὠθεῦνθ᾽ ὥσπερ ὕες ("It's really a crowd; / they're thrusting
like pigs"; 72–73). Praxinoa's comment is her way to apologize, for although she calls the crowd "pigs,"[42] the crowd does not now include the
polite man. Word repetitions further link the polite man with the
women. At home Gorgo consoles Praxinoa's child with the phrase θάρσει, Ζωπυρίων ("Take courage, Zopyrion"; 13), and on the street Gorgo
encourages Praxinoa similarly: θάρσει, Πραξινόα ("Take courage, Praxinoa"; 56). Now at the entrance to the festival grounds, the polite man
heartens Praxinoa with the same exhortation: θάρσει, γύναι ("Take
courage, lady"; 73).

The stranger's courteous manner changes Praxinoa's behavior and affects her use of language. When he brings Praxinoa and her companions
into the clear with the assurance θάρσει, γύναι· ἐν καλῷ εἰμές ("Take
courage, lady; we are in a good position"; 73), Praxinoa's expression of
gratitude exceeds his in politeness, as well as in elevation of language:

κῆς ὥρας κἤπειτα, φίλ᾽ ἀνδρῶν, ἐν καλῷ εἴης,
ἄμμε περιστέλλων. χρηστῶ κοἰκτίρμονος ἀνδρός.

(74–75)

And forever more then, may you be in a good position, dear man,
in return for protecting us. What a helpful and compassionate man.

Although Praxinoa initially treats him as if he were a slave (ἄνθρωπε,
71), she now addresses him as a friend and describes him as "helpful and
compassionate." Further, Praxinoa's reply revitalizes the aesthetic language underlying the stranger's colloquial reassurance by refashioning
his use of the expression ἐν καλῷ εἰμές ("we are in a good position,"

73): κῆς ὥρας κῆπειτα, φίλ' ἀνδρῶν, ἐν καλῷ εἴης ("And forever more
then, may you be in a good [beautiful] position, dear man"; 74). Harmony now characterizes this encounter, not the eristics of power. Rather
than shut the women out, this courtly stranger helps them gain public
access.

The encounter with a solicitous man affects Praxinoa's future interactions with men by showing her the limitations of her preconceptions,
and this demonstration of the civility to which men and women can rise
in their relations with one another helps strengthen Praxinoa's indigna-
tion when she later encounters a man who behaves rudely. In exploring
what is possible in the relations between men and women, *Idyll* 15 approaches an important issue in the Hellenistic age, for the rules were
changing and women who were mobile or had immigrated from home
might have to seek male friends outside the family to serve as *kurioi* instead of the customary close relatives.

A change in the language Praxinoa uses to address her personal slaves
underscores the change in Praxinoa that results from the encounter with
the nice man. In her treatment of Eunoa at home, Praxinoa is presented
as a virago: while washing and dressing Praxinoa, Eunoa can do nothing
right. But that is Praxinoa's way of asserting power over the slave:
through language. Before the polite man's intervention, Praxinoa addresses Eunoa abusively (αἰνόδρυπτε, "scratchface," 27; λᾳστρί, "thief,"
30; δύστανε, "wretched girl," 31; κυνοθαρσής, "fearless hound," 53).
Afterward however, Praxinoa becomes more solicitous and addresses
Eunoa compassionately as δειλά ("you poor thing," 76).[43] This echo of
Praxinoa's self-description when she discovers a tear in her shawl (ὄιμοι
δειλαία; "alas, poor me"; 69) underscores a lessening of distance between slave and mistress and reinforces a sense of temporary common-
ality among the women against outside threats, as evident in the hand-
clasping between mistresses and slaves in an attempt to effect inseparable
passage through the crowd (66–68). Through Praxinoa's and Gorgo's
changing relations with slaves and men, the poet shows how social context can change dynamics of inclusion and exclusion, domination and
subordination.

In naming fictive characters, Theocritus wryly highlights the typical
significance of the social relationships *Idyll* 15 explores.[44] Significant
names in fictions are by no means new (e.g., Aristophanes' Lysistrata,
dissolver of armies), but the Hellenistic age's intensified interest in the
representation of human types is shown by such recent works as Theophrastus's *Characters*, as well as the increasing attention to realistic vi-

sual portraiture.[45] *Idyll* 15 begins in the house of Praxinoa, a woman with her mind on her work[46] and thus naturally resistant to taking the morning off to attend a festival: ἀεργοῖς αἰὲν ἑορτά ("It's always holiday for those who don't work," 26). It takes a friend called Gorgo, whose name can signify danger and also female power,[47] to entice her out of the house. Their husbands' names highlight Gorgo's and Praxinoa's domestic discontent: Praxinoa's husband is named Dinon, the terrible; and Gorgo's is Diokleidas, ordained key-master. Praxinoa has a child named Zopyrion, little spark of fire: fearing lest his fragile spark be extinguished in the public streets, she leaves him at home. Praxinoa also has a servant called Eunoa (good sense), who carelessly handles the soap and water Praxinoa uses when preparing to leave the house.[48] This servant accompanies Praxinoa to the festival. Gorgo's servant, named Eutychis (good luck), is only mentioned once in the poem: when the women reach the doors to the palace, Praxinoa advises Eunoa to take Eutychis's hand (67). The women need more than just good sense to enter through the crowded doorway: "good sense" must combine with "good luck" to succeed. Thus significant names highlight the typical significance of *Idyll* 15's characters and plot. In addition, by wryly offering an allegory here, Theocritus can amuse a sophisticated audience familiar with the practice of allegorically interpreting myths[49] and also make a passing allusion to Tyche (luck), a personified deity rising in popularity in third-century Alexandria.[50]

The third encounter with a man in *Idyll* 15 takes place within the ceremonial space of the Adonia. A public festival, particularly one that includes works of art on display, constitutes a situation where persons not otherwise linked tend to interact with one another: exchange ideas, affirm values, and create a sense of community. When Praxinoa and Gorgo enter through a congested doorway to a ceremonial space where they pause to admire tapestries, their elevated remarks reinforce the ceremonial mood of the Adonia. The male bystander, on the other hand, instead of joining the women in admiring the tapestries, disrupts the ceremonial mood of the occasion by ridiculing the way Praxinoa and Gorgo speak.[51] Insofar as speech is immediately expressive of cultural identity and class, by introducing a fictive bystander critical of the women's speech, the poet can underscore the social boundaries that arise between men and women, and between Greeks of one ethnicity and another.

The bystander's hostile encounter with Praxinoa and Gorgo brings the issue of gender and power to a thematic level in the poem. A housewife can exercise dominance in the private world of the home: at the start of the poem, Praxinoa behaves authoritatively when she abuses her servant and scolds her child, and she speaks in front of her child as if he were not present and must be reminded that the child can understand. But in the public realm, Greek culture traditionally assigned dominance to men and subordination to women. Thus the male bystander is policing violations of the hierarchical social order when he orders the women to be silent and then tries to validate his attempt to exclude them from participation in the public experience by speaking in front of them as if they were not present:

παύσασθ᾽, ὦ δύστανοι, ἀνάνυτα κωτίλλοισαι,
τρυγόνες· ἐκκναισεῦντι πλατειάσδοισαι ἅπαντα.

(87–88)

You wretched women, stop that endless twittering—
like turtle doves they'll grate on you, with all their broad vowels.

The bystander's objections to the women reflect basic cultural presuppositions about gender and decorum; his behavior coincides with the patriarchal tradition of associating women with children and slaves in terms of their diminished capacity for understanding and self-control.[52]

The bystander's remarks can reflect male prejudice against what the women are doing and what the popular festival of Adonis is facilitating: the women have broken out of their place. They have cut loose from the ties of the domestic world, and their incursion into the public realm involves risk: for themselves, of reputation; for the men they encounter, of normative social dynamics. Even if one disregards the extremist view Thucydides presents in his version of Pericles' funeral oration (2.46), still, from the dominant culture's point of view, the semantic content of Praxinoa and Gorgo's speech transgresses normative expectations of women's speech in the public arena. They presume to pass evaluative judgments on a work of art, and although their speech corresponds to the pictorial imagery of the tapestries, their praise brings into the public realm speech that is private, domestic, and meant to be heard at home, or even restricted to the bedroom.[53]

Praxinoa dares in public to speak of eros. She describes Adonis at that liminal moment of boyhood when he still can look sexually ambiguous;[54] the first down is spreading from his temples; he has not yet shaved:

αὐτὸς δ᾽ ὡς θαητὸς ἐπ᾽ ἀργυρέας κατάκειται
κλισμῷ, πρᾶτον ἴουλον ἀπὸ κροτάφων καταβάλλων,
ὁ τριφίλητος Ἄδωνις, ὁ κἠν Ἀχέροντι φιληθείς.

(84–86)

And Adonis himself, how marvelous he is, reclining on a silver
couch, with the first youthful down spreading from his temples,
thrice-loved Adonis, loved even in Acheron [Hades].

This is the threshold of gender definition, the moment of gender doubt.
If he shaves now, Adonis will look androgynous again; but he is at the
point of turning into a man.[55] This is a moment when men can find boys
most alluring. But Theocritus's Praxinoa also finds this stage of gender
doubt erotic, and her description of Adonis makes evident the eroticism
of her gaze. The recurrent cycle of Adonis's death ensures the continued
appeal of his unaging vulnerability and passivity.[56] By experiencing eros
through viewing the tapestries, by desiring what is forbidden and alien
(Adonis, a passive young boy), Praxinoa is transported into the world of
the Adonia. But the bystander is oblivious to how Praxinoa's experience
is appropriate to the festive occasion; instead he objects to her violation
of patriarchal social norms for women's behavior in a public space.

The confrontation between the bystander and the Syracusan women
highlights issues of heterosexual power. The bystander's aim is to silence
the women and keep them from speaking. Through eavesdropping, the
bystander puts the women's private life on display for public consumption. His mockery makes their private life public, as Theocritus's poem
makes it public. The bystander's use of Doric here is sufficiently exagger-
ated to seem sarcastic rather than simply incongruous.[57]

Praxinoa rises to the challenge: she refuses to let him silence her and
thus legislate her public identity. She asserts her right to be heard and
affirms her identity by making a judicial response. Her mocking response to the bystander shows her "reading" of his speech and the social
and cultural stereotypes she understands to be informing his speech:

μᾶ, πόθεν ὤνθρωπος; τί δὲ τίν, εἰ κωτίλαι εἰμές;
πασάμενος ἐπίτασσε· Συρακοσίαις ἐπιτάσσεις.
ὡς εἰδῇς καὶ τοῦτο, Κορίνθιαι εἰμὲς ἄνωθεν,
ὡς καὶ ὁ Βελλεροφῶν. Πελοποννασιστὶ λαλεῦμες,
Δωρίσδειν δ' ἔξεστι, δοκῶ, τοῖς Δωριέεσσι.
μὴ φύη, Μελιτῶδες, ὃς ἁμῶν καρτερὸς εἴη,
πλὰν ἑνός. οὐκ ἀλέγω. μή μοι κενεὰν ἀπομάξῃς.

(89–95)

Mother, where does this man come from? What's it to you if we twitter?
If you have slaves, order them around. You're giving orders to
    Syracusans.
And let me assure you: we are Corinthians by descent,
like Bellerophon. We "babble" in the Peloponnesian manner;
Dorians are permitted, I think, to speak Doric.

Let there be no master over us, honey-goddess,
except one. I don't care: don't level off an empty jar on my account.

First, Praxinoa understands the bystander to be expressing linguistic chauvinism when he characterizes their speech as dovelike twittering, and her response defiantly exaggerates the female aspect of her speech by beginning and ending with exclamations characteristic of women: μᾶ ("mother," 89), Μελιτῶδες ("honey-goddess," 94), and μή μοι κενεὰν ἀπομάξῃς ("don't level off an empty jar on my account," 95).[58] The first word of her reply, μᾶ, also defiantly highlights the Doric accent that "grates" on the bystander's ears.[59] Praxinoa's self-assertion underscores her right to speak differently from the bystander. Second, Praxinoa understands that the bystander is attempting to exclude Gorgo and herself from the social community by editorializing about them in the third person (88); and she reverses the insult by speaking of him in the third person (πόθεν ὤνθρωπος; "where does this man come from?" 89). She also identifies herself and Gorgo with a regional group (Syracusans) that excludes him (Συρακοσίαις ἐπιτάσσεις, "You're giving orders to Syracusans," 90). Third, Praxinoa understands the bystander to be calling Gorgo and herself slaves: he gives orders to them (παύσασθ', ὦ δύστανοι; "stop, you wretched women"; 87) in the same way Praxinoa gives orders to her slave (δύστανε . . . παῦε; "wretched woman, stop"; 31–32), and she tells him to save that language for his slaves: πασάμενος ἐπίτασσε ("If you have slaves, order them around"; 90). Fourth, Praxinoa understands the bystander to be denying the women freedom during a festival that grants them license, and her reply shows that she values autonomy: μὴ φύῃ, Μελιτῶδες, ὃς ἁμῶν καρτερὸς εἴη, / πλὰν ἑνός ("Let there be no master over us, honey-goddess, / except one"; 94–95).

Gow identifies the master here "as the king, rather than her husband for whom in any case she has scant respect."[60] Dover agrees with this identification, but points out the incongruity in these circumstances of such a politically motivated clause: "We may doubt whether an indignant Syracusan housewife at Alexandria, reproving an impertinent stranger, would remember this humble compliment to Ptolemy."[61] But the nonspecificity of the language leaves the question of identity open and invites speculation. I would like to suggest that the language could also imply Adonis as master. It would not be uncharacteristic for Praxinoa, in the context of the Adonia, after a bystander expresses disgust at her praise of Adonis, to insinuate slyly that she would not mind having Adonis as "master." Such a desire would not jeopardize her claim to autonomy. Praxinoa will not be mastered: she has already shown that her husband is not a god to her. Further, Praxinoa's invocation of Melitodes, if this "honey-goddess" is Persephone (as the scholia suggest), would also support an interpretation of the "one master" as Adonis, since Praxinoa's underlying *hypomnesis* (precedent for the goddess's attention to her appeal) would be Persephone's own interest in Adonis (she is his mistress for a third of the year).

Praxinoa's final injunction μή μοι κενεὰν ἀπομάξῃς ("don't level off an empty jar on my account," 95) underscores the distance between Praxinoa and the male bystander. Basically, she is saying that the bystander's effort to silence her is a waste of time. Through this colloquial phrase, Praxinoa asserts her right to be there and to say anything she wants. Also, by having Praxinoa use rhetoric from the kitchen, the poet artfully illumines the social issues at stake here. The Adonia is traditionally a women's festival, women's discourse is appropriate for this environment, and the bystander has no right to complain. The movement of the festival from private to public brings women into the public realm and with them women's rhetoric.

Praxinoa's reply shows how common language, characterized by domestic proverbs and female oaths, can incorporate high culture's literary language as well, for she responds to the bystander's challenge, with its underlying presumption of a speech code that excludes women, by appropriating the male heroic strategies of a verbal duel. She validates her social history by tracing the lineage of the Doric dialect back to the hero Bellerophon. Her use of Homeric diction and a genealogical self-defense bridges the distanced world of myth and her own time.[62] The juxtaposition of the epic verb form φύη and the typically female invocation of Μελιτῶδες (94) exemplifies the blending of generic and linguistic styles that characterizes her speech.

Praxinoa appropriates diction and theme from the male-defined, militaristic world of Homeric duels to challenge a man who attempts to silence her. Her street tactics include cleverly recasting her opponent's insults. She defuses the bystander's insulting description of herself and Gorgo as κωτίλλοισαι ("twittering," 87) by first appropriating the cognate noun (τί δὲ τίν, εἰ κωτίλαι εἰμές; "What's it to you if we twitter?" 89), then neatly transforming this defiant assertion into a declaration of genealogy, matched in phoneme and phraseology: Κορίνθιαι εἰμὲς ἄνωθεν / ὡς καὶ ὁ Βελλεροφῶν ("We are Corinthians by descent, / like Bellerophon"; 91–92). The bystander's remarks indicate that the women's speech is as foreign to him as the twittering of birds. Praxinoa's retort, on the other hand, shows that she not only understands, but can also appropriate the rhetoric of the dominant male world.[63] Praxinoa's choice of Bellerophon as heroic ancestor, who is characterized like

Adonis by youthful vulnerability and a talent for attracting powerful, older women (e.g., Proetus's wife),[64] also contributes toward her refashioning of normative gender behavior.

By linking Praxinoa's focus on Adonis's androgyny with Praxinoa's rebellious attitude toward the bystander's criticism of her speech, the poet also connects gender doubt (a sexuality that can evoke eros in both men and women) with gender freedom. Praxinoa demonstrates gender freedom by publicly engaging in a verbal duel with a male stranger, a behavior customarily restricted in Greek society to men. So too Adonis's ambivalent model of manhood opposes the agonistic ideal that shapes the behavior of the bellicose bystander.

The bystander claims that Praxinoa and Gorgo are broadening and flattening their sounds. But the sounds that they make are definitely not flattened. Praxinoa's speech in praise of Adonis is Hellenistic in its variegation of detail and shape; it is also the language of epiphany spoken by poets like Sappho. Praxinoa characterizes her language as an international Doric that unites realms opposite in value and historical perspective, e.g., the Peloponnese, in general unrefined, and cultivated Corinth. Further, Praxinoa and Gorgo have brought this speech from Syracuse, Sicily, to Alexandria, Egypt. The sounds of a speech that brings together such diverse worlds should not be tedious. Praxinoa acclaims her international status. In a time marked by historical change and syncretism of language, she will not let her speech be squashed or confined to a single style, genre, diction. Instead she revels in its motley architecture and defiantly exalts the emergence of her folk language into the public realm. Thus Praxinoa's reply becomes a resonant linguistic moment in which the poet expresses programmatic values (e.g., the value of mixing levels of diction such as Homeric and folk-Doric in a single poem).[65] Praxinoa's language reflects her life: she rejects the bystander's attempt to homogenize and dismiss people. She asserts her right to be a Doric speaker, a Syracusan, and a woman.

How has Praxinoa, initially timid on the street, afraid of horses and men, come to this point of defiance against the bystander's attempt to control her? She treats the man who interrupts her praise of the tapestries differently from the way she treats the man who helps her with her cloak. During the encounter with the polite man (70–75), his considerate treatment changes her attitude and her language. Calling the crowd "pigs" is her way to apologize to the nice man who said, "I can't protect you but I will do my best" (my paraphrase of 72), for she associates him with herself and her companions in opposition to the "pigs." Her experience affects her, and she now speaks gracious language in regard to the helpful man: ἐν καλῷ εἴης ("May you be in beauty," 74). In the next encounter with a man (87–95), an eavesdropping bystander insults the Syracusan women when they are responding to the dimension of eros in religion and art. But this time, when someone abuses Praxinoa on a crude level, she puts him down with Theocritean manners (niceness).[66] Instead of responding with Callimachean "iambics" (the vile Assyrian river),[67] she uses Theocritean irony, a universalizing rhetoric that adopts eristics to make harmony.

The parallels between Praxinoa and Gorgo's fictive biography and the poet's own also can affect the reader's perceptions of the interaction between the bystander and the Syracusan women. Like Praxinoa and Gorgo, Theocritus himself is an immigrant from Syracuse. The bystander is slandering Doric, but the poet's native dialect is Doric, and his poems, written primarily in Doric, are trying to find audience in the Alexandrian court. By double voicing this passage, by addressing the bystander's remarks as much to the poem's "real" audience as to the Adonia's fictive crowd, the poet can anticipate responses to the poem itself, as well as to the hybridization characteristic of his poetry as a whole:[68] his presentation in hexameter poetry of "low" speech (everyday, domestic, Doric) and marginal characters (herdsmen, women, mercenaries, monsters), which involves the piquant mixing of "low" and "high" levels of style, genre, language, and character. Thus, in *Idyll* 15, the immigrant poet exploits the voice of immigrants in a witty self-irony which could also deflect criticism of his poetic enterprise.

The question naturally arises: after hearing Praxinoa's remarks about Adonis and the bystander's rebuff, is the poem's "real" audience going to side with the bystander or Praxinoa? Many have sided with the bystander. He represents a culturally validated prejudice against marginal figures. But the choices are not limited to a simple dichotomy. The poem is polysemous. The bystander represents a break for the poet from imaginatively projecting into Praxinoa's and Gorgo's experiences. The women live their lives; the bystander observes, and his mockery is ironically and self-consciously interrogated.

Women and Power

Traditionally in the ancient Greek world men attained power through physical force and public political activity. Women had fewer avenues to power: generally smaller and physically weaker than men, they were excluded from military power and also from public political life. In the Hellenistic world, however, men were losing their sense of public power due to the ascendancy of autocratic hegemonies and mercenary soldiery, and women were becoming more visible in the public arena, as shown by, e.g., terracotta representations of girls wearing cloaks and carrying tablets, presumably on their way to school.[69] The public presence of Hellenistic queens offered women a new model of feminine power and Greek males a gendered reminder of their relative powerlessness in the state. Greek men and women in Egypt especially, with its long tradition of relative equality for women, were witnessing different modes of gender behavior. The changing social conditions, both on the public and the private level, were destabilizing traditional Greek assumptions about relations of power between men and women.

Theocritus's three urban mimes, *Idylls* 2, 14, and 15, all feature self-assertive women retaliating against traditional male acts that threaten their sense of self: in *Idyll* 2, when Delphis cavalierly deserts her, Simaetha takes active retaliatory steps through magic; in *Idyll* 14, when Aeschinas beats her, Cynisca protests by leaving his symposium (and his life); in *Idyll* 15, when a male bystander tries to shame Praxinoa into silence, Praxinoa vigorously asserts her right to public speech. The previous section focused on representations of direct male-female interactions in Theocritus's urban mimes. This section examines other ways in which the topic of women's power emerges in Theocritus's poems as a central thematic concern, with attention to the themes of magic, motherhood, and the relations of powerful females and subordinate males. Select works of other Hellenistic poets are also included for comparative purposes.

The resources available to a woman mistreated by a man in ancient Greek society varied depending on class, status, and ethnicity. If a Greek woman had a *kurios* (male guardian) available, she could rely on him to take appropriate measures on her behalf. But a mobile world intensified problems of female protection and retribution. The rise of marriage contracts in the Hellenistic age addressed some of these problems by specifically spelling out the obligations of both partners and by allowing the woman, in the case of a dispute, to appeal directly to outside parties approved by both husband and wife.[70] But contracts were not available to cover other tricky situations, such as the plight of a woman who, abandoned by a male lover, finds herself without kin to defend her publicly (e.g., Theocritus's Simaetha).

Witchcraft offered one countercultural, private source of psychological power to women who were seemingly without recourse. The story of Medea, one of the three great witches in Greek literature and myth (the other two being Hecate and Circe), shows the kind of isolation that could provoke the use of magic. In Apollonius Rhodius's *Argonautica*, Medea's appeal to Jason to take her with him to the Greek world underscores the vulnerable position of a woman immigrant separated from her family:

> μηδ᾽ ἔνθεν ἑκαστέρω ὁρμηθεῖσαν
> χήτεϊ κηδεμόνων ὀνοτὴν καὶ ἀεικέα θείης.
> (*Argon.* 4.90–91 *O.C.T.*)

Do not expose me to insult and disgrace when I have left my country far away and have no kinsmen to protect me.

(trans. Rieu, Apollonius, 149)

Euripides' *Medea* illustrates what can happen when a man disregards such an injunction and deserts an inconvenient woman in order to marry into power.[71] Isolated in Corinth, an alien woman without official support, Medea turns to Hecate, the sinister goddess of witchcraft, to help her avenge her injuries:

> οὐ γὰρ μὰ τὴν δέσποιναν ἣν ἐγὼ σέβω
> μάλιστα πάντων καὶ ξυνεργὸν εἱλόμην,
> Ἑκάτην, μυχοῖς ναίουσαν ἑστίας ἐμῆς,
> χαίρων τις αὐτῶν τοὐμὸν ἀλγυνεῖ κέαρ.
> (395–98 *O.C.T.*)

It shall not be — I swear it by her, my mistress,
Whom most I honor and have chosen as partner,
Hecate, who dwells in the recesses of my hearth —
That any man shall be glad to have injured me.

(trans. Warner, Medea, 72)

By having Medea locate Hecate, goddess of public crossroads, at the heart of her household,[72] Euripides suggests Medea has turned the house against its former master, Jason, and remade it into a nucleus of power from which she moves against Corinth's hegemony.

Theocritus's *Idyll* 2 provides an elaborated and sustained representation of a woman empowering herself against an aristocratic Greek male's assumption of sexual privilege and social domination. Hecate, Circe, and Medea (Circe's niece) dominate the Greek literary and mythic tradition of witchcraft. In *Idyll* 2, by invoking her powerful predecessors in moving against Delphis, Simaetha shows that she understands herself to be participating in a strong female tradition of witchcraft:

χαῖρ᾽, Ἑκάτα δασπλῆτι, καὶ ἐς τέλος ἄμμιν ὀπάδει,
φάρμακα ταῦτ᾽ ἔρδοισα χερείονα μήτε τι Κίρκας
μήτε τι Μηδείας μήτε ξανθᾶς Περιμήδας.

(14–16)

Hail, dread Hecate, and attend me to the end,
making my drugs as strong as Circe's
or Medea's or blond Perimede's.

Delphis is at the center of a male-dominated elitist Greek world, defined by gymnasia and symposia. To counter his position of power, Simaetha is relocating herself into an alternative world of magic that privileges women rather than men.

A consideration of how Theocritus shapes Simaetha's magic is central to a discussion of the theme of women and power in Theocritus's poetry, for Simaetha's magic aims at subverting Delphis's public self and male autonomy.[73] Repetitions of vocabulary and themes in Simaetha's magic rites and self-narration show Simaetha acting out the reversal of normative relations of dominance and subordination she wishes to effect between herself and Delphis.

First, Simaetha is seeking through magic to dominate Delphis by evoking in him the love symptoms he induced in her. Thus she evokes the symptoms of burning (Δέλφις ἐνὶ φλογὶ σάρκ᾽ ἀμαθύνοι, "may Delphis's flesh be destroyed in the flame," 26; ἐπὶ τήνῳ πᾶσα κατιτ́θομαι, "I am all on fire for him," 40); consumption (τάκοιθ᾽ ὑπ᾽ ἔρωτος, "may he waste with love for me," 29; τὸ δὲ κάλλος ἐτάκετο, "my beauty wasted for him," 83); and madness (καὶ ἐς τόδε δῶμα περᾶσαι / μαινομένῳ ἴκελος, "like a man driven mad / may he come to this house," 50–51; χὠς ἴδον, ὡς ἐμάνην, "when I saw him I was driven mad," 82).

Second, in her magic rites Simaetha appropriates symbols of Delphis's patriarchal world and uses them against him. In preparation for a binding-spell against Delphis, Simaetha orders her slave to wreathe a bowl with crimson wool (2), and she calls the bowl a κελέβα, a term applied to vessels used at symposia.[74] Delphis described himself to Simaetha as a would-be sympotic *komastes* (reveller), wearing a wreath entwined with crimson bands (121), and Simaetha learned of his defection when a woman reported that he left a symposium to wreathe a house with garlands (153). The *komastes* typically performs ritual acts of seduc-

tion (a *komos*) at the beloved's house door: Simaetha's slave Thestylis is
to perform ritual acts on Delphis's doorstep (60–62). Further, by cast-
ing a spell to make Delphis turn at her door like the bronze rhomb she
whirls (30–31),[75] Simaetha would trap Delphis in a dizzying command
performance of a *komos* ritual.

Third, in reversing their gendered roles of power, Simaetha uses Delphis's most characteristic trait, his fickleness, against him:

εἴτε γυνὰ τήνῳ παρακέκλιται εἴτε καὶ ἀνήρ,
τόσσον ἔχοι λάθας ὅσσον ποκὰ Θησέα φαντί
ἐν Δίᾳ λασθῆμεν ἐυπλοκάμω Ἀριάδνας.

(44–46)

Whether a woman is lying by him or a man,
may he be as forgetful of them as Theseus, they say,
once forgot fair-haired Ariadne on Dia.

In using an analogy suited to herself (an Ariadne forgotten by a Theseus), Simaetha seeks to rewrite the mythic story. In her revisionist version, Ariadne will triumph over Theseus: Delphis will forget his current
lover and return to her.

Delphis, a star member of the gymnastic and sympotic set, repeatedly
left his oil flask with Simaetha: she interprets this act as a sign of her
power over his world (155–58). Now that Delphis has abandoned her,
Simaetha seeks, through magic, to separate Delphis from the sport-
ing life:

καὶ ἐς τόδε δῶμα περάσαι
μαινομένῳ ἴκελος λιπαρᾶς ἔκτοσθε παλαίστρας.

(50–51)

And like a man driven mad
may he come to this house from the shiny palaestra.

The repetition in the poem of the verb μαίνεσθαι (to be driven mad) in
association with sites of athletic activity (50–51, 80, 82) underscores the
theme of power reversal. Simaetha was driven mad by the sight of Delphis, glistening, fresh from the gymnasium (79–80, 82). Now she wants
him driven mad and forced outside (ἔκτοσθε) the shiny palaestra, back
into her domestic world.[76] By showing how Simaetha's ritual overturns
conventions of Delphis's world, the poet evokes male fears that women
might use magic to control and redefine them, that through witchcraft
women might redefine terms of sexual discourse.

Repetitions of the word κακός in *Idyll* 2 show how language can reinforce positions of power and also mirror the shifting of power rela-

tions. Delphis had plunged Simaetha into a crisis of self-identity: ἀντὶ γυναικὸς ἔθηκε κακὰν καὶ ἀπάρθενον ἧμεν ("He has made me, instead of a wife, a bad woman, and a maid no more"; 41). But Simaetha moves away from a patriarchal world that ranks her as κακάν (bad) by her sexual relations with men into an alternative realm in which κακά (bad things) can work in her favor. Empowered by Hecate in a world of witchcraft, Simaetha is bringing κακά against Delphis: σαύραν τοι τρί-ψασα κακὸν ποτὸν αὔριον οἰσῶ ("I'll mash a lizard and bring Delphis a bad drink tomorrow," 58).[77] Delphis, now making love toasts with un-mixed wine (151–52), will drink a κακὸν ποτόν instead and learn what it means to be a victim rather than an agent of κακά. Although Simaetha begins her self-narration by seeing herself as victim of a κακόν whose causation she is struggling to understand (τίς μοι κακὸν ἄγαγε τοῦτο; "Who brought this badness upon me?" 65), by the poem's end Simaetha has established herself in the position of controlling subject rather than victim:

> νῦν μὲν τοῖς φίλτροις καταδήσομαι· αἰ δ' ἔτι κά με
> λυπῇ, τὰν Ἀίδαο πύλαν, ναὶ Μοίρας, ἀραξεῖ·
> τοῖά οἱ ἐν κίστᾳ κακὰ φάρμακα φαμὶ φυλάσσειν.
>
> (159–61)

Now with spells I will bind him; and if he hurts me still,
by the Fates, he shall knock on Hades' gate,
such bad drugs, I swear, I keep for him in my box.

Simaetha's redescription of Delphis's and her relationship ends by af-firming the power reversal between Delphis and herself: when Delphis had been her suitor, he regularly knocked at her "door" (6); now, if he continues to play komastes elsewhere, she will use bad drugs (from her "box") against him. She will reverse the terms of eroticism and send him to play komastes at Hades' door.

Through the emotional experience of magic rites, by acting out matching retributions for her maltreatment, Simaetha releases herself from her dependency on Delphis and from society's hierarchical con-straints: the poem starts with her resolve to go to Delphis's wrestling school tomorrow and reproach him (8–9), but it ends with her vow to kill him if necessary (159–62). The crisis of identity and emotional tur-moil caused by Delphis separates Simaetha from her environment:

> ἠνίδε σιγῇ μὲν πόντος, σιγῶντι δ' ἀῆται·
> ἁ δ' ἐμὰ οὐ σιγῇ στέρνων ἔντοσθεν ἀνία.
>
> (38–39)

The sea is still, and the breezes are still;
yet the anguish in my breast will not be still.

In the course of the poem, through sympathetic magic and reciprocal self-narration, Simaetha changes the terms of sexual discourse and moves toward creating a more satisfactory world and self-identity for herself.

Allegory further enhances *Idyll* 2's presentation of Simaetha's process of reclaiming herself. Midway to Lycon's place (place of the wolf, a wild predator), Simaetha saw Delphis, and the sight distracted her from Artemis's festival: οὐκέτι πομπᾶς / τήνας ἐφρασάμαν ("No longer did I take notice of / that procession," 83–84). She turned away from her path toward Artemis, mistress of fierce beasts (67–68), chaste goddess of the wild, to pursue Delphis (an Apollo figure, Artemis's seductive twin).[78] At the poem's end, Simaetha is finding a way to return to her former path, to regain a sense of power over herself and her world. Her willingness to kill her violator Delphis (159–60), her desire to rid herself of his intrusion into her life, also suggests a turning back toward Artemis, goddess of independence from men, the goddess who destroyed Actaeon for seeing her naked.[79]

At the poem's end, Simaetha transfers the quality of shining from Delphis and his friend (στήθεα δὲ στίλβοντα πολὺ πλέον ἢ τύ, Σελάνα; "[whose] breasts were far more shining than you, Selene [the Moon]"; 79)[80] to Selene, invoked as λιπαρόθρονε ("of the shining throne," 165). Griffiths suggests that this reversal signifies Simaetha's move away from her own world: "Though Simaetha is venturing again into somewhat heightened poetic usages, she is no longer applying them to her own experiences. She is, rather, finding momentary release by projecting her sensuality into a removed aesthetic realm."[81] Yet by having Simaetha strip Delphis of his adjective and give it to the Moon, her ally in magic, Theocritus also shows Simaetha deconstructing her image of Delphis and returning from her obsession with his world to reclaim her own life.[82] Thus Simaetha's farewell to the moon and the night (εὔκαλος νύξ, "tranquil night," 166) suggests movement away from the turmoil caused by Delphis:

χαῖρε, Σελαναία λιπαρόθρονε, χαίρετε δ' ἄλλοι
ἀστέρες, εὐκάλοιο κατ' ἄντυγα Νυκτὸς ὀπαδοί.

(165–66)

Farewell, Selene of the shining throne, and farewell you other stars that attend upon the chariot of tranquil Night.

The night is over, and the moon has played her role as confidant in Simaetha's ritual therapy.

Idyll 2 reflects male concerns about the increased visibility of women in the Hellenistic world by suggesting the possibility of fearful female vengeance in the everyday world. Egypt's long tradition of rituals of enchantment, now more visible to Greeks due to Egypt's prominence in the Hellenistic Greek world,[83] may have strengthened Greek male anxieties about aliens and others (e.g., females) using magic to limit Greek male autonomy.

Ritual activities that particularly encouraged the acting out of oppositional positions toward gender roles and institutions of power among the Greeks include Dionysiac rites, witchcraft, and the worship of foreign gods. Theocritus's poems featuring women's religious activities highlight their countercultural aspects. In *Idyll* 26, bacchantes perform mystic rituals and then ecstatically dismember Pentheus, Thebe's king (and Agave's son). In *Idyll* 2, Simaetha first saw Delphis, whom she unconventionally pursued, at a festival of Artemis, goddess of the hunt (68), female initiations, and the wild. Simaetha's ritual magic also involves invoking Hecate, goddess of witchcraft, and Selene, the Moon goddess, both outside the Olympian establishment. *Idyll* 15 represents an Adonia, which celebrates Aphrodite's extramarital reunion with Adonis, a subordinated young male related to the Babylonian Tammuz, among others.[84] The Adonia was traditionally a countercultural festival celebrated privately by women; in *Idyll* 15, Theocritus explores the social dynamics involved when this formerly subversive festival is sponsored by Queen Arsinoe and celebrated in the center of the Ptolemaic state.

The subject of the capacity of women's communities and religious rituals to subvert traditional male power was popular among other Hellenistic Greek poets as well. Apollonius Rhodius's *Argonautica* features several oppositional or intrusive female communities: Medea and her sister Chalciope plot against their father, Colchis's ruler; the Lemnian women threaten to abort Jason's heroic quest; Aphrodite, Hera, and Athena plot to manipulate Jason and Medea. Callimachus's *Hymn* 6 includes the story of how Demeter punished a man for violating her grove by having him consume his family's estate; Callimachus's *Hymn* 5, how Athena punished a boy with blindness for gazing on her naked. Several of Herodas's mimes starring women also focus on ways female activities and friendships can overturn male assumptions of dominance and power (*Mimes* 3 and 6 are discussed later in this chapter).

Throughout Greek history, religious ceremonies, including funerals, provided standard occasions for women to enter the public domain, where they might encounter men,[85] and Hellenistic poets follow an established poetic tradition in using religious rituals to facilitate fictive encounters between men and women (e.g., Men. *Citharista* 93–97, *Sam.* 38–49 *O.C.T.*). As mentioned above, in Theocritus's *Idyll* 2, Simaetha was accompanying a friend to a festival of Artemis when she saw Delphis and fell in love. So too in *Idyll* 15, Praxinoa and Gorgo, on their way to the festival of Adonis, encounter several men (and an old woman).[86] Also, in Herodas's *Mime* 1, Metriche's athletic suitor first saw her at a festival of the goddess Mise (56),[87] and in Callimachus's *Aetia* 3, frs. 67–75, Acontius fell in love with Cydippe at a Delian festival of Apollo (frs. 67.5–6, 70).

Other Hellenistic poems featuring more benign women's religious activities include Herodas's *Mime* 4, which represents women visiting a shrine of Asclepius (see chapter 3 for discussion). Further, Theocritus's *Idyll* 24, an epic narrative, highlights a mother's religious role: Teiresias directs Alcmene to burn at midnight the snakes that attacked her sons, to have them cast from the community at dawn, to fumigate the house, and then to sacrifice a boar.[88] Callimachus's poetry also features women's religious communities, e.g., *Hymn* 5's female celebrants of Athena, as well as Athena and her company of maidens, and *Hymn* 6's female celebrants of Demeter.[89]

The motif of hostilities between male intruders and female celebrants is traditional in literary representations of women's ceremonies: in Aristophanes' *Thesmophoriazusae*, Euripides' relation Mnesilochus dresses in drag to infiltrate the Thesmophoria; in Euripides' *Bacchae,* Pentheus dresses in drag to spy on bacchantes. In Theocritus's *Idyll* 26, also featuring bacchantes, the poet heightens the sense of male violation of female space by having Pentheus spy on women engaged in the most secret ritual activities: removing holy things from a mystic chest and laying them on altars (7–8).[90] But by focusing on human agency in the destruction of Pentheus, not divine agency, the poet can underscore the fearsome power of women to destroy men.[91] Callimachus's *Hymns* 5 and 6 also underscore the exclusion of males from female religious celebrations through cautionary stories that reinforce the principle of female inviolability.[92] But in both these poems, unlike Theocritus's *Idyll* 26, the agent of the male's destruction is a goddess, not a mortal female: in *Hymn* 5, Teiresias sees Athena naked and she blinds him; in *Hymn* 6, Erysichthon violates Demeter's sacred grove to cut trees for a dining hall and she curses him with insatiable hunger.[93]

Differences in the ways Theocritus and Callimachus handle the topic of childbirth exemplify differences in their approaches to the issue of women and power. Theocritus's *Idyll* 17, Ptolemy's encomium, features the theme of Ptolemy II's birth from Berenice. Childbirth is a conventional hymnic topic (e.g., *Hymn. Hom. Ap.*; Callim. *Hymn* 1, to Zeus, and *Hymn* 4, to Delos), and *Idyll* 17's poet-narrator conventionally enhances the theme of Ptolemy's birth by associating it with legendary warrior births: the Argive woman's bearing Diomedes to Tydeus and Thetis's bearing Achilles to Peleus (53–56). But in commemorating the marriage union of Ptolemy's parents, the poet also emphasizes sources of male matrimonial anxiety:

ἀστόργου δὲ γυναικὸς ἐπ' ἀλλοτρίῳ νόος αἰεί,
ῥηίδιοι δὲ γοναί, τέκνα δ' οὐ ποτεοικότα πατρί.

(43–44)

But if a woman know not conjugal love, her mind is ever set on others; easily she gives birth, but the children resemble not their sire.

(trans. Gow, *Theocritus* 1:133)

Further, assurances of legitimacy precede the narrative of Ptolemy's birth too: ὃ δὲ πατρὶ ἐοικώς / παῖς ἀγαπητὸς ἔγεντο ("And in his father's likeness / was he born, a child beloved"; trans. Gow, *Theocritus* 1: 135; 63–64). The focus here is the woman's power over her husband in determining the legitimacy of offspring and the danger a wife's infidelity would create in a household (and in the Ptolemies' case, the state). Thus Ptolemy's encomium, *Idyll* 17, includes the theme of a woman's power to determine the legitimacy and claim of a child to patrimony and also raises the issue of a woman's role in a patriarchal system. Matrilineal identifications emphasize the themes of motherhood and female transmission of power in *Idyll* 17: Berenice, Ptolemy's mother, is identified as Antigone's daughter (61); Aphrodite, as Dione's daughter (36).[94] Further, *Idyll* 18's wedding song exalts Helen's importance (and undermines Menelaus's) by wishing they might have a child resembling its mother, not its father (21).[95]

Lysias's Euphiletus, in defending his killing of his wife's seducer Eratosthenes, shows the depth of male, patriarchal anxiety about the possibility of a woman having an extramarital affair:

τοὺς δὲ πείσαντας οὕτως αὐτῶν τὰς ψυχὰς διαφθείρειν, ὥστ' οἰκειοτέρας αὑτοῖς ποιεῖν τὰς ἀλλοτρίας γυναῖκας ἢ τοῖς ἀνδράσι, καὶ πᾶσαν ἐπ' ἐκείνοις τὴν οἰκίαν γεγονέναι, καὶ τοὺς παῖδας ἀδήλους εἶναι ὁποτέρων τυγχάνουσιν ὄντες, τῶν ἀνδρῶν ἢ τῶν μοιχῶν. (Lys. 1.33 O.C.T.)

Those who have got their way by persuasion corrupt women's minds, in such a way as to make other men's wives more attached to themselves than to their husbands, so that the whole house is in their power, and it is uncertain who is the children's father, the husband or the lover.

(trans. Freeman, "Killing of Eratosthenes," 49)

Herodas too pays special attention to the issue of female sexual fidelity in a mobile world. In *Mime* 1, an old bawd urges a young married woman to have an extramarital affair while her husband is away in Egypt. *Mime* 6 evokes male anxieties about sexual roles and the problem of infidelity: two women discuss dildoes, which Koritto claims, if well made, can be more than adequate substitutes for men (69–71). The importance of wifely loyalty for legitimate offspring is an ongoing motif in marriage songs (e.g., Cat. 61.217–26) and also in descriptions of ideal or alternative worlds (e.g., Hes. *Op.* 235; Hor. *Od.* 4.5.23; Mart. 6.27.3–4).

When Callimachus's poetry features the theme of childbirth, the focus is on the birthing process itself, with emphasis on female vulnerability and suffering. The emphasis on suffering in childbirth is not new with Callimachus, of course: the high risks of childbirth in the ancient world were notable.[96] But the point here is that suffering in childbirth is the focus of Callimachus's representations of childbirth and that this focus contrasts dramatically with Theocritus's focus on women's power in relation to children's legitimacy. Callimachus's *Hymn* 1 includes the story of how Rhea gave birth to Zeus and searched in distress for water afterwards (10–41). *Hymn* 3 identifies the unjust city as a place where women suffer and die in childbirth and bear lame children (126–28). *Hymn* 4 features the story of the unhappy wanderings of pregnant Leto (55–263), persecuted by Hera and dominated by her unborn son, who issues orders from the womb (162–95; cf. 86–99). Also in *Hymn* 4, Hera curses Zeus's mistresses with unhappy, difficult childbirth:

> καὶ τίκτοιτε κεκρυμμένα, μηδ' ὅθι δειλαί
> δυστοκέες μογέουσιν ἀλετρίδες, ἀλλ' ὅθι φῶκαι
> εἰνάλιαι τίκτουσιν, ἐνὶ σπιλάδεσσιν ἐρήμοις.

(241–43)

And [may you] bring forth in darkness, not even where the poor
mill-women bring forth in difficult labour, but where the seals
of the sea bring forth, amid the desolate rocks.

(trans. Mair, "Callimachus," 105)

Further, *Epigram* 53, in giving thanks to Eileithuia for the easy birth of a daughter and praying for the easy birth of a son, reflects the theme of difficult childbirth and the long tradition of Greek women's prayers and offerings to Eileithuia and other birth goddesses.[97]

Writing in a Hellenistic world defined by autocratic hegemonies, which denied Greek men political self-determination and placed them in positions of dependency instead, Theocritus repeatedly introduces into his poems the motif of strong mothers and dependent sons. *Idyll* 11 exemplifies the Theocritean theme of the complicated interdependency between mothers and sons. An adolescent cyclops blames his mother for not assisting him in his courtship of Galatea, but he also expresses confidence that she will empathize with his suffering if he tells her of it:

ἁ μάτηρ ἀδικεῖ με μόνα, καὶ μέμφομαι αὐτᾷ·
οὐδὲν πήποχ' ὅλως ποτὶ τὶν φίλον εἶπεν ὑπέρ μευ,
καὶ ταῦτ' ἆμαρ ἐπ' ἆμαρ ὀρεῦσά με λεπτύνοντα.
φασῶ τὰν κεφαλὰν καὶ τὼς πόδας ἀμφοτέρως μευ
σφύσδειν, ὡς ἀνιαθῇ, ἐπεὶ κἠγὼν ἀνιῶμαι.

(67–71)

My mother alone it is who wrongs me, and her I blame;
for never once has she spoken a kindly word for me to thee,
though she sees me growing thinner day by day.
I will tell her my head throbs, and both my feet,
that she may suffer since I too suffer.

(trans. Gow, *Theocritus* 1:91)

Idyll 11 emphasizes a mother's striking independence from family concerns: she consorts with a female friend (Galatea) and ignores her son's needs and demands. Further, the role that Polyphemus assigns his mother of arranging courtship/marriage was traditionally assigned to the father in the Greek world.[98] But in Theocritus's *Idyll* 11, no mention of a father interferes with the strained relations between Polyphemus and his mother.[99]

Idyll 24, on Heracles' infancy and early childhood, also focuses on a mother's relations with her sons. Although the poem includes a father, his less-than-attentive presence contrasts with Alcmene's dominating role in her sons' upbringing: she roused her husband, still sleeping, when baby Iphicles cried in fright; she summoned Teiresias to learn the meaning of the snake incident after her husband had gone back to bed; she directed Heracles' education, even choosing his tutors. More incidental mentions of close relationships between mothers and sons appear in *Idylls* 10 and 12: *Idyll* 10's Milon mockingly urges the lovelorn Bucaeus to complain to his mother when she rises in the morning (57–58);

Idyll 12's poet-narrator notes that the winner of a boys' kissing contest returns, laden with garlands, to his mother (32–33). *Idyll* 26 represents the most dysfunctional of Theocritus's mother-son relationships: the *sparagmos* (dismemberment) of Pentheus at the hands of his mother and aunts.[100] Further, *Idyll* 26's narrator's suggestion that a similar fate might yet befall some nine- or ten-year-old male child (28–29) brings the threat of the terrible, destroying mother figure into the contemporary world.[101]

In *Idyll* 15, Theocritus offers a paradigm of the process of power reversal between mothers and sons, as sons grow up. Within the context of the household, women can exercise power over males: Praxinoa and Gorgo complain about their husbands and Praxinoa invokes the female bogey Mormo, a surrogate dread mother, to scare her male child. Praxinoa's repetition of the verb ἀποκλᾴειν (to lock up), used first when she leaves the house (43) and again when she and her companions enter the palace grounds (77), signifies how relations change, however, between mothers and male children. While a son is still young, a mother can lock him at home, invoke the biting horse and bogeywoman, protect him from the outside world:

> οὐκ ἀξῶ τυ, τέκνον. Μορμώ, δάκνει ἵππος.
> δάκρυ’ ὅσσα θέλεις, χωλὸν δ’ οὐ δεῖ τυ γενέσθαι.
> ἕρπωμες. Φρυγία, τὸν μικκὸν παῖσδε λαβοῖσα,
> τὰν κύν’ ἔσω κάλεσον, τὰν αὐλείαν ἀπόκλαξον.
>
> (40–43)
>
> I will not take you, child. Mormo, the horse bites.
> Cry however much you like, but I won't have you maimed.
> Let's go. Phrygia, take the little one and play with him.
> Call the female dog inside; lock up the front door.

But when a child becomes a man, the power shifts and he now does the locking up: "ἔνδοι πᾶσαι", ὁ τὰν νυὸν εἶπ’ ἀποκλάξας ("'All women inside,' said the man, locking the door on the bride"; 77). Through Praxinoa's use of this proverb as the women reach the festival grounds of the Adonia, a celebration of the extramarital union of a goddess and her young consort, the poet underscores how the Adonia subverts normative, gendered relations: a bridegroom may dominate a bride, but not when the principals are Adonis and Aphrodite. Further, the Adonia offers women respite from their husbands' locks.[102] Also, by having Praxinoa use this phrase as she herself appropriates the bridegroom's power in ushering her companions inside the palace grounds,[103] Theocritus wryly highlights the distance between normative, traditional expectations about gender relations (and women's submissive behavior) and Alexandria's changing social world (as represented in the poem by, e.g., Praxinoa's assertion of liberty on public streets).

Matrilineal identifications underscore the thematic importance of women in *Idyll* 15: the hymnist is identified as the Argive woman's daughter (97), Arsinoe as Berenice's daughter (110), and Aphrodite as Dione's daughter (106). A further matrilineal description occurs in the catalogue of heroes, for the hymnist identifies Hector as Hecuba's eldest son (139).[104] Further, no identifications by father are made for women throughout the poem. By focusing on matrilineal identifications in the context of representing a festival sponsored by Queen Arsinoe and honoring her mother, Theocritus also emphasizes the transmission of power and identity from mother to daughter.

Herodas's poetry too includes the theme of the terrible, domineering mother. In *Mime* 3, Metrotime (honored mother) urges her son's schoolteacher Lampriskos[105] to beat her son:

οὕτω τί σοι δοίησαν αἱ φίλαι Μῦσαι,
Λαμπρίσκε, τερπνὸν τῆς ζοῆς τ᾽ ἐπαυρέσθαι,
τοῦτον κατ᾽ ὤμου δεῖρον, ἄχρις ἡ ψυχή
αὐτοῦ ἐπὶ χειλέων μοῦνον ἡ κακὴ λειφθῆι.

(1–4)

As you wish for any pleasure from the dear Muses,
Lampriskos, and to enjoy your life,
so do you beat this fellow a-shoulder, till his life —
curse it — remain hanging on his lips.

(trans. Knox, in Headlam and Knox, *Herodas*, 111)

Like Theocritus's *Idyll* 24, *Mime* 3 puts emphasis on the mother's role in her son's education:

ἔγωγ᾽ εἶπα
ἄνουν ἐμαυτήν, ἥτις οὐκ ὄνους βόσκειν
αὐτὸν διδάσκω, γραμμάτων δὲ παιδείην,
δοκεῦσ᾽ ἀρωγὸν τῆς ἀωρίης ἕξειν.

(26–29)

[I called]
myself a fool for not teaching him
to feed asses, rather than to learn letters
in the hope that I might have a support in my old age.

(trans. Knox, in Headlam and Knox,
Herodas, 111–13)

The parents share in the son's training: the son was expected to recite tragic speeches to either Metrotime or his father by command (30–31).[106] Through Metrotime's description of her husband as elderly and hard of hearing and sight (32), the poet emphasizes how the natural age discrepancy between men and women in a Greek household might result in an inversion of gender authority in the household over time: the mother would be better able to hear the son's recitations. The mother here takes charge of disciplining the son, even to the point of going to his school and giving orders to his teacher.

In *Mime* 3, the socioeconomic status of the family is low: they live in joint housing; the son's education and his damage to the tenement's roof tiling take up most of the household budget; the family grandma is illiterate and destitute. Metrotime's use of analogy emphasizes her frustrated ambitions for her son:

> ὄρη δ' ὀκοίως τὴν ῥάκιν λελέπρηκε
> πᾶσαν, κατ' ὕλην, οἷα Δήλιος κυρτεύς
> ἐν τῆι θαλάσσηι, τὠμβλὺ τῆς ζοῆς τρίβων.
>
> (50–52)

See now in what a state of grime all his back has become,
in his wanderings on the hills, as with some Delian
lobster-catcher wasting his dull life on the sea.

(trans. Knox, in Headlam and Knox, Herodas, 113)

Metrotime's bitter severity against her son reflects an understanding that she must rely on him for security in old age (29).[107] The emphasis in Herodas's *Mime* 3, as well as Theocritus's *Idyll* 24, on a mother's concern about her son's education may also reflect the increased urgency in a mobile Hellenistic world for women to secure their futures for themselves. So too the rise in educational opportunities for girls during the Hellenistic period would have familiarized more women with teaching techniques: in Herodas's *Mime* 3, the mother helps her son with his homework and advises the schoolmaster; in Theocritus's *Idyll* 24, the mother chooses her son's tutors.

Mime 3's Metrotime resents the thanklessness of her sacrifices for her son. Instead of writing on the wax tablets she so carefully prepares, he throws them down or scrapes off their wax (14–18); he knows the way to the gambling den but not to school (8–13); rather than attend class or study, he gambles (5–21), sits on the rooftop (40–41), eats grandma's food (38–39), and roams about (50–52). Metrotime's resolve at the poem's close underscores her controlling, aggressive urges toward her son (and her dominance over her husband). When the schoolmaster stops flogging her son, despite her insistence that he continue (87–92), Metrotime announces she will fetch footstraps from home so that her son might be publicly fettered for humiliation (94–97). She does not propose to discuss the course of action with her husband, but simply to inform him (94): her disrespect is shown by the term she uses for him, γέρων (old man).

The diminishment of the husband's authority in the household is also a theme in Herodas's *Mime* 5, in which the mistress of the household, Bitinna, has taken a young male slave, Gastron, as sexual consort.[108] In a world restricting extramarital sex to men,[109] Bitinna, a married woman, claims extramarital privilege and challenges the tradition that only free males could consider slaves as sexual opportunities.[110] The poem opens with Bitinna's suspicion that Gastron (Glutton) has become so ὑπερ-κορής (overfull) with sexual privilege that he now consorts with another married woman as well (1–3). Gastron's infidelity diminishes Bitinna's self-image and authority in the household: she tries to reassert her position as mistress of the house by having him bound and publicly flogged. Bitinna's oath by a female tyrant (οὐ τὴν Τύραννον; "no, by the female tyrant"; 77) underscores her assumption of a tyrant's role over Gastron (and the household).[111] In Herodas's poems, as well as in some of Theocritus's poems featuring women (e.g., *Idylls* 2 and 15), the notable absence of male *kurioi* (guardians) — e.g., husbands, fathers, and other male relatives[112] — which may reflect a growing reality related to mobility,[113] puts an emphasis on women's attempts to make a way for themselves in the world.

In Callimachus's poetry, unlike Theocritus's and Herodas's, fathers (not mothers) typically take aggressive action in the case of household disruptions. In the *Aetia*'s story of Acontius and Cydippe, when Cydippe became ill, her father responds by consulting the oracle about her marriage and then questioning her about her condition (*Aet.* 3, fr. 75.20–39). So too in *Hymn* 6, when Erysichthon becomes insatiably hungry, his father seeks outside help (96–106), while his mother just turns down embarrassing social invitations (75–86) and weeps (94–95). By contrast, in Theocritus's *Idyll* 24, as discussed above, the mother Alcmene (not the father) consults a seer about her son's strange powers over snakes. Another of Callimachus's poems that highlights the father's power is Callimachus's *Hymn* 3, which features Artemis's appeal to her father Zeus for perpetual virginity.

Callimachus's poetry, like Theocritus's, includes representations of relations between mothers and sons. But while Theocritus's fictive mothers take strong, aggressive roles (e.g., *Idyll* 24's Alcmene), Callimachus's fictive mothers are generally put in weak or subordinated positions. In Callimachus's *Hymns* 5 and 6, mortal mothers cannot save their sons from the terrible punishments goddesses give them: Chariclo cannot save Teiresias from Athena's blinding him (*Hymn* 5); Erysichthon's parents cannot save him from Demeter's curse of insatiable hunger (*Hymn* 6).[114] Instead of Theocritus's strong and controlling mothers, sorrowing mothers are an important theme in Callimachus's poetry.[115] In *Hymn* 5's cautionary tale, Chariclo grieves for her blinded son Teiresias (93–95). In *Hymn* 6's cautionary tale, Erysichthon's mother (with other women of the household) bemoans her son's insatiable hunger (94–95). Also, the start of *Hymn* 6 features Demeter's sad search for her daughter Persephone (10–17), Greek mythology's most paradigmatic example of the sorrowing mother theme. In *Hymn* 2, the hymnist-narrator quiets celebrants by noting that Apollo's paean can silence even the laments of Thetis and Niobe, also mythic paradigms of sorrowing mothers (20–24).

A related theme in Callimachus's poems is nurturant reciprocity between younger males and older, maternal females, mourned after their death.[116] *Epigram* 40 commemorates an old priestess who died in the arms of her two sons; *Epigram* 50, a Phrygian nurse, whom Miccus, a former nurseling, cared for in her old age and honored with a statue after her death. Callimachus's epic poem *Hecale*, which features an old woman who offers a young hero hospitality on his journey, elaborates the theme of the nurturing older woman, lamented after death by the young male she helped. When Theseus returns from his heroic exploit and seeks Hecale, he discovers she has died, and the poem includes Hecale's posthumous honors (*Hecale* frs. 79–83, Hollis, pp. 263–69).

In contrast to the sorrowing, maternal figures who nurture young males in Callimachus's poetry, older women in Theocritus's idylls are typically strong, and their relationships with young males are often non-nurturant,[117] erotic,[118] and even magic (old women are valued for their magic charms and powers).[119] Theocritus's extant poetry does not feature sorrowing mothers, even when such a plot motif might seem natural: thus in *Idyll* 26, Agave does not lament after dismembering her son.[120] *Idylls* 1 and 15 feature the related theme of how a young male's premature death affects females (other than his mother). But here too the theme of lamentation is displaced and diminished. In *Idyll* 1, Daphnis's story deflects the theme of female lamention for Daphnis to the animal kingdom.

The Muses, nymphs, and Aphrodite do not sorrow for Daphnis (despite the Muses' love and nymphs' fondness for him [141], and Aphrodite's regret when he dies [138–39]). Instead jackals, wolves, a lion, and cattle bewail Daphnis (71–75). Further, Thyrsis begins his song by reproaching the nymphs for their absence while Daphnis suffered (66–69). In *Idyll* 15, although the hymnist elaborates how women will lament the death of Adonis the next day (132–35), still Aphrodite's personal sorrow or lamentation is not mentioned,[121] and women celebrants participating in a ritual, communal lament are far from Callimachus's "sorrowing mother" theme. In both *Idylls* 1 and 15, moreover, the relationships are oriented around eros (and Aphrodite) rather than "motherlove."

The subject of passionate love, the kind of love that disrupts everyday life and overturns normative values, pervades Theocritus's poetry, and Aphrodite, goddess of love, plays a major role, especially in *Idylls* 1 and 15. In *Idyll* 1, the subject of Thyrsis's song is Daphnis and his unhappy interactions with Aphrodite. Further, Aphrodite has one of the rare speaking roles for a god in Theocritus's poetry: in Thyrsis's song she admonishes Daphnis and he responds (*Id.* 1.97–113).[122] *Idyll* 15's Adonia celebrates the passionate reunion of Adonis and Aphrodite: the hymnist invokes Aphrodite (100–11), and the tableau's centerpiece is a couch on which Aphrodite and Adonis figures embrace (128, 131). References to Aphrodite are also frequent elsewhere in Theocritus, especially in contexts of passionate, sexual love: heterosexual, extramarital love (*Id.* 2.130–31, *Id.* 10.33, *Id.* 11.16); mutual, married love (*Id.* 18.51, *Id.* 17.36); homosexual love (*Id.* 7.55); either-sexed love (*Id.* 2.7). Other references to Aphrodite involve a variety of subjects. In *Idyll* 2, Simaetha links Aphrodite's powers with the rhombus, which she uses in an effort to bewitch Delphis (30). In *Idylls* 15 and 17, more courtly poems, Aphrodite is credited with immortalizing Alexandria's old Queen Berenice (*Id.* 15.106–8, *Id.* 17.45) and also explicitly linked with the current queen, Arsinoe (*Id.* 15.109–11).[123] *Idyll* 28 highlights an Aphrodite-precinct in describing Miletus, home of Nicias and Theugenis (4). *Epigram* 13 represents an inscription on a statue of Aphrodite Urania in honor of a chaste matron.[124]

In Theocritus's poetry, *Idyll* 13's descriptions of the interactions between Hylas, a young boy, and insomniac water nymphs, δειναὶ θεαὶ ἀγροιώταις ("dread goddesses for country folk"; trans. Gow, *Theocritus* 1:99; 44), perhaps best exemplify the dangerous entanglement of erotic and maternal impulses in the relations of powerful women and youths.[125] For example:

Νύμφαι μὲν σφετέροις ἐπὶ γούνασι κοῦρον ἔχοισαι
δακρυόεντ᾽ ἀγανοῖσι παρεψύχοντ᾽ ἐπέεσσιν.

(53–54)

There in their laps the Nymphs sought to comfort
the weeping lad with gentle words.

(trans. Gow, *Theocritus* 1 : 99)

The most prominent (and domineering) goddess in Theocritus's poetry is Aphrodite, goddess of passionate, womanly love, a threatening figure for young Daphnis in *Idyll* 1 and a dominating figure for youthful Adonis in *Idyll* 15.[126] But this major erotic power in Theocritus's poetry receives mostly incidental mention in Callimachus's poetry, and typically not in the context of passionate, sexual love.[127] Callimachus's poems do not focus on female erotic subjectivity and do not link mothers with powerful, frustrated erotic impulses that can emerge in ambivalent feelings and hostilities directed toward the male child.[128] Instead, as shown by Callimachus's hymns, the focus is on chaste and/or matronly goddesses: Artemis (*Hymn* 3), Athena (*Hymn* 5), Demeter (*Hymn* 6), and Hera (whose jealousy in *Hymn* 4 [to Delos] focuses on her female rivals, not their progeny).

Another central theme in Theocritus's poetry is the destruction of young males' lives through powerful females.[129] This theme is developed on both mundane and elevated levels, and eros typically plays a role. On the divine and heroic level, *Idyll* 1's Daphnis commits suicide to escape Aphrodite's threatening, erotic power; *Idyll* 13's Hylas is pulled into a pool by loving water nymphs who drown him; *Idyll* 15's Adonis each year passionately reunites with Aphrodite and then dies. More incidental references to the theme of young, doomed consorts of powerful female deities include Endymion, Selene's lover, who sleeps forever (*Id.* 3.49–50), and Iasion, Demeter's lover, killed by a thunderbolt (*Id.* 3.49–50; see Hom. *Od.* 5.125–28). Two further poems develop the theme of the threatened youth on a more earthly plane: in *Idyll* 2, a young urban woman, Simaetha, assaults her youthful, male ex-lover through magic and poisonous drugs; in *Idyll* 3, a goatherd responds to his female beloved's indifference by threatening suicide.[130] Eros is not a factor in *Idyll* 26, in which Pentheus is killed by his mother Agave and her sisters, but the poem provides another example of the underlying theme of youth destroyed by powerful women.

Instead of Theocritus's young men intimidated and destroyed by powerful, erotic females (e.g., Daphnis, Hylas, Adonis), Callimachus's poetry includes vignettes of chaste girls who flee powerful, erotic males. *Hymn* 3's Britomartis leaped from a cliff into the sea to escape Minos (190–97); *Hymn* 4's Asteria leaped from heaven into an abyss to flee Zeus (36–38).[131] *Hymn* 3's attention to young Artemis's request for perpetual virginity underscores the theme of female flight from men and marriage.[132] The sexes of Callimachus's and Theocritus's bogey-monsters exemplify the reversals in Callimachus's and Theocritus's approaches to male-female power relations. Theocritus has a mother invoke a female bogey (Mormo) to frighten a male child (Theoc. *Id.* 15.40). Callimachus describes how mothers invoke male bogeys (cyclopes and Hermes) to frighten female children (*Hymn* 3.66–71; τὴν κούρην μορμύσσεται, "[Hermes] plays the bogey to the girl," 70).[133] Further, in Callimachus's *Hymn* 4, the marriage hymn itself frightens maidens in a bogeylike manner (μορμύσσεται, 296–97). In Theocritus's wedding song, on the other hand, a maidens' chorus mock the bridegroom's sexual inadequacies and extol the bride's accomplishments (*Id.* 18.54–55).

The topic of motherhood and sons also emerges elsewhere in Theocritus's poetry, most naturally in *Idyll* 18, Helen's wedding song.[134] Even in *Idyll* 22, Theocritus's most martial epic narrative, the poet-narrator introduces Castor and Polydeuces as the sons of Leda and Zeus (1) and again as the sons of Thestius's daughter (Leda, 5), and later highlights their adversary Idas's death through the poignant detail that his mother Laocoosa would not see him married (205–6). Also, *Idyll* 26, a narrative hymnic poem on Pentheus's death, underscores the importance of Dionysus's mother, Semele: the poem begins by describing how the bacchantes set up three altars for Semele and nine for Dionysus (6), and the poem ends by saluting Dionysus, then Semele and her sisters (33–37). Further, the poem's final greeting to Dionysus recalls, in a relative clause, his babyhood and birth from Zeus's thigh (33–34), which leads back to Semele, his mother (35).[135] The relative importance of the theme of motherhood in Theocritus's poetry, in contrast with fatherhood, is reflected in the prevalence of imagery featuring relations between mothers and children and the rarity of imagery of fathers and their young.[136]

The recurring theme in Theocritus's poetry of men (and women) seeking help from old crones and sorceresses also draws attention to the issue of gender and power.[137] In *Idyll* 2, Simaetha goes to the houses of old women to seek charms to cure her of love (90–91). In *Idyll* 3, the goatherd reports that Agroeo, a sieve diviner, told him his love was not reciprocated (31–33). In *Idyll* 6, Damoetas ends his song by reporting that he spit into his bosom to avert the evil eye, as the old woman Cotyttaris showed him. In *Idyll* 7, Simichidas ends his song with the wish for a crone ἅτις ἐπιφθύζοισα τὰ μὴ καλὰ νόσφιν ἐρύκοι ("to spit on us and keep unlovely things away"; trans. Gow, *Theocritus* 1 : 65; 126–27). In *Idyll* 15, a mysterious old woman appears and gives directions to the palace grounds (60–64).[138]

In summary, much of Theocritus's poetry features strong women — e.g., mothers who dominate and even destroy their sons; young women who threaten their lovers; Aphrodite, a powerful goddess, who subordinates young mortal males. Theocritus's urban mimes pay special attention to the issue of women's roles and access to power in a mobile world: particularly *Idylls* 2 and 15, which star women characters, but also *Idyll* 14, which includes a self-willed woman who disrupts a male-defined symposium. Several of Theocritus's poems also show how women isolated from their families or typically disregarded in patriarchal societies (such as old women) can find power in alternative realms of magic and cult; for example, *Idyll* 2's Simaetha attacks Delphis through witchcraft, and several poems feature old women giving advice to the superstitious.

These themes are not unique to Theocritus among Hellenistic poets. Herodas's poetry too includes the themes of the powerful, domineering mother and of self-willed females out in the world. Callimachus's poetry seems to approach women differently, however. When his poems feature mortal women, the focus is generally on women's vulnerability and suffering: sorrowing, nurturing mothers (and mother figures) and vulnerable, chaste maidens (mostly victimized by Zeus). The topic of female erotic subjectivity — prominent in Theocritus's *Idyll* 2 and also featured in such poems as *Idylls* 14 and 15, central to several of Herodas's mimes and Apollonius Rhodius's epic — is largely absent from Callimachus's poetry. Aphrodite, a central and dangerous erotic deity in Theocritus's poetry, invoked repeatedly in contexts of passionate love, seems sanitized in Callimachus's poetry, which mentions her only incidentally. Instead, Callimachus's hymns feature chaste Olympian goddesses such as Artemis, Demeter, and Athena. While in Theocritus's poetry, young males suffer intimidation and death at the hands of powerful erotic female deities (e.g., *Idyll* 1's Aphrodite and *Idyll* 13's water nymphs), in Callimachus's poetry, young mortals threatened by powerful, erotic immortals are typically chaste young females fleeing adulterous Zeus (a tricky theme in a state run by Ptolemy, notorious for his amorous adventures and likened by Callimachus himself to Zeus).[139]

Adonis and Sexual Ambiguity

A fashion in Hellenistic literature was to highlight feminine attributes in young males. This seems to correspond to a trend in statuary and painting, starting in the late fifth century and intensifying in the fourth century and Hellenistic age, to soften such male gods as Dionysus and Hermes by making them more youthful, beardless, and even effeminate (especially Dionysus),[140] and to further soften the perennially youthful Apollo.[141] Although during the democratized fifth century homosexual behavior, closely associated with the archaic age's privileged leisure class and privatized sympotic occasions, declined in visibility,[142] the rise of homoerotic epigrams during the Hellenistic period drew attention again to homoerotic culture, Dover suggests that the growing fashion in visual art and literature to feminize males, especially young males, may reflect a rising taste for effeminate *eromenoi* (male objects of homoerotic desire: generally boys).[143] But, as shown earlier, the Hellenistic age was also characterized by a trend toward heterosexuality, evident in the rising taste for the female nude in visual art and in the attention paid in literature to female erotic subjectivity. In representing female desire, the Alexandrian male poets seem to have borrowed from current trends in representing male homoerotic desire and thus to stress points of correspondence rather than difference between male and female eros, a continuum of sexual desires rather than a gendered dichotomy. Sculptural representations of hermaphrodites, which began to appear with more frequency during the Hellenistic period,[144] provide a visual example of fluidity of boundaries between male and female.

Several of Theocritus's poems, and particularly his urban mimes, underscore the gender ambiguity of young males by drawing attention to their erotic impact on both men and women. *Idyll* 2's Delphis provides a key example. Simaetha admires Delphis in terms that highlight his potential appeal to men, for her desire is aroused by how Delphis glistens after exercising in the wrestling school (80), a sight which could also provide erotic stimulus for Greek men who loiter around wrestling schools and gymnasia to gaze at boys.[145] Simaetha highlights Delphis's androgynous qualities by comparing his gleam to that of the goddess Selene (79). Further, Simaetha's informant is unsure whether Delphis's new love is male or female (150, 44).

Delphis's self-praise also highlights the fuzziness of his erotic placement between men and women: he reports that he is considered hand-some and nimble among the young men (124–25). In a seductive speech addressed to Simaetha, Delphis describes his eagerness to comply with Simaetha's summons by using an analogy that evokes the homoerotic ethos of the gymnasium:

> ἦ ῥά με, Σιμαίθα, τόσον ἔφθασας, ὅσσον ἐγώ θην
> πρᾶν ποκα τὸν χαρίεντα τράχων ἔφθασσα Φιλῖνον,
> ἐς τὸ τεὸν καλέσασα τόδε στέγος ἢ 'μὲ παρῆμεν.
>
> (114–16)

Truly, Simaetha, you barely beat me — by no more than I
the other day outran the graceful Philinos —
in summoning me to your house before I came unasked.

By having Delphis use the adjective χαρίεις (graceful) of Philinus when other adjectives might seem more suitable to running, the poet suggests that Delphis's interest in Philinus extends beyond the running field. Further, as noted in the previous discussion of *Idyll* 2's male-female interac-tions, the analogy Delphis uses to end his seduction speech also high-lights his sexual ambiguity, for in describing the passion that might have consumed him (had Simaetha not preempted it), he puts himself in the positions of a maiden and a bride victimized by Eros (136–38).

Before moving to a detailed consideration of *Idyll* 15's Adonis, another key example in a discussion of the representation of sexually ambiguous males in Theocritus's poetry, I would like to point out two other places in Theocritus's poetry where homosexual and heterosexual desire over-lap. In *Idyll* 13, the narration of Heracles and Hylas's story shows that water nymphs too find Heracles' boyfriend Hylas attractive (48–49). Segal aptly stresses Hylas's sexual ambiguities: "Love in his case veers ambiguously between male and female roles and between eroticism and maternal dependence."[146] In *Idyll* 7, Simichidas tries to diminish Phili-nus in his lover Aratus's eyes, by reporting how women are teasing him as he reaches maturity:

> καὶ δὴ μὰν ἀπίοιο πεπαίτερος, αἱ δὲ γυναῖκες,
> "αἰαῖ," φαντί, "Φιλῖνε, τό τοι καλὸν ἄνθος ἀπορρεῖ."
>
> (120–21)

And truly riper than a pear is he, and the women cry,
"Alas, Philinus, thy fair bloom is falling from thee."
(trans. Gow, *Theocritus* 1: 65)

Although *Idyll* 14 does not explore sexual ambiguity *per se*, the poem represents a male's confusion concerning gendered self-identity. When abandoned by Cynisca, his former lover, Aeschinas likens her behavior in leaving him to a bull's, and he likens himself to a mouse and a starving Megarian. These analogies underscore how Cynisca's act of self-assertion at a male-defined symposium has convoluted normative gender identities for Aeschinas: he now views Cynisca as powerful and dominant and himself, a man who formerly felt entitled to beat his girlfriend, as subordinated and powerless. A related example of role reversal occurs in *Idyll* 6: Damoetas's Polyphemus fantasizes that Galatea will appropriate the male's role of komastically courting him and he will take the subordinated role of barring his door to her (32).

Idyll 15's Adonis is central to a consideration of the theme of feminized males in Theocritus's poetry. Adonis is unusual among Greek heroes and gods in that he was already a figure of gender ambiguity in Greek poetry of the archaic age. In his first extant appearance in Greek literature, he is described as ἁβρός ("delicate"; Sappho fr. 244.1 Page).[147] In Hellenistic poetry, the adjective ἁβρός continues to spotlight feminized male beauty, for example, in a homoerotic epigram by Philostratus:

> τί τὸν ἡδὺν ἐπηυγάσσασθε καὶ ἁβρόν
> Στασικράτη, Παφίης ἔρνος ἰοστεφάνου;
> > (*Ep.* 1.5–6 Gow and Page [= *A.P.* 12.91])

Why did you gaze upon sweet, delicate
Stasicrates, a sapling of violet-crowned Aphrodite?

In *Idyll* 15, Theocritus's shaping of Praxinoa's gaze upon the Adonis figure represented in the woven tapestry underscores characteristics in Adonis that can make him sexually attractive to both men and women (πρᾶτον ἴουλον ἀπὸ κροτάφων καταβάλλων, "with the first youthful down spreading from his temples," 85). Youth was traditionally a valued quality in *eromenoi* (beloved boys) and "youthful down" imagery appears regularly in homoerotic poems.[148] The homoerotic appeal of "down" imagery in the Hellenistic age can also be seen in a wry Hellenistic epigram attributed to Asclepiades:[149]

> νῦν αἰτεῖς ὅτε λεπτὸς ὑπὸ κροτάφοισιν ἴουλος
> ἕρπει καὶ μηροῖς ὀξὺς ἔπεστι χνόος.
> > (*Ep.* 46.1–2 Gow and Page [= *A.P.* 12.36.1–2])

Now you offer yourself, when the delicate down is spreading
under your temples and there is a prickly bloom on your thighs.
> > (trans. based on Paton, *Greek Anthology* 4:299).

Callimachus, whose work includes many homoerotic epigrams, also uses down imagery to describe a youth's appearance:

ἀρμοῖ που κἀκείνῳ ἐπέτρεχε λεπτὸς ἴουλος
ἄνθει ἐλιχρύσῳ ἐναλίγκιος.

(*Hecale*, fr. 274)

A delicate down, like the helichryse's blossom,
was just starting to spread on him too.

The sex of the speaker is unspecified and could be female, but from the imagery, the speaker's sex could just as well be male.[150] Further, the element of down is also traditional in descriptions of males who die young, for example, Homer's description of young giants killed before reaching manhood:

πρίν σφῶϊν ὑπὸ κροτάφοισιν ἰούλους
ἀνθῆσαι πυκάσαι τε γένυς ἐυανθέϊ λάχνῃ.

(*Od.* 11.319–20 *O.C.T.*)

before the down blossomed beneath their temples
and covered their chins with freshly blooming beard.

(trans. A. T. Murray, *Odyssey* 1:409, rev.)

Thus when *Idyll* 15's Praxinoa gazes on a tapestry representing the dead or dying Adonis and comments on the youthful down on his face, she focuses on qualities (his youthfulness, the incipience of a beard) that make his sexuality available to both men and women (and that also emphasize the poignancy of his premature death).[151]

In Theocritus's *Idyll* 15, the poet intensifies Adonis's ambiguity as a sexual figure by having the hymnist highlight Adonis's association with Ganymede, an object of Zeus's homoerotic desire,[152] as well as with the Erotes, young male figures often represented hermaphroditically.[153] On Aphrodite and Adonis's couch, the centerpiece of *Idyll* 15's Adonis celebration, carved ivory eagles transport Ganymede to Zeus (123–24), and Erotes fly overhead in the arbors. Both Ganymede and Erotes, like Adonis, traditionally represented youthful homoerotic beauty, and Theocritus uses Ganymede elsewhere in explicitly homoerotic contexts. Thus in *Idyll* 12, the *erastes*-narrator uses Ganymede in the closure of a homoerotic courtship speech addressed to his *eromenos*:

ὄλβιος ὅστις παισὶ φιλήματα κεῖνα διαιτᾷ.
ἦ που τὸν χαροπὸν Γανυμήδεα πόλλ' ἐπιβῶται
Λυδίῃ ἶσον ἔχειν πέτρῃ στόμα, χρυσὸν ὁποίη
πεύθονται, μὴ φαῦλος, ἐτήτυμον ἀργυραμοιβοί.

(34–37)

Happy he who judges those kisses for the boys,
and surely long he prays to radiant Ganymede

that his lips may be as the Lydian touchstone whereby
the money-changers try true gold to see it be not false.

(trans. Gow, Theocritus 1 : 95)

Callimachus's *Epigram* 52 also underscores Ganymede's value in homoerotic contexts, for the *erastes*-narrator, in courting an *eromenos* named
Theocritus,[154] uses Ganymede to invoke Zeus: [155]

ναίχι πρὸς εὐχαίτεω Γανυμήδεος, οὐράνιε Ζεῦ,
καὶ σύ ποτ᾽ ἠράσθης.

(3–4)

Yea, by Ganymede of the fair locks, O Zeus in heaven,
thou too hast loved.

(trans. Mair, "Callimachus," 175 [his Ep. 53])

Thus in Theocritus's *Idyll* 15, the association with the Erotes and Ganymede (like Adonis, a beautiful boy who never grows up and a subordinated lover) emphasizes Adonis's sexual ambiguity as a passive, sexual
object on display for both men's and women's gazes.[156] The elements of
youth and passivity in Praxinoa's description of Adonis's appearance take
him beyond sexual dichotomy to suggest more androgynous appeal.[157]

Ovid too emphasizes the element of gender doubt in Adonis's erotic
appeal (*Met.* 10.519–739). Venus, in telling the story of Atalanta to
Adonis, highlights Adonis's androgyny by comparing Atalanta's face and
naked body[158] to Adonis's (as well as her own):

Ut faciem et posito corpus velamine vidit,
Quale meum, vel quale tuum, si femina fias,
Obstipuit.

(Met. 10.578–80; Anderson,
Ovid's Metamorphoses)

But when Hippomenes saw Atalanta's face and unclothed body —
a body like my own, or like yours, Adonis, if you were a woman —
he was struck with wonder.

Venus's flattery of Adonis here emphasizes the sexual ambiguity of his
appearance. In Ovid's version,[159] Venus, in Diana's dress, participates in
Adonis's liminal world of hunting (535–39) by feminizing it, transforming it into an erotic playground. In restricting the hunt to small animals,
especially deer and rabbits (traditional love-gifts),[160] Venus reorients the
hunt around the goal of embracing on the grass afterwards (554–59). But
for a Greek youth, the hunt represented a passage to manhood: [161]
Adonis ignores Venus's cautionary tale, rejects her hunting proscrip-
tions, and chases a boar. But he fails to pass to manhood, for the boar

kills him (708–16). Venus commemorates his youthful death by instituting an annual reenactment of her grief, and she transforms his blood into the anemone (717–39), a reminder of ephemerality and sexual ambiguity.[162]

The link between eros and death is a central theme in Adonis's representations in Greek literature. Thus Sappho emphasizes through the adjective ἄβρος (delicate) the poignancy of Adonis's tender death: κατθνάισκει, Κυθέρη᾽, ἄβρος Ἄδωνις ("Delicate Adonis is dying, Kythereia [Aphrodite]"; fr. 244.1 Page).[163] *Idyll* 15's representation of the Adonis festival exploits the linkage between eros and death. Praxinoa admires a representation of Adonis by describing him as one who evokes love even in death (86). The hymnist's description of the grieving female celebrants' appearance also highlights this linkage:

> ἀῶθεν δ᾽ ἄμμες νιν ἅμα δρόσῳ ἀθρόαι ἔξω
> οἰσεῦμες ποτὶ κύματ᾽ ἐπ᾽ ἀιόνι πτύοντα,
> λύσασαι δὲ κόμαν καὶ ἐπὶ σφυρὰ κόλπον ἀνεῖσαι
> στήθεσι φαινομένοις λιγυρᾶς ἀρξεύμεθ᾽ ἀοιδᾶς.
>
> (132–35)

At dawn we will gather with the dew and carry him outside
to the waves crashing on the shore,
and with hair unbound, robes in folds at our ankles,
breasts bare, we shall begin the funereal song.

The Adonia traditionally offered a poetic forum for heteroerotic voyeurism. For example, in Menander's *Samia*, a youth's spying activities at a private Adonia result in his impregnating his neighbor's daughter (38–50). A Hellenistic epigram by Dioscorides also highlights the heteroeroticism of the ritualized Adonis lament:

> Ἡ τρυφερή μ᾽ ἤγρευσε Κλεὼ τὰ γαλάκτιν᾽, Ἄδωνι,
>   τῇ σῇ κοψαμένη στήθεα παννυχίδι.
> εἰ δώσει κἀμοὶ ταύτην χάριν, ἢν ἀποπνεύσω,
>   μὴ προφάσεις, σύμπλουν σύν με λαβὼν †ἀγέτω.
>
> (*Ep.* 4 Gow and Page [= *A.P.* 5.193])

Tender Cleo took me captive, Adonis, as she beat her breasts
    white as milk at thy night funeral feast.
Will she but do me the same honour, if I die,
    I hesitate not; take me with thee on thy voyage.

                    (trans. Paton, *Greek Anthology* 1:223–25)

By personalizing the eros inherent to the Adonia, Dioscorides' speaker transforms the Adonis lament into a site of personal, heteroerotic seduction.[164] Later Ovid too recommends the Adonia as an opportunity to find women: "nec te praetereat Veneri ploratus Adonis" ("Do not let Adonis, bewailed by Venus, escape your notice"; *Ars Am.* 1.75).

Theocritus's poetry romanticizes deaths of other young males besides Adonis, in both heterosexual and homosexual contexts. *Idyll* 13 combines the two: amorous water nymphs steal Hylas from Heracles by pulling him into a pond:

πασάων γὰρ ἔρως ἁπαλὰς φρένας ἐξεφόβησεν
'Αργείῳ ἐπὶ παιδί.

(48–49)

For love of the Argive lad had fluttered
all their tender hearts.

(trans. Gow, *Theocritus* 1:99)

Idyll 1's Daphnis, a rebel, seeks to escape the tyranny of love through death: Daphnis vows to continue to give love (Eros) grief even in Hades (103), and Thyrsis's description of Daphnis's death stresses the muses' and the nymphs' tenderness for him (140–41). Throughout Theocritus's poetry, fictive characters connect love and death. In heterosexual contexts, *Idyll* 2's Simaetha threatens to kill her beloved (159–62, 58) and *Idyll* 3's goatherd threatens to commit suicide for love (25–27, 53). In homoerotic contexts, lovers also highlight their love through death references, but less violently. *Idyll* 12's *erastes* desires that even two hundred generations later, in Acheron (Hades), he might learn of his love affair's lasting fame (18–21). *Idyll* 29's *erastes* claims he would fetch Cerberus, keeper of the dead, for his beloved (38). *Idyll* 12 offers an amusing variation of the use of the eroticism of death motif in a seduction strategy: an *erastes* ends his courtship speech to his *eromenos* by describing an annual boys' kissing contest held at Diocles' tomb in Megara to commemorate his homoerotic passion (27–37).[165]

Callimachus's poems that feature young males also typically represent their attractiveness in ways that heighten their homoerotic appeal, even when the context for their appearance is heterosexual (as in the case of a male-female marriage). For example, in Callimachus's *Aetia* 3, frs. 67–75 (the marriage of Acontius and Cydippe), the poet-narrator underscores Acontius's attractiveness by describing the attention he is given in settings that typically attract the homoerotic gaze: Acontius receives notice on his way to school or to the bath (fr. 68), and at symposia male admirers play the game *kottabos* in his honor (fr. 69). Further, Callimachus describes only Acontius's response on the wedding night, not Cydippe's, and he uses imagery that reflects a homoerotic world oriented around the gymnasium:[166]

οὔ σε δοκέω τημοῦτος, ᾿Ακόντιε, νυκτὸς ἐκείνης
    ἀντί κε, τῇ μίτρης ἥψαο παρθενίης,
οὐ σφυρὸν ᾿Ιφίκλειον ἐπιτρέχον ἀσταχύεσσιν
....
δέξασθαι.

(*Aet.* 3, fr. 75.44–48)

Then, I deem, Acontius, that for that night,
    wherein you touched her maiden girdle,
you would [not] have accepted . . . the ankle of Iphicles
....
who ran upon the corn-ears.

(trans. Trypanis, "Callimachus," 59)

Callimachus also underscores the effeminancy of the god Apollo:[167]

καὶ μὲν ἀεὶ καλὸς καὶ ἀεὶ νέος· οὔποτε Φοίβου
θηλείαις οὐδ᾿ ὅσσον ἐπὶ χνόος ἦλθε παρειαῖς.

(*Hymn* 2.36–37)

And ever beautiful is he and ever young: never on the girl
cheeks of Apollo hath come so much as the down of manhood.

(trans. Mair, "Callimachus," 51–53)

This feminized Apollo may correspond to (or anticipate) a trend in Hellenistic statuary representing Apollo: as Smith suggests, "Apollo had always been represented as young and beautiful, but Hellenistic Apollo often takes on a soft, languorous, effeminate style."[168] Callimachus also highlights the homoerotic aspect of Apollo's relationship with Admetus: ζευγίτιδας ἔτρεφεν ἵππους / ἠιθέου ὑπ᾿ ἔρωτι κεκαυμένος ᾿Αδμήτοιο ("He tended the yokemares, / fired with love of young Admetus"; trans. Mair, "Callimachus," 53; *Hymn* 2.48–49).[169]

In Callimachus's *Iambus* 3, the *erastes*-narrator's wish to overturn his sexual identity highlights Callimachus's preoccupation with gender róles: he claims that he would rather be a celebrant of Cybebe (Cybele) or participate in the ritual lament for Adonis (that is, he would rather be a eunuch or a woman) than be a poet in a materialistic age when poets are not honored (or a lover of boys when boys have turned mercenary).[170] This poem stresses the degraded aspect of the *erastes*-narrator's wish by describing Adonis, the proposed object of worship, as Aphrodite's ἄνθρωπος ("slave [or mortal]," *Iambus* 3, fr. 193.37).

In addition to feminized males, boyish females appear in many of Theocritus's and Callimachus's poems.[171] In Theocritus's *Idyll* 18, for example, a maiden chorus underscore their own athleticism:

ἄμμες δ' αἱ πᾶσαι συνομάλικες, αἷς δρόμος ωὑτός
χρισαμέναις ἀνδριστὶ παρ' Εὐρώταο λοετροῖς.

(22–23)

And we, the full tale of her coevals, together anoint ourselves in manly
    fashion
by the bathing places in Eurotas and run there together.

(trans. Gow, *Theocritus* 1:143)

Similarly, Callimachus's *Hymn* 5 praises Athena by highlighting her boyish charms (13–32). The festival director instructs the celebrants not to bring Athena perfume, alabasters, or mirror, for her red blush comes from running and from simple unguents:[172]

τῶι καὶ νῦν ἄρσεν τι κομίσσατε μῶνον ἔλαιον,
    ὧι Κάστωρ, ὧι καὶ χρίεται Ἡρακλέης.

(29–30 Bulloch, *Callimachus*)

So now too bring something manly, just olive oil,
    the anointing oil of Castor, of Heracles.

(trans. Bulloch, *Callimachus*, 95)

Theocritus's urban mimes also include examples of women engaging in conventionally male behavior. *Idyll* 2's Simaetha takes an active (male) role in courtship behavior: she falls in love when she sees Delphis on the street, and she summons him to her. *Idyll* 15's Syracusan women take the active roles of subjects as they gaze upon male objects of desire (the Adonis figures), and Praxinoa defies a male stranger and asserts her right to public speech. *Idyll* 14's Cynisca claims the traditional male right of a self-willed love, and when Aeschinas beats her for her disloyalty, she asserts her power by leaving him.

A key simile can illustrate the theme of gender ambiguity in Apollonius Rhodius's *Argonautica*, for Jason's joy when he has attained the golden fleece, the object of his heroic quest, is compared to a girl's delight in catching the moonlight on her robe:

ὡς δὲ σεληναίης διχομήνιδα παρθένος αἴγλην
ὑψόθεν †ἀνέχουσαν ὑπωρόφιον θαλάμοιο
λεπταλέῳ ἑανῷ ὑποΐσχεται, ἐν δέ οἱ ἦτορ
χαίρει δερκομένης καλὸν σέλας — ὡς τότ' Ἰήσων

γηθόσυνος μέγα κῶας ἑαῖς ἀναείρετο χερσίν,
καί οἱ ἐπὶ ξανθῇσι παρηίσιν ἠδὲ μετώπῳ
μαρμαρυγῇ ληνέων φλογὶ εἴκελον ἷζεν ἔρευθος.

(*Argon.* 4.167–73 *O.C.T.*)

And as a maiden catches on her finely wrought robe
the gleam of the moon at the full, as it rises above
her high-roofed chamber; and her heart rejoices
as she beholds the fair ray; so at that time did Jason
uplift the great fleece in his hands;
and from the shimmering of the flocks of wool
there settled on his fair cheeks and brow a red flush like a flame.

(trans. Seaton, *Argonautica,* 305, rev.)

Medea has performed the crucial feat of putting the serpent to sleep, while Jason has simply taken the fleece afterward. This simile not only feminizes Jason's response to the fleece, but also seems to eroticize it by evoking imagery appropriate to marriage readiness and by emphasizing Jason's sexual attractiveness (the flush on his cheeks and brow).[173]

The gender ambiguity characteristic of much of Hellenistic poetry may reflect uncertainty about gender roles in a world in which Greek men's public roles were being curtailed and women's were opening up. Just as boundaries between males and females were fluctuating in Hellenistic society, so too in poetry and art. The trend toward feminizing males in Hellenistic visual art and literature may reflect the political subordination of males in a new Greek world defined by autocratic hegemonies. Hellenistic poets were living in a period of change: gendered roles in society — such as the equation of public and political with male, and private and immobile with female — were in flux due to the rise of mobility and the domination of autocratic hegemonies. Through representations of sexual desire and interrelations, poets were able to explore the changing gendered conditions of their world.

CHAPTER 3

Ekphrasis and the Reception of Works of Art

The topic of aesthetic reception rose in popularity among creative artists and writers after the fifth century B.C. Anecdotal accounts of fourth-century artists' lives illustrate the lively interest in viewer response. For example, Pliny reports that Apelles habitually placed his paintings in a public gallery in order to eavesdrop on the criticism of passersby, since he judged the public a more observant critic than himself.[1] Vase paintings also indicate the fourth-century artist's attention to the relationship between viewer, creator, and work of art — e.g., a fourth-century column-krater from Southern Italy shows Heracles, Zeus, and Nike observing a man painting a statue of Heracles.[2] So too, a Pompeian wall-painting (a copy of a Hellenistic original) shows Thetis seated in Hephaestus's workshop gazing at Achilles' shield and seeing herself reflected back.[3] In addition to exploring optical effects, this painting also raises the question of the subjectivity of experiencing art: do we look into a picture to see ourselves reflected back?[4] Fourth-century philosophers, as well, attest to the artist's increased attention to the subjectivity involved in "reading" works of art. For example, Plato expresses concerns about the deceptiveness of the fourth-century artist's practice of altering "true" proportions to enhance the optical effect (*Sophist*, esp. 235e-236c).[5] Further, the fourth-century interest in the psychology of reception manifests itself in Plato's and Aristotle's troubled explorations of art's potential to harm character. Although Aristotle expands the definition of pleasurable art to include the ugly (*Poetics* 1448b17–19), still his moral program provincially forbids juveniles to view Pauson's paintings, since Pauson represents persons as worse than they are (*Politics*

1340a35–38). Plato goes further and excludes paintings from his "ideal" state (*Republic*, book 10).

Despite the moral strictures of fourth-century philosophers, "trivial" themes, genre scenes, and grotesque subjects increasingly engaged artists and writers anxious to create works not submerged by the authority of the past, and the problematic topics of subjectivity in the reception of art, psychological characterization in art, the aesthetic value of ugliness, art's potential to affect character, and the relationship between public and private aspects of art continued as vital concerns in the Hellenistic age. The device of *ekphrasis* (a rhetorical description of a work of art),[6] which complicates reception by mediating between verbal and visual representations, became a popular poetic forum in which to explore such concerns.

Theocritus's *Idyll* 15 represents two women attending a festival where elaborate tapestries and a hymn to Adonis enliven the celebration. Many scholars have expressed the belief that the poem mocks the aesthetic taste of the fictive women (who "express naïve wonder at the lifelikeness of the tapestries").[7] Recent articles include descriptions of the fictive women as "ignorant city girls mindlessly admir[ing] tapestries"[8] and their taste as "sublime[ly] bad — at once ignorant and pretentious."[9] After all, the argument goes, for the first half of the poem the women are represented as gossipy, quarrelsome housewives, and if an author brings such creatures into the presence of works of art, what can he possibly intend except ironic collusion between himself and the reader against these female characters? But given that the realistic mode of representation was highly valued by creative artists and writers of the Hellenistic period and their most sophisticated contemporaries,[10] the assumption that the author intended to mock Gorgo and Praxinoa's aesthetic orientation deserves closer examination.

The tone of Herodas's *Mime* 4, the other Hellenistic poem in which women view works of art in a ceremonial setting,[11] has often been cited to reinforce assessments of the mocking tone of *Idyll* 15.[12] The similarities between the two poems are striking: in both poems two women view works of art in a ceremonial setting and admire them for their realism, and both poems are written in the mode of dramatic dialogue. Yet stylistic differences between the two poems set them apart in intention and design: in meter and language, Herodas's mime recalls the low poetry of Hipponax, while Theocritus's poem recalls the high poetry of Homer. This chapter examines the rhetorical handling of the *ekphrases* of the two poems in order to sharpen our understanding of their different approaches to the topic of aesthetic responses.

Ekphrases per se were nothing new (e.g., the *Iliad*'s description of

Achilles' shield), but attention in poetry to the psychological process of viewing the work of art is characteristically Hellenistic. It is generally recognized how effectively later poetry uses the device of *ekphrasis*; e.g., in the nineteenth-century poem "My Last Duchess" by Robert Browning, the duke's description of the duchess's portrait clearly contributes to psychological characterization and to the manipulation of the reader's sympathies.[13] But in the study of Hellenistic poetry, little attention has been paid to the role of *ekphrasis* in exploring the psychology of aesthetic response in both Theocritus's *Idyll* 15 and Herodas's *Mime* 4, and the place of these poems in the tradition of exploring subjectivity through *ekphrasis* has been largely overlooked.[14] Yet the exploration of subjectivity through *ekphrasis*, by representing fictive characters describing works of art, is an important contribution of Hellenistic literature to later Greek and Latin writers.[15]

As in other aspects of Hellenistic artistry, such as techniques of complicating audience response,[16] Euripides anticipates the Hellenistic practice of using *ekphrases* to enrich psychological characterizations. For example, in the *Electra,* the choral ode that precedes the recognition scene describes Achilles' journey to Troy and includes an *ekphrasis* of Achilles' armor (452–79). The *ekphrasis* in this choral ode helps characterize Electra's psychological state.[17] Electra expects her brother to return aggressively, like Achilles (also an avenger of adultery, as the chorus reminds us). Shown locks of Orestes' hair, Electra rebukes the old man who brought them for thinking her fearless brother would sneak back in secret. By highlighting the gap between fantasy and reality, the *ekphrasis* reflects Electra's inflated expectations, which threaten to block recognition of her brother. This choral ode also shows, through the chorus's example, how easily one might sympathetically participate in Electra's lonely fantasies. The ode begins by calling attention to the theme of distance: the description of a ship's journey to Troy reflects the distance Orestes and Electra must travel to reach one another. As for the authority of the description of Achilles' shield, the chorus of Argive women did not themselves see the shield they describe; instead they call on an eyewitness's report. This distancing of the women from the work of art, reinforced by the Euripidean shield's distance from the Iliadic shield in time and design, intensifies the reader's perception of disjunction between Euripides' creatures and the monumental epic world from which they come.[18]

Theocritus's *Idyll* 15 and Herodas's *Mime* 4 also belong to a secondary tradition of *ekphrasis* wherein fictive characters view works of art in a ceremonial (religious) context. This secondary tradition includes the *parodos* (chorus's entry song) of Euripides' *Ion*.[19] This *parodos* consists of the talk of the chorus of slave women from Athens as they visit the precinct of Apollo's temple at Delphi and excitedly point out the works of art they see (184–218). Their *ekphrases* emphasize the psychological distance between the slave women's response to temple art and that of their mistress Creusa. The statues give pleasure to the chorus's eyes (231) but pain to Creusa's (242–44), because Apollo once raped her.[20]

The motif of "misreading" works of art, of selective viewing in terms of self-interest, is another important secondary tradition of *ekphrasis* in Greek and Latin literature. For example, in the passage above, because of her personal history, Creusa cannot feel joy at the sight of the sanctuary, but instead violates its celebratory intention with tears. The most familiar Latin example of "misreading" works of art is the passage from Vergil's *Aeneid* that describes Aeneas viewing pictures of Troy's fall on the walls of Juno's temple (1.450–93). In describing these pictures, the poet explores the relations between a work of art, the context of its viewing, and the viewer's preoccupations. The images of Troy's suffering reassure Aeneas, and he imputes to the artist his own feelings of sympathy for the fallen warriors. On the basis of these pictures he assumes that there is sympathy for Trojans in this place (see especially 459–63). Yet in the context of Juno's temple, images of Troy's fall function as a celebration and reminder of Juno's implacable anger against the Trojans.[21] Another example of the motif of "misreading" works of art occurs in Petronius's *Satyricon*, 83. The recently jilted Encolpius visits an art gallery, and from the many paintings displayed there he fixates on only those pictures and aspects of pictures that feed his own feelings of betrayal by his lover Giton and the friend who seduced Giton: an eagle abducting Ganymede, Hylas repulsing a naiad, and Apollo cursing his hands for murdering Hyacinth.

Theocritus's *Idyll* 15 and Herodas's *Mime* 4 are of seminal importance in the tradition of exploring subjectivity through *ekphrases*, for they both explore how context and viewer expectation and preoccupation can affect what is seen and not seen in works of art. In the next section, I compare *Idyll* 15's representation of aesthetic experiences with *Mime* 4's and show how differences between these representations underscore the different concerns of their poets. In the last section of this chapter, I examine how in *Idyll* 15, through the shaping of Gorgo's response to the hymn, the poet provides not only a passage for Gorgo from the world of art to her own fictive reality, but also a passage for his actual audience from the fictive world of poetry to their own reality. A poet can hardly represent a work of visual or verbal art, an inherently selective process, without reflecting on the intention of art and on the possibilities of art for representing human experiences. Insofar as the poet is himself creating a figment of life (a poem), by representing a fictive audience's response to a fictive work of art, the poet can also approach the issue of how real audiences might respond to his own works of art.

Reception of Art

Works of art, whether viewed in religious sanctuaries or elsewhere, can elicit many different reactions: awe, laughter, sorrow, desire, boredom. Much depends on the occasion and context of viewing, and the viewer's psychic state and aesthetic orientation.[22] In both Theocritus's *Idyll* 15 and Herodas's *Mime* 4, two women friends enter a ceremonial sanctuary and view a work of religious art before them and one of the friends gives a detailed *ekphrasis* of this work of art, which includes a three-line description of the figure of a young male and a silver object. Scholars typically conflate the viewing experiences of the women in these two poems.[23] Yet differences in the handling of *ekphrases* between these two poems reflect their different approaches to the issue of aesthetic response.

The terms that the women of *Idyll* 15 and *Mime* 4 use to describe viewing works of art exemplify the difference between the poets' approaches to their fictive women's aesthetic responses. In *Idyll* 15, Theocritus has Gorgo and Praxinoa describe their responses to art through the verb θεάομαι (behold with wonder), which frequently appears in contexts of ceremonial viewing.[24] Thus Gorgo uses this verb to urge Praxinoa to attend the Adonia: βᾶμες . . . / θασόμεναι τὸν Ἄδωνιν ("Let's go . . . to see the Adonis," 22–23). Standing in wonderment before the Adonis figure on display in the palace grounds fulfills this invitation. Praxinoa affirms the elevated mood of this occasion by using the corresponding verbal adjective θαητός (wondrous)[25] to call attention to the figure of Adonis: αὐτὸς δ' ὡς θαητός ("And Adonis himself, how marvelous he is"; 84).

In *Mime* 4, on the other hand, Kynno describes the proper response to Apelles' painting by the verb παμφαλάω (gaze with excitement):

> ὃς δ' ἐκεῖνον ἢ ἔργα τὰ ἐκείνου
> μὴ παμφαλήσας ἐκ δίκης ὀρώρηκεν,
> ποδὸς κρέμαιτ' ἐκεῖνος ἐν γναφέως οἴκωι.
>
> (76–78)

> And whoever does not gaze on the artist or his works
> in excited astonishment (as is just),
> may he hang by the foot in a fuller's shop.

The reduplicated verb παμφαλάω emphasizes the required intensity of aesthetic response. Further, Kynno prescribes a punishment for anyone who errs in responding to Apelles' art: to be treated with the violence used on dirty laundry. This hyperbolic description, with its imagery from everyday domestic concerns, underscores the inappropriateness of the violence to the offense, as well as to a visit to a shrine of Asclepius, the healer-god.

In Theocritus's *Idyll* 15, Praxinoa views a figured tapestry[26] which includes a representation of an Adonis figure reclining on a silver couch.[27] Her description of the Adonis figure makes evident the congruity of what she sees with the ceremonial context of her viewing:

> αὐτὸς δ' ὡς θαητὸς ἐπ' ἀργυρέας κατάκειται
> κλισμῷ, πρᾶτον ἴουλον ἀπὸ κροτάφων καταβάλλων,
> ὁ τριφίλητος Ἄδωνις, ὁ κἠν Ἀχέροντι φιληθείς.
>
> (84–86)

And Adonis himself, how marvelous he is, reclining on a silver couch,
with the first youthful down spreading from his temples,
thrice-loved Adonis, loved even in Acheron.

First, she describes his representation as a unified whole, for she associates the wonder appropriate to the figure of Adonis with the silver of the couch. Her integrated vision of the work of art is shown in the interlaced word placement of the description of Adonis reclining on a silver couch (an ABA pattern): ἀργυρέας κατάκειται / κλισμῷ (84–85). The wonder appropriate to the ceremonial Adonis figure is associated (by immediate juxtaposition) with the substance silver,[28] and this mutual enhancement of the figure of Adonis and his silver couch is phonetically mirrored by the repetition of kappas in the descriptions of where he reclines and how he looks (κατάκειται / κλισμῷ, . . . κροτάφων κατα-βάλλων; 83–84). Second, Praxinoa's description concentrates on those aspects of the work of art integral to the festival of Adonis: his incipient manhood, the love he inspires, and the transition between the realms of Aphrodite and of Persephone that the festival reenacts. Praxinoa "reads" the work of art in its context: the sensual pleasure of viewing Adonis's representation contributes to the religious experience that viewing him inspires. Her description reveals the ceremonial value of the pictorial ob-

ject, and the hymnic tone of the last line of the description contributes
to the elevation of the ceremonial occasion of the viewing.

In Herodas's *Mime* 4, as Kokkale[29] enters the inner sanctuary of Asclepius's temple, like Praxinoa she also views a representation of a young
boy, but she is transfixed by his nakedness. Kokkale's description exemplifies her obliviousness to the ceremonial context of the painting, for
she proposes to scratch the naked boy, a crude test of realism ill-suited
to the temple of Asclepius, the god of healing not injury:

> τὸν παῖδα δὴ ⟨τὸν⟩ γυμνὸν ἢν κνίσω τοῦτον
> οὐκ ἕλκος ἕξει, Κύννα; πρὸς γάρ οἱ κεῖνται
> αἱ σάρκες οἷα †θερμα† πηδῶσαι
> ἐν τῆι σανίσκηι.
>
> (59–62)

Look at this naked boy, if I scratch him,
will he not bleed, Kynno? For the flesh lies on him
pulsing like a warm liquid in the picture.

Next, silver fire tongs engage Kokkale's interest. But Kokkale's three-line
description of a young male and a silver object, unlike Praxinoa's description, does not reveal the function of the boy in the painting and does not
present the silver object and the boy as part of a unified artistic conception. Instead Kokkale focuses on a hypothetical audience foolish enough
to respond to painted silver fire tongs with the emotion of greed:

> τὠργύρευν δὲ πύραυστρον
> οὐκ ἢν ἴδηι Μύελλος ἢ Παταικίσκος
> ὁ Λαμπρίωνος, ἐκβαλεῦσι τὰς κούρας
> δοκεῦντες ὄντως ἀργύρευν πεποιῆσθαι;
>
> (62–65)

And the silver fire tongs,
if Myellos or Pataikiskos, son of Lamprion,
sees them, won't their eyes fall out
when they think those tongs made of real silver?

Then, after seven lines describing a naked boy and silver fire tongs
(59–65), suddenly in two lines Kokkale fills the picture with inhabitants
and activity:

> ὁ βοῦς δὲ κὠ ἄγων αὐτὸν ἥ τ' ὁμαρτεῦσα
> κὠ γρυπὸς οὗτος κὠ ἀνάσιλλος ἄνθρωπος.
>
> (66–67)

An ox and the man who leads him, and a woman attendant,
and this hook-nosed man, and a bristling-haired fellow.

But Kokkale is not interested in the world of the painting, and she never
puts the pieces of her description together. The picture is presented as a
riddle: the reader must participate, fill the interpretive gap, and create
the picture from the parts.[30] Scholars generally conjecture a sacrifice
scene, with the naked boy holding the silver fire tongs and tending a
sacrificial fire.[31] But the nakedness of the young boy in the painting distracts Kokkale: she never connects him with the silver fire tongs, and she
never indicates his possible function as sacrificial attendant. Kokkale's
description of the fire tongs exemplifies her indifference to how such a
painting might be integral to a god's sanctuary: she never describes the
possible ceremonial function of fire tongs but only the greed their realistic representation might arouse.

Kokkale demonstrates her familiarity with the popular aesthetic of the
day by admiring the lifelike illusion of the figures in the painting: οὐχὶ
ζοὴν βλέπουσι κἠμέρην πάντες; ("Do they not all have the look of
life?" 68). But she only experiences the realism of the representation of a
naked boy as it mirrors her libido. Further, her description of the painting concludes by measuring the realism of the painted ox by the fear it
inspires in her:

ἀνηλάλαξ᾽ ἄν, μή μ᾽ ὁ βοῦς τι πημήνηι.
οὕτω ἐπιλοξοῖ, Κυννί, τῆι ἐτέρηι κούρηι.

(70–71)

I should have cried aloud for fear the ox would harm me;
he gives such a sidelong look, Kynno, with one eye.

Kokkale first responds to the painting through desires to violate it:
she proposes to test its realism by scratching the boy (59–60); she certifies its realism by imagining other viewers coveting its painted silver
(63–65). The culmination of Kokkale's appreciation of the painting's realism is to impute to a mean-looking ox an intent as violent as her own.

To grasp the unity of a work of art can be a difficult process requiring
sympathetic and imaginative participation. This Kokkale does not do.
Instead Kokkale draws so close to the realism of the work, she admires
the details so intently, that she does not see the representation as a whole,
nor does she interpret it in the context of the temple of Asclepius. A
painting of a sacrifice can be appropriate in a temple. A sacrificial ox
pictured in the inner sanctuary of Asclepius's temple can substitute for

the rich offerings that poorer persons, such as Kokkale and her friend, cannot offer; Asclepius is covetous, according to Libanius, and particularly welcomes a sacrificial ox.[32] But the experience of viewing this painting distances Kokkale from its ceremonial context. She shows no interest in the painting's possible religious functions — instead she projects hostility and potential violence against herself into the ox's sidelong glance. Thus, Herodas's Kokkale responds to the realism of a picture in a way that distances her from the ceremonial world of the representation and the context of Asclepius's temple.

In Theocritus's *Idyll* 15, on the other hand, Praxinoa's viewing experience draws her into the ceremonial occasion of the Adonia. She sees the work of art in the context of the Adonia and admires realism in a way that enables her to participate in the mythological world represented on the tapestries. Insofar as the Adonia celebrates Adonis's annual revival, Praxinoa's remark on the life in the woven figures is relevant to the religious function of the art: ἔμψυχ᾿, οὐκ ἐνυφαντά ("They have life within them and are not woven in," 83). By admiring the life in the tapestries, by imaginatively and sympathetically experiencing Adonis's coming to life in the tapestries, the viewer recreates for that brief moment the magic of the resurrection of Adonis.

Mime 4's representation of how realism in art can heighten and mirror unpleasant aspects of life for viewers makes explicit an aesthetics of low life and the grotesque[33] which seems to permeate Herodas's poetry (e.g., *Mime* 5's representation of a jealous mistress's proposal of sordid punishment for a slave boy suspected of sexual infidelity).[34] In *Mime* 4, the choice to focus on certain aspects of the painting and items of statuary in the courtyard helps establish criteria of aesthetic valuation which could also favor Herodas's poetry. Thus when Kokkale and her friend view temple statuary in the courtyard outside Asclepius's temple, they pass over statues, such as that of an old man, to focus on statues that call up their excited astonishment:[35] a girl reaching desperately for an apple, a boy strangling a goose, and a woman whose name and stance seem to suggest questionable virtue.[36]

Mime 4 represents female viewers exercising their right to "read" the painting in their own way and without regard to the context of the viewing. The violent impulse Kokkale feels to wound the naked boy may seem discordant in a sanctuary of Asclepius, the god of healing, but it is not inappropriate to an erotic experience: metaphors connecting wounds and love are frequent among the Greek epigrammatists,[37] for example:

Ἡ λαμυρή μ᾽ ἔτρωσε Φιλαίνιον, εἰ δὲ τὸ τραῦμα
μὴ σαφές, ἀλλ᾽ ὁ πόνος δύεται εἰς ὄνυχα.
οἴχομ᾽, Ἔρωτες, ὄλωλα, διοίχομαι.
                    (Asclepiades *Ep.* 8.1–3 Gow and Page
                    [= *A.P.* 5.162.1–3])

Wanton Philainion has wounded me, and even if the wound
    does not show, still the pain reaches my fingertips.
I am ruined, Loves, I am undone, life has ended for me.

In *Mime* 4 Herodas's Kokkale does not let the context of the picture dominate her or obstruct the voyeurism of her gaze. Instead she responds to the painting by thinking of scratching the naked boy.[38]

Now let us consider Gorgo's response when she views the ceremonial tapestries hanging before her: λεπτὰ καὶ ὡς χαρίεντα ("how light and graceful they are," *Id.* 15.79). As Gow notes, Theocritus has Homer's *Odyssey* 10.222–23 specifically in mind.[39] In appendix 2, I discuss this allusion: how through Gorgo's use of this exclamation as she enters through doors to the palace grounds, Theocritus recalls Homer's representation of the moment Odysseus's men stood in Circe's gateway and saw Circe's woven materials hanging before them (which also includes a description of the weaving as λεπτά τε καὶ χαρίεντα, "light and graceful," *Od.* 10.223). Here our attention is focused on this allusion's possible role in characterizing Gorgo's subjectivity.

In the case of a specific allusion, the question necessarily arises: is the allusion meant to be perceived as intended by the character in the poem or only by the poet creating the character? Is Gorgo meant to be perceived as herself alluding to the Circe passage? The point of view such a Homeric allusion entails would be appropriate for the poet Theocritus, but strangely omniscient for the fictional character Gorgo. Most contemporary scholars limit the effect of Gorgo's and Praxinoa's use of Homerisms to humorous incongruity and deny the fictive characters the capacity to use such allusions appropriately, for example: "Gorgo and Praxinoa may owe their timeless appeal to their being so very like the woman next door, but the careful reader will be periodically startled by Homeric or other erudite allusions of varying nature in their chatter. These are sufficiently far apart for the easy flow of the dialogue not to be impaired, but constant enough to warrant the assumption that Theocritus has consciously and deliberately chosen incongruity as an ingredient of his humor."[40] Yet although Gorgo's admiration of the tapestries reaches a level of eloquence and allusive suggestiveness that coincides with Theocritus's own, it is also natural to her fictive character, for her

discussion and even allusions reflect interests Theocritus has already had
her show in the domestic arena. Gorgo expresses an interest in clothing
and cloth throughout the poem: she laments that her wastrel husband
does not buy quality wool for her work (18–20), tells Praxinoa what
to wear to the Adonia (21), admires Praxinoa's dress and asks its cost
(34–35), admires Praxinoa's dress again (38), and even describes the men
she encounters on the road to Praxinoa's by their boots and cloaks (6).
Thus, when Gorgo sees tapestries, it is natural for her to describe them
in terms of clothing.[41] Her vision is elevated: she describes the tapestries
as worthy to be gowns for gods (79).

Further, Gorgo's use of the phrase λεπτὰ καὶ ὡς χαρίεντα ("how
light and graceful they are," 79) heightens her description of the tapestries by recalling descriptions of Homeric woven materials. The adjectives λεπτός and χαρίεις occur together in only four Homeric passages,
all surely well-known, and all using this adjective-pair to describe a
woven fabric. At *Od.* 10.223 the phrase λεπτά τε καὶ χαρίεντα describes
the fabric Circe is weaving on her loom when Odysseus's men discover
her; at *Il.* 22.511 Andromache uses the phrase λεπτά τε καὶ χαρίεντα to
describe garments she will burn on Hector's pyre; at *Od.* 5.231 the phrase
λεπτὸν καὶ χαρίεν describes the gown Calypso wears when she helps
Odysseus prepare to depart; and at *Od.* 10.544 the phrase λεπτὸν καὶ
χαρίεν describes the gown Circe wears when she allows Odysseus and
his men to depart for Hades. It is not unreasonable to think that such a
standard Homeric phrase might naturally occur to Gorgo when she
looks for a way to express her admiration of a ceremonial tapestry, particularly a phrase found in important Homeric passages which feature in
every instance woven materials and women. Women who have themselves put on and admired their own woven garments, and who now
view woven materials representing a further dimension to the art of creation that they have already admired in their own more humble example,
might well be motivated to speak of such woven materials in terms
which evoke the most traditional and elevated (hence epic) instances of
such woven works.[42]

A Homeric phrase that includes the term λεπτός, a term fashionable
in Hellenistic discussions of literary merit,[43] to describe works of weaving would have been memorable to Theocritus's contemporary audience
and thus available for him to draw on with assurance of its recognition.[44]
But also, by showing a woman finding evidence in a tapestry of a quality
prized also in Hellenistic poetry, the quality of λεπτότης, Theocritus
can approach the issue of whether the academy's aesthetic standards

could transcend the cultural boundary between the academy and the Greek public. Qualities Gorgo and Praxinoa admire in the tapestries (and later the hymn) coincide with qualities prized by aestheticized Hellenistic poets, e.g., fineness and delicacy (λεπτά, χαρίεντα, 79), variegation (ποικίλα, 78), craftsmanship (ἐπόνασαν, 80; πονέονται, 115), realism (τἀκριβέα, 81; ὡς ἔτυμ', 82), and learnedness (σοφόν, 83; σοφώτατον, 145; πολύιδρις, 97).[45] Thus, *Idyll* 15 shows ordinary housewives using the terms of discourse of the academy. What can that mean? Scholars who assume a mocking tone in Theocritus might suppose that the poet is ironizing the learned discourse by using the wrong speakers for it.[46] Another possibility is that Theocritus is raising the question of whether an experience of art can be enriched simply because the viewer has been sensitized to the academy's values.[47] A third and perhaps more likely possibility is that Theocritus is showing how the academy's values happen to coincide with female values. This idea is supported by Skinner's recent discussion of Nossis, a female Hellenistic poet, in which she suggests that women writers naturally adopted the values that emerged as the advanced aesthetics of the Alexandrian academy: "[Women], because of the exigencies of their private lives, were less likely to attempt the *mega biblion* or 'weighty masterpiece' that Callimachus, a generation later, would magisterially condemn."[48] In addition, by making the qualities that Gorgo and Praxinoa praise in works of art coincide with those admired by the sophisticated Hellenistic reader, the poet discourages the audience of the poem from identifying with the eavesdropping bystander who crudely claims to be unable to understand the women's speech.

The final clause of Gorgo's tapestry description exemplifies the economy of Theocritus's art of characterization: θεῶν περονάματα φασεῖς ("You'll say they are gowns worthy of the gods," 79). Although Horstmann cites this clause only to reinforce his dismissal of the phrase λεπτὰ καὶ ὡς χαρίεντα (79), which "trägt aber im Grunde nicht viel zur Charakterisierung des Gesehenen bei, ebensowenig wie das anschliessende θεῶν περονάματα φασεῖς (79),"[49] this slight clause contributes in two key ways to the characterizations in *Idyll* 15. First, as a corollary detail it helps make the specific allusion to *Od.* 10.223 more probable, as shown in appendix 2. Second, the vocabulary and structure used in this phrase associate the ceremonial tapestries with Praxinoa's garments. The word περονάματα is rare, occurring only at *Id.* 15.79 to describe garments.[50] But twice earlier in *Idyll* 15, Gorgo uses cognate words which are equally rare, and both times these rare and therefore memorable words refer to

Praxinoa's garment: περονατρίς ("wrap," 21), a word found elsewhere only once (as a possibly restored adjective, *A.P.* 7.413), and ἐμπερόναμα ("garment," 34), a word not found elsewhere.[51] That Gorgo's association of ceremonial tapestries and Praxinoa's clothing is meant to be perceived by the reader is made more probable by Gorgo's use of a hypothetical statement in the second person to express admiration of both Praxinoa's garments (ἀλλὰ κατὰ γνώμαν ἀπέβα τοι· τοῦτό κεν εἴπαις; "it suits your style; this you can say"; 38) and the tapestries (θεῶν περονάματα φασεῖς, "you'll say they are gowns worthy of the gods," 79). Thus through a deft and economic use of Homeric allusion, Theocritus enriches his characterization of Gorgo. Further, by using rare cognate words to describe both gowns fit for gods (θεῶν περονάματα, 79) and Praxinoa's more humble clothing (περονατρίς, 21; ἐμπερόναμα, 34), Theocritus can associate lower and higher classes, cross social boundaries, and mix genres. By showing how language can provide a means for associating ceremonial and everyday woven materials, Theocritus explores poetry's capacity to transform perceptions of the ordinary world.

When in a work of literature a poet describes a work of art, the poet can use that *ekphrasis* to say something about his or her fictive characters and their relation to life by showing their relation to a representation of life. When the context of viewing art is religious, a poet can also use the *ekphrasis* to explore the psychology of religious experience, a topic of some delicacy at the time of Herodas and Theocritus, when Greek rulers were beginning to cohabit shrines and claim divinization.[52] Herodas's and Theocritus's use of *ekphrasis* in exploring the nature of aesthetic reception in ceremonial contexts reflects the growing interest in the ethical and religious value of works of art, a topic that becomes increasingly important in later Greek and Roman thought.[53]

The aesthetic orientations of the women in Herodas's *Mime* 4 and Theocritus's *Idyll* 15 complement the kinds of religious experience the poems are each exploring. Egoism and subjectivity characterize the worship of Asclepius: private pains, private offerings, and private cures. Help is available throughout the year as individually needed. Thus, in Herodas's *Mime* 4, Kokkale and Kynno visit a sanctuary of Asclepius to make private offerings in private thanks for a private boon; there they admire private offerings and individualized works of art. Kokkale asks for the specific names of the statuary's artist and dedicator (21–22), and Kynno reads the inscription on a statue's base: Praxiteles' sons are the artists, and Euthies, Prexon's son, is the dedicator (23–25). So too Kynno identifies the ox-sacrifice picture displayed in the inner sanctum

as the specific creation of Apelles, whom she characterizes as an individualistic artist, autonomous — free to indulge his own whim:

ἀλλ᾽ ὧι ἐπὶ νοῦν γένοιτο καὶ θέων ψαύειν
ἠπείγετ᾽.

(75–76)

whatever came to mind, he eagerly hastened
to give it a go.

In Theocritus's *Idyll* 15, on the other hand, Praxinoa and Gorgo attend
a public celebration of the Adonia, a seasonal festival, where they view
costly tapestries and listen to the public performance of a hymn. Unlike
Mime 4, *Idyll* 15 emphasizes communal aspects of the religious experience: works of art are admired as collaborative creations by anonymous
men and women. Thus Praxinoa begins her description of the tapestries
by praising the men and women who worked together to create them:

πότνι᾽ Ἀθαναία, ποῖαί σφ᾽ ἐπόνασαν ἔριθοι,
ποῖοι ζωογράφοι τἀκριβέα γράμματ᾽ ἔγραψαν.

(80–81)

Lady Athena, what excellent women wove the tapestries,
what excellent artists, the men who outlined the drawings.

The hymnist, too, describes objects displayed in the Adonis tableau as
anonymous and collaborative creations: the shaped cakes created by
anonymous women (115) and the ceremonial coverlets which "Miletus"
and a Samian shepherd helped make (126–27).

Both poems, then, show how the dominant mode of the religious
event (public or private, universalizing or individualistic) can affect aesthetic experience. Further, insofar as *Idyll* 15 commemorates a public
celebration of the Adonia, sponsored by Arsinoe, by emphasizing the
anonymity of the artists involved in creating the ceremonial setting, the
poem can reflect goals of Greek collectivity under the Ptolemies. In
chapter 4, I return to these issues in discussing in more detail Arsinoe's
patronage and the shaping of the hymnist's song in *Idyll* 15.

In both Herodas's *Mime* 4 and Theocritus's *Idyll* 15, the relation between audience and art is raised to a subject of thematic interest: the
poems' readers have, within the fiction of the poems, people looking at
art, and outside the fiction of the poems, themselves looking at art.
Thus, in the experience of fictive viewers of art, readers can see their own
interpretive problems mirrored. In *Mime* 4, Herodas's ironic portrait

of Kokkale and Kynno underscores how they willfully misunderstand works of art. Kokkale and Kynno do not see the universalizing dimension of art and they look for qualities in works of art other than the classic norm of beauty. The picture they view is presented as a riddle and never explicitly solved. The conjecture of the poem's real audience must remain a conjecture, although the imaginative act of interpretation may encourage a feeling of ironic superiority to the fictive women.

In *Idyll* 15, on the other hand, Praxinoa's and Gorgo's descriptions of the pictorial tapestries draw the poem's real audience into the mood of celebrating the Adonia and away from the cynical stance some readers might adopt at the start of a poem focusing on ordinary housewives. Gorgo's and Praxinoa's remarks support the proposition that the women's praise of the tapestries is meant to be more privileged than the bystander's complaints about their speech, for Gorgo's and Praxinoa's evocative and allusive language is Theocritus's own: his signature appears in their talk. In focusing on Praxinoa's and Gorgo's aesthetic experiences in the context of a public Adonia, Theocritus seems to be refuting Callimachus's position that art and imagination should no longer seek a public audience and suggesting instead that the experience of art in the Hellenistic age can still have an enriching public role, for if Praxinoa and Gorgo transcend themselves in describing the tapestries, art has enabled them to do so.

But *Idyll* 15's seeming valorization of Gorgo and Praxinoa's discourse on the tapestries is immediately mediated by an ironic swerve on the part of Theocritus as he introduces a mocking bystander:

παύσασθ', ὦ δύστανοι, ἀνάνυτα κωτίλλοισαι,
τρυγόνες· ἐκκναισεῦντι πλατειάσδοισαι ἄπαντα.
(87–88)

You wretched women, stop that endless twittering —
like turtle doves they'll grate on you, with all their broad vowels.

By including a critical response to the women's remarks, the poet invites the reader to agree or disagree with the bystander's point of view on the women. *Idyll* 15's readers have traditionally endorsed the fictive eavesdropper's remarks: descriptions of Gorgo and Praxinoa often echo the bystander's (examples include "buzzing housewives" and "chattering viragoes"),[54] and one scholar even attributes the bystander's remarks directly to the poet: "Wir gehen wohl nicht fehl in der Annahme, dass sich hinter dem Vorwurf des Fremden auch die Meinung des Dichters verbirgt."⁵⁵ Yet the bystander's disregard for his ceremonial surroundings and his crude and commonplace response to the women undermines any presumed mocking collusion between poet and reader against the women.⁵⁶ The Hellenistic age can be characterized by irony, and among the aestheticized Alexandrian poets and their audience, the ironic response is the expectable norm. But by undermining the irony in the case of the bystander, *Idyll* 15 discourages the complacency of an unreflecting mocking reader's stance. If some readers momentarily identify with the bystander, it is more consistent with Theocritus's thematic treatments of friendship and song that he should encourage the experience of wry self-recognition for these readers rather than complacent self-congratulation.⁵⁷

Other poems of Theocritus also reflect the contemporary interest in rhetorical descriptions of art objects. *Idyll* 1 includes Theocritus's most famous *ekphrasis*, a goatherd's elaborate description of a drinking cup. Parallels between *Idylls* 1 and 15 encourage comparisons of the two poems: they both include important examples of *ekphrasis* and they both include songs that concern Aphrodite's relations with a young male.⁵⁸ Both poems also illustrate Theocritus's artful attention to balance and contrast. In *Idyll* 1, the goatherd's diminutively Homeric *ekphrasis* of a rustic cup⁵⁹ balances the bucolic yet heroic story of the relations between Aphrodite and Daphnis (who sets himself against Diomedes in defying Aphrodite).⁶⁰ In *Idyll* 15, the hymnist's description of the Adonia, a celebration of Aphrodite's reunion with Adonis (who, as the hymnist claims, surpasses heroes in that he can return repeatedly from Hades), balances the representation of the fictive women's experiences at home and on city streets. *Idyll* 1's *ekphrasis* of a cup has been much discussed elsewhere,⁶¹ but one scene represented on the cup is of particular interest to our study of Theocritus's urban mimes, since it is another example of Theocritus's thematic interest in powerful women and subordinated men. It is the first cup decoration the goatherd describes: a representation of a woman dominating two men through her indifferently shifting gaze:⁶²

> ἔντοσθεν δὲ γυνά, τι θεῶν δαίδαλμα, τέτυκται,
> ἀσκητὰ πέπλῳ τε καὶ ἄμπυκι· πὰρ δέ οἱ ἄνδρες
> καλὸν ἐθειράζοντες ἀμοιβαδὶς ἄλλοθεν ἄλλος
> νεικείουσ' ἐπέεσσι· τὰ δ' οὐ φρενὸς ἅπτεται αὐτᾶς·
> ἀλλ' ὅκα μὲν τῆνον ποτιδέρκεται ἄνδρα γέλαισα,
> ἄλλοκα δ' αὖ ποτὶ τὸν ῥιπτεῖ νόον· οἳ δ' ὑπ' ἔρωτος
> δηθὰ κυλοιδιόωντες ἐτώσια μοχθίζοντι.

                                                    (32–38)

And within is wrought a woman, such a thing as the gods might
    fashion,
bedecked with cloak and circlet. And by her two men
with long fair locks contend from either side
in alternate speech. Yet these things touch not her heart,
but now she looks on one and smiles,
and now to the other she shifts her thought, while they,
long hollow-eyed from love, labour to no purpose.

(trans. Gow, Theocritus 1:7)

In *Idyll* 5, a goatherd pairs a bowl he describes as made by Praxiteles with
a pail of cypress wood (105–6). By having the goatherd name Praxiteles
(if this is the famous sculptor, then he is an unlikely craftsman of a goatherd's bowl), Theocritus can perhaps highlight the naive pretensions of
his goatherd.[63] Since the fourth century, art had been increasingly re-
oriented toward private functions: thus, for example, paintings were being created for elite private homes.[64] In *Idyll* 5, by having the goatherd
keep both objects equally as gifts for his girlfriend, Theocritus might also
be raising the issue of the value and function of art (both elite and folk
art) for ordinary persons.

Idyll 28 focuses on a distaff, a common household item. But by invoking a distaff in hymnic fashion (with epithets), the poet-narrator elevates
the domestic and everyday:

Γλαύκας, ὦ φιλέριθ' ἀλακάτα, δῶρον 'Αθανάας
γύναιξιν νόος οἰκωφελίας αἶσιν ἐπάβολος.

(1–2)

Distaff, friend of them that spin, grey-eyed Athena's gift
to women who know the art of housewifery.

(trans. Gow, Theocritus 1:227)

The distaff also attains the status of aesthetic object: σὲ τὰν ἐλέφαντος
πολυμόχθω γεγενημέναν / δῶρον ("thee, my gift created of wrought
ivory"; trans. Gow, *Theocritus* 1:227; 8–9). Several of Theocritus's
poems highlight the presence of women among audiences of art—
especially the women audience members (both internal and implied) in
Idyll 15, but also the girlfriend recipient of Praxiteles' bowl in *Idyll* 5, and
Theugenis and her women friends, potential admirers of the distaff in
Idyll 28. Further, the focus on women's items and values in these poems
(and elsewhere) seems to suggest correspondences between women's
traditional focus on small and private objects and Callimachean aesthetics. Thus *Idyll* 28 ends with the poet-narrator forecasting how ordinary

persons viewing the distaff will set a value on smallness compatible with
the most elite, "Callimachean" fashion for miniaturization:

κῆνο γάρ τις ἔρει τὦπος ἰδων σ'· 'ἦ μεγάλα χάρις
δώρῳ σὺν ὀλίγῳ· πάντα δὲ τίματα τὰ πὰρ φίλων.'

(24–25)

For seeing thee someone will say, "Truly great love
goes with a little gift, and all that comes from friends is precious."

(trans. Gow, *Theocritus* I : 227)

Other poems of Herodas too, besides *Mime* 4, feature the theme of
viewing creative artifacts. For example, in the domestic context of
Mime 6, women praise dildoes for their craftsmanship. Also, in the commercial context of *Mime* 7, a cobbler offers shoes to women for their
admiration and purchase.[65] Interestingly, language and thematic motif
link *Mime* 6's low discussion of dildoes[66] not only with *Mime* 7's low
discussion of shoes, but also with *Mime* 4's *ekphrases* in the elevated context of Asclepius's sanctuary, as well as with Theocritus's *Idyll* 15's *ekphrases* in the elevated context of an Adonia. First, in all these poems,
whether in the context of elevated viewing experiences or not, Athena
is invoked to emphasize the fine craftsmanship of creative artifacts. In
Theocritus's *Idyll* 15, in the elevated context of an Adonia, Praxinoa invokes Athena in praising the workmanship of the tapestry artists:

πότνι' 'Αθαναία, ποῖαί σφ' ἐπόνασαν ἔριθοι,
ποῖοι ζωογράφοι τἀκριβέα γράμματ' ἔγραψαν.

(80–81)

Lady Athena, what excellent women wove the tapestries,
what excellent artists, the men who outlined the drawings.

Again, in Herodas's *Mime* 4, in the elevated context of Asclepius's
temple, Kokkale praises the chiseled works she views:

οἶ' ἔργα κεῖ 'νῆν· ταῦτ' ἐρεῖς 'Αθηναίην
γλύψαι τὰ καλά.

(57–58)

Look at these works — you'll say that Athena
chiseled them in their beauty.

In Herodas's *Mime* 6, in the ordinary context of Koritto's house, Koritto praises well-made dildoes by also associating them with Athena's
craftsmanship:

ἀλλ' ἔργα, κοῖ' ἐστ' ἔργα· τῆς 'Αθηναίης
αὐτῆς ὀρῆν τὰς χεῖρας, οὐχὶ Κέρδωνος,
δόξεις.

(65–67)

But his works, his works are truly Koan: you'll think
you see the hands of Athena herself, not those of Kerdon.

Again, in Herodas's *Mime* 7, in the humble context of a cobbler's shop, the cobbler Kerdon praises the shoe he puts on Metro's foot as worthy of Athena:

αὐτὴν ἐρεῖς τὸ πέλμα τὴν 'Αθηναίην
τεμεῖν.

(116–17)

Athena herself, you'll say, cut out the sole
of the shoe.

Mime 7's cobbler also certifies his honesty by claiming he would not lower the price even for Athena (80–82).

Second, both Herodas's *Mimes* 4 and 6 focus on the artist's identity. As discussed above, *Mime* 4's Kokkale asks the identities of the craftsman and the dedicator (21–22) when she views dedicatory statues in an elevated context; and Kynno responds that Praxiteles' sons made them and Euthies was dedicator (23–25, cf. 72). *Mime* 6's Metro, in an ordinary context, asks Koritto repeatedly who made the dildo and who gave it to Nossis (17–19, 22, 43, 47, 48), and Korrito responds that Kerdon (48) of Chios or Erythrae (58) made it and Eubule gave it to Nossis (25–26).

Third, both *Mimes* 4 and 6 feature similar descriptions of aesthetic responses. In *Mime* 4, in an elevated context, Kokkale posits the responses of two hypothetical viewers when they see a silver fire tongs in Apelles' painting: ἐκβαλεῦσι τὰς κούρας ("Won't their eyes fall out?" 64–65). In *Mime* 6, in an ordinary context, Koritto describes her first response to Kerdon's display of two dildoes to her: ἰδοῦσ' ἅμ' ἰδμῆι τὤμματ' ἐξεκύμηνα ("At first sight, my eyes burst out of my head," 68).

Fourth, *Mime* 6's dildoes and *Mime* 7's cobbler's wares share evaluative terms with *Mime* 4's paintings and *Idyll* 15's ceremonial tapestries and coverlets. In *Idyll* 15, the hymnist describes the coverlets on Adonis's couch as μαλακώτεροι ὕπνω ("softer than sleep," 125); similarly, in *Mime* 6, Koritto describes two dildoes as ἡ μαλακότης ὕπνος ("as soft as sleep," 71).[67] In *Mime* 7, the cobbler forecasts Metro's pleasure in viewing his wares: . . . . Μη]τροῖ, / οἶ᾽ ἔργ᾽ ἐπόψεσθ᾽ ("Oh Metro, how fortunate you are! What works you will view!" trans. Knox, in Headlam and Knox, *Herodas*, 319, rev.; 17–18); similarly in *Mime* 4, Kokkale calls Kynno's attention to the works of art in the inner sanctuary: οὐκ ὀρῆις, φίλη Κυννοῖ; / οἶ᾽ ἔργα κεῖ ᾽νῆν ("Only look, dear Kynno, what works are those there!" trans. Knox, in Headlam and Knox, *Herodas*, 171; 56–57). Again in *Mime* 7 an anonymous woman describes the cobbler's works as beautiful (καλῶν ἔργων, 84); so too in *Mime* 4, Kokkale adds the epithet καλά (58). Further, in *Mime* 4, Kynno suggests truth as a criterion of good painting (72–73); in *Idyll* 15, truth is part of Praxinoa's criteria for evaluating ceremonial tapestries (81–82); and in *Mime* 7, truth is emphasized in the valuation of cobbler's goods (31–35, 70, 120–21).

Thus, language and thematic motif link these three mimes by Herodas and Theocritus's *Idyll* 15.[68] Since we do not know the relative dates of the poems of Herodas, the direction of influence is uncertain, as is the connection of these poems with Theocritus's *Idyll* 15. The similarities may in part reflect common sources in Sophron's poetry, which includes a poem on dildoes and one on women attending an Isthmian festival.[69] By linking the terms women use to praise dildoes in the home (*Mime* 6) and wares in a cobbler's shop (*Mime* 7) with terms women use to admire statues and paintings in ceremonial sanctuaries (*Mime* 4), Herodas comically suggests a continuity between sacred and commercial realms of value and perhaps also in the process wryly destabilizes the academy's elevation of certain cultural goods over others. The similarities also suggest that Herodas in *Mime* 6 is deliberately presenting women's admiration of well-crafted dildoes in terms also suitable for more elevated viewing experiences.

Theocritus's *Idyll* 16 laments the economic greed of his day which is resulting in a failure to value and support the cultural life:

> νενίκηνται δ᾽ ὑπὸ κερδέων.
> πᾶς δ᾽ ὑπὸ κόλπου χεῖρας ἔχων πόθεν οἴσεται ἀθρεῖ
> ἄργυρον, οὐδέ κεν ἰὸν ἀποτρίψας τινὶ δοίη,
> ἀλλ᾽ εὐθὺς μυθεῖται . . .
> . . . .
> ῾οὗτος ἀοιδῶν λῷστος, ὃς ἐξ ἐμεῦ οἴσεται οὐδέν.᾽

(15–18, 21)

[Men] are enslaved by gain;
and each, his hand within his purse-fold, looks to see whence

he may win money, and will not rub the very rust therefrom to give
   another,
but straight answering rather, . . .
....
"He is the best of poets who shall get naught of me."

(trans. Gow, Theocritus 1 : 123, rev.)

Idyll 16 also explicitly raises the issue of the market-value of modern poetry by positing the popular view: τίς δέ κεν ἄλλου ἀκούσαι; ἅλις πάντεσσιν "Ομηρος ("Who would listen to another? Homer is enough for
all"; trans. Gow, *Theocritus* 1 : 123; 20). Further, in many of Theocritus's
poems, the motif of fictive judges of art may raise the issue of the difficulty of determining the value of cultural goods.

Herodas's poetry also reflects the increasingly commercial values of
the Hellenistic age, for several of his mimes focus directly on the mar-
ketplace and on mediators of market value—e.g., *Mime* 1's old bawd,
who tries to match consumers with goods; *Mime* 2's pander, who compares his goods (girls) with those of a merchant of wheat (e.g., 19–20);
Mime 6's Kerdon, whose dildoes (and marketing skills) women praise in
the poem; and *Mime* 7's Kerdon, a cobbler who displays his wares to
women consumers. *Mime* 7 underscores the issue of market value, when
the cobbler invites his customer to determine price:

αὐτὴ σὺ καὶ τίμησον, εἰ θέλεις, αὐτό
καὶ στῆσον ἧς κότ' ἐστιν ἄξιον τιμῆς.

(67–68)

You yourself assess it, if you please, and
determine a worthy payment.

The world of art in the Hellenistic age included past masterpieces as
well as contemporary creations. The geographically diverse Hellenistic
world offered a multiplicity of commercial and aesthetic possibilities, as
Herodas's *Mime* 7 dramatically illustrates through a cobbler's list of geographically and stylistically diverse wares:

θήσεσθε δ' ὑμ[εῖς·] γένεα ταῦτα πα[ν]τοῖα·
Σικυώνι', 'Αμβρακίδια, Νοσσίδες, λεῖαι,
ψιττάκια, κανναβίσκα, βαυκίδες, βλαῦται,
'Ιωνίκ' ἀμφίσφαιρα, νυκτιπήδηκες,
ἀκροσφύρια, καρκίνια, σάμβαλ' 'Αργεῖα,
κοκκίδες, ἔφηβοι, διάβαθρ·' ὧν ἐρᾶι θυμός
ὑμέων ἑκάστης εἴπατ'.

(56–62)

You will see; here are all kinds,
Sicyonian, Ambraciot, Nossis-shoes, plain,
parrots, hempen, saffron shoes, common shoes,
Ionian button-boots, "night-hoppers,"
"ankle-tops," red shoes, Argive sandals,
scarlet, "youths," "steps"; just say each of you
what your heart desires.

> (trans. Knox, in Headlam and Knox,
> *Herodas*, 323, rev.)

Much of Hellenistic poetry reflects a loss of faith in hierarchical traditions and old-fashioned establishment values; instead, novelty is crucial. But the audience willing to support advanced Hellenistic art also seems to be limited. Theocritus's *Idylls* 15 and 16, as well as Herodas's *Mimes* 4, 6, and 7, raise the issue of contingencies of value in a mobile and multitudinous world.

Transitions between Art and Reality

A problem implicit in the experience of art is how to make the transition back to the real world. Because of its spatial movement from the outskirts of Alexandria to its royal center, *Idyll* 15 explores crossing boundaries more than any other of Theocritus's poems. In the realm of physical motion, boundaries are crossed between home and street, ordinary world and ceremonial precinct, land and sea; in the spiritual realm, between male and female, public and private, life and death, god and mortal, and joy and grief. This section shows how through Gorgo's response to the hymn's performance and her resolution to return home to her husband, the poet can bring together the themes of audience reception and gender relations and create a passage (for both the fictive women and the poem's real audience) between fantasy and reality, art and life.

Before looking at how Theocritus handles the ending of *Idyll* 15, we will consider the ending of *Idyll* 1 as another dramatic example of how Theocritus moves from a mythic world represented in song back to a fictive audience's more commonplace world. Thematic similarities between *Idylls* 1 and 15 suggest the usefulness of comparing how they handle transitions between art and reality: both poems include a description of a work of art, feature a central performance of a song about a

young man's involvement with Aphrodite, and end by representing a
fictive audience's response to the song performance.[70] I am interested
here in how Theocritus shapes an internal audience's passage from a
world evoked in song to his or her own fictive reality. For example, *Idyll*
1's goatherd moves from a song that recreates Daphnis's mythic world
back to his own fictive reality of goats and herding, and *Idyll* 15's women
move from a hymn that evokes the ceremonial world of Adonis back to
their reality of husbands and housekeeping. Such a fictive passage can
also represent a passage for the poem's readers.

Rhetorical strategies useful at moments of transition and also popular among advanced Hellenistic poets include mixing levels of diction,
which can destabilize boundaries between elevated and ordinary worlds,
and framing grand stories with plain style narratives.[71] Such transitions
(from *ekphrases*, from inset songs) occur often at the ends of poems, but
not always.[72] The way Thyrsis ends the lengthy Daphnis song in *Idyll* 1
illustrates Theocritus's technique of making the boundary between song
and frame fluctuate. Thyrsis momentarily interrupts the song's elevated
mood with a plain style request for the promised goat and bowl:

καὶ τὺ δίδου τὰν αἶγα τό τε σκύφος, ὥς κεν ἀμέλξας
σπείσω ταῖς Μοίσαις.

(143–44)

Now you must give me the goat and the bowl, so I may, after milking,
Pour a libation of milk to the Muses.

(trans. Hine, *Theocritus*, 7)

But the linkage between goat's milk and libations to the Muses modu-
lates the song back to the elevated mood of a hymnic farewell to the
Muses:

ὦ χαίρετε πολλάκι, Μοῖσαι,
χαίρετ'· ἐγὼ δ' ὔμμιν καὶ ἐς ὕστερον ἅδιον ἀσῶ.

(144–45)

Farewell to you, Muses,
Frequent farewell. I shall sing you a sweeter refrain in the future.

(trans. Hine, *Theocritus*, 7)

Thus the ending of Thyrsis's song offers a passage from Daphnis's
mythic world to the world of Thyrsis's fictive audience, a goatherd.

The goatherd's response to Thyrsis's song shows the goatherd com-
pleting the process of transition from the fantasy of Daphnis's mythic

world to the reality of his own. The goatherd starts by praising Thyrsis, but the awards he gives Thyrsis, a cup and goat's milk, lead him back to his flock:

πλῆρές τοι μέλιτος τὸ καλὸν στόμα, Θύρσι, γένοιτο,
πλῆρες δὲ σχαδόνων, καὶ ἀπ᾽ Αἰγίλω ἰσχάδα τρώγοις
ἀδεῖαν, τέττιγος ἐπεὶ τύγα φέρτερον ᾄδεις.
ἠνίδε τοι τὸ δέπας· θᾶσαι, φίλος, ὡς καλὸν ὄσδει·
Ὡρᾶν πεπλύσθαι νιν ἐπὶ κράναισι δοκησεῖς.
ὧδ᾽ ἴθι, Κισσαίθα· τὺ δ᾽ ἄμελγέ νιν. αἱ δὲ χίμαιραι,
οὐ μὴ σκιρτασῆτε, μὴ ὁ τράγος ὔμμιν ἀναστῇ.

(*Id.* 1.146–52)

Thyrsis, I pray that your beautiful mouth may be filled full of honey,
Filled full of honeycomb, furthermore that you may munch the sweet
    figs of
Aigila, seeing your singing's superior to the cicada's.
Look, here's the goblet, dear friend, only notice its beautiful odour:
You might suppose that this cup had been dipped in the spring of the
    Hours.
Come here, Cissaetha! You milk her, she's yours now. Be careful, you
    she-goats,
Don't be so frisky, for fear that the he-goat will get an erection.

(trans. Hine, *Theocritus*, 7)

The warning to she-goats not to rouse the he-goat not only reflects the goatherd's everyday world but also transfigures the poem, for the goatherd's final recognition of eros's power in his daily affairs contrasts with Daphnis's assertion of independence from Aphrodite's demands. Further, by making the goatherd's world — a fantasy realm for urban audiences — seem realistic and commonplace in contrast to Daphnis's more distanced mythic realm, Theocritus can explore poetry's power to create paradigmatic "fictional worlds."[73] His later fame as "father of pastoral poetry" underscores his success in this ambitious creative project.

A similar boundary fluctuation between fantasy and reality takes place at the end of *Idyll* 15 when Gorgo responds to the Adonis hymn by first disrupting the ceremonial mood and then renewing it:

Πραξινόα, τὸ χρῆμα σοφώτατον ἁ θήλεια·
ὀλβία ὅσσα ἴσατι, πανολβία ὡς γλυκὺ φωνεῖ.
ὥρα ὅμως κῆς οἶκον. ἀνάριστος Διοκλείδας·
χὠνὴρ ὄξος ἅπαν, πεινᾶντι δὲ μηδὲ ποτένθῃς.
χαῖρε, Ἄδων ἀγαπατέ, καὶ ἐς χαίροντας ἀφικνεῦ.

(145–49)

Praxinoa, this woman is a creature of exceeding wisdom;
wealthy in the arts she knows, and truly wealthy in the sweetness of her
    voice.
Still, it is time to go home. Diokleidas hasn't been fed;
and the man is all vinegar — don't even approach him when he's hungry.
Farewell, beloved Adonis, and may you find us rejoicing on your return.

Gorgo's response to the Adonis hymn, by including a reminder of her
husband's mealtime needs, highlights the contrast between the homely
demands of a woman's daily life and the fantasy of sensuality and female
dominance represented by the Adonia. A hungry husband may resemble
an impatient he-goat, and food, like sex, can revitalize. But the last lines
of *Idylls* 1 and 15 reflect crucial differences in the closure strategies of the
two poems.[74] *Idyll* 1 ends with the goatherd distracted by his herd's behavior. *Idyll* 15 ends with Gorgo refocused on the Adonia, for Gorgo's
last words echo the hymn and renew its mood of formal invocation.[75]
By showing how the hymnist's performance inspires Gorgo to join the
Adonis song,[76] Theocritus can explore the power of art and ritual to
draw audiences into alternative worlds. The state could try to control
disruptive religious behavior by sponsoring cult festivals and thus regulating them. Yet by showing Gorgo appending her own private farewell
to the public Adonis hymn, Theocritus also explores private responses
to the public program.

Gorgo's farewell to Adonis uses an inclusive form of the participle
(χαίροντας) to signify the celebrant community: χαῖρε, ᾿Αδων ἀγαπατέ, καὶ ἐς χαίροντας ἀφικνεῦ (149).[77] The hymnist's farewell to
Adonis, on the other hand, maintains the traditional composition of
the celebrant community by using a feminine form of the participle
(εὐθυμεύσαις):

ἵλαος, ὦ φίλ᾽ ᾿Αδωνι, καὶ ἐς νέωτ᾽· εὐθυμεύσαις
καὶ νῦν ἦνθες, ᾿Αδωνι, καί, ὅκκ᾽ ἀφίκῃ, φίλος ἡξεῖς.

(143–44)

Be gracious, dear Adonis, in the new year too. Now your coming
has brought us women joy. When you return, we will welcome you with
    love.

Does Gorgo's use of a generic participle in line 149 (χαίροντας) under-
mine the suggestion produced by the hymnist's use of a feminine participle in line 143 (εὐθυμεύσαις) that critical gender-related aspects of the
cult have not changed with state appropriation? Or does it reflect a more
gender-inclusive attitude prompted by Gorgo's street encounter with a

man whose civility wins her approval (70–75)? The poem's careful attention to gender difference elsewhere is marked (even the tapestry makers are distinguished in sex), which makes it less likely, I think, that the gender difference between the participles signifying the celebrant community is merely indifferent, a poetic convenience. After all, Gorgo's response to the hymn begins with a description highlighting the hymnist's sex: τὸ χρῆμα σοφώτατον ἀ θήλεια ("This woman is a creature of exceeding wisdom," 145).[78] This admiring description echoes Praxinoa's phraseology in admiring the tapestry makers' collaborative male-female artistry: σοφόν τι χρῆμ' ἄνθρωπος ("Man [generic] is a creature of wisdom," 83). In the middle of the poem Praxinoa associates women who weave with men who draw outlines, their collaborative effort resulting in an exemplification of σοφία (wisdom);[79] at the end of the poem, Gorgo describes a woman's solo performance as in itself exemplifying σοφία. The echo of phraseology emphasizes the gender specificity of Gorgo's description of the hymnist and reinforces the view that Theocritus is paying special attention to gender concerns in this poem. In a world in which women are attaining public visibility, *Idyll* 15 shows how the movement of the Adonia (traditionally a private, women's festival) into the public realm also brings women's art into the public realm. Thus the Syracusan women admire tapestries created by the collaborative artistry of men and women, and the hymnist sings of ceremonial shaped cakes created by women alone. But most importantly, Arsinoe's public Adonia provides a public forum in which a woman hymnist can perform an Adonis hymn before a mixed-sex audience, whose mixed composition is attested by Gorgo's use of a generic participle in line 149 (χαίροντας).

Scholars typically consider Gorgo's admiration of the hymnist's craftsmanship as part of Theocritus's mockery of the aesthetic taste of the fictive women, e.g.: "Any appreciation of the significance of the occasion or of the meaning of the hymn is overshadowed by a naive awe at the technical mastery of the performer and then by Gorgo's preoccupation with the trivialities of her own mundane existence."[80] But anecdotes report how artists valued recognition of their craftsmanship. For example, the painter Zeuxis shunned the public for not admiring his technical artistry (Lucian *Zeuxis* 7). Further, Gorgo's use of aesthetic terminology is not markedly naive: terms relating to σοφία were long privileged in evaluations of verbal and plastic art,[81] and to call a hymnist who can also win dirge contests a πολύιδρις ἀοιδός ("a very learned singer," 97) coincides with Callimachus's valorization of artistic diversity and learnedness.[82] Thus in proposing a standard for judging new poetry, Callimachus calls poetry σοφίη and privileges craft:

αὖθι δὲ τέχνῃ
κρίνετε,]ₗμὴ σχοίνῳ Περσίδι τὴₗνₗ σοφίην.
(*Aet.* 1, fr. 1.17–18)

Henceforth judge poetry
by its craft and not the Persian league.
(trans. Bulloch, "Hellenistic Poetry," 559)

The point is not to defend or belittle Gorgo's response to the hymn: an author can have fun with fictive characters and endorse their values at the same time. Instead the focus is on how a fictive character's response to a hymn performance provides a forum for exploring issues of poetic closure and audience response.

By highlighting linkages between social and ceremonial rituals, a poem can explore intersections between fantasy and reality. On the social level, Gorgo's decision to return home to feed her husband can reflect the subordination of women in the Hellenistic age and show the patriarchal order recontaining the women at the poem's end. Yet on a ritual level, the husband's hunger can also represent the need for a transitional activity mediating between ceremonial and everyday worlds. After experiencing the virtual death of Adonis's departure, an audience too might rejuvenate through eating, insofar as food can represent life and renewal.[83]

Word repetitions and wordplay help connect the women's daily realities with the ceremonial realm of the Adonia. For example, the polarization of the terms γλυκύς (sweet) and ὄξος (vinegar) helps reinforce the theme of transitions in relations between men and women in the course of the poem. Gorgo and Praxinoa are both distanced from their husbands at the poem's start, but during an excursion through crowded streets they encounter a polite man whose civility represents the possibility of harmony between men and women. Gorgo sees sweetness in a child (13) and a hymnist (146) and tartness in her husband (148).[84] Gorgo's use of the term γλυκύς in evaluating the hymnist's artistry heightens the contrast between Gorgo's experience of the Adonia and the "all vinegar" reception she expects at home. Gorgo's husband is "all vinegar" when he has not eaten (147–48), which implies that he is fine if fed. Gorgo knows what he needs and what she can do to bring about at least a degree of domestic harmony.

Word repetitions also emphasize linkages between ceremonial and commonplace activities: πόνος (labor) is expended in weaving (ἐπόνασαν, 80) and making cakes (πονέονται, 115), and σοφία is admired in the artistry of tapestry makers (σοφόν τι χρῆμ' ἄνθρωπος, "Man [generic] is a creature of wisdom," 83) and a hymnist (τὸ χρῆμα σοφώτα-τον ἁ θήλεια, "this woman is a creature of exceeding wisdom," 145). One can sew garments and ceremonial tapestries, prepare foodstuffs for a ceremony and for one's husband, talk about the shortcomings of husbands and praise aesthetic achievements. By making these linkages, Theocritus both glorifies the value of everyday activities and also highlights the influence ordinary life can have on aesthetic experience.

A repetition of the term ὄλβιος (wealthy) highlights the passage of the Syracusan women from isolation to inclusion, from the city's outskirts to the palace grounds. The term ὄλβιος appears four times, twice in each of two lines. Early in the poem, Praxinoa responds to Gorgo's invitation to the Adonia with a proverb that limits the term to the financially wealthy: ἐν ὀλβίω ὄλβια πάντα ("In a rich person's house, everything's rich," 24). This economic definition naturally excludes the Syracusan women. At the end of the poem, however, Gorgo recasts this proverb when she praises the hymnist: ὀλβία ὅσσα ἴσατι, πανολβία ὡς γλυκὺ φωνεῖ ("Wealthy in the arts she knows, and truly wealthy in the sweetness of her voice," 146); and her reapplication of the term ὄλβιος, in an established ritual usage, enlarges its definition to include spiritual wealth.[85] Gorgo's praise of the singer also illustrates the multidimensionality of meaning that can emerge from word repetition in Theocritus's poetry. The potential inclusiveness of Gorgo's use of ὄλβιος (ὀλβία ὅσσα ἴσατι, "wealthy in the arts she knows," 146) is ironized by its echo of Praxinoa's wry response to the old woman's remarks: πάντα γυναῖκες ἴσαντι ("Women know everything," 64). On the other hand, Gorgo's praise of the singer can also imply a poet's sense of entitlement—that a singer's/poet's σοφία (art) should translate into ὄλβια (material reward). The theme of a poet's role in a materialistic world and the difficulties inherent to a patronage system emerges elsewhere in his poetry, particularly in *Idyll* 16 (24, 29–35) and *Idyll* 17 (112–14). This multivalent reading of Gorgo's remarks illustrates how word repetitions enable Theocritus to explore poetry's capacity to create passages for internal (and external) audiences without losing its self-ironic edge.

The repeated theme of cyclicity reinforces the linkages between ceremonial and commonplace activities established through word repetitions. By having Gorgo resolve to return home to feed her husband at the poem's end, the poet connects everyday patterns of cyclicity (e.g., recurrent mealtimes) with Adonis's seasonal pattern of departure and return. The repetition of the verb χαίρω in Gorgo's farewell underscores the Adonia's cyclicity, for the verb both salutes Adonis on departure and signifies the celebrants' joy on his return: χαῖρε, ῎Αδων ἀγαπατέ, καὶ ἐς χαίροντας ἀφικνεῦ ("Farewell, beloved Adonis, and may you find us rejoicing on your return," 149). The Adonia offers models of renewal: the Hours convey Adonis to Aphrodite and the eagles convey Ganymede to Zeus; so too Gorgo conveys Praxinoa to the magical realm of the Adonia, and the women can renew their participation in Adonis's cyclical myth of return by returning for next year's Adonia. Thus, by showing Gorgo and Praxinoa's passage from their fictive everyday world into a ceremonial and mythic community, and by reinforcing that passage through the suggestion of contiguities between aesthetic, mythic, and commonplace activities, the poet explores art's capacity to transfigure everyday life.

At the same time, there is a prevalence of disruptive events in *Idyll* 15 for example, a maid spills water, a horse rears up, a cloak is torn, and a bystander interrupts. These disruptive events contrast with the shared cyclical patterns in *Idyll* 15's representations of ceremonial and everyday worlds. By highlighting these disruptive events, even while establishing parallels between the Syracusan women's experiences and the Adonia's mythic world, Theocritus underscores the complexity of representing real life in art: the tension between art's implicit patterns and borders and the unruliness of the everyday world.[86]

Storytelling emerges as a thematic concern in *Idyll* 15 when Gorgo urges Praxinoa to attend the festival by reminding her of the importance of having a tale to tell: ὧν ἴδες, ὧν εἴπαις κεν ἰδοῖσα τὺ τῷ μὴ ἰδόντι ("Things you've seen, you can talk about, once you've seen them, to someone who hasn't seen them"; 25). At the end of *Idyll* 15, Gorgo and Praxinoa can return home to tell the tale of their experiences, and they will be able to renew the experience at will, each time they tell the story.

By renewing the ceremonial mood of the Adonia, Gorgo's farewell to Adonis turns the poem into a ritual of transformation in which the real audience can participate as well as the fictive women. A consolation available for the fictive women, the poet, and the reader/listener is that the contingencies of the real world, its unruly life, can be refigured and made intelligible through storytelling (poetry). The hymn can do for these Syracusan women what art can do for life; and the experience of art is renewable. Gorgo's hymnic farewell to Adonis merges Gorgo's everyday world with the fantasy world represented by the Adonia.

At the close of the poem, the time comes for the real as well as the fictive audience to return home, to leave the world of fantasy. By showing the Syracusan women coming to terms with returning home after experiencing the Adonia, Theocritus creates a bridge for the reader/ listener as well between the fantasy represented by the poem and real life. Just as *Idyll* 15 provides passageways for the fictive women between mortal and divine, outlander and court, and fantasy and reality, so too the poem provides a passageway for the poem's real audience.

CHAPTER 4

Patronage

Patronage of cultural projects by kings and tyrants was an established tradition in the ancient Greek world.[1] In Hellenistic Alexandria, the Ptolemies added their own innovations to the patronage system by establishing official institutions — a museum and library — in which sponsored scholars worked, ate common meals, and earned royal stipends.[2] The generosity of Ptolemaic patronage attracted poets, scientists, and scholars, particularly from areas under Ptolemaic influence, such as Samos, Cyrene, and Cos,[3] but also from elsewhere (e.g., Demetrius of Phaleron, fugitive Athenian dictator and peripatetic philosopher).[4] Theocritus, although attracted for a time by the splendors of Alexandria and its court, seems to have avoided attaching himself directly to the Ptolemaic institutions.[5] Timon of Phlius, a philosopher-poet and another outsider, mocks those living within the bounds of the museum:

πολλοὶ μὲν βόσκονται ἐν Αἰγύπτῳ πολυφύλῳ
βιβλιακοὶ χαρακῖται ἀπείριτα δηριόωντες
Μουσέων ἐν ταλάρῳ.

(Ath. 1.22d)

Many ruminate in multiethnic Egypt —
cloistered bookish men who quarrel endlessly
in the birdcage of the Muses.

The identities of the royal tutors suggest the Ptolemaic family's ongoing desire to attain cultural competence and authority. Thus, to tutor young Ptolemy II and not improbably his sister Arsinoe II as well,[6] the royal court retained in turn Philitas of Cos, poet and scholar; Straton of Lampsacus, philosopher and scientist; Zenodotus of Ephesus, scholar and chief librarian.[7] The frequent appointment of the same man as royal tutor and chief librarian (e.g., Zenodotus and Apollonius Rhodius)[8] illustrates the Ptolemies' program of merging courtly and cultural institutions.

An additional factor in the cultural life at Alexandria was the presence of strong women at court. Arsinoe II, an important patron during Theocritus's time, followed her influential mother, Berenice, as well as a tradition of visible and combative Macedonian royal women (e.g., Cynane, Adea-Eurydice, and Olympias).[9] Berenice's intelligence and passion had attracted Ptolemy I, who set aside his second wife Eurydice to marry her.[10] Anecdotes attest to Berenice's power at court: when Pyrrhus came as hostage to Egypt, noting Berenice's great influence and intelligence, he concentrated on winning her favor (Plut. *Pyrrh.* 4). She may well have participated in the selection of royal tutors for the children, and she may also have ensured that Arsinoe II have the same opportunities as Ptolemy II to acquire cultural competence.[11]

Unlike her brother Ptolemy II, Arsinoe II spent a great deal of time living abroad, apart from her family, where she acquired sources of wealth (for example, her elderly husband Lysimachus gave her his prize city of Heraclea)[12] and learned to use her money to advantage. At Samothrace, an international cult center, she dedicated a magnificent rotunda to the "Great Gods" at Samothrace,[13] and Frazer has recently proposed that Arsinoe may be "the effective patron" also of Ptolemy II's Propylon at Samothrace.[14] Also, when as Lysimachus's widow she had to escape assassins at Arsinoea (Ephesus) through disguise as a maidservant, she nonetheless had the presence of mind (and understanding of power) to choose to flee to Cassandreia, where Lysimachus had been proclaimed a god,[15] and there to use her wealth to hire soldiers[16] and to sponsor a lavish festival (Just. 24.3). Arsinoe finally returned, an experienced woman of the world, to Alexandria, and her brother Ptolemy II set aside his wife Arsinoe I, her stepdaughter, to marry her.

Alexandrian poets attest to Arsinoe II's high visibility in the cultural world and at court:[17] Theocritus's *Idyll* 15 celebrates her sponsorship of the worship of Aphrodite and Adonis,[18] and *Idyll* 22 may reflect her interest in the Dioskouroi, deities comparable to the savior gods at Samothrace.[19] Arsinoe's presence was recognized in other areas as well: Ptolemy II took her to the Suez on an inspection of defences in 274/273,[20] and the Decree of Chremonides gives credit to Arsinoe for influencing

Ptolemy II's policy of liberating Greek city-states.[21] Thus, while the public political life of Greek men was diminishing, royal women at the Ptolemaic court were becoming visibly influential, as shown by Berenice and her daughter Arsinoe.

Royal patronage and the establishment of royal institutions of knowledge heightened the separation between ordinary persons and the literati. Unlike in fifth-century Athens, the creative artist in Alexandria did not have to rely on popular support and public visibility: instead Alexandrian literati, mostly Greek outlanders with ties just to the court, constituted a court-sponsored enclave. Timon's satiric verse, cited above, emphasizes the diversity of the world from which the Alexandrian scholarly community turns[22] — an Alexandria made up of a mixed population of natives, settlers, and itinerants: Egyptians, Jews, slaves of various ethnicities, as well as diverse Greeks (both citizens and noncitizens).[23]

Topics that arise in considering works created in such an environment include the influence of court patronage on the direction and shape of literary works and on the tone of literary voices. By establishing institutions of culture and by acquiring and cataloguing books, the Ptolemies seem to have been moving toward a position of regulating knowledge and high culture. Alexandrian poets, however, writing in the context of a library where texts were being separated by such criteria as genre and verse form and contained within an institution of knowledge, showed an unruly tendency to mix genres and create verse not easy to classify.[24]

What kind of cultural experiences did the Ptolemies make available to persons outside the institutions? To live in Alexandria was to be made constantly aware of the Ptolemies and their power: visible evidence included streets named after Arsinoe II, and such architectural sights as new and impressive temples (e.g., of the Theoi Soteres, Ptolemy I and Berenice) and the splendid royal palaces.[25] The Ptolemies also sponsored spectacular, public events, such as Ptolemy II's *Pompe* (Grand Procession)[26] and Arsinoe II's Adonia. Also, Ptolemy II declared his parents gods, and then Ptolemy II and Arsinoe II themselves became proclaimed gods,[27] which enabled ordinary persons (outside the court) to approach the royals less directly, e.g., through dedicatory offerings.[28] But the pervasive self-display of the Ptolemies also emphasized the diminishment of public political life for Greek males, even as Arsinoe's prominence (both before and after death) helped set a new standard of public visibility, at least at the highest levels, for Greek women.

In *Idylls* 14 and 15, Theocritus took advantage of the forum of urban mimes to project praise of Arsinoe and Ptolemy, patrons of high culture and public spectacles, into the mouths of fictive characters. This chapter shows how these two poems approach Alexandria's court (and the issue of patronage) from the margins, from the positions of outsiders. Further, Theocritus highlights gender and gender relations in his urban mimes that approach the royal patrons: *Idyll* 14, which includes praise of Ptolemy, features two male friends; *Idyll* 15, which spotlights the Adonia, a female-defined festival sponsored by Arsinoe, features two female friends. Many scholars have seen praise of the court as the most important element in the poems. But, as shown in previous chapters, these two poems open up the discourse to include other than courtly perspectives on issues of gender relations, ethnicity, and mobility. This chapter focuses on how these two poems handle the topic of patronage.

Ptolemy

Idyll 14 features the male-dominated world of unruly symposiasts and mercenary soldiers, and it ends with an encomium of Ptolemy. Earlier we considered *Idyll* 14's handling of gender and mobility issues in its representation of Aeschinas's experiences as sympotic host and as jilted lover. Now our attention is directed to how in this poem Theocritus approaches the issue of patronage. Seeking to escape his lovesick state, Aeschinas resolves to go abroad and become a mercenary soldier. Through Thyonichus's endorsement of Aeschinas's decision, Theocritus directs the poem toward Ptolemy, Egypt's king and patron of arts:[29]

εἰ δ' οὕτως ἄρα τοι δοκεῖ ὥστ' ἀποδαμεῖν,
μισθοδότας Πτολεμαῖος ἐλευθέρῳ οἷος ἄριστος.

(58–59)

But if you're so inclined, then, as to go abroad,
Ptolemy's the best paymaster for a free man.

An encomium of Ptolemy follows, motivated by Aeschinas's query about Ptolemy's other qualities (60). For some readers the encomium represents the purpose of the poem; others regard it as a digression.[30] The encomium's function becomes clearer when we relate it to *Idyll* 14's central thematic concern with sympotic culture.

Gow notes that "it may be remarked that the panegyric which follows, though it answers Aeschinas's question, does not provide much information likely to profit him when he enlists as a private soldier."[31] But the information could profit Aeschinas as symposium host, for the qualities Thyonichus praises in Ptolemy coincide with those approved in the male sympotic culture: cultural sophistication, erotic discernment, and generosity:[32]

εὐγνώμων, φιλόμουσος, ἐρωτικός, εἰς ἄκρον ἀδύς,
εἰδὼς τὸν φιλέοντα, τὸν οὐ φιλέοντ᾽ ἔτι μᾶλλον,
πολλοῖς πολλὰ διδούς, αἰτεύμενος οὐκ ἀνανεύων,
οἷα χρὴ βασιλῆ᾽· αἰτεῖν δὲ δεῖ οὐκ ἐπὶ παντί,
Αἰσχίνα.

(61–65)

Kindly, a lover of culture, amorous, exceedingly pleasant;
knowing who loves him and, even more, who doesn't;
giving generously to many, and when asked not refusing;
a model of kingship — but you shouldn't always be asking,
Aeschinas.

The repetition of the word ἀδύς ("pleasant," used at 17 to describe the symposium and at 61 to describe Ptolemy) suggests a link between Ptolemy's character and sympotic values. Further, Ptolemy's particular virtues offer a contrast to Aeschinas's unhappy experience as symposium host. Aeschinas's most obvious problem was that, unlike Ptolemy, he did not know who loved him and who did not (62). Because he could not recognize signs of affection and disaffection, the revelation of Cynisca's disloyalty shocked him and caused a major disruption at the symposium.[33]

Hasty and immoderate in his desires (10–11), quick to anger and violent (34–35), Aeschinas needs a new role model. On *Idyll* 14's scale of manhood, which includes an ascetic philosopher and an overpassionate lover, Ptolemy represents a complex and temperate mean. Aeschinas's prolonged lovesick response to Cynisca's abandonment of him two months earlier demonstrates his obsessive tendency to limit himself to a single plane of being: the marginalized activity of love had become central and overwhelmed his ability to engage in other business.[34] Thyonichus's Ptolemy, on the other hand, has the capacity to play many roles: an army paymaster, a lover (ἐρωτικός), a generous and cultured leader, a man of discerning kindness (εὐγνώμων).

Through Thyonichus's praise of Ptolemy, Theocritus also approaches the issue of the relationship between patron and poet. Like the fictive Aeschinas, Theocritus too came to Ptolemy's Egypt from abroad (Syracuse), with questions about Ptolemy. He too would have been reassured by reports of generous patronage. Thyonichus's praise of Ptolemy does not actively exhort, but instead describes him with qualities appreciated by poets seeking patronage: kindly discernment, love of culture, generosity.[35] By having Thyonichus also include the quality of ἐρωτικός (amorousness), Theocritus can flatter Ptolemy by showing confidence in his sophistication and tolerance. Further, Ptolemy's notable fondness for mistresses might have encouraged the expectation that he would welcome a good poem on the theme of heterosexual love and sympotic culture.[36] Reports on the many statues in Alexandria of Ptolemy's cupbearer Cleino, holding a drinking-horn, and the houses named after Ptolemy's girlfriends (the actress Myrtion and the flute girls Mnesis and Potheine) further attest to Ptolemy's enjoyment of heterosexual sympotic entertainments.[37]

Thyonichus underscores Aeschinas's need to change by including in his praise of Ptolemy's generosity an exhortation to Aeschinas to limit his desires:

πολλοῖς πολλὰ διδούς, αἰτεύμενος οὐκ ἀνανεύων,
οἷα χρὴ βασιλῆ· αἰτεῖν δὲ δεῖ οὐκ ἐπὶ παντί,
Αἰσχίνα.

(63–65)

Giving generously to many, and when asked not refusing,
he is a model of kingship — but you shouldn't always be asking,
Aeschinas.

Thyonichus's recommendation to Aeschinas represents a projection of what Aeschinas might do given his character: Aeschinas will want too much, as he does in love.[38] Still, within the fiction of *Idyll* 14, the advice Thyonichus gives Aeschinas not to make too many requests of Ptolemy is strange: as a lowly mercenary, Aeschinas will not be in a position to ask Ptolemy for favors. Yet Thyonichus's advice presupposes an egalitarian social world in which such requests might be made. And it may also represent Theocritus's ironic self-admonition not to make too many requests of his patron.

Although Ptolemy's power was autocratic, the fiction of more democratic social (and political) freedoms continued to appeal to Greeks in the Hellenistic world.[39] Insofar as traditional sympotic culture valued reciprocity and egalitarianism (guests drank equal amounts and participated equally in contests), the symposium theme allows the poet to assume a stance of equality with Ptolemy. But by putting the praise in

Thyonichus's mouth, Theocritus can both ironize the praise and flatter Ptolemy by displaying confidence in his appreciation of wit and irony.[40] Friendship traditionally played a central role in a poet's representation of his relationship with his patron, as shown, for example, by Pindar's artful approaches to his patrons. So too in *Idyll* 14, Thyonichus notes that Ptolemy knows his friends (62), and the poem displays Theocritus's worthiness to be counted a friend (sophisticated, witty, able to create poetry that can both flatter and amuse). Thus the focus of *Idyll* 14 on the symposium, with its tradition of social equality, enables the poet to approach a patron-king by projecting the theme of friendship from Aeschinas and Thyonichus's privatized fictive world to the public and historical realm of Ptolemy's Egypt.[41]

Idyll 15 also embeds the issue of royal patronage within the fictive world of a mime, and here too recreational activities, in this case an Adonis festival sponsored by Arsinoe, offer a forum for exploring and reflecting the ideology of the hegemony. Later in this chapter we see how *Idyll* 15's representation of Arsinoe's Adonia approaches the issue of Arsinoe's patronage. Here we focus on *Idyll* 15's praise of Ptolemy. The following incident illustrates Theocritus's strategy of using the vantage of marginalized fictive characters to present wry defenses of the autocracy that also suggest questions about it. On leaving the insular world of her house, Praxinoa expresses consternation at the crowded, unruly public streets (44–45) and then praises Ptolemy:

πολλά τοι, ὦ Πτολεμαῖε, πεποίηται καλὰ ἔργα,
ἐξ ὧ ἐν ἀθανάτοις ὁ τεκών· οὐδεὶς κακοεργός
δαλεῖται τὸν ἰόντα παρέρπων Αἰγυπτιστί,
οἷα πρὶν ἐξ ἀπάτας κεκροτημένοι ἄνδρες ἔπαισδον,
ἀλλάλοις ὁμαλοί, κακὰ παίχνια, πάντες ἀραῖοι.

(46–50)

You have accomplished many good deeds, Ptolemy,
since your father took his place among the immortals; no evildoer
sneaks up to someone on the street, Egyptian style, and hurts him,
doing tricks that men forged from deceit used to play,
each rascal as bad as the other, wicked pranksters, curse them all.

Praxinoa's description of Ptolemy's accomplishments also reflects a linkage between cultural prejudice and fear, for Praxinoa makes the crowded streets seem less threatening by focusing, with a colonialist's xenophobia, on the disappearance of Egyptian ruffians. Thus, by showing how Praxinoa transforms Ptolemy's public identity into something she can

understand and value, Theocritus wryly explores a king's place in an ordinary person's private world.

Ptolemy's deification of his parents posed a tactical problem for
Greeks: how could one recognize mortal rulers as potentially gods?[42] By
embedding notice of the deification of Ptolemy's father in Praxinoa's
self-interested assessment of Ptolemy's achievements, the poet can suggest a secular point of reference — Ptolemy is a potential god for us insofar as he makes the streets safe. The Ptolemies were trying to create an
imperial myth; *Idyll* 15 shows how subjects could enable themselves
(through fictions) to give qualified, "conditional assent."[43] So too in
Thyonichus's remarks at the end of *Idyll* 14, Theocritus explores how
ordinary persons (and poets) can try to humanize, and hence compre-
hend, the autocratic hegemony by evaluating it in the context of private
concerns, e.g., love and money.[44]

But Praxinoa's valorization of the king's law-and-order campaign is
immediately mediated by the threatening appearance of the king's
horses:

ἀδίστα Γοργώ, τί γενώμεθα; τοὶ πολεμισταί
ἵπποι τῶ βασιλῆος. ἄνερ φίλε, μή με πατήσῃς.
ὀρθὸς ἀνέστα ὁ πυρρός· ἴδ᾽ ὡς ἄγριος.

(51–53)

Sweetest Gorgo, what will become of us? Warhorses,
the king's cavalry. Dear man, don't trample me.
The chestnut horse has reared up; look how fierce he is.

Danger emanates from the hegemonic system that guarantees order:
Ptolemy clears the streets of Egyptian ruffians only to fill them with
fierce horses. Phonetic similarities reinforce the interchangeability of the
threats presented by the Egyptian ruffian (δαλεῖται τὸν ἰόντα, 48) and
by the king's horse (διαχρησεῖται τὸν ἄγοντα, 54). The juxtaposition
of Praxinoa's gratitude for the king's law-and-order campaign with her
fright at the sudden appearance of the king's horses suggests the ambiguous nature of autocracy and also underscores the instability of Alexandria's streets — a realm in which a king, characterized by καλὰ ἔργα
("good deeds," 46), can transmute into κακοεργός ("evildoer," 47),
child's play (42) become thievery (49–50), and childhood fears (40, 58)[45]
materialize as king's horses (51–52).

A brief consideration of Theocritus's *Idyll* 10, a rustic mime, may suggest additional subtleties in Theocritus's approaches to Ptolemy.[46] In a
recent article, Cameron connects Ptolemy II's mistress named Didyme,

a native Egyptian (Ath. 13.576e–f) and thus probably dark skinned, with the Didyme praised in an epigram by Asclepiades:[47]

εἰ δὲ μέλαινα, τί τοῦτο; καὶ ἄνθρακες· ἀλλ' ὅτε κείνους
θάλψωμεν λάμπουσ' ὡς ῥόδεαι κάλυκες.
(Ep. 5.3–4 Gow and Page [= A.P. 5.210.3–4])

If she is black, so what? So are the coals.
But when we burn them, they glow like rosebuds.
(trans. Cameron, "Two Mistresses," 287 n. 2)

Similarly Theocritus's *Idyll* 10, in which a reaper expresses love for the dusky flute girl Bombyca, may be more oriented toward the Ptolemaic court than previously thought:[48]

Βομβύκα χαρίεσσα, Σύραν καλέοντί τυ πάντες,
ἰσχνάν, ἁλιόκαυστον, ἐγὼ δὲ μόνος μελίχλωρον.
(26–27)

Charming Bombyca, all call thee the Syrian,
lean and sun-scorched, and I alone, honey-hued.
(trans. Gow, Theocritus 1:83)

Perhaps too Bucaeus's longing to erect golden statues of himself and Bombyca in simple attire reflects Ptolemy's own predilection for amorous self-display:

αἴθε μοι ἦς ὅσσα Κροῖσόν ποκα φαντὶ πεπᾶσθαι·
χρύσεοι ἀμφότεροί κ' ἀνεκείμεθα τᾷ Ἀφροδίτᾳ,
τὼς αὐλὼς μὲν ἔχοισα καὶ ἢ ῥόδον ἢ τύγε μᾶλον,
σχῆμα δ' ἐγὼ καὶ καινὰς ἐπ' ἀμφοτέροισιν ἀμύκλας.
(32–35)

Would I had such wealth as Croesus, in the tales, once owned.
Then should we both stand in gold as offerings to Aphrodite—
thou with thy pipes, and a rosebud or an apple,
and I with raiment new and new shoes of Amyclae on either foot.
(trans. Gow, Theocritus 1:83)

Throughout Alexandria, Ptolemy set up statues representing his cup-bearer Cleino dressed in a simple tunic and holding a drinking cup, a tool of her trade (like Bombyca's pipes).[49] Further, Ptolemy, a comparative Croesus in wealth,[50] was renowned for setting up golden statues,[51] as *Idyll* 10's Bucaeus wishes he could, and the Ptolemies too would dedicate such statues to Aphrodite: Berenice, Ptolemy's mother, was placed after death in Aphrodite's temple as a patroness of lovers

(Theoc. *Id.* 17.50–52), and Arsinoe II cultivated the connection with Aphrodite.[52]

Other elements might also associate *Idyll* 10 with Ptolemy. First, evidence attests to Ptolemy's special fondness for flute girls (like Bombyca): he honored two such girls by naming fine houses for them (Ath. 13.576f). In *Idyll* 10, Theocritus underscores Bombyca's occupation by naming her for a flute (βόμβυξ).[53] Second, the name of Bombyca's "master,"[54] Polybotas (*Id.* 10.15), also refers to a giant associated with Cos[55] (where Ptolemy was born). Third, Milon's description of Bucaeus's inactivity (*Id.* 10.5–6) seems to contrast pointedly with another Alexandrian poet's description of Ptolemy's propensity for action (Callim. *Hymn* 1):[56]

> ἑσπέριος κεῖνός γε τελεῖ τά κεν ἦρι νοήσῃ·
> ἑσπέριος τὰ μέγιστα, τὰ μείονα δ᾽, εὖτε νοήσῃ.
>
> (87–88)[57]

At evening he accomplishes that whereon he thinks in the morning;
at evening the greatest things, but the lesser as soon as he thinks
    on them.

(trans. Mair, "Callimachus," 45, rev.)

Theocritus's *Idyll* 10 begins with Milon mocking Bucaeus's failure to reach such a standard:

> ποῖός τις δείλαν τὺ καὶ ἐκ μέσω ἄματος ἐσσῇ,
> ὃς νῦν ἀρχόμενος τᾶς αὔλακος οὐκ ἀποτρώγεις;
>
> (5–6)

What will you be like in the evening, or afternoon even,
if now at the start you can't get your teeth into your row?

(trans. Gow, *Theocritus* 1:81)

This suggestion of Ptolemaic undertones in Theocritus's *Idyll* 10 is, of course, highly speculative, since we do not know the dates of Ptolemy's relationships with his various mistresses nor of his public monuments honoring them, and we do not know the date of Theocritus's *Idyll* 10 nor its place of writing. But if *Idyll* 10 is somehow linked with Ptolemy's relations with his mistresses (and written when Arsinoe II was still alive), then the poem can illustrate a clever strategy for approaching a bipartite royal house, for by discreetly distancing his fictive characters, Theocritus could perhaps avoid offending the queen, an important patron, while still amusing the king.

Arsinoe

Since large cities such as Alexandria included many Greek local interest groups, public productions had to become more inclusive for greater impact and appeal.[58] Some Greeks advocated withdrawal from the civic community (e.g., Epicureans and Cynics);[59] others looked to magic, astrology, and mysteries for private spiritual guidance. Traditionally in the Greek world, foreign and mystery cults, philosophical cults, witchcraft, and enthusiastic rites offered alternative sources of power and control for those whose access to official power was limited. In the Hellenistic age of kingdoms governed by autocratic hegemonies, such alternatives rose in general popularity, especially in multiethnic Egypt, a center for magic and traditionally regarded by Greeks as a source of mystery cults.[60] The Ptolemies, usurpers of royal power (like the rest of Alexander the Great's successors), sought to legitimize their power by associating themselves with various gods, including Dionysus and Aphrodite.[61] By cultivating the association with Dionysus and Aphrodite, gods traditionally linked with popular cult worship that transcended spatial and class boundaries, the Ptolemies could not only promote their personal ascendancy (and the official hegemony),[62] but also expand their popular appeal among displaced Greeks.

Ptolemy II advertised his family's linkage with Dionysus in a magnificent procession described by Callixeinus (Ath. 5.197e–201e). A central spectacle was Dionysus's triumphant return from India (200d–201c), which emphasized the link with Alexander and thus also supported Ptolemaic imperialism.[63] The official Ptolemaic cultural program was in evidence, for the entire Dionysiac artists' guild, a professional association sponsored by Ptolemy,[64] walked in the procession (198b–c). But countercultural figures were also on show: men dressed as satyrs and sileni (197e–198b; 199a–b; 200e), Dionysian priests and priestesses, and women dressed as bacchantes (198e). By bringing such cult figures into the public light, by incorporating, e.g., bacchantes holding snakes and daggers into a court-sponsored parade, the Ptolemies could also move toward defusing potentially subversive cult activities.

Aphrodite's attractive features for the Ptolemies may have included her close connection with Cyprus, an important Ptolemaic external possession,[65] as well as her association with passionate love in marriage.[66] Theocritus's *Idylls* 15 and 17 show that after Arsinoe and Ptolemy's marriage, Aphrodite played a crucial role in the official mythology of the Ptolemies: both poems assume the marriage of Ptolemy II and Arsinoe II and both poems credit Aphrodite with immortalizing Berenice, their mother. Further, *Idyll* 17 describes Berenice sharing temple honors with Aphrodite (50–52), and *Idyll* 15 highlights Arsinoe's sponsorship of a public Adonia in Aphrodite's honor (23–24, 109–11). The court's official project of identifying Ptolemaic women with Aphrodite, as well as the court patronage of poets, makes political concerns a vital factor in the reception of poetry written in Ptolemaic Alexandria and featuring Aphrodite.[67]

Although, as Gutzwiller has recently emphasized, celebrations of Aphrodite as patroness of married life would have offered clear benefits for the Ptolemaic court,[68] Arsinoe II's choice to promote her association with Aphrodite through an Adonia, traditionally a private, countercultural women's festival linked with prostitution and extramarital love, seems a bit odd:[69] for instance, the Adonia's focus on relations between a powerful, self-willed female (Aphrodite) and a subordinated, younger male (Adonis) might have reinforced attitudes of cynicism toward a court featuring the marriage of Arsinoe and her brother Ptolemy, eight years younger and sickly.[70] Further, in a world that separated wives and mistresses, the linkage of an Adonia with the deification of Berenice, Arsinoe's mother, might have seemed to highlight an awkwardness in Berenice's history, for Berenice broke up Ptolemy I's marriage to her aunt by having an extramarital love affair with him.[71]

The evidence for Arsinoe's patronage of a public Adonia is Theocritus's *Idyll* 15. *Idyll* 15's Adonis hymn is also our most important witness for celebration of the Adonia in the Hellenistic age.[72] Almost all the other Hellenistic poems extant that include the Adonis theme highlight countercultural, even salacious, aspects of Adonis worship.[73] Thus *Idyll* 15's representation of Arsinoe's Adonia offers an unusual vantage on Arsinoe as an important sponsor of Alexandrian cultural life and on Arsinoe's cultural program. This section explores how Theocritus's *Idyll* 15 handles the tricky subject of Arsinoe's public Adonia, suggests ideological implications of Ptolemaic court sponsorship of a public Adonia, and then briefly contrasts Callimachus's and Theocritus's approaches to the incestuous Ptolemaic marriage.

A crucial and unresolved issue is the tone of *Idyll* 15's Adonis hymn: whether it is parody or not. Our judgment of the hymn's tone affects our understanding of *Idyll* 15's poetic orientation to the court. Does *Idyll* 15's representation of an Adonis hymn reinforce or question the hegemony's ideology? Does it offer alternative values? The standard approach has been to criticize the hymn, if not for dwelling on vulgar elements of luxury, then for general ineptitude (e.g., Helmbold, Gow, Griffiths, Dover, Wells).[74] The only audiences that could applaud such a hymn, it has been suggested, would be those whose "thoughts and tastes, like those of Gorgo and Praxinoa, existed only as strings of cliches."[75] Recently the hymn has found admirers, too (e.g., Bulloch, Zanker, Hutchinson).[76] But the issue of tone remains undecided (e.g., Goldhill).[77] The following discussion proposes ways in which aspects of the hymn most commonly perceived as ineptitudes are instead conscious refinements contributing to the overall effectiveness of a strikingly unconventional hymn. I then question the hymn's so-called vulgar insistence on luxury and focus on a more interesting aspect of the hymn that has been overlooked, an aspect that contributes significantly to the overall design and tone of the hymn when considered in the cultural context of a public Adonia sponsored by Arsinoe II in the palace grounds.

A brief review of the position of the hymn in the overall structure of the poem may be helpful here. *Idyll* 15, a mimetic poem in dialogue form, presents two Syracusan women's experiences as they go from Praxinoa's house through the crowded streets of Alexandria to the Ptolemaic palace to attend an Adonis celebration. At the palace, they view a ceremonial display and listen to an Adonis hymn sung by a female hymnist (the Argive woman's daughter). The length of the hymn (almost a third of the poem) underscores its climactic importance, and the hymn, along with the women's praise of the tapestries, provides the details of the Adonia display: tapestries; green bowers decorated with Erotes; a central tableau featuring models of Adonis and Aphrodite lying on a couch with coverlets; and offerings displayed by the couch, many probably provided by Arsinoe (e.g., silver baskets, not wicker or terracotta), but including foodstuffs typical of private offerings.

I propose the following question as central to an appreciation of the hymn's tone: what would the reading of this hymn be like if embedded in the cultural context of a public celebration of an Adonia? Certainly the Adonis hymn of *Idyll* 15 develops in an unusual manner. It had to: *Idyll* 15 commemorates a public Adonia sponsored by Arsinoe at the center of the state. Yet traditionally the Adonia was a private, countercultural festival celebrated principally by women and not incorporated in state rituals.[78] Writers of old and new comedy represent it as a countercultural festival of sensuality, providing occasion for mistresses, courtesans, prostitutes, and wives to consort with selected "Adonis substitutes,"[79] and for women to disrupt state affairs with unruly and indecent behavior (as on the eve of the Sicilian expedition).[80]

Problems arise for a poet interested in presenting a public Adonia and still maintaining the goodwill of the court. How can one celebrate the bringing of such a ceremony into the public realm? What can one say? A conventional hymn includes a narration of the genealogy, the exploits, and the powers of the gods.[81] But what can a hymnist say about Adonis: that he was the child of an incestuous union between Myrrha and her father? Such a topic might be sensitive to an Arsinoe who married her full brother and whose worship came to coincide with that of Aphrodite, Adonis's lover.[82] Or should the hymnist tell the story of how Adonis was born from a tree after Myrrha changed form to escape the wrath of her father, who was trying to murder her?[83] Ptolemy Ceraunus and Arsinoe could both attest to the high rate of kinship murders among the dynasts. The one line we have extant from Sotades' poem entitled "Adonis" suggests that other Hellenistic poets too were not unaware of the tactical difficulties of handling the topic of Adonis in a courtly environment: Τίνα τῶν παλαιῶν ἱστοριῶν θέλετ᾽ ἐσακοῦσαι; ("Which of the narratives of old [on Adonis] are you willing to hear?" fr. 3 Powell, Coll. Alex.).[84] Sotades' query, a sly varient of the aporia motif (I have many things I could say, but nothing my audience wants to hear), seems to address an implied audience that includes a Ptolemaic court invested in Arsinoe's Adonia and uneasy about its reception.

Theocritus evades the issue of Adonis's past history. Instead of starting with Adonis's genealogy, Idyll 15's Adonis hymn describes how the Hours convey Adonis from Acheron to Aphrodite for this current celebration. Theocritus does not present a conventional hymnic narrative of the exploits of the gods involved and risk emphasizing aspects of the story of Adonis and Aphrodite unflattering to the Ptolemaic house. For example, the hymn does not say that Adonis was loved by a powerful older woman; nor does it say that two goddesses vied for his love (Arsinoe II displaced her own stepdaughter to become Ptolemy's wife). Other parallels might be more dangerous: the hymn does not describe how Adonis was killed by a boar (a failed initiation into manhood), nor that he was born from sensual myrrh and later hidden away in limp, impotent lettuce.[85] Instead of describing Adonis's exploits or powers, his credentials justifying a celebration, the hymn elaborates the characteristics of the Hours, Adonis's escorts to the celebration. Rather than linger over a narrative of what Aphrodite and Adonis do together (a sensitive enterprise at best), the hymn first describes where they do it: the setting, the offerings, the atmosphere, the seductive mood, the ambiance. The hymn discretely concentrates on the mechanics of the ritual occasion and the ceremonial display sponsored by Arsinoe rather than the traditional hymnic motifs.

The challenge was to write a public hymn that celebrated the Adonia and did not cause embarrassment to the royal court. The artistry of the hymn has to do with the tact of evading controversial points of Adonis's story. Theocritus uses the technique of hymnic evasion repeatedly in his poems: Griffiths examines the evasive strategy used in *Idyll* 16 in praising Hieron, the still unproven new leader of Syracuse (to paraphrase, "when you do something praiseworthy, then I will praise you"; see especially 73–75).[86] Similarly in *Idyll* 15's hymn, a strategy of evasion is a tactful way to handle diplomatic problems that arise, and variations on hymnic techniques divert attention from the ambiguities of Adonis's traditional status as a countercultural hero. But because the hymn's use of the tactic of evasion has been overlooked, the artistry of the hymn has not been recognized.

The two main points on which scholars fault the hymn are, first, the hymn's effusive exclamation on the couch carved with a representation of Ganymede, and second, the circular, unstructured catalogue of heroes found at the end of the hymn.[87] But if placed in the context of a tactic of evasion, these "ineptitudes" must be understood differently. First, the effusive quality of the apostrophe to the couch's luxurious materials highlights the magnificence of the display and deflects attention from the hymn's evasion of disconcerting aspects of Adonis's story:

> ὦ ἔβενος, ὦ χρυσός, ὦ ἐκ λευκῶ ἐλέφαντος
> αἰετοὶ οἰνοχόον Κρονίδᾳ Διὶ παῖδα φέροντες.
>
> (123–24)

O ebony, o gold, o eagles of ivory white
conveying the cupbearing boy to Zeus.

Thus the hymnist represents herself as so powerfully affected by the luxurious display that she cannot help but dwell on its material aspects. This artfully effusive exclamation also intervenes between the couch, with its representation of Ganymede, and Adonis's story, for Ganymede, like Adonis, is snatched before he reaches manhood; trapped now forever in a stage of gender doubt, he too is victim of the erotic caprice of gods. The chiastic structure of line 124 mimetically signifies Ganymede's transposition and Zeus's new centrality in Ganymede's world, and the Erotes suspended above the couch (120–22) reinforce the symbolic constellation of sexual impulses and ambiguities.[88]

A keynote of the hymn is love, tactfully modulated and wryly reflecting back on the preoccupations evident in the fictive audience's everyday lives.[89] The hymn begins by highlighting φιλία (love) in describing Aphrodite's relations to her cult sites, Δέσποιν', ἃ Γολγώς τε καὶ Ἰδάλιον ἐφίλησας ("Mistress who cherishes Golgi and Idalium," 100),[90] and the hymn ends by underscoring φιλία as Adonis's characteristic quality, for the adjective φίλος frames the final couplet:

ἵλαος, ὦ φίλ' ῎Αδωνι, καὶ ἐς νέωτ'· εὐθυμεύσαις
καὶ νῦν ἦνθες, ῎Αδωνι, καί, ὅκκ' ἀφίκη, φίλος ἡξεῖς.

(143–44)

Be gracious, dear Adonis, in the new year too. Now your coming
has brought us women joy. When you return, we will welcome you with
    love.

Further, the ending of Praxinoa's description of the tapestries' Adonis figure anticipates the hymn's emphasis on φιλία:

ὁ τριφίλητος ῎Αδωνις, ὁ κἠν Ἀχέροντι φιληθείς.

(86)

Thrice-loved Adonis, loved even in Acheron.

Repetitions of words underscore changes in mood as the women move from the safe mimetic space of home through crowded streets to Adonis's enclave at court: what is innocent when a boy does it at home (παῖσδε, "play," 42) and sinister when ruffians do it in the streets (ἔπαισδον, "[tricks] they used to play," 49) becomes sensually elevated when Aphrodite does it among the gods (χρυσῷ παίζοισα, "playing with gold," 101).[91]

The hymn's tact in representing the sensuality of Adonis contrasts with the Syracusan women's blunt appraisals of their husbands. For example, the hymn's elevated description of Adonis as ὁ ῥοδόπαχυς ῎Αδωνις ("rosy-armed," 128) and ὀκτωκαιδεκετὴς ἢ ἐννεακαίδεχ' ὁ γαμβρός ("eighteen or nineteen years old, the bridegroom," 129) recalls Praxinoa's deflating epic characterization of her husband as ἀνὴρ τρισκαιδεκάπαχυς ("our thirteen-cubit hero," 17). Also, the description of Adonis's incipient sexuality, ἔτι οἱ περὶ χείλεα πυρρά ("reddish down still lies upon his lip," 130), recalls the name of Praxinoa's child: Ζωπυρίων ("little spark of fire").[92] Thus, through phonetic and thematic echoes, the poet underscores the complicated response that a sexually ambiguous

Adonis can evoke in a largely female audience of an Adonia and also emphasizes the contrast between the romance evoked through a festival display and the fictive Syracusan housewives' everyday life.

The hymn's tact is also evident in the mythological excursus at the hymn's end, the negative catalogue of heroes that comes full circle, for how can the hymn praise Adonis further? He is young and his kisses are not rough (129–30). This minimalist description of Aphrodite and Adonis's embrace forestalls charges of self-indulgent eroticism. What else can the hymn say? Since the hymn cannot praise Adonis for manly heroic deeds (he did not conquer the boar; he did not live to reach manhood),[93] it praises him instead for surpassing exemplars of who he is not:

ἔρπεις, ὦ φίλ' Ἄδωνι, καὶ ἐνθάδε κῆς Ἀχέροντα
ἡμιθέων, ὡς φαντί, μονώτατος. οὔτ' Ἀγαμέμνων
τοῦτ' ἔπαθ' οὔτ' Αἴας ὁ μέγας, βαρυμάνιος ἥρως,
οὔθ' Ἕκτωρ, Ἑκάβας ὁ γεραίτατος εἴκατι παίδων,
οὐ Πατροκλῆς, οὐ Πύρρος ἀπὸ Τροίας ἐπανενθών,
οὔθ' οἱ ἔτι πρότεροι Λαπίθαι καὶ Δευκαλίωνες,
οὐ Πελοπηιάδαι τε καὶ Ἄργεος ἄκρα Πελασγοί.

(136–42)

Dear Adonis, you travel both here and to Acheron;
this you alone can do among demigods, so they say. Agamemnon
did not undergo this, nor mighty Ajax, a hero of great wrath,
nor Hector, the eldest of Hecuba's twenty sons,
nor Patrokles, nor Pyrrhus when he returned from Troy,
nor still earlier the Lapiths and Deukalion's clan,
nor the house of Pelops and the Pelasgian nobles of Argos.

But even this seemingly disordered list of manly heroes is mediated for the predominantly female audience of the Adonia. The leading Trojan warrior Hector is identified as the eldest of Hecuba's twenty sons. Further, the list of warrior-heroes highlights other youthful and vulnerable male figures: Patrokles (Achilles' surrogate, who cries like a girl) and Achilles' son Pyrrhus.[94] By calling Achilles' son Pyrrhus (flame-haired) not Neoptolemus (new warrior),[95] the poet recalls Praxinoa's son Zopyrion (little spark of fire) and Adonis (πυρρός, "with reddish down," 130). Again, through the free play of phonetic and thematic echoes, the poet can suggest a mother's subjective response to her aesthetic experience — the flow of Praxinoa's associations which connect her young son Zopyrion, Adonis, a vulnerable and beautiful youth, and Pyrrhus, a young warrior from Troy.[96]

The mention of Hecuba, queen of a besieged city, who lost husband

and sons to war, whose husband's friend betrayed her by murdering her only remaining boy-child,[97] might also draw in Arsinoe herself, the Adonia's sponsor and Theocritus's patron, a queen who lost her first husband in war, who had to flee a city no longer safe for her, whose half-brother/husband Ceraunus betrayed her by having two of her three sons murdered,[98] and who as queen of Egypt had left to her only an eldest son (cf. doomed Hector, "eldest of Hecuba's sons," *Id*. 15.139). How much of Arsinoe's history was known in Alexandria (and by whom) can only be a matter of conjecture, but Arsinoe's parallels with Hecuba, even if fortuitous on the poet's part, might have added another level to *Idyll* 15's reception at court. Further, Adonis is not an ambitious warrior-king like Agamemnon; he does not sacrifice himself for honor like Ajax. But in the context of a female-defined Adonia, in front of an internal audience of mothers and wives (the Syracusan women), a catalogue that devalues old-fashioned individualistic, death-dealing heroism in favor of Adonis (brought back to life through a female's love) is certainly not out of place.

The individually named warriors featured in *Idyll* 15's catalogue all fought at Troy, but Achilles himself is notably missing as is Diomedes. Since in *Idyll* 17 Theocritus associates both Achilles and Diomedes with Ptolemy (55),[99] perhaps their omission in *Idyll* 15 is a tactical move on the poet's part: Ptolemy, a famous lover but not so clearly accomplished as a warrior,[100] and younger than his sister-wife by eight years, might not have appreciated the implications of a virile Achilles' subordination to a feminized Adonis dominated by a powerful female. But the identities of other warriors on the list — Agamemnon (leader of the Greek forces), Ajax (best of the Achaeans after Achilles), Hector (best of the Trojan warriors, killed by Achilles), Patrokles (Achilles' best friend), Pyrrhus (Achilles' son) — seem to emphasize the omission of Achilles. Thus the poet exploits the opportunity available in the Adonia to contrast different ideologies of life and of aesthetics, for the catalogue's suppression of warrior-heroes also corresponds to Alexandrian poetry's resistance to old-fashioned martial epic (and its mode of praising kings and heroes).[101]

Thus far, in looking at the Adonis hymn, we have seen artistic (and political) sense where critics often see feminine failings.[102] The "feminine failings" argument falls down even more when we turn to a closer consideration of the hymn's descriptions of the offerings and setting, and thus to a consideration of the second charge against the hymn, the charge of vulgarity: that "the rococo flamboyance of the festival epitomizes bad taste."[103]

The hymn, along with the women's praise of the tapestries, describes an Adonis display that includes the following luxurious items: silver baskets and golden perfume containers (113–14); fruits and cakes (112, 115–18); a carved couch of ebony, gold, and ivory (123–24); soft purple coverlets (125–27); embroidered tapestries (78–86); and green bowers with figures of Erotes overhead (119–22). The charge that this display is inordinately lavish forms a cornerstone of claims that the hymn lacks aesthetic balance. Yet luxurious display was expected in offerings to gods: generosity to the gods, as exemplified in magnificent displays and shows, was traditionally regarded as important to the welfare of the state and the glory of a ruler,[104] and *luxus* particularly characterizes festivals of Dionysus and Aphrodite, gods favored by the Ptolemies. Literary representations of other celebrations sponsored by royal persons typically include similar objects and settings,[105] and the Ptolemies were, in any case, known for splendid displays of wealth.[106] Further, in *Idyll* 15 the hymn's emphasis on the material abundance of the festivities helps deflect attention from Adonis's weak credentials as a hero for the Ptolemaic hegemony.

More notable than emphasis on luxury in the fictive hymnist's description of an Adonia display is the unusual attention given to the contributions of common persons (the makers of cakes and coverlets) to the ceremonial display.[107] The traditional reading has tried to explain away the attention to cakes—for example, the magisterial Gow understands the final item to be meats not shaped cakes (otherwise the display ends on an indecorous note, he explains).[108] Most translators and scholars follow Gow's lead and assume meats are part of the display.[109] But in the context of Arsinoe's court, we can read the attention to these items with a different eye.

There are two passages to consider—the passage describing the offerings (112–18) and the passage describing the setting for the tableau (119–27)—and they are structurally very similar. Both passages start with standard lists of botanical and luxury items appropriate to the occasion and end by focusing on the creation of ceremonial objects. The seven-line description of the offerings displayed by the couch ends with four lines describing the shaped cakes:

πὰρ μέν οἱ ὥρια κεῖται, ὅσα δρυὸς ἄκρα φέροντι,
πὰρ δ' ἁπαλοὶ κᾶποι πεφυλαγμένοι ἐν ταλαρίσκοις
ἀργυρέοις, Συρίῳ δὲ μύρῳ χρύσει' ἀλάβαστρα,
εἴδατά θ' ὅσσα γυναῖκες ἐπὶ πλαθάνῳ πονέονται
ἄνθεα μίσγοισαι λευκῷ παντοῖα μαλεύρῳ,

ὅσσα τ' ἀπὸ γλυκερῶ μέλιτος τά τ' ἐν ὑγρῷ ἐλαίῳ,
πάντ' αὐτῷ πετεηνὰ καὶ ἑρπετὰ τεῖδε πάρεστι.[110]

(112–18)

By him are all the seasonal fruits that grow on trees,
beside him delicate gardens kept in silver baskets,
and golden vessels of Syrian perfume,
and cakes, all that women work on kneading-tray,
mixing colors of every hue with white flour,
and cakes made of sweet honey and in smooth oil,
all shaped like creatures that fly and creep, here they are beside him.

After three lines describing fruits, gardens in baskets, and flasks of perfume, the last four lines describe only one kind of offering, cakes; and rather than simply describing what they look like in the display, the singer gives a detailed description of how they are made: who makes them (γυναῖκες, "women," 115), what tools they use (πλάθανον, "kneading-tray," 115), how they combine ingredients (μίσγοισαι, "by mixing," 116), and what ingredients they mix (ἄνθεα παντοῖα, "colors of every hue," 116; λευκόν μάλευρον, "white flour," 116; γλυκερὸν μέλι, "sweet honey," 117; and ὑγρὸν ἔλαιον, "smooth oil," 117). Notice how affectionately Theocritus has the singer describe making cakes. Must we assume, as some readers do, that "the rococo flamboyance of the festival epitomizes bad taste, and therefore Theocritus can share a laugh with his patron by memorializing the masses' susceptibility to such vulgarity in his own impeccably refined verse"?[111] A comparison of the description of the offerings with the description of the setting for the tableau enables us to interpret the attention to shaped cakes differently.

The description of the setting for the tableau has a similar structure:

χλωραὶ δὲ σκιάδες μαλακῷ βρίθοισαι ἀνήθῳ
δέδμανθ'· οἱ δέ τε κῶροι ὑπερπωτῶνται Ἔρωτες,
οἷοι ἀηδονιδῆες ἀεξομενᾶν ἐπὶ δένδρῳ
πωτῶνται πτερύγων πειρώμενοι ὄζον ἀπ' ὄζω.
ὢ ἔβενος, ὢ χρυσός, ὢ ἐκ λευκῶ ἐλέφαντος
αἰετοὶ οἰνοχόον Κρονίδᾳ Διὶ παῖδα φέροντες,
πορφύρεοι δὲ τάπητες ἄνω μαλακώτεροι ὕπνω·
ἁ Μίλατος ἐρεῖ χὢ τὰν Σαμίαν καταβόσκων,
'ἔστρωται κλίνα τὠδώνιδι τῷ καλῷ ἁμά.'

(119–27)[112]

And green bowers laden with tender dill
have been built; and boyish Loves flutter overhead,
like nightingales that flutter on the tree

from branch to branch testing their fledgling wings.
O ebony, o gold, o eagles of ivory white
conveying to Zeus, son of Cronos, the cupbearing boy.
Purple coverlets above, softer than sleep.
Miletus will say and the shepherd who herds sheep in Samos,
"The couch covered for the fair Adonis is our work."

The order of naming the materials that make up the offerings and the setting is parallel in the two passages. The description of the offerings (112–18) starts with botanical substances (fruits, 112), moves through costly materials (silver baskets, golden vessels, and Syrian perfume, 114), and ends with objects linked with their makers (a four-line description of the cakes that women make, 115–18). The description of the setting (119–27) starts with botanical substances (green bowers and tender dill, 120), moves through costly materials (ebony, gold, and ivory, 124), and ends with objects linked with their makers (a description of the coverlets that "Miletus" and a Samian shepherd make, 125–27). Thus, there is a structural similarity between the passages describing the ceremonial offerings (112–18) and the setting for the tableau (119–27), and they both highlight the descriptions of objects linked with their makers.

But what is the thematic value of such descriptions? By focusing on transitory and collaborative arts (e.g., shaped cakes), the hymnist can reinforce the transitory nature of the Adonia: its fragile gardens and ephemeral hero. So too the emphasis on how carefully the cakes are crafted suggests an analogy to the hymnist's craft in composing a hymn, as well as to the poet's own craft.[113] But why then highlight a Samian shepherd's contribution rather than that of a craftperson such as a woolworker or carpenter? A reference to Samos and Miletus, recent acquisitions of the Ptolemaic kingdom,[114] would compliment the royal house. But why include the hypothetical response of the lowliest member of the production chain?

I would like to suggest another possibility than the usual proposal of ineptitude on the hymnist's part, a mocking amplification of trivial details. Instead I propose that the unusual emphasis in the hymn on the production of cakes and coverlets may have to do with the public nature of the Adonia represented in the poem. A problem in composing a hymn for a public celebration of the Adonia is, how could it speak to the traditional audience members of the Adonia (mostly housewives and prostitutes) and make them feel welcome in a public festival enacted on the palace grounds? A description of how cakes are made and a mention of a shepherd's contribution to the making of coverlets might represent a suitable rhetorical strategy to draw in less elite audience members, those who normally feel excluded from the glittering palace society of Alexandria.[115] By suggesting that a hypothetical shepherd (were he to attend such an Adonia)[116] might be most moved by coverlets he helped make, *Idyll* 15's hymn raises the issue of how private experiences might enhance the appreciation of ceremonial displays. So too women sensitive to the qualities of woven materials in daily life (*Id*. 15.18–20, 34–38) can linger over figured ceremonial tapestries (78–86); a woman responsible for preparing food at home (147–48) can praise a hymn featuring a description of women making cakes. Most dramatically, the hymnist of *Idyll* 15 urges women audience members to participate in the next day's ritual lament (132–35), and in the last line of the poem, Gorgo herself joins the song, when she gives the final hymnic closure to both the Adonis song and *Idyll* 15 itself: χαῖρε, ᾽Ἄδων ἀγαπατέ, καὶ ἐς χαίροντας ἀφικνεῦ ("Farewell, beloved Adonis, and may your return find us happy"; 149).

But if there is a case to be made for the possibility that in this poem at least, under the self-protective ironical aegis of a modernist woman hymnist and two housewives, Theocritus is denying the cloistered limitations of the Alexandrian academy and suggesting that the aesthetic experience might yet have an active, public, and liberating effect in the world, such a case would be strengthened were it grounded in cultural context. The emergence of the Adonia as a public festival in Hellenistic Alexandria seems to provide such a context, for in *Idyll* 15, the Adonia is described as a public festival, sponsored by Arsinoe II, and inclusive rather than exclusive, its audience including both men and women, commoner and royal in a communal celebration.

I am going to be more speculative here and suggest a few reasons for the Alexandrian court's public celebration of the traditionally private Adonis festival. The Ptolemies were trying to establish a Greek way of life in Egypt:[117] the Greeks had a code of law separate from the Egyptians,[118] and Koinè was the basic language of state. Alexandria's museum and libraries attracted the Greek intellectual elite to the Ptolemaic court, and freeborn male Greeks could reinforce their ethnic identity in the gymnasia. But Greeks of lower status had more difficulty maintaining a strong Greek identity and community, and a public Adonia, traditionally a festival important to women, might draw more marginal figures to the palace grounds.[119] But whatever social program might lie beyond the fiction of the poem, the Greek population presented in *Idyll* 15 reflects Alexandria's Greek population in its multiplicity: each separately might exhibit local pride,[120] but the hymn shows how together they can form a ceremonial community. Thus, when Praxinoa and the hymnist describe the collaborative productions of anonymous men and women artisans, the inclusive spirit of their descriptions underscores the inclusive spirit of Arsinoe's Adonia, as Theocritus represents it in *Idyll* 15. Also, by showing how the aesthetic and the political can merge in *Idyll* 15, the poet explores how Alexandrian poetry and art, generally characterized by an aesthetic philosophy of "art for art's sake," can still assume a public role.

Also, a public celebration of the Adonia had the potential for broad appeal in multiethnic Alexandria, insofar as the relationship of Aphrodite and Adonis shared traits with those of Phoenician Astarte and Tammuz, Phrygian Cybele and Attis, Sumerian Inanna and Dumuzi,[121] and Egyptian Isis and Osiris.[122] The tendency toward syncretism of gods in the Hellenistic age may also have increased the appeal of Dionysus and Aphrodite for the Ptolemies: the Greek Dionysus was easily identified with the Egyptian Osiris (the chthonic Sarapis),[123] and in Memphis, funerary rites of the bull Apis were associated with Dionysiac mysteries.[124] So too Aphrodite was early identified with the Phoenician Astarte and the Egyptian Isis.[125] But any inclusiveness suggested in Theocritus's representation of an Adonia would not extend beyond the Greek community, for *Idyll* 15's Praxinoa specifically bars Egyptians and projects her discriminatory impulse into the court itself (47–48).[126]

In sponsoring a public Adonia, Arsinoe officially recognized and authorized the most marginalized women's activities and made these activities part of the public forum. The Adonia's celebration at court brought ordinary women into the palace grounds and encouraged women to enter the public realm to attend the festival. In the context of a hegemony that included a powerful female, Theocritus's celebration of Arsinoe's Adonia shows women claiming the right to speech in the public realm, e.g., Praxinoa's retort to the bystander. Arsinoe's Adonia made available an official forum in which women artists, such as *Idyll* 15's female hymnist, could perform (at court) for an audience that featured women. Cratinus, an early Attic comic poet, in his play *The Herdsmen* had dismissed the aesthetic demands of representing an Adonis ode: he mocks another poet's incompetence by asserting that he gave a chorus to a man Cratinus himself would not hire to produce a choral ode even for an Adonia (Ath. 14.638f). But in *Idyll* 15's Alexandria, a woman patron has taken charge of producing a public Adonia and has authorized an Argive woman's daughter to sing. Theocritus's subtle shaping of women's interests in the hymnist's song and throughout *Idyll* 15 distances him from the (male) tradition of ridiculing the Adonia for loose morals and shrill behavior (e.g., Ar. *Lys.* 387–98; Men. *Sam.* 38–50; Dioscorides *Ep.* 3 and 4 Gow and Page [= *A.P.* 5.53, 5.193]). Instead *Idyll* 15 shows that "the *need* for authenticity and creativity do[es] not belong only to the advanced, the educated, or the elite. These forces are played out in different forms for women in differing circumstances, but they are necessities for all."[127]

In *Idyll* 15, Theocritus appropriates a woman hymnist's voice to address a female patron. Theocritus's identification of the hymnist as an Argive woman's daughter advances the celebratory tone of a poem commemorating a festival sponsored by a Ptolemaic queen in her mother's honor. In addition, the woman hymnist's connection with Argos through her mother may reflect the Ptolemies' own claim to a connection with Alexander through the Argead dynasty of Macedonia.[128] The mother's importance in establishing the connection of the hymnist and Argos also illustrates Theocritus's thematic concern with the motifs of motherhood and legitimation.[129] In this context, Gorgo's praise of the hymnist does not seem aesthetically ignorant.[130] Insofar as Theocritus's Adonis hymn is addressed to women (*Id.* 15.143) and focuses on women's concerns, a woman like Gorgo might be able to judge its effectiveness and art better than at least the kind of man the bystander represents.

Theocritus's thematic interest in women's song is apparent elsewhere in his poetry. In *Idyll* 24, Teiresias assures Alcmene that Greek women will sing of her by name as they work yarn and that Argive women will honor her (76–78). *Idyll* 18 presents a chorus of women celebrating Helen's marriage, and they praise Helen's skill at playing the lyre and performing hymns of Artemis and Athena (32–37). In *Idyll* 2, Theocritus shapes Simaetha's incantation and self-narration through refrains and hymnic invocations, queries, and closures. Also, *Idyll* 4 includes mention of the songs of Glauce, most likely a reference to a famous Hellenistic female poet.[131] Women also frequently appear in Theocritus's poems as audiences, both for male performances (e.g., *Id.* 1.34–38, *Id.* 2.112–39, *Id.* 3, *Id.* 4.35–37, etc.) and for female achievements (e.g., *Idyll* 28's poet-narrator describes how Theugenis will gain fame among housewives for her skilled use of a distaff [22]; *Idyll* 26 ends by praising the Cadmean women as "honored by many heroines" [36]).

The nonstandard voices presented by Theocritus and other Alexandrian poets (the voices of, e.g., ordinary housewives, herdsmen, and pimps) challenge traditional patriarchal values by giving access to a multiplicity of alternative, deviant worlds (e.g., Herod. *Mime* 6's women, who describe dildoes as works of art).[132] But Arsinoe's Adonia offered Theocritus a special, court-sponsored excuse to explore a public suspension of traditional patriarchal values: to look at how carnivals, even those connected with courts, can offer forums for inverting hierarchies (e.g., male over female), dissolving boundaries (e.g., insider vs. outsider), and deconstructing assumptions of power (e.g., the bystander's over the Syracusan women). But *Idyll* 15 also shows how festivals can enable a hegemony to reset social boundaries to encompass and contain what used to be marginal (women immigrants).

In addition to favoring Aphrodite and Adonis, Arsinoe paid special attention to deities who offered salvation at sea: she sponsored Samothracian deities[133] and probably the Dioskouroi as well.[134] (Arsinoe, who twice escaped assassination by fleeing in ships — from Arsinoea [Ephesus] to Macedonia and from Cassandreia to Samothrace — and who made successful voyages to and from Egypt, probably felt a special thankfulness to saviors at sea.) Arsinoe's patronage of saviors at sea reinforces our perception that the choice of sponsoring an Adonia was perhaps deliberately iconoclastic (a breaking of the boundary between private and public), for Arsinoe could have honored Aphrodite as patroness of sea travel, e.g., Aphrodite Euploia (of a fair voyage) or Aphrodite Pontia (of the sea),[135] instead of as patroness of illicit love. Since Berenice and her husband Ptolemy I were called Theoi Soteres (Savior Gods),[136] a celebration of Aphrodite as savior at sea might have also suited the occasion of Berenice's deification. But Arsinoe sponsored the Adonia instead, traditionally a countercultural, female festival celebrating the passionate relations of a strong woman and a subordinated younger male.

Arsinoe's sponsorship of a public Adonia, traditionally a private festival celebrating an extramarital affair, may also be part of an ongoing dialogue with a Ptolemy notoriously ἐρωτικός (amorous), as Theocritus remarks in *Idyll* 14 (61), and perhaps openly unfaithful. Ptolemy certainly advanced such a dialogue, even if only after Arsinoe's death, by publicly flaunting his mistresses and bestowing Arsinoe's attributes and honors on them. Ptolemy set up public statues of his mistress Cleino, wearing only a tunic, but holding the drinking cup he had ordered made to be a special attribute of Arsinoe on her statues (Polyb. 14.11; Ath. 10.425e–f, 11.497b–e). For his mistress Bilistiche, Ptolemy dedicated temples and shrines of Bilistiche-Aphrodite (Plut. *Mor.* 753e), which recalled those of Arsinoe-Aphrodite.[137] Ptolemy also named fine houses in Alexandria for his girlfriends and set up a great monument near the sea at Ephesus in honor of his mistress Stratonice (Ath. 13.576f). Thus as Bouché-Leclercq remarks: "Arsinoé n'était pas oubliée. Elle servait d'original pour les copies."[138]

Although we do not know the strategies whereby Arsinoe exerted her patronage, the focus on gender dynamics in many of Theocritus's poems seems to reflect attention to Arsinoe's authority in Alexandrian cultural life. Thus Arsinoe's sponsorship of the Adonia in Alexandria could itself be a statement of power. In any case, Theocritus's *Idyll* 15 moves away from a patriarchal state, with its male-dominated streets, toward a realm controlled by Arsinoe and Aphrodite.

The historical Arsinoe, having returned home a sorrowing mother, a troubled refugee, moved from the private realm into Alexandria's public forum through political influence, marriage, and cultural patronage. In *Idyll* 15, by moving fictive women out of the private sphere into the center of the Ptolemaic state, the poet draws attention to the innovation of Arsinoe's public Adonia and the vital public presence of women at court. Through representations of powerful (and threatening) women (e.g., *Idyll* 1's Aphrodite, *Idyll* 26's bacchantes),[139] Theocritus can suggest disconcerting aspects of a strong woman's position at court for Greek men used to political dominance. But by projecting himself into a female's subjective consciousness, as he does in two of the urban mimes (*Idylls* 2 and 15), Theocritus makes female sensibilities public and thus also part of the public discourse.

A brief reconsideration of the gender dynamics of *Idyll* 17, a hymnic encomium of Ptolemy, underscores Theocritus's attention to the powerful female presence within the Ptolemaic court. In this poem, which celebrates Ptolemy's achievements in the Syrian war (86–90), Theocritus also emphasizes the power of the Ptolemaic women at court. For Alexander's usurping successors and their self-legitimizing dynasties, a wife's loyalty was crucial. *Idyll* 17 highlights male anxieties concerning a wife's power in determining the legitimacy of her children (43–44). Written at a time in which traditional boundaries between public and private, men and women, political and domestic were becoming more fluid, *Idyll* 17 draws attention to the importance of motherhood and marriage in the Ptolemaic discourse. By bringing private (female) life into the public (male) realm and by emphasizing the significance of the private realm to the public self, the poem suggests the weakness of an ideology that polarizes private and public, and it shows a Ptolemaic court of shared power, a hegemony constituted not as a patriarchal monologue but rather as a dialogue between male and female.

Let us now examine how Theocritus uses the motif of the relations of Hera and Zeus to approach the theme of Ptolemy and Arsinoe's (incestuous) relations. In *Idyll* 17, the motif of Hera and Zeus's wedding is directly compared with Ptolemy and Arsinoe's:

αὐτός τ᾽ ἰφθίμα τ᾽ ἄλοχος, τᾶς οὔτις ἀρείων
νυμφίον ἐν μεγάροισι γυνὰ περιβάλλετ᾽ ἀγοστῷ,
ἐκ θυμοῦ στέργοισα κασίγνητόν τε πόσιν τε.
ὧδε καὶ ἀθανάτων ἱερὸς γάμος ἐξετελέσθη
οὓς τέκετο κρείουσα Ῥέα βασιλῆας Ὀλύμπου·
ἓν δὲ λέχος στόρνυσιν ἰαύειν Ζηνὶ καὶ Ἥρῃ
χεῖρας φοιβήσασα μύροις ἔτι παρθένος Ἶρις.

(128–34)

He and his noble wife [Ptolemy and Arsinoe], than whom none better
clasps in her arms a husband in his halls,
loving with all her heart her brother and her spouse.
After this fashion was accomplished the sacred bridal also
of the immortals whom Queen Rhea bore to rule Olympus;
and single is the couch that Iris, virgin still, her hands made
pure with perfumes, strews for the sleep of Zeus and Hera.

(trans. Gow, *Theocritus* 1:139)

Gow proposes that "the comparison of the Ptolemies to Zeus and Hera seems both blasphemous and sycophantic."[140] But the analogy seems to have been popular from the marriage's start: thus the famous story of a rhapsode who evidently started his song at Ptolemy and Arsinoe's wedding with a reference to Zeus and Hera (Ζεὺς δ᾽ Ἥρην ἐκάλεσσε κα-σιγνήτην ἄλοχόν τε; "Zeus called to Hera, his wife and sister"; Plut. *Mor.* 736e–f).[141] Further, the Ptolemies themselves may have encouraged this analogy.[142] More importantly for our discussion, *Idyll* 17's passage on Zeus and Hera, with its highlight on how Rhea bore them to be joint rulers (βασιλῆας) of Olympus (132), intensifies *Idyll* 17's thematic focus on the mother's importance in determining dynastic succession and on hegemonic power that is shared between male and female.

Callimachus's representations of Hera's relations with Zeus also seem suggestive of male-female relations at the Ptolemaic court and thus provide a useful comparison with Theocritus's approach to Arsinoe and Ptolemy's sibling marriage.[143] Many scholars see in Callimachus's *Hymn* 1 (to Zeus) an implicit comparison between Zeus's and Ptolemy II's accession to the throne.[144] Hera does not appear in *Hymn* 1, which is generally dated before Ptolemy II's marriage to Arsinoe,[145] but she does appear in *Hymns* 3 (to Artemis) and 4 (to Delos). *Hymn* 4 is typically dated to Philadelphus's reign and generally after Arsinoe and Ptolemy's marriage;[146] *Hymn* 3 offers less scope for dating.[147] The discussion that follows is necessarily highly speculative, since the dating of all three of these hymns is problematic, but let us consider whether in the context of a court defined by a brother-sister marriage, Callimachus's hymnic references to Hera and Zeus's marital relations might seem wryly polysemous (especially to the members of Callimachus's courtly audience who were already feeling distanced by the incest of the Ptolemaic marriage).[148]

Hymns 3 and 4, which highlight Hera's oppositional position to Zeus, raise the issue of the difficulties of balancing male and female power at the hegemonic level, an issue most pertinent to the Ptolemaic court. Thus in *Hymn* 4, a jealous and vindictive Hera curses Zeus's mistresses:

> οὕτω νῦν, ὦ Ζηνὸς ὀνείδεα, καὶ γαμέοισθε
> λάθρια καὶ τίκτοιτε κεκρυμμένα, μηδ' ὅθι δειλαί
> δυστοκέες μογέουσιν ἀλετρίδες, ἀλλ' ὅθι φῶκαι
> εἰνάλιαι τίκτουσιν, ἐνὶ σπιλάδεσσιν ἐρήμοις.
>
> (240–43)

So now, O shameful creatures of Zeus, may ye all wed
in secret and bring forth in darkness, not even where the poor
mill-women bring forth in difficult labour, but where the seals
of the sea bring forth, amid the desolate rocks.

(trans. Mair, "Callimachus," 105)

Hera's relations with Zeus are mostly unfruitful (Ares was their only son together); in *Hymn* 3, Callimachus's Zeus boasts to young Artemis sitting on his knees that he has other sources for children:

> ὅτε μοι τοιαῦτα θέαιναι
> τίκτοιεν, τυτθόν κεν ἐγὼ ζηλήμονος Ἥρης
> χωομένης ἀλέγοιμι.
>
> (29–31)

When goddesses bear me children like this,
little need I heed the wrath of jealous Hera.

(trans. Mair, "Callimachus," 63)

An analogy seems possible here with the Ptolemies' relationship, for Arsinoe reportedly did not bear Ptolemy children,[149] and Ptolemy was famous for his many mistresses.[150] *Hymn* 4's Hera presents the criterion through which a female might attain favor in her court:[151]

ἀλλά μιν ἔκπαγλόν τι σεβίζομαι, οὕνεκ' ἐμεῖο
δέμνιον οὐκ ἐπάτησε, Διὸς δ' ἀνθείλετο πόντον.
(247–48)

Howbeit I honour her exceedingly for that she did not
desecrate my bed, but instead of Zeus preferred the sea.

(trans. Mair, "Callimachus," 105)

Hymn 3's description of the happy city, with its focus on kinship factionalism within well-established houses, also may seem suggestive of
Ptolemaic family history:

οὐδὲ διχοστασίη τρώει γένος, ἥ τε καὶ εὖ περ
οἴκους ἐστηῶτας ἐσίνατο· ταὶ δὲ θυωρόν
εἰνάτερες γαλόῳ τε μίαν πέρι δίφρα τίθενται.
(133–35)

Nor does faction wound their race — faction which ravages
even well-established houses: but brother's wife
and husband's sister set their chairs around one board.

(trans. Mair, "Callimachus," 71)

Arsinoe II had much experience of complicated kinship factionalism between women in well-established houses. In her first husband Lysimachus's house, her interests conflicted with those of her husband's son
Agathocles and his wife, her half-sister Lysandra: the conflict ended with
Agathocles' execution, his widow's self-exile, and Lysimachus's death in
battle.[152] At her brother Ptolemy's court, Arsinoe II's interests conflicted
with those of Ptolemy's wife Arsinoe I, Lysimachus's daughter and
hence Arsinoe II's step-daughter.[153] This conflict ended with Arsinoe I's
exile and Arsinoe II's marriage to her brother. At the Ptolemaic table,
peace between kinswomen seems to have come only when brother's wife
and husband's sister (γάλοῳ, Callim. *Hymn* 3.135) were one and the
same — Arsinoe II herself. Thus Callimachus's representations of relations between Zeus and Hera, as well as other marriage themes, raise
issues that might have seemed relevant also to the Ptolemaic court,
whose marital discourse also included incest and extramarital affairs.[154]

A major difference between Callimachus's and Theocritus's approach
to the theme of heterosexual relations is that Theocritus sometimes suggests the possibility, however ironized, of mutual love — e.g., *Id.* 15.128
(Aphrodite and Adonis); *Id.* 18.52–53, 54–55 (Helen and Menelaus);[155]
Id. 17.38–40 (Ptolemy and Berenice); *Id.* 17.42 (an anonymous loving
married couple).[156] In Callimachus's poetry, on the other hand, the most
prominent (and repeating) examples of the marital loyalty theme are

Zeus's infidelities and Hera's powerful expressions of anger against his helpless, young mistresses (e.g., Leto in *Hymn* 4).[157] In Herodas's poetry, too, passionate love for one's spouse is not a theme: even *Mime* 1's Metriche, who refuses to cuckold her husband, refuses not for love but to preserve her husband's reputation (77).[158]

Although *Idyll* 17's representation of Hera and Zeus's relations, unlike most of Callimachus's representations, seems to reinforce the theme of passionate, married love (with emphasis here on Arsinoe's love for Ptolemy),[159] Theocritus also offers a more ironic view of the divine incestuous marriage in a remark of *Idyll* 15's Praxinoa: πάντα γυναῖκες ἴσαντι, καὶ ὡς Ζεὺς ἀγάγεθ' Ἥραν ("Women know all things, even how Zeus married Hera"; 64). Here, through the voice of a low-status Syracusan immigrant woman, Theocritus underscores the liberty of private speech (and poetry) to make Zeus and Hera's incestuous marriage (and perhaps by analogy the Ptolemies') into town talk.[160]

As Griffiths has shown, Theocritus's poetry focuses on gods and heroes favored by the Ptolemaic court, e.g., *Idylls* 1 and 15 feature Aphrodite; *Idylls* 13 and 24, Heracles; *Idyll* 26, Dionysus; *Idyll* 18, Helen; *Idyll* 22, the Dioskouroi; *Idyll* 17, Zeus, the deified Alexander, Heracles, Aphrodite, and Hera.[161] But reservations about hegemonic power also seem to emerge in aspects the poet emphasizes from their stories.[162] For example, in *Idyll* 26, bacchantes, incited through Dionysus, tear a king limb from limb. Although featured in the procession of Ptolemy described by Callixeinus, Dionysus is conspicuously absent from *Idyll* 17, Theocritus's encomium of Ptolemy.[163] Also, in *Idyll* 13, love distracts an unhappy Heracles from his heroic business.

In Herodas's *Mime* 1, through an old bawd's review of the famous attractions of Alexandria, the poet seems to highlight the importance of Arsinoe at court. The list of attractions begins and ends with females and even the brother-sister sharing of power is mentioned before the king by himself:[164]

> κεῖ δ᾽ ἐστὶν οἶκος τῆς θεοῦ· τὰ γὰρ πάντα,
> ὅσσ᾽ ἔστι κου καὶ γίνετ᾽, ἔστ᾽ ἐν Αἰγύπτωι·
> πλοῦτος, παλαίστρη, δύναμις, εὐδίη, δόξα,
> θέαι, φιλόσοφοι, χρυσίον, νεηνίσκοι,
> θεῶν ἀδελφῶν τέμενος, ὁ βασιλεὺς χρηστός,
> Μουσῆιον, οἶνος, ἀγαθὰ πάντ᾽ ὅσ᾽ ἂν χρήιζηι,
> γυναῖκες, ὀκόσους οὐ μὰ τὴν Ἄιδεω Κούρην
> ἀστέρας ἐνεγκεῖν οὐραν[ὸ]ς κεκαύχηται,
> τὴν δ᾽ ὄψιν οἷαι πρὸς Πάριν κοτ᾽ ὥρμησαν
> .] [κρ]ιθῆναι καλλονήν — λάθοιμ᾽ αὐτάς.

(26–35)

Egypt is the very home of the goddess; for all
that exists and is produced in the world is in Egypt:
wealth, wrestling grounds, might, peace, renown,
shows, philosophers, money, young men,
the domain of the Θεοὶ ἀδελφοί [the brother-sister gods],[165] the king
  a good one,
the museum, wine, all good things one can desire,
women more in number — I swear by Kore wife of Hades —
than the sky boasts of stars,
and in charms like the goddesses who went on a time to Paris
to have their beauty judged — I pray they may not hear me.

(trans. Knox, in Headlam and Knox, Herodas, 5)

Headlam suggests that the ἡ θεός (goddess) of the first line of this passage refers to Aphrodite, since the poem's theme is love, but ἡ θεός could also refer to Arsinoe, who was identified with Aphrodite but was also herself called θεά (goddess), even before her death.[166]

Hellenistic poetry attests Arsinoe's prominent position in the cultural life of Alexandria. But the Alexandrian poets approached the theme of the power relations between Ptolemy and Arsinoe in complex and sophisticated ways, often by placing praise in low voices, but also possibly through veiled analogies to such figures as Aphrodite and Adonis, Zeus and Hera, and Helen and Menelaus.[167] Thus, for instance, through representations of Hera's relations with Zeus, Callimachus seems to approach the difficult theme of the relations of Arsinoe and Ptolemy with some degree of cynicism. Arthur's apt description of the Hera featured in the *Homeric Hymn to Apollo* seems to suit Callimachus's Hera (and perhaps Arsinoe II as well): "Hera appears as a powerful and formidable foe to Zeus, conscious of her own prerogatives, jealous of their usurpation by Zeus, and altogether capable of retaliation."[168] Theocritus, on the other hand, in *Idyll* 17 uses the marriage of Zeus and Hera to highlight the theme of shared hegemonic power. In *Idyll* 15, Theocritus emphasizes Arsinoe's power in the Ptolemaic court by focusing on her patronage of a public Adonia, which brings women's discourse and women's arts into the public realm, and also by emphasizing parallels between Arsinoe and Aphrodite.

In the case of the royal hegemony at Alexandria, the official voice was not exclusively male. Arsinoe's female voice made itself heard as well, through, for example, the sponsorship of a public Adonia, traditionally a private, women's festival celebrating the relations of a dominant female with a younger, subordinate male, now brought by Arsinoe into the public discourse. A juxtaposition of Theocritus's *Idylls* 14 and 15 highlights gendered differences between male and female patronage: *Idyll* 14, which includes an encomium of Ptolemy, features two male friends and the male-defined world of the symposium; *Idyll* 15, which highlights Arsinoe's patronage, features two female friends and the female-defined world of the Adonia. Both poems also feature the theme of relations of power between males and females. The dialogue form, favored by Theocritus in many of his poems, was especially useful for testing and challenging official monologues. In Alexandria under the Ptolemies, Arsinoe's forceful presence at court introduced diversity of voice and gender difference. Thus in a cultural environment defined by two royal voices — Arsinoe's and Ptolemy's — Alexandrian poets, not least Theocritus, wrote poems drawing attention not only to the heteroglossia offered by little, nonelite voices (e.g., the voices of immigrant housewives in *Idyll* 15), in contrast to the dominant hegemony, but also to the dialogue of male and female, Ptolemy and Arsinoe, within the official hegemony itself.

Conclusion

This study shows the value of approaching Theocritus's urban mimes with attention to the themes of mobility and internationalism, gender and identity, art and audience reception, and patronage and the poetic project. The result is a multifaceted reading of these poems that is more complete and consistent than traditional approaches allow. This study also illustrates how careful attention to such themes in reading Hellenistic poetry can significantly enrich our conception of Hellenistic Greek life.[1]

Themes of mobility and internationalism, notable characteristics of the Hellenistic world, pervade Theocritus's urban mimes. They highlight their fictive characters' ethnicities and their identities as immigrants or settlers, and they focus on conditions of life in a mobile world: the attraction of such mobile occupations as mercenary soldiery, the function of symposia and festivals as gathering places for mobile and dislocated persons, and the role of private friendships in offsetting feelings of isolation and alienation.

Theocritus's urban mimes also explore issues of gender and power. Poetic explorations of such issues were especially pertinent in a world of changing gendered roles, where Greek males were experiencing diminished public political power and females were becoming increasingly visible. The urban mimes explore male-female interactions, female friendships, female claims to power and public visibility, and sexual ambiguity in young males.

The theme of aesthetic reception is critical in *Idyll* 15's representation of Arsinoe's Adonia. By viewing works of art through the eyes of immigrant housewives, Theocritus suggests the possibility of reaching beyond the elite court to a more public audience as well. Also, Theocritus's representations of the passage between art and reality for a poem's internal audiences offer metaphors for the transition between art and reality for the external audience as well.

Ptolemaic patronage is clearly an important factor in the production of poetry and art in Alexandria. Theocritus's sophisticated artistry is evident in his ability to acknowledge (and compliment) his royal patrons while at the same time wryly exploring the hegemony's role in the world. By including encomia of Ptolemy and a representation of Arsinoe's public Adonia, the urban mimes explore possible meanings of hegemony in the private lives of ordinary men and women, underscore the importance of Arsinoe at court, and draw attention to the possibility of male-female dialogue within the Ptolemaic hegemony itself.

A brief review of how these themes emerge in each of the urban mimes shows how alertness to these issues and a consideration of these mimes as a group can illuminate aspects of the poems that have often been slighted or unrecognized. *Idyll* 2, Simaetha's monologue, underscores the difference between the options available to males and to females in a mobile world. Delphis, an elite outlander, can establish himself as a star member of the local sympotic/gymnastic set. But Simaetha, seemingly a local, nonelite woman, in the absence of a *kurios* has to look out for herself in a male-defined world. Her recourse to magic reflects the limited options available to women and also highlights the attractiveness of alternative realms of power for privatized persons outside the official hegemony, e.g., the realms of magic, foreign cults, ecstatic rites.

Idyll 14, a dialogue between two male friends, Thyonichus and Aeschinas, features the male worlds of symposiasts and mercenary soldiers. But this mime changes the traditional male-defined dynamics of the symposium. The host's obsessive love isolates him from the other symposiasts, and the woman of his affections, instead of passively submitting to his needs and his violence, asserts her right to a self-willed passion of her own and, when maltreated, leaves him. Thus the poem raises the issue of the viability of traditional, patriarchal assumptions about gender relations in a changing Hellenistic world (e.g., more mobile, heterosexual). A male jilted lover has more options than a female: he can leave town to join a mercenary force. Aeschinas's decision prompts Thyonichus's encomium of Ptolemy, which focuses on qualities attractive in sympotic contexts. This encomium works within the fiction of the poem by providing a model for Aeschinas of a balanced life, in which soldiery does not exclude symposia and balanced love affairs, and also works as a poet's sly approach to a patron famous for heterosexual affairs and sympotic amusements. The poem also underscores Alexandria's position as a cultural and economic mecca for displaced Hellenistic Greeks.

Idyll 15's motif of a road leading immigrant Syracusan housewives from the outskirts of Alexandria to the palace grounds highlights issues of mobility and cultural alienation. The women's encounters with men on the public streets raise issues of ethnicity and gender, and the very fact of a public Adonia brings into the center of the city marginalized persons customarily excluded from palace activities. The central *ekphrasis* of the figure of Adonis woven into tapestries raises to a thematic level issues of aesthetics and the relations of audience and work of art. In addition, Theocritus's *Idyll* 15, which represents Arsinoe's Adonia (in part through a woman hymnist's performance), provides our best example of Theocritus's relations with Arsinoe, a powerful cultural patron in Alexandria.

Singers, songs, personal stories, objects of art, and internal audiences and judges are featured throughout Theocritus's poetry. The prevalence of these motifs shows Theocritus's special interest in audience reception and the function and nature of poetry. Herdsmen-poets repeatedly compete in song with one another. *Idyll* 18 even specifies that the skills of Helen include singing hymns and playing the lyre (38). Theocritus's emphasis on the importance of poetry, the value he sets on telling stories, is exemplified in *Idyll* 15, for Gorgo explicitly urges Praxinoa to attend the Adonia in order to have a story to tell: ὧν ἴδες, ὧν εἴπαις κεν ἰδοῖσα τὺ τῷ μὴ ἰδόντι ("Things you've seen, you can talk about, once you've seen them, to someone who hasn't seen them"; 25). *Idyll* 1 further stresses the urgency of telling one's story (singing one's song): a goatherd tells Thyrsis to sing while he can, since he will forget his song in Hades (62–63). *Idyll* 12 shows how storytelling can serve as a vehicle to commemorate lives: a lover prays that he and his beloved become a song for all time (11). Also, by frequently providing fictive audiences and judges for songs within the poems, Theocritus invites the real audience to participate in the judgments, to involve themselves imaginatively in the world of the poems. Thus fictive witnesses often flatter singers into performing or otherwise indicate the internal audience's level of expectation. For example, in *Idyll* 1, the goatherd invites Thyrsis to perform by acknowledging his mastery of bucolic song (19–20); in *Idyll* 7, Simichidas invites Lycidas to a song contest by acknowledging his reputation as the best piper of herdsmen and reapers (27–28) and by citing his own reputation as best singer (38); and in *Idyll* 15, Gorgo cites the singer's success last year in the dirge contest as a probable guarantee of excellence in performing an Adonis hymn this year (96–99).

An important issue for Theocritus, in the increasingly privatized Hellenistic world, is the diminishment of public support for his poetry. In *Idyll* 16, the poet-narrator personifies his poems as Graces and sends them out to find an audience, but they return unheard:

τίς γὰρ τῶν ὁπόσοι γλαυκὰν ναίουσιν ὑπ᾽ ἠῶ
ἡμετέρας Χάριτας πετάσας ὑποδέξεται οἴκῳ
ἀσπασίως, οὐδ᾽ αὖθις ἀδωρήτους ἀποπέμψει;
αἳ δὲ σκυζόμεναι γυμνοῖς ποσὶν οἴκαδ᾽ ἴασι,
πολλά με τωθάζοισαι, ὅτ᾽ ἀλιθίην ὁδὸν ἦλθον.

(5–9)

Who, of all that dwell beneath the bright daylight,
will with open house receive our Graces [poems]
gladly, nor send them back without a guerdon?
Instead they come bare-foot home complaining,
and much upbraid me that their journey has been vain.

(trans. Gow, *Theocritus* 1 : 123, rev.)

In Alexandria, the Ptolemies sponsored a museum and library, which provided an enclaved, supportive environment for creative artists and scientists. Thus one response to public indifference in the Hellenistic age was to withdraw into an alternative world and shun the public domain. Callimachus responds to the decline in public support for poetry by extolling his distance from public taste, for example:

Ἐχθαίρω τὸ ποίημα τὸ κυκλικόν, οὐδὲ κελεύθῳ
χαίρω, τίς πολλοὺς ὧδε καὶ ὧδε φέρει.

(*Ep.* 28.1–2)

I hate the cyclic poem, nor do I take pleasure
in the road which carries many to and fro.

(trans. Mair, "Callimachus," 157 [his *Ep.* 30])

But withdrawal into the world of the academy might also lead to feelings of isolation. Theocritus's poetry frequently underscores the isolation of individuals in the world. Theocritus's *Idyll* 7 offers a dramatic parallel to the poet's own situation in the story of how a king imprisons the legendary singer Comatas in a coffer and leaves him to be fed by bees.[2] Poems that underscore the isolation of ordinary persons include *Idyll* 2 and *Idyll* 14. In *Idyll* 2, Simaetha finds herself alone, deserted by her elitist male lover and without public recourse. In *Idyll* 14, Aeschinas too is alone, abandoned by his lover and disconnected from his former sympotic life.

As an alternative to this isolation, Theocritus's poems often include individuals talking with one another: fictive characters entertain one another with stories, songs, and conversation. Most of Theocritus's poems explore the private lives of ordinary persons: herdsmen, slaves, women, mercenary soldiers, etc. Many of these poems depict the difficulties of human relationships and show the role talking, telling stories, and singing songs can play in establishing identities and in making connections with others. Thus Theocritus's poetry underscores the community-engendering potential of telling stories and singing songs and thereby highlights traditions and functions for poetry in realms outside the elitist court and academy.

Although Theocritus's poetic universe is various, including bucolic, urban, and mythic landscapes, constant elements uniting his poetry are the value placed on friendship and private relationships and the role that song can play in sustaining friendships. The theme of friendship in Theocritus's poetry also becomes a metaphor for friendship between a poet and his "real" audience. In three poems, this metaphor is made explicit: in *Idylls* 11, 13, and 28, the poems themselves are presented as letters addressed to friends. Theocritus recognized that a value that literature could still offer an increasingly privatized and mobile audience was friendship,[3] and one of Theocritus's greatest contributions was to energize the experience of poetry by bringing the topic of friendship through song to the center of his poetic project. Further, in making friendship central to his poetics, Theocritus offers an alternative value for literature to the traditional privileging of didacticism and the rising aestheticism of his own day.

This study focuses on Theocritus's urban mimes, since their representations of persons trying to make their way in the contemporary urban world offer Theocritus's richest forums for exploring a wide range of important issues of his day. The issues highlighted in this study include the impact of mobility on personal identity, the relations of gender, ethnicity, and power, the linkages between audience reception and art, and the effects of patronage on poetry. But the value of suspending preconceptions about elitism and aestheticism and instead interposing questions about contemporary social and cultural issues extends beyond Theocritus's urban mimes, both to the rest of his corpus and to works of other Hellenistic poets as well.

APPENDIX I

Translations of Theocritus's
Urban Mimes

I have provided these translations for the reader's convenience. The
translations do not pretend to literary merit (for more artful translations,
the reader might consult Hine, *Theocritus,* and Wells, *Theocritus,* among
others). My aim was to reproduce fairly closely in English the effects I
saw in the Greek. The Greek text used is that in Gow, *Theocritus.*[1]

Idyll 2

Where are my laurel leaves? Fetch them, Thestylis. And where are my
   charms?
Wreathe the bowl with fine crimson wool
that I may bind my love, who has been abusive to me.
He hasn't visited me for eleven days now, the louse,
and he doesn't even know if I'm dead or alive,   5
and he hasn't even knocked on my door, the rat. Eros
and Aphrodite must have flown elsewhere with his fickle heart.
Tomorrow I'll go to Timagetus's wrestling school
to see him and complain of how he treats me.
But now I'll bind him with spells. Shine brightly, Selene,   10
for I will sing softly to you, goddess,
and to earthly Hecate — before whom even dogs shiver
as she comes among the tombs of the dead and the black blood.
Hail, dread Hecate, and attend me to the end,
making my drugs as strong as Circe's   15
or Medea's or blond Perimede's.

    Magic wheel, draw that man to my house.

Barley burns in the fire first. So strew it,
Thestylis. Wretched girl, where are your wits?
Am I a source of fun, then, even to you, foul creature?   20
Strew it and say: "I'm strewing Delphis's bones."

    Magic wheel, draw that man to my house.

Delphis made me suffer, and so I burn laurel
for Delphis. And just as the laurel crackles loudly in the fire
and suddenly flares up so we can't see even its ashes,   25
so too may Delphis's flesh be destroyed in the flame.

    Magic wheel, draw that man to my house.

Now I'll burn the bran. And you, Artemis, can move even   33
Hades' adamant and anything else as firm —
Thestylis, listen, the dogs are howling through the city;   35
the goddess is at the crossroads. Quickly, sound the bronze.

    Magic wheel, draw that man to my house.

The sea is still, and the breezes are still.
Yet the anguish in my breast will not be still,
but I am all on fire for the man who made me   40
miserable, instead of a wife, a bad woman, and a maid no more.

    Magic wheel, draw that man to my house.

As I melt this wax, with the goddess's help,   28
so may Myndian Delphis waste swiftly with love.   29
And as this bronze rhomb turns by Aphrodite's power,   30
so may that man turn ever at my door.   31

    Magic wheel, draw that man to my house.   32

Three times I pour libations, lady, and three times I speak these words: 43
whether a woman is lying by him or a man,
may he be as forgetful of them as Theseus, they say,   45
once forgot fair-haired Ariadne on Dia.

    Magic wheel, draw that man to my house.

There is a plant, Hippomanes, in Arcadia, and for it
all the foals and swift mares go mad on the hills.
So may I see Delphis, and like a man driven mad   50
may he come to this house from the shiny palaestra.

    Magic wheel, draw that man to my house.

This fringe Delphis lost from his cloak,
and I now shred and throw it in the fierce fire.
Ah, cruel Love, why have you sucked all the black blood from my body,   55
clinging like a leech from the marsh?

    Magic wheel, draw that man to my house.

I'll mash a lizard and bring Delphis a bad drink tomorrow,
Thestylis, but now take these herbs and knead them
above Delphis's threshold, while it's still night,   60
and whisper, "I'm kneading Delphis's bones."   62

   Magic wheel, draw that man to my house.

   Now left alone, from what point shall I lament my love?
Where shall I begin? Who brought this badness upon me?   65
Euboulus's daughter, our Anaxo, went as basket bearer
to the grove of Artemis, in whose honor many wild beasts
were parading about that day, and among them a lioness.

   Consider whence came my love, lady Selene.

And Theumaridas's Thracian nurse, now passed away,   70
who lived next door, begged and entreated me
to see the procession. And I, doomed woman,
went with her — trailing a lovely linen frock
and wrapped in Clearista's robe.

   Consider whence came my love, lady Selene.   75

And I was already midway on the road, at Lycon's place,
when I saw Delphis walking with Eudamippus.
And their beards were more golden than helichryse,
and their breasts were far more shining than you, Selene,
for they had freshly left the gymnasium's fair exercise.   80

   Consider whence came my love, lady Selene.

And when I saw him I went mad, and my hapless heart caught fire,
and my beauty began to waste. No longer did I take notice of
that procession, and I don't know how I came
back home, but a burning fever shook me hard,   85
and I lay on my couch for ten days and ten nights.

   Consider whence came my love, lady Selene.

And my skin would often turn the color of fustic,
and all my hair was falling from my head, and skin
and bones alone were left. And whose house didn't I visit? 90
What old woman who casts spells did I leave out?
But it was no light matter, and time was flying by.

   Consider whence came my love, lady Selene.

And so I told the truth to my slave-girl:
"Come, Thestylis, find a cure for my cruel sickness.   95
The Myndian possesses me totally. Go then,
keep watch at Timagetus's wrestling-school,
for that's where he goes and where he likes to lounge.

   Consider whence came my love, lady Selene.

And when you know he's alone, nod quietly,   100
and say 'Simaetha summons you,' and lead him here."
So I spoke, and she went and brought the shiny-skinned
Delphis to my house. And as soon as I saw him
stepping over my threshold with light foot—

    Consider whence came my love, lady Selene.   105

I froze all over, colder than snow, and from my brow
sweat poured like damp dew,
and I couldn't make a sound, not even the whimper
children make when calling in sleep for their mother,
but I became stiff all through my fair body, like a wax doll.   110

    Consider whence came my love, lady Selene.

And with a glance at me, the heartless fellow fixed his eyes on the ground,
sat on my couch, and told his tale:
"Truly, Simaetha, you barely beat me—by no more than I
the other day outran the graceful Philinos—   115
in summoning me to your house before I came unasked.

    Consider whence came my love, lady Selene.

For I would have come, by sweet Eros I would have come,
with two or three friends, at nightfall,
carrying Dionysus's apples in the folds of my tunic,   120
and on my head a wreath of white poplar, Heracles' holy plant,
all entwined with crimson bands.

    Consider whence came my love, lady Selene.

And if you had received me, that would have been pleasing
(for I'm considered agile and fair among all the young men),   125
and I would have slept, if I only had kissed your lovely mouth.
But if you had sent me elsewhere and your door had been barred,
axes and torches would certainly have come against you.

    Consider whence came my love, lady Selene.

But as it is, I declare that I owe thanks first to Cypris,   130
and after Cypris, you second caught me from the fire,
woman, by summoning me, already half-burnt,
to this house of yours. And truly Eros often kindles a blaze
more brightly fierce than Hephaestus Liparaios.

    Consider whence came my love, lady Selene.   135

And with bad madness he rouses a maid from her chamber
and a bride to leave her husband's bed, still warm."
    Thus he spoke, and I, too quick to trust,

took him by the hand and drew him down on the soft bed;
and quickly flesh warmed to flesh, and faces grew   140
hotter than before, and we whispered sweetly.
And not to prolong the story, dear Selene,
the ultimate act was done: we both attained our desire.
And he didn't find fault with me nor I with him
until yesterday at least. But today the mother of Philista   145
our flute player and of Melixo came to me,
as horses were swiftly bearing
rosy Dawn from ocean to sky,
and she told me many other things, but also how Delphis was in love.
Whether love for a woman or a man possessed him,   150
she couldn't really say, but only this, that he
always toasted Love in unmixed wine, and at last he ran off
saying he would wreathe that house with garlands.
This is the story my visitor told me, and she's right.
For truly he used to come to me three and four times a day,   155
and he often left his Doric oil-flask with me.
But now eleven days have passed since I last saw him.
Mustn't it be that he has some other delight and has forgotten me?
Now with spells I will bind him; and if he hurts me still,
by the Fates, he shall knock on Hades' gate,   160
such bad drugs, I swear, I keep for him in my box,
having learned, lady, from an Assyrian stranger.
But farewell, lady, and turn your horses toward ocean.
I'll bear my longing as I have borne it.
Farewell, Selene of the shining throne, and farewell you other   165
stars that attend upon the chariot of tranquil Night.

Idyll 14

AESCHINAS
  Warm greetings, Thyonichus, old friend.

THYONICHUS
                              The same to you, Aeschinas.
  It's been a long time.

AESCHINAS
                  Long indeed.

THYONICHUS
                              What's the trouble?

AESCHINAS
  I'm not doing very well, Thyonichus.

thyonichus

That explains your thinness, then,
and your shaggy mustache and squalid locks.
You look like a Pythagorean who came by the other day,   5
pale and unshod, claiming to be an Athenian.

aeschinas

Was that fellow in love too?

thyonichus

I think so — with baked bread.

aeschinas

You're always joking, my friend. But as for me, the lovely Cynisca
maltreats me, and I'll go suddenly mad one day — I'm just a hair's
    breadth away.

thyonichus

You're always like this, Aeschinas, a bit impulsive,   10
wanting everything just so. Still, tell me what's new.

aeschinas

The Argive and I, and the Thessalian horse trainer,
Agis, and Cleunicus the soldier, were drinking
at my country place. I killed two chickens
and a suckling pig, opened Bibline wine for them —   15
almost as fragrant at four years as the day it was pressed —
put out onions and snails. It was a pleasant drinking-party.
And when the party was well along, we decided to toast
our favorites; only we had to name names.
So while we were drinking and calling out names, as agreed,   20
she said nothing, though I was right there! How do you think I felt?
"Won't you speak? Have you seen a wolf?" someone teased. "How
    clever," she said,
and her cheeks blazed; you could have lit a lamp from her easily.
There is a Wolf, a Wolf I say, my neighbor Labes' son, Lycus,
tall, soft, many say handsome.   25
For him she burned with that famous love of hers.
A faint rumor of this reached my ears once,
but I didn't investigate, so little use is my beard and manhood.
By then we four were already deep in our drinking,
and the Larissan was singing "My Wolf" from the start,   30
a Thessalian song, the wicked wit. And Cynisca
suddenly started crying, worse than a six-year-old
who longs for her mother's lap.
Then I — you know me, Thyonichus — I struck her with my fist
on the temple, and then I struck her again. She drew up her skirts,   35
and was quickly gone. "Bane of my life, don't I please you?
Is another, sweeter lover nestling in your lap? Go and warm
your other friend. Your tears are for him? Let them flow like apples."

A swallow gives morsels to her nestlings under the eaves
and flies swiftly off again to fetch more food.   40
More swiftly flew that woman from her soft couch
straight through passage and door, where her feet led.
A certain proverb goes "A bull once went through the woods."
Twenty, then eight, nine, and another ten,
today it's the eleventh. Add two, and it's two months   45
since we've been apart. I might have a Thracian haircut,
for all she knows. Now Lycus is everything; her door's open to Lycus
    even at night.
But as for me, I'm not worth notice or account,
like the miserable Megarians, in last place.
If only I'd stop loving her, everything would come out right.   50
But as it is, how can it? I'm like the mouse caught in pitch, as they say,
    Thyonichus.
And what is the cure for helpless love,
I don't know; except that Simus, who had fallen in love with a brazen
    girl,
sailed away and returned cured — a man my age.
I too will sail across the sea; a soldier's not the worst   55
nor the first, perhaps, but an ordinary sort.

THYONICHUS
I wish that your desires had turned out as you wanted,
Aeschinas. But if you're so inclined, then, as to go abroad,
Ptolemy's the best paymaster for a free man.

AESCHINAS
What's he like in other respects?   60

THYONICHUS
                                    The best possible:
kindly, a lover of culture, amorous, exceedingly pleasant;
knowing who loves him and, even more, who doesn't;
giving generously to many, and when asked not refusing;
a model of kingship — but you shouldn't always be asking,
Aeschinas. So if pinning your cloak on your right shoulder   65
suits you, and if you can stand firm on your feet
and bravely meet a bold soldier's assault,
go straightway to Egypt. We're all growing old
from the temple, and whitening time creeps hair by hair
toward the cheek. One must act while the knee's still supple.   70

Idyll 15

GORGO
Is Praxinoa at home?

PRAXINOA

Dear Gorgo, I'm home. How long a time it's been.
I wonder that you have come even now. Bring a chair for her, Eunoa.
Toss a cushion on top as well.

GORGO

It's perfectly fine as is.

PRAXINOA

Do sit down.

GORGO

How distraught I've been; it was difficult to reach your house safely,
Praxinoa: the crowd was so big, the chariots so numerous;   5
everywhere boots, everywhere men in military cloaks.
The road is endless; you live farther away all the time.

PRAXINOA

It's that absurd husband of mine—he went to the ends of the world
and bought a hutch not a home, to keep us from being neighbors to one
    another,
and he did it for spite, the jealous scoundrel, always the same.   10

GORGO

Don't say such things of your husband Dinon, dear,
with your little one present; see, lady, how he looks at you.
Cheer up, Zopyrion, sweet child. She doesn't mean papa.

PRAXINOA

The child understands, by the goddess.

GORGO

Good papa.

PRAXINOA

Well, that papa, just the other day we said to him—just the other day   15
then: "papa, buy soda and red dye from the store."
He came back with salt for us, our thirteen-cubit hero.

GORGO

My husband likewise: Diokleidas, waster of silver.
Five fleeces he bought yesterday, seven drachmas worth of dog hairs,
the pluckings of old wallets, all filthy, nothing but work.   20
But come on, fetch your wrap and dress.
Let's go to the palace of rich king Ptolemy
to see the Adonis; I hear the queen
is arranging a fine festival.

PRAXINOA

In a rich person's house, everything's rich.

GORGO

Things you've seen, you can talk about, once you've seen them,   25
to someone who hasn't seen them. It must be time to go.

PRAXINOA

It's always holiday for those who don't work.
Eunoa, pick up the spinning and put it back in the middle,
scratchface: weasels like to sleep in soft beds.
So, hurry; bring me water quickly. I need water first,
and she brings soap. Give it to me anyway. Not so much, thief.   30
Now pour the water. Wretched girl, why are you watering my frock?
Stop already; I've done as much washing as the gods willed.
The key to the big chest, where is it? Bring it to me.

GORGO

Praxinoa, this billowing garment is very flattering to you.
Tell me, how much did it cost to come down from the loom?   35

PRAXINOA

Don't remind me, Gorgo; more than two minas of pure silver;
and I put my soul into the work as well.

GORGO

But it's a success: it suits your style; this you can say.

PRAXINOA

Bring me my wrap and sun-hat. Arrange them on me
becomingly. I will not take you, child. Mormo, the horse bites.   40
Cry however much you like, but I won't have you maimed.
Let's go. Phrygia, take the little one and play with him.
Call the female dog inside; lock up the front door.

Oh gods, what a huge crowd. How and when are we to get through
this dreadful mob? Like ants, innumerable and incalculable.   45
You have accomplished many good deeds, Ptolemy,
since your father took his place among the immortals; no evildoer
sneaks up to someone on the street, Egyptian style, and hurts him,
doing tricks that men forged from deceit used to play,
each rascal as bad as the other, wicked pranksters, curse them all.   50
Sweetest Gorgo, what will become of us? Warhorses,
the king's cavalry. Dear man, don't trample me.
The chestnut horse has reared up; look how fierce he is. Eunoa,
fearless hound, won't you run? He will destroy the man who's leading
    him.
I am very glad that I left my baby at home.   55

GORGO

Take courage, Praxinoa. Now we are behind them;
they've gone on to their station.

PRAXINOA

And I too am regaining my composure now.
From childhood on I've been most fearful of horses and cold snakes.
Let's hurry; we're being engulfed by a huge crowd.

GORGO

Are you from the palace, mother?   60

GRAUS (OLD WOMAN)

                              I am, my children.

GORGO

                                                  Then is it easy to get

in?

GRAUS

The Achaeans got into Troy by trying,
my young beauties; all things are accomplished by trying.

GORGO

The old woman has gone off, having spoken her oracles.

PRAXINOA

Women know all things, even how Zeus married Hera.

GORGO

Look, Praxinoa, what a huge crowd is around the doors.   65

PRAXINOA

An awe-inspiring crowd. Gorgo, give me your hand; you too, Eunoa,
take hold of Eutychis's hand; watch out or you'll get separated from her.
Let's all go in together; hold onto us tightly, Eunoa.
Alas, poor me, my summer cloak is already rent in two, Gorgo.
By Zeus, if you would hope for good fortune, man,   70
watch out for my wrap.

XENOS (MALE STRANGER)

It is not in my power; all the same, I will take care.

PRAXINOA

                              It's really a crowd;
they're thrusting like pigs.

XENOS

                    Take courage, lady; we are in a good position.

PRAXINOA

And forever more then, may you be in a good position, dear man,
in return for protecting us. What a helpful and compassionate man.   75
Our Eunoa's being crushed; come on, you poor thing, force your way
through.
Perfectly done. "All women inside," said the man, locking the door on
the bride.

GORGO

Praxinoa, come over here. Gaze first at the broidered tapestries,
how light and graceful they are; you'll say they are gowns worthy of the
gods.

PRAXINOA

Lady Athena, what excellent women wove the tapestries,   80

what excellent artists, the men who outlined the drawings.
How realistically the figures stand; how realistically they twirl.
They have life within them and are not woven in. Man is a creature of
　　wisdom.
And Adonis himself, how marvelous he is, reclining on a silver couch,
with the first youthful down spreading from his temples,　　　　　　85
thrice-loved Adonis, loved even in Acheron.

HETEROS XENOS (SECOND MALE STRANGER)
　　You wretched women, stop that endless twittering–
　　like turtle doves they'll grate on you, with all their broad vowels.

PRAXINOA
　　Mother, where does this man come from? What's it to you if we twitter?
　　If you have slaves, order them around. You're giving orders to　　　90
　　　　Syracusans.
　　And let me assure you: we are Corinthians by descent,
　　like Bellerophon. We "babble" in the Peloponnesian manner;
　　Dorians are permitted, I think, to speak Doric.
　　Let there be no master over us, honey-goddess,
　　except one. I don't care: don't level off an empty jar on my account.　　95

GORGO
　　Silence, Praxinoa. She's about to sing the Adonis hymn;
　　it's the Argive woman's daughter, a very learned singer,
　　who last year also performed best in the dirge competition.
　　She'll sing something beautiful, I am certain. She's clearing her throat
　　　　now.

GUNE AOIDOS (WOMAN SINGER)
　　Mistress who cherishes Golgi and Idalium　　　　　　　　　　　100
　　and sheer Eryx, Aphrodite with the golden toys,
　　see what a fine Adonis the soft-footed Hours have brought you,
　　in the twelfth month, from ever-flowing Acheron,
　　the beloved Hours, slowest of the blessed ones; but yearned for,
　　they come to every mortal and always bear a gift.　　　　　　　105

　　Cypris, Dione's daughter, you made immortal
　　mortal Berenice, as human legend tells,
　　letting ambrosia flow into her womanly breast.
　　To please you, lady of many names and many shrines,
　　Berenice's daughter, Helen's peer,　　　　　　　　　　　　　110
　　Arsinoe delights Adonis with all agreeable things.

　　Beside him lie all the seasonal fruits that tree-tops bear,
　　beside him delicate gardens cared for in silver baskets,
　　and golden vessels full of Syrian perfume.
　　And cakes, all that women work on baking tray,　　　　　　　115
　　mixing blossoms of every color with white flour,

cakes made from sweet honey and those in smooth oil,
shaped like all flying and creeping creatures, are here beside him.

And green bowers laden with tender dill
have been built; and boyish Loves flutter overhead,   120
like nightingales that flutter on the tree
from branch to branch testing their fledgling wings.

O ebony, o gold, o eagles of ivory white
conveying to Zeus, son of Cronos, the cupbearing boy,
and the purple coverlets above, softer than sleep;   125
Miletus will say and the shepherd who herds sheep in Samos,
"The couch covered for fair Adonis is our work."

Cypris embraces him; the rosy-armed Adonis holds her.
Eighteen or nineteen years old, the bridegroom;
his kiss does not scratch; reddish down still lies upon his lip.   130

Now we must bid Cypris farewell, as she holds her man;
at dawn we will gather with the dew and carry him outside
to the waves crashing on the shore,
and with hair unbound, robes in folds at our ankles,
breasts bare, we shall begin the funereal song.   135

Dear Adonis, you travel both here and to Acheron;
this you alone can do among demigods, so they say. Agamemnon
did not undergo this, nor mighty Ajax, a hero of great wrath,
nor Hector, the eldest of Hecuba's twenty sons,
nor Patrokles, nor Pyrrhus when he returned from Troy,   140
nor still earlier the Lapiths and Deukalion's clan,
nor the house of Pelops and the Pelasgian nobles of Argos.

Be gracious, dear Adonis, in the new year too; now your coming
has brought us women joy. When you return, we will welcome you with
    love.

GORGO
Praxinoa, this woman is a creature of exceeding wisdom;   145
wealthy in the arts she knows, and truly wealthy in the sweetness of her
    voice.
Still, it is time to go home. Diokleidas hasn't been fed;
and the man is all vinegar—don't even approach him when he's hungry.
Farewell, beloved Adonis, and may you find us rejoicing on your return.

Circe Allusion (*Id*. 15.79)

This appendix explores implications of Theocritus's use of Homeric allusion in Gorgo's description of the tapestries as λεπτὰ καὶ ὡς χαρίεντα:

Πραξινόα, πόταγ' ὧδε. τὰ ποικίλα πρᾶτον ἄθρησον,
λεπτὰ καὶ ὡς χαρίεντα· θεῶν περονάματα φασεῖς.

(78–79)

Praxinoa, come over here. Gaze first at the broidered tapestries,
how light and graceful they are; you'll say they are gowns worthy of
the gods.

Scholars routinely acknowledge that the phrase λεπτὰ καὶ ὡς χαρίεντα (79) is reminiscent of Homer and usually cite one or more of the four Homeric passages in which the two adjectives λεπτός and χαρίεις occur together: *Od*. 5.231, 10.223, 10.544, and *Il*. 22.511. Some scholars claim, in addition, that the phrase alludes to a specific passage in the *Odyssey*. Thus Gow declares without argument and unequivocally (*Theocritus* 2.287): "Theocritus is thinking of *Od*. 10.222 [to 223]." Early editions of Theocritus also mention this specific allusion (e.g., Wordsworth, *Theocritus* [1877], Fritzsche, *Theokrits Gedichte* [1881], and Cholmeley, *Idylls of Theocritus* [1906]).[1] The questions that arise in a consideration of a possible allusion are, of course, difficult ones. First, is the audience just meant to perceive a general evocation of high poetic style, or, in addition, a specific allusion to Homer? Second, if the allusion is specific, what effect does such an allusion have in this context? Third, is the allusion meant to be perceived as intended by the character in the poem or only by the poet creating the character?

Both linguistic content and the specific occasion in which the phrase λεπτὰ καὶ ὡς χαρίεντα occurs in *Idyll* 15 (79) make it probable that Theocritus, qua poet, has the memorable Homeric passage in mind:

ἔσταν δ' ἐν προθύροισι θεᾶς καλλιπλοκάμοιο,
Κίρκης δ' ἔνδον ἄκουον ἀειδούσης ὀπὶ καλῇ,
ἱστὸν ἐποιχομένης μέγαν ἄμβροτον, οἷα θεάων
λεπτά τε καὶ χαρίεντα καὶ ἀγλαὰ ἔργα πέλονται.
                                        (*Od.* 10.220–23 O.C.T.)

They stood in the doorway of the fair-haired goddess,
and within they heard Circe singing with her beautiful voice,
as she went back and forth before a great immortal web, such as are
the light and graceful, and glorious works of goddesses.

At both *Od.* 10.223 and *Id.* 15.79, the adjectives λεπτά and χαρίεντα are plural in number, stand first in their lines, refer to woven materials, and are qualified by a genitive plural of θεός in close proximity. Further, in *Idyll* 15's passage, the qualifying clause θεῶν περονάματα φασεῖς (*Id.* 15.79) directly follows the adjectives, and in *Odyssey* 10's passage the words οἷα θεάων directly precede the adjectives.

Similarities of circumstance reinforce the linkage between *Od.* 10.223 and *Id.* 15.79 in several ways. First, when Odysseus's men enter the doorway of Circe's house, they see Circe and the woven materials she is working on her loom. So too when the Syracusan women enter through doors to the palace grounds, they see woven materials hanging before them (78). Second, brutish crowds jostle both Odysseus's men and the Syracusan women on their way to these respective realms. Around Circe's house, Odysseus's men encounter animals under Circe's spell (*Od.* 10.212–19). As the Syracusan women approach the palace grounds, they encounter a crowd Praxinoa describes as shoving like swine: ὄχλος ἀλαθέως. / ὠθεῦνθ' ὥσπερ ὕες (*Id.* 15.73–74). Odysseus's men are subsequently transformed into swine (*Od.* 10.239–40). Circe changes men into animals literally; Praxinoa, metaphorically. Third, Odysseus's men and the Syracusan women are both entering realms different from their normal worlds, realms that are magical and seductive in their allure.

By alluding to the Circe passage at this point in *Idyll* 15, the poet can evoke the hesitancy, fearfulness, and awe that characterize Odysseus's men as they approach Circe, as they cross that elusive boundary between reality and fantasy (one of them not to return). The Syracusan women are also crossing a boundary between the everyday world and the fantasy represented by the Adonia, and they will hear a hymn about Adonis for whom the seductive fantasy has become reality. Further, by heightening through the Circe allusion the fluidity of boundaries between mythic and everyday life, between Adonis's, Arsinoe's, and the Syracusan women's intersecting worlds, Theocritus also raises the problematic issue of how readers experience fictive worlds and subjects.[2]

Thus, the specific allusion to *Od.* 10.223 invites the reader to recall the whole approach to Circe's house and all the parallels in atmosphere and expectations with *Idyll* 15. In representing the liminal moment of viewing ceremonial tapestries, Theocritus also, by evoking Circe, conjures up an atmosphere of change, transformation, and magic.[3]

Details of subject, occasion, theme, and circumstance lend authority to Gow's bold assertion (*Theocritus* 2.287) that Theocritus specifically has *Od.* 10.223 in mind when he uses the phrase $\lambda \epsilon \pi \tau \grave{\alpha}$ $\kappa \alpha \grave{\iota}$ $\overset{\varsigma}{\omega}$ $\chi \alpha \rho \acute{\iota} \epsilon \nu \tau \alpha$. Gow, however, is the last of generations of critics to recognize the allusion as a specific one. Some contemporary scholars dismiss the fashion for citation of parallels that was a hallmark of edition-making in the nineteenth century, and with it they dismiss some important observations. This is particularly unfortunate in the case of the Hellenistic poets, since they are perhaps best characterized by their scholarly capacity for edition-making and their familiarity with parallels and precedents.[4] But if contemporary scholars raise the question of the significance of the Homeric phrase $\lambda \epsilon \pi \tau \grave{\alpha}$ $\kappa \alpha \grave{\iota}$ $\overset{\varsigma}{\omega}$ $\chi \alpha \rho \acute{\iota} \epsilon \nu \tau \alpha$ at all, they typically raise the question only to dismiss it, claiming that the phrase does not affect characterization in any noteworthy way, e.g., Horstmann: "Die homerische Formel $\lambda \epsilon \pi \tau \grave{\alpha}$ $\kappa \alpha \grave{\iota}$ $\overset{\varsigma}{\omega}$ $\chi \alpha \rho \acute{\iota} \epsilon \nu \tau \alpha$ (79) verleiht ihrer Bewunderung zwar den erhabenen Klang epischer Sprache, trägt aber im Grunde nicht viel zur Charakterisierung des Gesehenen bei."[5] I submit that, on the contrary, the phrase $\lambda \epsilon \pi \tau \grave{\alpha}$ $\kappa \alpha \grave{\iota}$ $\overset{\varsigma}{\omega}$ $\chi \alpha \rho \acute{\iota} \epsilon \nu \tau \alpha$ is used at *Id.* 15.79 in precisely those interests of characterization and of thematic design that contribute to the significance intended in the poem.

Notes

Introduction

1. Recent collections of papers illustrate the crucial attention now being paid to gender issues in classical studies: Helene P. Foley, ed., *Reflections of Women in Antiquity* (New York: Gordon and Breach Science Publishers, 1981); Averil Cameron and Amélie Kuhrt, eds., *Images of Women in Antiquity* (Detroit: Wayne State University Press, 1983); John Peradotto and J. P. Sullivan, eds., *Women in the Ancient World: The* Arethusa *Papers* (Albany: State University of New York Press, 1984); David M. Halperin, John J. Winkler, and Froma I. Zeitlin, eds. *Before Sexuality: The Construction of Erotic Experience in the Ancient Greek World* (Princeton: Princeton University Press, 1990); Sarah B. Pomeroy, ed., *Women's History and Ancient History* (Chapel Hill: University of North Carolina Press, 1991); Amy Richlin, ed. *Pornography and Representation in Greece and Rome* (New York and Oxford: Oxford University Press, 1992); Nancy Sorkin Rabinowitz and Amy Richlin, eds., *Feminist Theory and the Classics* (New York: Routledge, 1993); Léonie J. Archer, Susan Fischler, and Maria Wyke, eds., *Women in Ancient Societies: "An Illusion of the Night,"* (New York: Routledge, 1994). On the vital topics of ethnicity and class, see, e.g., Koen Goudriaan, *Ethnicity in Ptolemaic Egypt* (Amsterdam: J. C. Gieben, 1988); Per Bilde et al., eds., *Ethnicity in Hellenistic Egypt* (Aarhus: Aarhus University Press, 1992); Gayatri Chakravorty Spivak, *In Other Worlds: Essays in Cultural Politics* (New York: Methuen, 1987).

2. For a useful introduction to the area of postcolonial studies, see Bill Ashcroft, Gareth Griffiths, and Helen Tiffin, *The Empire Writes Back: Theory and Practice in Post-Colonial Literatures* (London and New York: Routledge, 1989). On patronage in ancient Greece and Rome, see Barbara K. Gold, *Literary Patronage in Greece and Rome* (Chapel Hill: University of North Carolina Press, 1987), 15–37. For a useful collection of papers on issues in Renaissance patronage, see Guy Fitch Lytle and Stephen Orgel, eds., *Patronage in the Renaissance*

(Princeton: Princeton University Press, 1981). On the tension between private patronage and public taste, see Thomas E. Crow, *Painters and Public Life in Eighteenth-Century Paris* (New Haven: Yale University Press, 1985).

3. Important recent books on the subject of aesthetic evaluation include Pierre Bourdieu, *La distinction: Critique sociale du jugement* (Paris: Les éditions de minuit, 1979); and Barbara Herrnstein Smith, *Contingencies of Value: Alternative Perspectives for Critical Theory* (Cambridge: Harvard University Press, 1988).

4. Since Theocritus, unlike the other two major Alexandrian poets of his day, Callimachus and Apollonius Rhodius, has left no evidence of employment at the library, this support may be less compelling in his case.

5. See Frederick T. Griffiths, "Home before Lunch: The Emancipated Woman in Theocritus," in Foley, *Reflections of Women,* 247–73; Sarah B. Pomeroy, *Women in Hellenistic Egypt: From Alexander to Cleopatra* (New York: Schocken Books, 1984), esp. 67–82; Kathryn J. Gutzwiller and Ann Norris Michelini, "Women and Other Strangers: Feminist Perspectives in Classical Literature," in *(En) Gendering Knowledge: Feminists in Academe,* ed. Joan E. Hartman and Ellen Messer-Davidow (Knoxville: University of Tennessee Press, 1991), 72–75; Kathryn J. Gutzwiller, "Callimachus' *Lock of Berenice*: Fantasy, Romance, and Propaganda," *American Journal of Philology* 113 (1992), 359–85.

6. See, e.g., Graham Zanker, *Realism in Alexandrian Poetry: A Literature and Its Audience* (London and Wolfeboro, N.H.: Croom Helm, 1987), esp. 19–22. On the trend toward mobility see, e.g., Paul McKechnie, *Outsiders in the Greek Cities in the Fourth Century BC* (London and New York: Routledge, 1989).

7. Matthew Arnold, "Pagan and Mediaeval Religious Sentiment," in *Essays in Criticism* (Boston: Ticknor and Fields, 1865), 174–99; Wahib Atallah, *Adonis dans la littérature et l'art grecs* (Paris: C. Klincksieck, 1966), 105–35; Peter Green, *Alexander to Actium: The Historical Evolution of the Hellenistic Age* (Berkeley and Los Angeles: University of California Press, 1990), 597–98; John J. Winkler, "The Constraints of Eros," in *Magika Hiera: Ancient Greek Magic and Religion,* ed. Christopher A. Faraone and Dirk Obbink (New York: Oxford University Press, 1991), 228; Ross Shepard Kraemer, *Her Share of the Blessings: Women's Religions among Pagans, Jews, and Christians in the Greco-Roman World* (New York and Oxford: Oxford University Press, 1992), 31–35.

8. P. M. Fraser, *Ptolemaic Alexandria,* 3 vols. (Oxford: Clarendon Press, 1972), 1:65; Green, *Alexander to Actium,* 169–70; R. R. R. Smith, *Hellenistic Sculpture: A Handbook* (London: Thames and Hudson, 1991), 82.

9. Charles Seltman, *Women in Antiquity* (London and New York: Thames and Hudson, 1956), 153–55; Carl Schneider, *Kulturgeschichte des Hellenismus* (Munich: C. H. Beck, 1967), 1:107; Pomeroy, *Women in Hellenistic Egypt,* esp. 71, 73, 93–94, 161, 164; Griffiths, "Home before Lunch," 247–73.

10. Jean H. Hagstrum, *The Sister Arts: The Tradition of Literary Pictorialism and English Poetry from Dryden to Gray* (Chicago: University of Chicago Press, 1958), 26–27; Zanker, *Realism in Alexandrian Poetry,* esp. 42–47; Green, *Alexander to Actium,* 246–47.

11. E.g., Stanley M. Burstein, "Arsinoe II Philadelphos: A Revisionist View," in *Philip II, Alexander the Great, and the Macedonian Heritage,* ed. W. Lindsay Adams and Eugene N. Borza (Washington, D.C.: University Press of America,

1982), 202 (with n. 26: "There is no reason to doubt the historicity of this event").

12. See also Joan B. Burton, "The Function of the Symposium Theme in Theocritus' *Idyll* 14," *Greek, Roman, and Byzantine Studies* 33 (1992), 227–45.

13. E.g., T. G. Rosenmeyer, *The Green Cabinet: Theocritus and the European Pastoral Lyric* (Berkeley and Los Angeles: University of California Press, 1969); Charles Segal, *Poetry and Myth in Ancient Pastoral: Essays on Theocritus and Virgil* (Princeton: Princeton University Press, 1981); David M. Halperin, *Before Pastoral: Theocritus and the Ancient Tradition of Bucolic Poetry* (New Haven: Yale University Press, 1983); Kathryn J. Gutzwiller, *Theocritus' Pastoral Analogies: The Formation of a Genre* (Madison: University of Wisconsin Press, 1991).

14. On Arsinoe's career before marrying Ptolemy II, see, e.g., Grace Harriet Macurdy, *Hellenistic Queens: A Study of Woman-Power in Macedonia, Seleucid Syria, and Ptolemaic Egypt* (Baltimore: Johns Hopkins Press, 1932), 111–16; Gabriella Longega, *Arsinoë II* (Rome: «L'Erma» di Bretschneider, 1968), 13–67, 127–31; Burstein, "Arsinoe II," 198–200.

15. On the marriage between Lysimachus and Arsinoe, see, e.g., Paus. 1.10.3.

16. On the marital machinations between Ceraunus and Arsinoe, see Just. *Epit.* 24.2–3.

17. On Arsinoe's career after returning to Egypt, see Macurdy, *Hellenistic Queens*, 116–30; Longega, *Arsinoë II*, 69–124, 131–34; Burstein, "Arsinoe II," 200–212. Hans Hauben, "Arsinoé II et la politique extérieure de l'Égypte," in *Egypt and the Hellenistic World*, Proceedings of the International Colloquium, Leuven, 24–26 May 1982, ed. E. van't Dack, P. van Dessel, and W. van Gucht, Studia Hellenistica, no. 27 (Louvain, 1983), 99–127, argues that Arsinoe's tenure as queen of Egypt was a period of profound changes politically and militarily, and he addresses the revisionist devaluation of Arsinoe's influence, as represented by, e.g., Burstein's judicious approach. But although the question of Arsinoe's political and military influence remains unresolved, there is general consensus on the importance of her cultural influence: "The extraordinary honors she enjoyed before and after her death are sufficient evidence of the prominent and popular role she played in the life of Egypt and its empire during her brother's reign" (Burstein, "Arsinoe II," 202).

18. See Elizabeth D. Carney, "The Reappearance of Royal Sibling Marriage in Ptolemaic Egypt," *La parola del passato* 42 (1987), 427–28 (with n. 18), who cautions that the scholia (on Theoc. *Id.* 17.128) credit Ptolemy alone with exiling his first wife.

19. Thus Arsinoe becomes called the second, since she was the second Arsinoe married to Ptolemy II; his first wife, Lysimachus's daughter, was also named Arsinoe and is sometimes referred to as Arsinoe I (I do not use her name to avoid confusion in the narration). All references to "Arsinoe" in the text should be taken to mean Arsinoe II.

20. On how the Ptolemies' practice of brother-sister marriage might have reassured Egyptian subjects, see, e.g., P. M. Fraser, *Ptolemaic Alexandria* 1:217; Carney, "Reappearance of Sibling Marriage," esp. 431–35.

21. P. M. Fraser, *Ptolemaic Alexandria*, 1:217; see also 2:366 n. 223. For a linkage of the title *Philadelphos* with Egyptian beliefs, see Ludwig Koenen, "Die

Adaptation ägyptischer Königsideologie am Ptolemäerhof," in van't Dack, van Dessel, and van Gucht, *Egypt,* esp. 157–61; idem, "The Ptolemaic King as a Religious Figure," in *Images and Ideologies: Self-Definition in the Hellenistic World,* ed. Anthony W. Bulloch et al. (Berkeley and Los Angeles: University of California Press, 1993), 61–62.

22. Cf. Ulrich Kahrstedt, "Frauen auf antiken Münzen," *Klio* 10 (1910), 261ff., who argues that coinage emphasizes the disparity in power between Ptolemaic kings and queens, since dead deified queens could appear on gold and silver coins, while living queens had to settle for copper. But if Arsinoe was deified during her lifetime, coins showing the royal siblings on the obverse, with *adelphon* inscribed above, and their parents Ptolemy I and Berenice on the reverse, with the inscription *theon,* could have been issued during Arsinoe's lifetime to celebrate the deification of the royal siblings—e.g., the golden octadrachm illustrated as 293a in J. J. Pollitt, *Art in the Hellenistic Age* (Cambridge and New York: Cambridge University Press, 1986), 272. For the view that such coins could have been issued during Arsinoe's lifetime, see Longega, *Arsinoë II,* 111; Dorothy Burr Thompson, *Ptolemaic Oinochoai and Portraits in Faience: Aspects of the Ruler-Cult* (Oxford: Clarendon Press, 1973), 56 n. 3. This view is strengthened by the recent redating of Arsinoe's death to 268. On the redating, see Erhard Grzybek, "La mort d'Arsinoé II Philadelphe," in *Du calendrier macédonien au calendrier ptolémaïque: Problèmes de chronologie hellénistique* (Basel: Friedrich Reinhardt, 1990), 103–12; see also Koenen, "Ptolemaic King," 51–52, esp. n. 61. After Arsinoe and Ptolemy II, Ptolemaic kings and queens customarily became deified during their lifetimes (P. M. Fraser, *Ptolemaic Alexandria,* 1:219).

23. On the historical and cultural significance of Arsinoe and Ptolemy's sibling marriage, see Carney, "Reappearance of Sibling Marriage," 424–35. For discussion of the political implications of poetic references to deities, see Frederick T. Griffiths, *Theocritus at Court* (Leiden: E. J. Brill, 1979).

24. Ath. 14.620f–621a = Sotades 1 Powell, *Coll. Alex.* (see discussion in P. M. Fraser, *Ptolemaic Alexandria* 1:117–18 and 2:210 nn. 203–5). Cf. Theocritus's *Id.* 7 in which a king imprisons a poet in a coffer (and *Id.* 13 in which Hylas meets a watery fate). For the dating of Sotades' execution to 266, see Marcel Launey, "L'exécution de Sotadès et l'expédition de Patroklos dans la mer Égée (266 av. J.C.)," *Revue des études anciennes* 47 (1945), 33–45. For the suggestion that an unflattering poem on Ptolemy II's mistress Bilistiche may have been "the final straw," see Alan Cameron, "Two Mistresses of Ptolemy Philadelphus," *Greek, Roman, and Byzantine Studies* 30 (1989), 301 n. 48 (cf. P. M. Fraser, *Ptolemaic Alexandria* 1:118, 2:206).

25. See, e.g., Sarah B. Pomeroy, *Goddesses, Whores, Wives, and Slaves: Women in Classical Antiquity* (New York: Schocken Books, 1975), 142–46; Barbara Hughes Fowler, *The Hellenistic Aesthetic* (Madison: University of Wisconsin Press, 1989), esp. 137–38; Green, *Alexander to Actium,* esp. 100; R. R. R. Smith, *Hellenistic Sculpture,* 79–83. On the Knidian Aphrodite, see, e.g., Pliny *HN* 36.20–22; for a convenient collection of ancient writings on the Knidian Aphrodite, see J. J. Pollitt, *The Art of Ancient Greece: Sources and Documents,* 2d ed. (Cambridge and New York: Cambridge University Press, 1990), 84–88.

26. On Hellenistic marriage contracts, see Claire Préaux, "Le statut de la

femme à l'époque hellénistique, principalement en Égypte," in *La Femme,* Recueils de la Société Jean Bodin pour l'histoire comparative des institutions, vol. 11 (Brussels: Éditions de la Librairie encyclopédique, 1959), 1:147–64; Claude Vatin, *Recherches sur le mariage et la condition de la femme mariée à l'époque hellénistique* (Paris: Éditions E. de Boccard, 1970), 163–80; Pomeroy, *Women in Hellenistic Egypt,* esp. 83–98 (for further references, with useful commentary, see 194 n. 4).

27. See Sarah B. Pomeroy, "Technikai kai Mousikai: The Education of Women in the Fourth Century and in the Hellenistic Age," *American Journal of Ancient History* 2 (1977), 51–68; Susan Guettel Cole, "Could Greek Women Read and Write?" in Foley, *Reflections of Women,* 219–45.

28. On women philosophers in the Hellenistic period, see, e.g., Bernard Frischer, *The Sculpted Word: Epicureanism and Philosophical Recruitment in Ancient Greece* (Berkeley and Los Angeles: University of California Press, 1982), 61–62; Pomeroy, *Women in Hellenistic Egypt,* 61–71; Jane McIntosh Snyder, *The Woman and the Lyre: Women Writers in Classical Greece and Rome* (Carbondale: Southern Illinois University Press, 1989), 101–8. See also Richard Hawley, "The Problem of Women Philosophers in Ancient Greece," ch. 4 in Archer, Fischler, and Wyke, *Women in Ancient Societies,* 70–87.

29. See, e.g., Pomeroy, *Goddesses,* 136–39. For an epigram that seems to represent a response to a female singer's public recital (Gow and Page's suggestion), see Dioscorides *Ep.* 2 Gow and Page (= *A.P.* 5.138) in A. S. F. Gow and D. L. Page, *The Greek Anthology: Hellenistic Epigrams,* 2 vols. (Cambridge: Cambridge University Press, 1965), 2:237. On Hellenistic women poets in general, see Snyder, *Woman and the Lyre,* 64–98.

30. *Idylls* 2 and 15 are Theocritus's only mimetic poems presented through female characters. On the functions of women's friendships in a patriarchal society, see, e.g., Robinette Kennedy, "Women's Friendships on Crete: A Psychological Perspective," in *Gender and Power in Rural Greece,* ed. Jill Dubisch (Princeton: Princeton University Press, 1986), 121–38.

31. Seltman, *Women in Antiquity,* 155.

32. See Griffiths, "Home before Lunch," esp. 247–48.

33. Griffiths, "Home before Lunch," 256.

34. Griffiths, "Home before Lunch," 256 (cf. 258: "What *The Syracusan Women* establishes above all is that nature has picked its housewives well, even as it has picked its queens"), followed by Kraemer, *Her Share,* 33–34. At its most extreme, this approach can result in a characterization of Alexandrian poets as "toadies" (see Green, *Alexander to Actium,* esp. 182 on Callimachus; cf. review by Jasper Griffin, "Decadence Revisited," *The New York Review of Books* 38.9 [1990], 57–62).

35. Ernst-Richard Schwinge, *Künstlichkeit von Kunst: Zur Geschichtlichkeit der alexandrinischen Poesie* (Munich: C. H. Beck, 1986).

36. E.g., in regard to the encomium of Ptolemy in Theocritus's *Idyll* 14, Schwinge assumes Ptolemy would not notice the playful ambiguity of the poet's use of the epithet ἐρωτικός (amorous), in view of Ptolemy's notorious philandering (*Künstlichkeit von Kunst,* 61); and Schwinge considers the second half of Ptolemy's description as εἰδὼς τὸν φιλέοντα, τὸν οὐ φιλέοντ' ἔτι μᾶλλον

(knowing who loves him and, even more, who doesn't; *Id.* 14.62) "rashly" self-referential of Theocritus's own relations with Ptolemy (65). See also Graham Zanker, "Current Trends in the Study of Hellenic Myth in Early Third-Century Alexandrian Poetry: The Case of Theocritus," *Antike und Abendland* 35 (1989), 88–91.

37. Green, *Alexander to Actium*, 241. Syme characterizes Augustan poetry similarly and perhaps draws on Timon's unflattering description of the Alexandrian poets to disassociate Catullus from the Augustan poets: "Catullus, however, could not have been domesticated, tamely to chant the regeneration of high society, the reiterated nuptials of Julia or the frugal virtues of upstarts enriched by the Civil Wars" (Ronald Syme, *The Roman Revolution* [1939; reprint, London and New York: Oxford University Press, 1960], 461).

38. Green, *Alexander to Actium*, 246. So too Giuseppe Giangrande, "Interpretation of Herodas," *Quaderni urbinati di cultura classica* 15 (1973), 92–94: "In sum: we must not forget that both Herodas and Theocritus skilfully make their characters say very silly and ridiculous things" (94). A greater and corollary danger of the "elitist" construct is that it can preclude readers from finding any pleasure in the poems: thus Green's summary judgment of the fictive women of Herod. *Mime* 4 and Theoc. *Id.* 15 contributes to his assessment of Herodas's poetry in general: "It is all very Hellenistic, and ultimately very depressing" (Green, *Alexander to Actium*, 246).

39. E.g., Halperin, *Before Pastoral*, 180: "The lovelorn teenager of Idyll 2, the mercenaries of Idyll 14, or the Syracusan housewives of Idyll 15, sketched with a wealth of telling and veristic detail, would have aroused in Theocritus and his colleagues a social response hardly differentiated from that evoked by the countrymen of the pastoral Idylls; both groups are sufficiently distant from the poet's own social environment to facilitate a sense of aesthetic detachment, yet neither is excessively exotic" (so too Halperin's remarks following Peter Levi, "People in a Landscape: Theokritos," in *Hellenistic History and Culture*, ed. Peter Green [Berkeley and Los Angeles: University of California Press, 1993], 135–36). See also Gary B. Miles, "Characterization and the Ideal of Innocence in Theocritus' Idylls," *Ramus* 6 (1977), 156: "The settings of the two *Idylls* [*Idylls* 1 and 15] may be quite different, but the mentality of the characters [*Idyll* 1's goatherd and *Idyll* 15's Gorgo] is the same."

40. Hellenistic women poets — e.g., Glauce, mentioned in Theoc. *Id.* 4.31; Anyte, who, like Theocritus, wrote in Doric; Nossis, an older poet — might have felt an especially keen interest in Theocritus's attempts to represent women's experiences.

Chapter 1. Mobility and Immigration

1. For a brief overview of the varied patterns of Hellenistic Greek settlements see, e.g., Simon Price, "The History of the Hellenistic Period," ch. 13 in *The Oxford History of the Classical World*, ed. John Boardman, Jasper Griffin, and Oswyn Murray (Oxford: Oxford University Press, 1986), 321–23. On the large number of cities founded by the Seleucids, see, e.g., Susan Sherwin-White and

Amélie Kuhrt, *From Samarkhand to Sardis: A New Approach to the Seleucid Empire* (Berkeley and Los Angeles: University of California Press, 1993), 143.

2. On the attractions of Ptolemaic Egypt for Greeks, see, e.g., Koenen, "Ptolemaic King," 29–30; on advantages of being considered Greek in Ptolemaic Egypt, see ibid., 35–36.

3. On how Ai Khanum, a Greek city founded in central Asia during Alexander's campaigns, maintained its Greek identity, see, e.g., Paul Bernard, "An Ancient Greek City in Central Asia," *Scientific American* 247 (Jan. 1982), 148–59; Green, *Alexander to Actium*, 332–34; Sherwin-White and Kuhrt, *From Samarkhand to Sardis*, esp. 178–79; F. W. Walbank, *The Hellenistic World*, rev. ed. (1992; reissue, Cambridge: Harvard University Press, 1993), 60–62.

4. On mobility and colonization during the archaic period see, e.g., Andrew Robert Burn, *The Lyric Age of Greece* (London: E. Arnold, 1960); John Boardman, *The Greeks Overseas: Their Early Colonies and Trade*, rev. and enl. ed. (New York: Thames and Hudson, 1980); Oswyn Murray, *Early Greece*, 2d ed. (Cambridge: Harvard University Press, 1993), 102–23.

5. For a discussion of Herodotus's account of city relocations in response to the coming of the Persians, see Nancy H. Demand, *Urban Relocation in Archaic and Classical Greece: Flight and Consolidation* (Norman: University of Oklahoma Press, 1990), 34–44. See also O. Murray, *Early Greece*, 260: "One long term consequence of the pressure of the Persians from 546 onwards was the increased emigration westwards of Ionian communities and individuals."

6. On economic effects of the Peloponnesian war, see, e.g., Simon Hornblower, *The Greek World, 479–323 BC*, reprint, with corrections (London and New York: Methuen, 1985), esp. 162, 170–76 (with references): "In the fourth century, by contrast [with the archaic period], mercenary service has ceased to be the near monopoly of the places just mentioned [e.g., Krete, Arkadia, Karia], because economic problems had now hit the great states of Old Greece as well" (162). Further, on the linkage of "the material debilitation of the old city-states" with the "Greek exodus to Sicily in the 340s," see Hornblower, *Greek World*, 241; Moses I. Finley, *Ancient Sicily*, rev. ed. (London: Book Club Associates, by arrangement with Chatto and Windus, 1979), 95. On the increase in political exiles during the fourth century, see McKechnie, *Outsiders*, esp. 23–29.

7. On Theocritus's connection with Syracuse, see, e.g., A. S. F. Gow, *Theocritus*, 2d ed., 2 vols. (Cambridge: Cambridge University Press, 1952), esp. 1:xv–xviii (with citations from Suidas and the scholia); Kenneth J. Dover, *Theocritus: Select Poems* (Basingstoke and London: MacMillan Education, 1971), xix; Green, *Alexander to Actium*, 240.

8. Thuc. 6.3.2 is our source for the traditional date of the foundation of Syracuse; for discussion, see A. W. Gomme, A. Andrewes, and K. J. Dover, *A Historical Commentary on Thucydides* (Oxford: Oxford University Press, 1970), 4: 198–210; J. B. Bury and Russell Meiggs, *A History of Greece: To the Death of Alexander the Great*, 4th ed. (New York: St. Martin's, 1975), 522 n. 8 (with references).

9. Gelon destroyed the city of Camarina and moved its population to Syracuse, where they were enfranchised. Also, he moved people from Megara and Euboea (Sicilian cities) to Syracuse, where he enfranchised the rich and sold the

poor as slaves for export (Hdt. 7.156). Gelon also enfranchised large numbers of mercenaries (Diod. Sic. 11.72.3). For discussion, see, e.g., T. J. Dunbabin, *The Western Greeks: The History of Sicily and South Italy from the Foundation of the Greek Colonies to 480 B.C.* (Oxford: Clarendon Press, 1948), 415–18; Demand, *Urban Relocation*, 46–50.

10. Hieron moved the populations of Naxos and Catana to Leontini, refounded Catana as Aetna, and repopulated Naxos and Aetna with selected settlers from the Peloponnesus and Syracuse (Diod. Sic. 11.49.1–3).

11. An ancient tradition of thought links the rise of the art of rhetoric in Syracuse with the land disputes that resulted from the population shifts of this time (Arist. *ap.* Cic. *Brut.* 46; for discussion, see Finley, *Ancient Sicily*, 61; Demand, *Urban Relocation*, 53).

12. See, e.g., Diod. Sic. 13.111.3–6, 14.15; for discussion, see Demand, *Urban Relocation*, 98–106 (with references).

13. See Plut. *Tim.* 1, 22, 23, 35. For discussion of Timoleon's restoration of order, see, e.g., Finley, *Ancient Sicily*, esp. 98–99; Hornblower, *Greek World*, 241. See also R. J. A. Talbert, *Timoleon and the Revival of Greek Sicily: 344–317 B.C.* (Cambridge: Cambridge University Press, 1974).

14. On Agathocles, see, e.g., Diod. Sic. 19.1–21.17 (select passages); Just. 22.1–23.2; Finley, *Ancient Sicily*, 101–6; Édouard Will, *Histoire politique du monde hellénistique (323–30 av. J.-C.)*, 2d ed., 2 vols. (Nancy: Presses universitaires de Nancy, 1979–82), 1:114–20; K. Meister, "Agathocles," ch. 10 in *The Hellenistic World*, vol. 7.1 of *The Cambridge Ancient History*, ed. F. W. Walbank, A. E. Astin, M. W. Frederiksen, and R. M. Ogilvie, 2d ed. (London and New York: Cambridge University Press, 1984), 384–411; Green, *Alexander to Actium*, 220–24.

15. For discussion of date, see Meister, "Agathocles," 405 n. 19 (with references).

16. Diod. Sic. 22. 13ff; Polyb. 1.8.3–9.8; Just. 23.4; for discussion of date, see Gow, *Theocritus* 2:305–7.

17. On Theocritus's relations with Hieron, see Gow, *Theocritus* 1:xvii, xxv, 2:305–7; Dover, *Theocritus*, xxi-xxii.

18. See Victor Magnien, "Le Syracusain littéraire et l'Idylle XV de Théocrite," *Mémoires de la Société de linguistique de Paris* 21 (1920), 49–85, 112–38.

19. On the genre of the mime, see Hermann Reich, *Der Mimus: Ein litterarentwickelungsgeschichtlicher Versuch* (Berlin: Weidmann, 1903); I. C. Cunningham, *Herodas: Mimiambi* (Oxford: Clarendon Press, 1971), 3–17; Winfried Albert, *Das mimetische Gedicht in der Antike: Geschichte und Typologie von den Anfängen bis in die augusteische Zeit* (Frankfurt am Main: Athenäum, 1988), with an overview of scholarship, 3–19. On the Latin tradition of mime, see, e.g., R. Elaine Fantham, "Mime: The Missing Link in Roman Literary History," *Classical World* 82 (1989), 153–63 (with annotated bibliography).

20. Plato reportedly kept a copy of Sophron's mimes under his pillow and imitated Sophron's style of representing character (Diog. Laert. 3.18). Duris too notes Plato's fondness for Sophron (Ath. 11.504b), and Aristotle links Sophron's mimes with the Socratic dialogues (*Poet.* 1447b9–11).

21. For discussion of evidence, see, e.g., Gow, *Theocritus* 2:33–35, 265–66 (with references).

22. Arist. *Poet.* 1459b31–1460a5.

23. For discussion, see G. O. Hutchinson, *Hellenistic Poetry* (Oxford: Clarendon Press; New York: Oxford University Press, 1988), 200: "We may surely suppose that in these poems [*Idylls* 2, 14, 15], and to a lesser degree in others, the associations with a lowly form of literature on the one hand, and on the other the dignity which must still attach to the hexameter, will enhance the interplay of the base and sordid with the grand and intense. Similarly, the dramatic framework was at the least not the standard one in hexameter verse: this will have sharpened the exploitation of narrative levels." It should be noted, of course, that Theocritus uses dactylic hexameter in most of his poems, whether mimes or not. Scholars generally agree that the interplay of the genres epic and mime adds special piquancy to Theocritus's poetry: see, e.g., W. Kroll, "Die Kreuzung der Gattungen," in *Studien zum Verständnis der römischen Literatur* (Stuttgart: J. B. Metzler, 1924), esp. 204–5; J. Van Sickle, "Epic and Bucolic (Theocritus, *Id.* VII; Virgil, *Ecl.* I)," *Quaderni urbinati di cultura classica* 19 (1975), esp. 50–56; but cf. Halperin, *Before Pastoral*, esp. 207–9.

24. See, e.g., the remark of a fictive "common man" at Theoc. *Id.* 16.20: τίς δέ κεν ἄλλου ἀκούσαι; ἅλις πάντεσσιν Ὅμηρος ("Who would listen to another? Homer is enough for all"; trans. Gow, *Theocritus* 1:123). For evidence of Hellenistic rulers' taste for Homer, see, e.g., Ath. 5.207c–d (Hieron II had the whole story of Homer's *Iliad* represented in mosaic flooring on his ship the *Syracusia*); Ael. *VH* 13.22 (Ptolemy IV had a shrine built for Homer). The Ptolemies sponsored new scholarship on Homer (on the work of Zenodotus, first head of Alexandria's library, see Rudolf Pfeiffer, *History of Classical Scholarship*, vol. 1, *From the Beginnings to the End of the Hellenistic Age* [Oxford: Clarendon Press, 1968], 105–17). Alexander the Great offered a model for his successors: on campaign, he reportedly kept a copy of Homer's *Iliad* under his pillow (Plut. *Alex.* 8), and through his mother, he claimed a genealogical link with Achilles (Plut. *Alex.* 2). On how literary papyri show evidence of Homer's popularity in the Ptolemaic period, see Colin H. Roberts, "Literature and Society in the Papyri," *Museum Helveticum* 10 (1953), 267–68. See also C. O. Brink, "Ennius and the Hellenistic Worship of Homer," *American Journal of Philology* 93 (1972), 547–52.

25. Themes of mobility and ethnicity are, of course, pervasive throughout Greek literature, e.g., Hom. *Od.*, Ap. Rhod. *Argon.* Athenian drama too explores social problems related to mobility and ethnic difference, e.g., Aesch. *Supp.* (Egyptian women seek sanctuary in Argos), Eur. *Med.* (a woman from non-Greek Colchis seeks justice in Corinth), Eur. *IT* (a Greek woman resettled as a priestess among the non-Greek Taurians finds a way home to Greece). Greek lyric poems also often explore themes of mobility and colonialism (notably Pindar's odes; also, e.g., Archilochus's poems). On Greek narratives of colonization, see Carol Dougherty, "Linguistic Colonialism in Aeschylus' *Aetnaeae*," *Greek, Roman, and Byzantine Studies* 32 (1991), 119–32; idem, *The Poetics of Colonization: From City to Text in Archaic Greece* (New York and Oxford: Oxford University

Press, 1993), with special attention to Pind. *Pyth.* 1, 5, 9; Pind. *Ol.* 7; Bacchyl. *Ode* 11; Aesch. *Aetnaeae.*

26. Cf. the description of Alexandria at the start of book 5 in Achilles Tatius's Greek novel *Clitophon and Leucippe.*

27. On how Theocritus exploits the contrast between the safety of the house and the danger of the street, see below. On the opposition between house and street, see also Jill Dubisch, "Culture Enters through the Kitchen: Women, Food, and Social Boundaries in Rural Greece," in *Gender and Power in Rural Greece,* ed. Dubisch (Princeton: Princeton University Press, 1986), 200.

28. On liminal encounters, see Arnold van Gennep, *The Rites of Passage,* trans. Monika B. Vizedom and Gabrielle L. Caffee (Chicago: University of Chicago Press, 1960); Victor Turner, *From Ritual to Theatre: The Human Seriousness of Play* (New York: Performing Arts Journal Publications, 1982). See also Edmund Leach, *Culture and Communication: The Logic by Which Symbols Are Connected: An Introduction to the Use of Structuralist Analysis in Social Anthropology* (Cambridge and New York: Cambridge University Press, 1976), esp. 33–35, 77–79.

29. On the road motif's association with encounters, see esp. Mikhail M. Bakhtin, *The Dialogic Imagination: Four Essays,* ed. Michael Holquist, trans. Caryl Emerson and Michael Holquist (Austin: University of Texas Press, 1981), 243–45; on the motif of meetings, see 97–99.

30. Bakhtin, *Dialogic Imagination,* 243.

31. On the threshold motif, see esp. Bakhtin, *Dialogic Imagination,* 248–50.

32. The scholia identify the men as troops because of their military cloaks. Gow, *Theocritus,* 2 : 268 n. 6, proposes that these men are dressed in their holiday best to go to the racetrack. Monteil follows the scholia and suggests that the troops are part of the celebration (Pierre Monteil, *Théocrite: Idylles (II, V, VII, XI, XV)* [Paris: Presses universitaires de France, 1968], 147).

33. So too later, when Praxinoa encounters horses on the road, she exclaims τοὶ πολεμισταί / ἵπποι (51–52). Gow, *Theocritus* 2 : 281–82 n. 51, citing the Byzantine scholar Photius, identifies the horses as racehorses "on their way to the hippodrome" (Monteil, *Théocrite,* 154, and Dover, *Theocritus,* 204, agree). But whether Praxinoa sees them as warhorses or racehorses, she warns "the horse bites" as she leaves her child home (40).

34. Name-calling strategies are also used in direct confrontations of power; verbal duels regularly occur on battlefields, in boardrooms, and on urban street corners. Chapter 2 includes a discussion of *Idyll* 15's encounter between the bystander and Praxinoa in terms of verbal strategies of aggression familiar from meetings of warriors in the Homeric epics: the bystander employs the same strategies of dehumanization that the Syracusan women have been using throughout the poem, for his insults turn them metaphorically into birds. Thus too, Gorgo's description of men as "boots" seems not dissimilar to monolithic descriptions of women as "skirts": the aim is not to denote specific kinds of males or females, but rather to emphasize difference from oneself.

35. William Blake's poem "London" is a modern example of the continued power of the motif of walking through city streets to evoke a crowded city and imbue it with a mood of urban alienation.

36. For example, unlike Theocritus's Syracusan women, who as resident aliens are trying to make a place for themselves in cosmopolitan Alexandria, Juvenal's Umbricius, a reactionary Roman, is abandoning multicultural Rome. One factor affecting these poets' representations is the issue of patronage. Chapter 4 (on patronage) will discuss in more detail how Theocritus's poetry relates to the Ptolemaic court. But for now, I just want to point out that, like *Idyll* 15's Syracusan women, Theocritus himself was trying to find a place in Alexandria: his poetry was written in part within a context of patronage by Alexandria's Ptolemaic court (e.g., *Id.* 17). Juvenal's poetry, however, situates itself outside the court.

37. For a detailed discussion of the gender dynamics of this verbal interaction, see chapter 2.

38. On the important topic of the relations between Greeks and Egyptians in Egypt, see, e.g., Alan K. Bowman, *Egypt after the Pharaohs: 332 BC–AD 642: From Alexander to the Arab Conquest* (Berkeley and Los Angeles: University of California Press, 1986), esp. 121–64; Naphtali Lewis, *Greeks in Ptolemaic Egypt: Case Studies in the Social History of the Hellenistic World* (Oxford: Clarendon Press, 1986); Willy Peremans, "Les Lagides, les élites indigènes et la monarchie bicéphale," in *Le système palatial en Orient, en Grèce et à Rome*, Actes du Colloque de Strasbourg, 19–22 juin 1985, ed. E. Lévy, (Leiden: E. J. Brill, 1987), 327–43; Roger S. Bagnall, "Greeks and Egyptians: Ethnicity, Status, and Culture," in *Cleopatra's Egypt: Age of the Ptolemies*, catalog of an exhibition held at the Brooklyn Museum (New York: Brooklyn Museum, 1988), 21–27; Goudriaan, *Ethnicity in Ptolemaic Egypt*; Alan E. Samuel, *The Shifting Sands of History: Interpretations of Ptolemaic Egypt* (Lanham, Md.: University Press of America, 1989), esp. 35–49 (ch. 3: "Two Solitudes"); Koenen, "Ptolemaic King" (for a useful survey of scholarship, see 25–26 n. 2).

39. This is the only mention of Egyptians in Theocritus's extant poetry. Cf. Callimachus's literary tendency to insult others through ethnocentric analogies; for discussion, see Green, *Alexander to Actium*, 172, 201, who cites *Hymn* 2.108–9's linkage of literary rivals with the Euphrates, described as carrying filth in its waters, and the *Ibis* poem (fr. 381–82), unfortunately lost, which evidently associated a rival with the ibis, a bird native to Egypt and even worshipped there, but with foul habits. On the later denigration of Egyptians as "others" by both Jews and opponents of Jews, see Koen Goudriaan, "Ethnical Strategies in Graeco-Roman Egypt," in Bilde et al., *Ethnicity in Hellenistic Egypt*, esp. 86–89.

40. On Callimachus's special interest in *aitia*, see, e.g., P. M. Fraser, *Ptolemaic Alexandria*, esp. 1 : 514, 2 : 774–76.

41. The phrase πάντα τελεῖται occurs four times in the *Odyssey* and two times in the *Iliad*, always in the context of prophecies coming true: *Od.* 2.176, *Od.* 5.302, *Od.* 13.178, *Od.* 18.271, *Il.* 2.330, and *Il.* 14.48. On the old woman's Homeric language, see Magnien, "Syracusain littéraire," 128; Axel E.-A. Horstmann, *Ironie und Humor bei Theokrit* (Meisenheim am Glan: Anton Hain, 1976), 32.

42. But see Anna Lydia Motto and John R. Clark, "Idyllic Slumming 'Midst Urban Hordes: The Satiric Epos in Theocritus and Swift," *The Classical Bulletin* 47 (1971), 41.

43. See, e.g., Motto and Clark, "Idyllic Slumming," 41–42; R. W. Garson, "An Aspect of Theocritean Humor," *Classical Philology* 68 (1973), 296; Heather White, "Two Textual Problems in Theocritus' Idyll XV," ch. 8 in *Essays in Hellenistic Poetry* (Amsterdam: J. C. Gieben, 1980), esp. 63–64.

44. For a seminal study of Homeric type scenes, see Walter Arend, *Die typischen Scenen bei Homer* (Berlin: Weidmann, 1933), which includes the arrival scene, expandable into a visit (28, 35). *Idyll 7*'s journey features the motif of the encounter; the more elaborated context of *Idyll 15*'s journey includes more of these type-scenes. But both poems show how mythic paradigms (and poetry) can help shape the contingencies of everyday life.

45. E.g., at *Od.* 7.18 Odysseus, when about to enter the city of the Phaeacians, meets Athena (in the guise of a Phaeacian girl fetching water); at *Il.* 24.348 Priam, when heading for Achilles' hut, meets Hermes (in the guise of Achilles' squire); and at *Od.* 10.276 Odysseus, when approaching Circe's house, meets Hermes in disguise. See Vladímir Propp, *Morphology of the Folktale*, trans. Lawrence Scott, 2d ed., rev. and ed. Louis A. Wagner (Austin: University of Texas Press, 1968), a seminal study of the folktale, which describes the standard shape of encounters with mythic helpers (84).

46. I am adding "comments on infrequency of visits" to Arend's list of elements in *Typischen Scenen*, since it seems to become pervasive in later literary representations of reception scenes. Although Griffiths, *Theocritus at Court*, 116, interprets Praxinoa's remark in *Idyll 15* on the infrequency of Gorgo's visits (Γοργὼ φίλα, ὡς χρόνῳ, 2) as a sign of mental stress, the conventional nature of her remark is underscored by Thyonichus's similar remark in *Idyll 14*, on greeting Aeschinas (Αἰσχίνα. ὡς χρόνιος, 2).

47. Calypso's paradigmatic reception of Hermes includes all these elements (*Od.* 5.85–104). Hephaestus's and Charis's receptions of Thetis include greeting, seating, and remark on the infrequency of visits (*Il.* 18.380–90, 421–25), as do Cephalus's reception of Socrates (Pl. *Resp.* 328c) and Aphrodite's reception of Athena and Hera (Ap. Rhod. *Argon.* 3.47–54).

48. For an example of how boy and dog can represent an Odyssean journey for a reader, see John D. Niles, "Patterning in the Wandering of Odysseus," *Ramus* 7 (1978), 57. Other dogs whose appearances have epic resonance include "old Argus" in James Joyce's *Ulysses* (1922; rev. ed., corr. and reset, New York: Random House, 1961), 90, where Bloom recalls his father's dying wish for his dog; and the artificial watchdog at the doors to Trimalchio's house in Petronius's *Satyricon* (29), which recalls the gold and silver dogs guarding Alcinous's palace in *Od.* 7.91–93.

49. E.g., Gorgo's exhortation to Praxinoa's son (*Id.* 15.13), θάρσει, Ζωπυρίων, γλυκερὸν τέκος· οὐ λέγει ἀπφῦν ("Cheer up, Zopyrion, sweet child; she doesn't mean papa"), which recalls two memorable Homeric exhortations to children. First, it recalls Eumaeus's and Penelope's greetings to Telemachus when he returns home (*Od.* 16.23 = 17.41): ἦλθες, Τηλέμαχε, γλυκερὸν φάος· οὔ σ' ἔτ' ἐγώ γε ("you have come, Telemachus, sweet light; . . ."). (The adjective γλυκερός appears as a vocative in only these two instances in the Homeric epics.) Second, it recalls Zeus's address to Athena (*Il.* 8.39 = 22.183): θάρσει, Τριτογέ-

νεια, φίλον τέκος· οὖ νύ τι θυμῷ ("cheer up, Tritogeneia, dear child; . . . "). (The imperative θάρσει appears in only these two instances in the Homeric epics.)

50. Thompson's comprehensive index of folk-motifs includes the headings "old woman as prophet" (M301.2) and "wise woman as helper" (N828) (Stith Thompson, *Motif-Index of Folk-Literature: A Classification of Narrative Elements in Folktales, Ballads, Myths, Fables, Mediaeval Romances, Exempla, Fabliaux, Jest-Books, and Local Legends*, rev. and enl. ed., 6 vols. [Bloomington: Indiana University Press, 1955–58], 5 : 47, 136). Narrators in epic tales commonly sum up encounters with helpers by describing the helper's departure — e.g., Menelaus on his encounters with Eidothea and Proteus (ὣς εἰποῦσ᾽ ὑπὸ πόντον ἐδύσετο κυμαίνοντα, *Od.* 4.425=570).

51. Gow, *Theocritus* 2 : 283 n. 66, excuses the use here of the epic word θεσπέσιος: "It is prevailingly epic and seems in Praxinoa's mouth a considerable concession to the metre employed by her creator, unless . . . used colloquially." Cf. G. J. de Vries, "Theocritea," *Mnemosyne*, 4th ser., 20 (Leiden, 1967), 438. Horstmann, *Ironie und Humor*, 33, agrees with Gow: "Ein solches Wort ist in Praxinoas Mund sicher nicht." Yet the use here of the word θεσπέσιος contributes to the general elevation of tone of the door-sighting, which is reinforced by Gorgo's use of the elevated verb θᾶσαι (cf. the ceremonial uses of the verb at 23 and 84). Further, the use of the term ὅμιλος reinforces the Homeric tone here: ὅμιλος appears regularly in the Homeric epics, whereas the term ὄχλος does not. In fact, ὅμιλος's only other appearance in Theocritus's poems is in the epic context of *Id.* 22.7 (*Hymn to the Dioskouroi*).

52. Paradigmatic mythic paired helpers in which the female precedes the male include Circe and Teiresias in *Od.* 10, Eidothea and Proteus in *Od.* 5, and Hecate and Helios in the *Hom. H. Dem.* See Cora A. Sowa, *Traditional Themes and the Homeric Hymns* (Chicago: Bolchazy-Carducci Publishers, 1984), 223. Cf. A. B. Lord, *The Singer of Tales* (Cambridge: Harvard University Press, 1960), 165. S. Thompson, *Motif-Index of Folk-Literature* 5 : 135, includes under the heading "old person as helper" (N825) the subheading "succession of helpers on quest" (H1235).

53. See, e.g., V. Turner, *From Ritual to Theatre*; and van Gennep, *Rites of Passage*. For a useful discussion of the metaphor of passage (in the context of surrealism), see Mary Ann Caws, *A Metapoetics of the Passage: Architextures in Surrealism and After* (Hanover, N. H.: University Press of New England, 1981).

54. Ἀποκλᾴξας can mean locked in or out: probably in this case the bridegroom jokingly ushers his bride inside the bedroom. See discussion in Dover, *Theocritus*, 205–6; and Gow, *Theocritus* 2 : 285–86 n. 77.

55. For further exploration of this topic, see J. Hillis Miller, *The Linguistic Moment: From Wordsworth to Stevens* (Princeton: Princeton University Press, 1985).

56. See Gow, *Theocritus* 2 : 50 n. 70: "It is sometimes hard to be sure how far they [ethnics] are names and how far descriptive adjectives; here the disposition of the words points to the latter."

57. On Cos's famous medical schools (and the mobility of doctors), see, e.g., P. M. Fraser, *Ptolemaic Alexandria*, esp. 1 : 343–46; G. E. R. Lloyd, ed. and in-

tro., *Hippocratic Writings*, trans. J. Chadwick, W. N. Mann, I. M. Lonie, and E. T. Withington, enl. ed. (Harmondsworth: Penguin Books, 1978), 14–16; Susan M. Sherwin-White, *Ancient Cos: An Historical Study from the Dorian Settlement to the Imperial Period* (Göttingen: Vandenhoeck and Ruprecht, 1978), 256–89.

58. On Ptolemy's use of Cos as headquarters, see Diod. Sic. 20.27; Édouard Will, "The Succession to Alexander," ch. 2 in Walbank et al., *Hellenistic World*, 54. On Cos's connections with Ptolemaic Egypt, see P. M. Fraser, *Ptolemic Alexandria*, esp. 1: 307, 343–46, 2: 462 n. 11; Sherwin-White, *Ancient Cos*, 82–137.

59. See Ulrich von Wilamowitz-Moellendorff, "Aratos von Kos," *Nachrichten von der k. Gesellschaft der Wissenschaften zu Göttingen, Philologisch-historische Klasse* (1894), 183–84; Gow, *Theocritus* 2: 55 n. 115; Dover, *Theocritus*, 96–97.

60. So Walter Headlam and A. D. Knox, eds., *Herodas: The Mimes and Fragments* (Cambridge: Cambridge University Press, 1922), 17–18 (on Herod. 1.11); Gow, *Theocritus* 2: 62 (on Theoc. 2.160) concurs. For discussion, see Sherwin-White, *Ancient Cos*, 106 n. 122.

61. For a more detailed discussion of the gender issues raised through *Idyll* 2's threshold and road motifs, see chapter 2.

62. On the linkage between Herodas's poems and the genre of mime (and on the connection with Sophron's prose mimes), see, e.g., Cunningham, *Herodas*, 3–17; R. G. Ussher, "The Mimiamboi of Herodas," *Hermathena* 129 (1980), 66–67. For a detailed discussion of differences in tone between Herodas's *Mime* 4 and Theocritus's *Idyll* 15, both poems featuring women viewing works of art, see chapter 3.

63. On Herodas's use of Hipponax's meter and dialect, see Headlam and Knox, *Herodas*, esp. xxviii; Cunningham, *Herodas*, esp. 12–15. Most scholars believe that Herodas thus oriented his poetry toward an exclusive, educated audience—e.g., W. Geoffrey Arnott, "Herodas and the Kitchen Sink," *Greece and Rome*, 2d ser., 18 (1971), 123; Cunningham, *Herodas*, 16; Giuseppe Mastromarco, *The Public of Herondas* (Amsterdam: J. C. Gieben, 1984), 95; Neil Hopkinson, ed., *A Hellenistic Anthology* (Cambridge and New York: Cambridge University Press, 1988), 233. But the question of Herodas's ancient audience remains problematic (see, e.g., Green, *Alexander to Actium*, 246: "I cannot share the confidence of most modern scholars that Herodas was catering to select *littérateurs*, capable of picking up the most recondite allusions, rather than to the popular audience that enjoyed a lowbrow mime. At the very least I suspect there was something in Herodas for both categories to enjoy").

64. Hutchinson, *Hellenistic Poetry*, 236, stresses the greater mixture of tone and style in Theocritus's (and Callimachus's) poetry.

65. On dating Herodas, see I. C. Cunningham, "Herodas 4," *Classical Quarterly*, n.s., 16 (1966), 117–18; idem, *Herodas*, 2; P. M. Fraser, *Ptolemaic Alexandria* 2: 876–78 n. 30; Sherwin-White, *Ancient Cos*, 94–95 n. 60.

66. Cunningham supports an identification of Metriche as a *hetaira* (I. C. Cunningham, "Herodas 1.26ff.," *Classical Review* 15 [1965], 7 n. 1; idem, *Herodas*, 57). But as Konstan observes, "there is no explicit support for this assumption in the text" (David Konstan, *Sexual Symmetry: Love in the Ancient Novel and Related Genres* [Princeton: Princeton University Press, 1994], 166 n. 64).

67. Giangrande, "Interpretation of Herodas," 82–84, points out that "the inhabitants of Greece regarded Egypt as a Greek ἀποικία [settlement]" (83) in his argument supporting Crusius's preference for the reading ἀποικίης rather than the second hand's ἀγροικίης in Herod. 2.2.

68. Stern's densely mythic reading of Herodas's *Mime* I takes as its point of departure this epiphany motif (Jacob Stern, "Herodas' *Mimiamb* I," *Greek, Roman, and Byzantine Studies* 22 [1981], 161–65).

69. Compare the beginning of Pl. *Resp.* with Lys. 12 (*Against Eratosthenes*). On the status of metics in Athens, see L. B. Carter, *The Quiet Athenian* (Oxford: Oxford University Press, 1986), 126–28.

70. So too Herod. 2.28–30. On the adoption of Greek names by non-Greeks, see, e.g., Headlam and Knox, *Herodas*, 85 n. 38 (Herod. *Mime* 2). On social implications of the use of dual names (one Greek and one Egyptian) in Egypt, see Bagnall, "Greeks and Egyptians," esp. 22–24, with references.

71. On the general topic of relations between Greeks and non-Greeks, see, e.g., Marie-Françoise Baslez, *L'étranger dans la Grèce antique* (Paris: Société d'édition «Les belles lettres,» 1984). See also Claude Vatin, *Citoyens et non-citoyens dans le monde grec* (Paris: Société d'édition d'enseignement supérieur, 1984). On cosmopolitanism's effect on social categories in the Hellenistic period, see too Julia Kristeva, *Strangers to Ourselves*, trans. Leon S. Roudiez (New York: Columbia University Press, 1991), 61–63.

72. On the function of the gymnasium in the Hellenistic period, see, e.g., Claire Préaux, *Le monde hellénistique: La Grèce et l'Orient de la mort d'Alexandre à la conquête romaine de la Grèce (323–146 av. J.-C.)*, 2d ed., 2 vols. (Paris: Presses universitaires de France, 1987–88), 2:562–65; Adalberto Giovannini, "Greek Cities and Greek Commonwealth," in Bulloch et al., *Images and Ideologies*, 270–73: "the gymnasium was really felt by the Greeks to be a symbol of their cultural superiority, a symbol they were not ready to share" (273). See also Peter Bing, *The Well-Read Muse: Present and Past in Callimachus and the Hellenistic Poets* (Göttingen: Vandenhoeck and Ruprecht, 1988), 75 n. 41.

73. For important recent work on the symposium, see esp. Oswyn Murray, ed., *Sympotica: A Symposium on the* Symposion (Oxford: Clarendon Press, 1990); William J. Slater, ed., *Dining in a Classical Context* (Ann Arbor: University of Michigan Press, 1991). See also Oswyn Murray, "Symposion and Männerbund," in *Concilium Eirene* 16, ed. P. Oliva and A. Frolíková (Prague, 1982), 47–52.

74. The regulations of Mytilene's statesman Pittacus against drunkenness illustrate the disjunction between the sympotic community and the democratic statesman: the penalty was double for a crime committed while drunk (Arist. *Pol.* 1274b19–23 and *Eth. Nic.* 113b30–33; Diog. Laert. 1.76). The repeated lyric exhortations to drink written by Pittacus's aristocratic detractor Alcaeus oppose the political values that would challenge aristocratic claim to hybristic (sympotic) license.

75. See, e.g., Oswyn Murray, "The Affair of the Mysteries: Democracy and the Drinking Group," in Murray, *Sympotica*, 149–61; idem, "The Greek Symposion in History," in *Tria corda: Scritti in onore di Arnaldo Momigliano*, ed. E. Gabba (Como: Edizioni New Press, 1983), 269–70.

76. For Aristotle's and Xenocrates' treatises on sympotic manners, see

Ath. 5.186b; for Aristotle's treatise on drunkenness, see Ath. 11.464c, 496f. Plato's dialogues, too, include discussions of wine's social functions (notably *Prt.* 347e–348a; *Symp.* 176c–e; *Leg.* 1.645d–e, 2.671b–674c). Also, Theophrastus's *Characters* repeatedly mocks undesirable sympotic behavior. On wine's role in social life, see too Ath. 10.419b–448a (with attention to wine's role in violence at, e.g., 421a–b and 443c–d). Cf. Xenophanes' well-ordered symposium (1 West).

77. For examples of drunken violence at Philip's and Alexander's symposia, see Plut. *Alex.* 9 and 50–51. For examples of luxurious display and ostentation at Philip's and Alexander's symposia, see Dem. 19.192–95; Plut. *Alex.* 54; and Ath. 4.146c, 12.537e–540a. For examples of extravagant Hellenistic royal symposia, see, e.g., Ath. 5.195d, 5.196b, 12.540a–c. See also Eugene N. Borza, "The Symposium at Alexander's Court," in *Archaia Makedonia, III: Anakoinoseis kata to Trito Diethnes Symposio*, Thessalonike, 21–25 septemvriou 1977 (Thessaloniki, 1983), 45–55.

78. Oswyn Murray, "Symposium and Genre in the Poetry of Horace," *Journal of Roman Studies* 75 (1985), 44. On the Hellenistic epigram, see Giuseppe Giangrande's fundamental article, "Sympotic Literature and Epigram," in *L'épigramme grecque* (Geneva: Fondation Hardt, 1968), 91–177.

79. Portions of this section (and of "Ptolemy" in chapter 4) appear in Burton, "Function," which also includes an overview of the history of the Greek symposium.

80. Francis Cairns, *Generic Composition in Greek and Roman Poetry* (Edinburgh: Edinburgh University Press, 1972), 172–73, briefly discusses *Idyll* 14's symposium setting in connection with the "symptoms of love" genre within which he is classifying the poem.

81. On mercenaries, see, e.g., McKechnie, *Outsiders*, 79–100. (See also his discussion of prostitutes, 152–54.)

82. On nonelite symposia, see Ezio Pellizer, "Outlines of a Morphology of Sympotic Entertainment," trans. Catherine McLaughlin, in O. Murray, *Sympotica*, 181: "probably the use of the *symposion* was not limited to aristocratic or tyrannical circles (therefore élites), but must have been practised also in wider strata of society such as the mercantile, artisan, or peasant classes."

83. Dover, *Theocritus*, 189. See Gow, *Theocritus* 2:252 n. 21. The theme of physical violence against women at symposia was traditionally popular among makers of sympotic vessels (see, e.g., Robert F. Sutton Jr., "Pornography and Persuasion on Attic Pottery," in Richlin, *Pornography and Representation*, 11–12).

84. See, e.g., Préaux, "Statut de la femme"; Vatin, *Recherches sur le mariage*; Pomeroy, *Goddesses*, esp. 125–31, 128–39; J. K. Davies, "Cultural, Social, and Economic Features of the Hellenistic World," in Walbank et al., *Hellenistic World*, 311–13.

85. The aristocratic Hipparchia, Cynic Crates' wife, reportedly attended symposia with her husband (Diog. Laert. 6.97–98). Also, during the archaic period, Pythagorean philosophical societies admitted women (Diog. Laert. 8.41); later the Cynics and the Epicureans admitted women to their philosophical cults as well. Women admitted to philosophical societies might presumably have dined with men. Further, Aspasia, when she lived with Pericles, hosted intellectual

gatherings attended by Athenian women with their husbands (see, e.g., Plut. *Per.* 24). If she had experience as a *hetaira* and as an importer of *hetairai* (Ar. *Ach.* 524–29; Ath. 13.569f), she would have been familiar with sympotic customs and might well have modeled her gatherings on them. Also, two women are specifically mentioned among Plato's disciples, and they may well have attended philosophical symposia, especially since one of them, Axiothea of Phlius, reportedly dressed in men's clothing (Diog. Laert. 3.46).

86. Cameron too submits that "we need not automatically assume that any woman present at a symposium was a hetaira," and he cites *Idyll* 14's Cynisca as an example (Alan Cameron, "Asclepiades' Girl Friends," in Foley, *Reflections of Women*, 277: "there is no question of the depth and sincerity of her passion for Lykos").

87. Cf. the unclear social status of *Id.* 2's Simaetha and of the rustic characters in the bucolic poems.

88. See, e.g., O. Murray, "Greek Symposion in History," 268–69.

89. Love toasts with unmixed wine are customary. See, e.g., Theoc. *Id.* 2.151–52; Callim. *Epigrams* 5 and 8; Meleager *Epigrams* 42 and 43 (numeration from Gow and Page).

90. It is interesting to note that Aeschinas's "we four" here excludes Cynisca.

91. M. L. West, ed., *Delectus ex Iambis et Elegis Graecis* (Oxford: Clarendon Press; New York: Oxford University Press, 1980), 85–86 (fr. 6) = Ath. 10.432d–433b.

92. Tyrtaeus 10.31–32 West: ἀλλά τις εὖ διαβὰς μενέτω ποσὶν ἀμφοτέροισι / στηριχθεὶς ἐπὶ γῆς ("Let each man, firmly planting himself, stand fast on both feet upon the earth"); Archil. 114.4 West: ἀσφαλέως βεβηκὼς ποσσί, καρδίης πλέως ("firmly planted on his feet, full of heart").

93. See Ewen Bowie, "*Miles Ludens?* The Problem of Martial Exhortation in Early Greek Elegy," in O. Murray, *Sympotica*, 221–29.

94. See the numerous Hellenistic epigrams, particularly the fictive tomb and statue inscriptions, that focus on archaic poets. For example, on Anacreon, see the following epigrams: Theoc. 15, Leonidas of Tarentum 31 and 90, Dioscorides 19, Antip. Sid. 16 and 17 (all numeration taken from Gow and Page).

95. The strong association of the carpe diem theme with the sympotic world continues in Roman poetry (cf. Hor. *Epod.* 13.3–6). On Horace's handling of the carpe diem theme, see Gregson Davis, "Modes of Consolation: *Convivium* and *carpe diem*," ch. 3 in *Polyhymnia: The Rhetoric of Horatian Lyric Discourse* (Berkeley and Los Angeles: University of California Press, 1991), 145–88.

96. Aeschinas's fellow celebrants included a soldier and a horse trainer, Aeschinas himself later resolves to become a mercenary, and his friend Thyonichus displays knowledge about soldiering opportunities. Ancient anecdotes highlight the issue of wine's value for a soldier: wine can hearten soldiers in battle (Ath. 10.429a, 433b–c, 442c), and drinking parties can offer tests of "military skills" (e.g., Philip's drunken sword-attack on Alexander, Plut. *Alex.* 9). See Oswyn Murray, "War and the Symposium," in *Dining in a Classical Context*, ed. William J. Slater (Ann Arbor: University of Michigan Press, 1991), esp. 83–87.

97. Cf. the enclaved dinner parties popular among philosophers (Ath.

5.186a–b). Thus, for example, Epicurus restricts a party to Democritean philosophers (Ath. 5.187b). So too Antipater later hosted a party at which all guests had to discuss sophism (Ath. 5.186c).

98. Simaetha only learns of her lover's defection through hearsay: a flute player's mother reports on Delphis's behavior at a symposium (145–54).

99. On "star-groups," see V. Turner, *From Ritual to Theatre*, 69, 72; idem, *The Anthropology of Performance* (New York: Performing Arts Journal Publications, 1986), esp. 45–46.

100. These gender issues are discussed in more detail in chapter 2.

101. On "what Freud called the inflation of the love-object" in *Idyll* 3, see Charles Isenberg and David Konstan, "Pastoral Desire: The Third Idyll of Theocritus," *Dalhousie Review* 64 (1984), 306.

102. For thematic connections between *Idyll* 7's Philinus and *Idyll* 2's Philinus, with attention to the *komos* theme, see Gilbert Lawall, *Theocritus' Coan Pastorals: A Poetry Book* (Washington, D.C.: Center for Hellenic Studies, 1967), esp. 99–100; Charles Segal, "Running after Philinus (Theocritus, *Idyll* 2.114ff.)," *Estudios clásicos* 26 (1984), 347–50.

103. On the appropriation of Greek customs by ambitious non-Greeks, see Green, *Alexander to Actium*, 315–16.

104. On the motif of the *komos* in Hellenistic epigrams, see Sonya Lida Tarán, *The Art of Variation in the Hellenistic Epigram* (Leiden: E. J. Brill, 1979), 52–114. For references to Greek (and Latin) literature featuring the *komos* theme, see Headlam and Knox, *Herodas*, 82–84 (on Herod. *Mime* 2.34–37). For discussion of the *komos* theme in Greek literature (with a focus on the *paraclausithyron*, the song sung during a *komos* at the beloved's door), see Frank O. Copley, *Exclusus Amator: A Study in Latin Love Poetry*, American Philological Association Monograph Series, no. 17 (Baltimore, 1956), 1–27.

105. On *Mime* 2's *komos*, see Headlam and Knox, *Herodas*, 82–84 (on 34–37). See also Ussher, "Mimiamboi of Herodas," 72:13–14.

106. The transcendent nature of the appeal to pride in the city goes beyond the Athenian Ariston's argument against Conon for committing drunken battery: πότερον δ᾽ ὑμῶν ἑκάστῳ συμφέρει ἐξεῖναι τύπτειν καὶ ὑβρίζειν ἢ μή; ("Is it to the advantage of each one of you that a man be permitted to indulge in battery and outrage, or that he be not permitted?"; trans. A. T. Murray in *Demosthenes: Private Orations*, vol. 3, *Orations L–LIX* (Cambridge: Harvard University Press, 1939), 161; Dem. 54.43 *O.C.T.*). On the commonplace courtroom strategy of linking a legal case with a city-state's freedom, see Headlam and Knox, *Herodas*, 78 n. 25–27, with references. On Cos's autonomy, as implied by Herodas's *Mime* 2, see Sherwin-White, *Ancient Cos*, 94–95.

107. Scholars generally reserve such praise for Rhodes, "the one Greek power that preserved complete and genuine independence in Hellenistic times" (Green, *Alexander to Actium*, 378).

108. For the displaced Themistocles too, ostracized from Athens, making his home in Asia, symposia and festivals functioned as reminders of home: he founded a festival of Pitchers (the Anthesteria's second day), celebrated a Panathenaea, and held symposia (although he reportedly lamented that his friends could hardly fill a triclinium [Ath. 12.533e]). See too Ar. *Ach.*, in which the dis-

placed farmer Dicaiopolis celebrates his return to his farm with an Anthesteria (960) and a Country Dionysia. Thus Aristophanes awakens in his audience, secluded behind city walls, nostalgia for a time when war did not disrupt festivals associated with the countryside.

109. On the cultural and social functions of carnival, see Mikhail M. Bakhtin, *Rabelais and His World*, trans. Hélène Iswolsky (Bloomington: Indiana University Press, 1984), esp. 196–277.

110. On this aspect of Cleisthenes' reforms, see Robin Osborne, *Demos: The Discovery of Classical Attika* (Cambridge and New York: Cambridge University Press, 1985), 189; Ellen Meiksins Wood, *Peasant-Citizen and Slave: The Foundations of Athenian Democracy* (1988; reprint, with corrections, London and New York: Verso, 1989), esp. 101–8. For a seminal discussion of city and country in ancient Greece, see Sally C. Humphreys, *Anthropology and the Greeks* (London and Boston: Routledge and Kegan Paul, 1978), 130–35.

111. See R. Scodel, "Wine, Water, and the Anthesteria in Callimachus Fr. 178 Pf.," *Zeitschrift für Papyrologie und Epigraphik* 39 (1980), 37–40. See also Walter Burkert, *Greek Religion*, trans. John Raffan (Cambridge: Harvard University Press, 1985), 237–42.

112. On the intellectual symposium in the Hellenistic age, see Oswyn Murray, "Aristeas and Ptolemaic Kingship," *Journal of Theological Studies*, n.s., 18 (1967), esp. 346–47; idem, "Greek Symposion in History," 270–71.

113. Although later Ptolemy IV reportedly founded a flagon-bearing festival, which Athenaeus likens to the Anthesteria, Arsinoe III (Ptolemy IV's wife) called the festival "a shabby get-together," according to Eratosthenes in his *Arsinoe* treatise (Ath. 7.276b–c). On Eratosthenes' *Erigone* and the Anthesteria, see also T. B. L. Webster, *Hellenistic Poetry and Art* (London: Methuen, 1964), 136–38.

114. For discussion of the linkage between mobility and friendship (in Athens), see Humphreys, *Anthropology and the Greeks*, esp. 234: "Increased spatial and social mobility in any society tends to weaken status-based obligations, such as those attached to particular positions in a kinship system, and replace them with more flexible ties based on similarity of interests and compatibility of personality."

115. See the reference in an early Hellenistic marriage contract (311/310 B.C.: *P. Elephantine* 1) to "those representing Demetria" (trans. Pomeroy, *Women in Hellenistic Egypt*, 86; for discussion, see 91–92).

116. For example, on social functions of ancient mystery cults, see Walter Burkert, *Ancient Mystery Cults* (Cambridge: Harvard University Press, 1987), esp. 30–65 (ch. 2: "Organizations and Identities").

117. On the rise of Dionysiac guilds, see esp. Arthur Pickard-Cambridge, "The Artists of Dionysus," ch. 7 in *The Dramatic Festivals of Athens*, 2d ed., rev. John Gould and D. M. Lewis, reissue, with supplement and corrections (Oxford: Clarendon Press; New York: Oxford University Press, 1988), 279–323.

118. On the topic of friendship in ancient philosophy, see, e.g., Jean-Claude Fraisse, *Philia: La notion d'amitié dans la philosophie antique: Essai sur un problème perdu et retrouvé* (Paris: Philosophique J. Vrin, 1974). On the importance of reciprocity in Aristotle's notion of friendship, see Paul Ricoeur, *Oneself as Another*, trans. Kathleen Blamey (Chicago: University of Chicago Press, 1992), esp. 183–

88. On the Epicurean ideal of friendship, see, e.g., David K. O'Connor, "The Invulnerable Pleasures of Epicurean Friendship," *Greek, Roman, and Byzantine Studies* 31 (1990), 165–86.

119. On Simaetha's social status, see Gow, *Theocritus* 2:33; see also Dover, *Theocritus*, 95–96: "Perhaps we are meant to imagine that Simaitha's father was abroad, that her mother was dead, and that no officious uncle was to hand; and perhaps situations of this kind were sufficiently familiar to Theokritos to need no explanation" (96).

120. Cf. Ov. *Ars Am.* 1.729–38. Cairns, *Generic Composition*, 171–73, proposes the generic category "Symptoms of Love" as a key to *Idyll* 14. Jacob Stern's article, "Theocritus' *Idyll* 14," *Greek, Roman, and Byzantine Studies* 16 (1975), 51–58, expands on Cairns's approach by showing how *Idyll* 14 tests love conventions against reality.

121. Much attention was being paid during the Hellenistic period to women's talk and women's communities. Herodas's mimes, especially 1, 4, and 6, represent women talking among themselves. Apollonius Rhodius's *Argonautica* features women's communities (Medea and her sister Chalciope at Colchis; Aphrodite, Hera, and Athena in Olympus; the Lemnian women). Callimachus's *Hymns* 5 and 6 represent women's communal religious ceremonies, and *Hymn* 5 also explores the friendship between Athena and one of her attendants, the nymph Chariclo, Teiresias's mother.

122. Cf. Callim. *Ep.* 16, an epitaph for Crethis, which suggests an immigrant community of Samian women among whom Crethis was a star speaker (πολύμυθος, 1).

123. On literary and social functions of talk, see Patricia Meyer Spacks, *Gossip* (Chicago: University of Chicago Press, 1986).

Chapter 2. Gender and Power

1. On the linkage of soldiery with citizenship, see Nancy Fraser, *Unruly Practices: Power, Discourse, and Gender in Contemporary Social Theory* (Minneapolis: University of Minnesota Press, 1989), esp. 126–27.

2. For a judicious discussion of ways Greek males could continue to live political lives in Hellenistic Greek cities, see Albrecht Dihle, "Response," in Bulloch et al., *Images and Ideologies*, part 4, "Self-identity in Politics and Religion," esp. 287–90.

3. *Idyll* 7 takes men out of the city into the country to participate in a private ceremony; *Idyll* 15 takes women out of the suburbs into the city center to view a public festival. By showing women becoming more publicly visible and men retreating into the private sphere, these poems can suggest the social changes gender roles are undergoing in the Hellenistic age.

4. On the granting of honorary citizenship to the itinerant poet Aristodama of Smyrna, see *IG* 9.2.62 (for discussion, see Pomeroy, *Goddesses*, esp. 126–31). On the rise in female euergetism, esp. from the second century B.C. on, see Riet Van Bremen, "Woman and Wealth," in Cameron and Kuhrt, *Images of Women*, 223–42. See also Brunilde Sismondo Ridgway, "Ancient Greek Women and Art:

The Material Evidence," *American Journal of Archaeology*, 2d ser., 91 (1987), esp. 405–9.

5. See esp. *P. Elephantine* 1 (311/310 B.C.), which ends with the statement: "This contract shall be valid in every respect, wherever Heraclides may produce it against Demetria, or Demetria and those helping Demetria to exact payment may produce it against Heraclides, as though the contract had been made in that place" (trans. Pomeroy, *Goddesses*, 128). The full text (English translation) and a discussion of this contract can be found in Pomeroy, *Goddesses*, 127–29; idem, *Women in Hellenistic Egypt*, 86–98.

6. Leila Ahmed, *Women and Gender in Islam: Historical Roots of a Modern Debate* (New Haven: Yale University Press, 1992), 29–33. On the traditional Egyptian belief in equality of the sexes, see Jean Vercoutter, "La femme en Egypte ancienne," in *Préhistoire et antiquité*, vol. 1 of *Histoire mondiale de la femme*, ed. Pierre Grimal (Paris: Nouvelle librairie de France, 1965), 119; Christiane Desroches-Noblecourt, *La femme au temps des pharaons* (Paris: Stock/Laurence Pernoud, 1986), 170–71.

7. Pomeroy, *Women in Hellenistic Egypt*, 173; see also David M. Schaps, *Economic Rights of Women in Ancient Greece* (1979; reprint, Edinburgh: Edinburgh University Press, 1981), 96–97.

8. The sympotic toasting ritual is pivotal in revealing differences between *Idyll* 2's and *Idyll* 14's male symposiasts. *Idyll* 2's toasting ritual, as reported to Simaetha, revealed Delphis's autonomy of her, his complete involvement in a promiscuous sympotic community (from which she is excluded). *Idyll* 14's sympotic toasting ritual separated Aeschinas from the sympotic community and revealed his obsession with Cynisca.

9. *Idyll* 2, more than the other two urban mimes, has a tradition of readers sensitive to important gender issues—e.g., Steven F. Walker, *Theocritus* (Boston: Twayne Publishers, 1980), 95–98; Griffiths, "Home before Lunch," esp. 260–68; Charles Segal, "Space, Time, and Imagination in Theocritus' Second *Idyll*," *Classical Antiquity* 4 (1985), 103–19.

10. For a useful introduction to this interpretative strategy, see Ashcroft, Griffiths, and Tiffin, *Empire Writes Back*, 174–77. See also, for example, Spivak, *In Other Worlds*, 241–68 (ch. 14: "A Literary Representation of the Subaltern: A Woman's Text from the Third World").

11. On earth-centered religion as a source of power for native peoples against colonizers, see Victor Turner, *Dramas, Fields, and Metaphors: Symbolic Action in Human Society* (Ithaca: Cornell University Press, 1974), 234.

12. See Kenneth J. Dover, *Greek Homosexuality* (Cambridge: Harvard University Press, 1978), esp. 54–55.

13. The name Delphis may itself suggest androgyny: Delphis occurs as a girl's name at Diog. Laert. 8.88. On sexual ambiguity in Theocritus's representations of Simaetha and Delphis, see also Walker, *Theocritus*, 97–98; Griffiths, "Home before Lunch," 266; Segal, "Space, Time, and Imagination," 110.

14. Included among the meanings of ἐλαφρός in Liddell and Scott's lexicon are "light, easy to understand," "light in moving, nimble," and "light-minded, fickle" (Henry George Liddell and Robert Scott, *A Greek-English Lexicon*, 9th ed., with supplement [Oxford: Clarendon Press, 1968]).

15. Simaetha was quick to respond to Delphis after she committed herself, but she regrets this in retrospect (138–40).

16. See Segal, "Space, Time, and Imagination," 105–6.

17. See, e.g., Burkert, *Greek Religion*, 151–52.

18. Theocritus emphasizes the crucial moment of Delphis's crossing the threshold, and the crossing of sexual boundaries implied in that act, by having the sentence cross stanzas as well (the sentence breaks at 104 and continues in 106 after the refrain).

19. Cf. Callim. *Ep.* 25.6.

20. The distinction between maiden and wife which Delphis disregards at the end of his seduction speech (the critical element for Delphis is that Eros causes both to leave their bed-chambers) is crucial in a Greek female's life-sequence, but Delphis's actions have denied Simaetha both these identities.

21. At the time of the symposium, Aeschinas's blame was directed principally against Cynisca, whom he accosted as ἐμὸν κακόν ("bane of my life," 36), but Aeschinas's retrospective description of the Thessalian singing "My Wolf" as κα-καὶ φρένες ("a wicked wit," 31) shows that Aeschinas now views himself as a victim of his guests' games too.

22. Line 47's anaphora, phonetic repetitions (κ's, ν's, and τ's), and syllabic balance (especially in the second clause) reflect Aeschinas's compulsive linkage of Lycus, nighttime, and an accessible Cynisca.

23. E.g., Ph.-E. Legrand, *Étude sur Théocrite*, Bibliothèque des Écoles françaises d'Athènes et de Rome, no. 79 (Paris, 1898), 138.

24. E.g., Stern, "Theocritus' *Idyll* 14," 56–57; Griffiths, *Theocritus at Court*, 114–15. For a seminal discussion of Theocritus's use of incongruous images, see Garson, "An Aspect of Theocritean Humor."

25. Cf. Euripides' *Medea*, where the nurse mixes the image of a bull with that of a lioness with cubs to describe Medea (187–88). In Theocritus's *Idyll* 26, the narrator uses the fierce, feminine image of a lioness with cubs to describe Agave as she roars over her son's head (21): Agave is the lioness who destroys her own cub.

26. On instances of this proverb elsewhere in Greek literature, see Knox's note on Herodas's *Mime* 2.62 (in Headlam and Knox, *Herodas*).

27. On the bull fable, see Gow, *Theocritus* 2:256 n. 43.

28. See Marcel Detienne, *Dionysos Slain*, trans. Mireille Muellner and Leonard Muellner (Baltimore: Johns Hopkins University Press, 1979), esp. 25–26. Examples of persons who escape to the woods include Atalanta, Artemis and her nymphs, Hippolytus, and Melanion (Ar. *Lys.* 781–96).

29. See P. M. C. Forbes Irving, *Metamorphosis in Greek Myths* (Oxford: Clarendon Press, 1990), esp. 63–68, 72–76.

30. On the wolf as savage outsider, see Forbes Irving, *Metamorphosis in Greek Myths*, 77 and 92–94 (Lycaon).

31. See, e.g., the 500 B.C. red-figure alabastron from Athens, Kerameikos 2713, depicting a man offering a courtship gift of a hare to a woman sitting in a chair and spinning (pictured in Alain Schnapp, "Eros the Hunter," in *A City of Images: Iconography and Society in Ancient Greece*, by Claude Bérard et al., trans. Deborah Lyons [Princeton: Princeton University Press, 1989], 82–83 [figs. 112–

13, with discussion, 82: "The woman spinning in this modest pose is a hetaira who, by identifying herself with the wife, adds greater worth and distinction to her seduction"]). See also the Adolphseck 41 pelike (= ARV 566,6), depicting on one side, a man offering a purse to a standing woman with a workbasket, and on the other, a man with a walking stick offering a purse to a seated woman (pictured in Eva C. Keuls, *The Reign of the Phallus: Sexual Politics in Ancient Athens* [New York: Harper and Row, 1985], 228 [plates 205–6], with discussion, 224: "If my reading is correct, the pelike juxtaposes a man with his wife and the same man with a hetaera"; but cf. Martin F. Kilmer, *Greek Erotica* [London: Duckworth, 1993], 166–67: "It may also be that, for the purposes of such scenes as this, things were deliberately left ambiguous: the viewer could think of these as courting scenes taking place between free Athenians, or business transactions between prostitute and client; or there may have been other interpretations"). See also Makron's cup (Toledo, Ohio, 72.55), depicting on the outside band, men soliciting women, and on the tondo, a woman making offerings at an altar (pictured in Keuls, *Reign of the Phallus*, 167 [the outside band: plates 141–42], with discussion, 167–68; 227 [the tondo: plate 204], with discussion of the juxtaposition of tondo and outside band, 223–24). On difficulties distinguishing the status of women depicted on erotic Greek vases, see Kilmer, *Greek Erotica*, 159–67. For a discussion of Greek epigrams linking weavers and *hetairai* (as well as weaving and love), see Tarán, *Art of Variation*, 115–31.

32. On the blurring of female social categories, see Jasper Griffin, *Latin Poets and Roman Life* (1985; reprint, Chapel Hill: University of North Carolina Press, 1986), 27–28. On Roman wives acting as courtesans, see R. O. A. M. Lyne, *The Latin Love Poets: From Catullus to Horace* (Oxford: Clarendon Press, 1980), 13–16. On the inclusion of respectable women at Roman symposia, see O. Murray, "Symposium and Genre," 48–49.

33. For discussion of Cat. 68's use of the marriage motif and the Laodamia story in redescribing his relationship with the unfaithful Lesbia, see, e.g., Lyne, *Latin Love Poets*, 56–60. On Tib. 1.5.21–34, see Lyne, *Latin Love Poets*, 160–63.

34. Gow, *Theocritus* 2 : 253 n. 33.

35. For an evocative discussion of how attention to the literary echoes of Sappho and Homer can enhance the reader's experience of Theocritus's *Idyll* 2, see Charles Segal, "Underreading and Intertextuality: Sappho, Simaetha, and Odysseus in Theocritus' Second Idyll," *Arethusa* 17 (1984), 201–9.

36. In both cases, the tears initiate a process of physical violence leading to the loss of the subordinated partner: Cynisca's tears prompt Aeschinas to assail her with his fists, and she leaves the symposium (and his life); Patroclus's tears prompt Achilles to send him into battle, where Patroclus is killed.

37. Gow, *Theocritus* 1 : 107. I use the translation "brazen" here for euphony's sake, with the understanding that, as Dover, *Theocritus* 195 n. 53, points out, "χαλκός and its derivatives are not used metaphorically in the sense of English 'brazen.'" He suggests as possible meanings here "sunburnt" or "whom you could get for a bronze coin." ("Brazen," of course, can also mean "brass-colored.")

38. Thwarted lovers elsewhere in Theocritus's poems try other cures for disappointed love—for example, song (e.g., *Ids.* 10, 11) and suicide (e.g., *Ids.* 2, 3).

39. See Gow, *Theocritus* 2:249 n. 8. See also Headlam and Knox, *Herodas*, 183 (*Mime* 4.20). Gow also notes Archidamus's daughter Κυνίσκα (see in addition to Plut. *Ages.* 20; Paus. 3.8.1; 6.1.6; *A.P.* 13.16).

40. Cf. Lucian's later use of the name Κυνίσκος in the meaning "Little Cynic" for characters in the satiric dialogues *Zeus Elenchomenos* ("Zeus Refuted") and *Kataplous* ("The Voyage Down").

41. On the sexual symbolism of the snake, see, e.g., Burkert, *Ancient Mystery Cults*, 106.

42. Praxinoa is expressing a Callimachean sentiment, insofar as pigs can represent mud and filth; cf. the literary values expressed at the close of Callim. *Hymn* 2 (when Apollo rejects what he describes as the filthy Assyrian river, full of refuse, in favor of the pure stream, 108–12). Callimachus also scorns the crowded road, *Ep.* 28.1–2.

43. The adjective δειλός (wretched) often connotes compassion. See, e.g., Odysseus's self-description at *Od.* 5.299: ἐγὼ δειλός.

44. By using significant names that are not uncommon, Theocritus can reinforce characterizations without unduly interrupting the narrative. On the use of significant names in Homer's *Odyssey*, see, e.g., Norman Austin, "Name Magic in the Odyssey," *California Studies in Classical Antiquity* 5 (1972), 1–19.

45. On Herodas's use of appropriate names, see J. C. Austin, "The Significant Name in Herondas," *Transactions and Proceedings of the American Philological Association* 53 (1922), 16–17. On realistic portraiture, see, e.g., John Onians, *Art and Thought in the Hellenistic Age: The Greek World View, 350–50 BC* (London: Thames and Hudson, 1979), esp. 38–50; Christine M. Havelock, *Hellenistic Art*, 2d ed. (New York: W. W. Norton, 1981), esp. 141–47; Pollitt, *Art in the Hellenistic Age*, esp. 19–23.

46. Praxinoa's name links πρᾶξις (business) and νόος (mind). The verb πράσσω can mean "*achieve, manage* affairs, *do* business." (These definitions are all taken from Liddell and Scott, *Lexicon*.)

47. The name Γοργώ is also used to denote the Gorgon, a legendary female monster (e.g., Medusa), whose gaze turns men to stone. For discussion of the Gorgon, see, e.g., Jean-Pierre Vernant, "Death in the Eyes: Gorgo, Figure of the *Other*," ch. 6 in *Mortals and Immortals: Collected Essays*, ed. Froma I. Zeitlin (Princeton: Princeton University Press, 1991), 111–38.

48. If Theocritus were a fan of puns, one could imagine Praxinoa's abuse of Eunoa underscoring the household's lack of well-being, for a synergy of the names Praxinoa and Eunoa produces happiness: τὸ εὖ πράττειν (a definition endorsed by Aristotle in *Eth. Nic.* 1095a19–20).

49. This practice, popular among philosophers seeking hidden meanings in Homer's epics, was criticized in Plato's *Republic*, but gained momentum during the Hellenistic period, especially among Stoics and philosophers interpreting scripture (see David Dawson, *Allegorical Readers and Cultural Revision in Ancient Alexandria* [Berkeley and Los Angeles: University of California Press, 1992]).

50. See P. M. Fraser, *Ptolemaic Alexandria* 1:241–43.

51. The surprise of *Idyll* 15's hostile encounter between the bystander and the women might be intensified by the expectable literary motif that women who go

to festivals are often seduced (e.g., in Eur. *Ion*, new comedy in general, and Theocritus's *Idyll* 2). The Adonia in particular is a favorite literary occasion for seductions (e.g., Men. *Sam.* 41; cf. Theoc. *Idyll* 24.50, Theophr. *Char.* 2.4, Ar. *Lys.*). Before meeting the hostile bystander, Praxinoa thinks of erotic proverbs (the first concerning Hera and Zeus; the second, an anonymous bridegroom) after each encounter on the road to the Adonia. Some audience members might even expect that a seductive encounter would be the main concern of the poem. In *Idyll* 2, for example, the festival is not described, but simply provides an occasion for Simaetha to fall in love with Delphis. A hostile encounter between men and women at a festival, however, is not necessarily incongruous. An exchange of abusive insults is a traditional feature of such festivals as Demeter's at Pellene (Paus. 7.27.10) and Apollo's at Anaphe (Ap. Rhod. *Argon.* 4.1726). Apollodorus (1.5.1) attributes the traditional jesting at the festival of the Thesmophoria to the incident of Demeter's arrival at the house of Celeus, when Iambe jests to make her smile (*Hom. H. Dem.* 202–4). In *Idyll* 15, Praxinoa's invocations of μᾶ (89) (possibly Demeter) and Μελιτῶδες (94) (whom the scholia identify as Persephone) in reply to insults from a man perhaps recall a ritual of abusive exchanges between men and women, typical of Demeter's festival (for the scholia, see C. Wendel, *Scholia in Theocritum Vetera; Scholia in Technopaegnia Scripta* [Leipzig: B. G. Teubner, 1914], 313).

52. E.g., Arist. *Pol.* 1259a–1260b. Cf. Arist. *Poet.* 1454a22–24 on gender and decorum. The patriarchal tradition's exclusivity, represented by Aristotle, was already being challenged in the fourth century B.C. when Epicureans and Cynics began to allow women and slaves to participate in the philosophical experience.

53. White argues that Praxinoa is describing the Adonis statue rather than an Adonis figure on the tapestries (Heather White, "Theocritus' 'Adonis Song,'" *Museum Philologum Londiniense* 4 (1981), 199–203; so too Schwinge, *Künstlichkeit von Kunst*, 57 n. 27). In this discussion, I follow Gow and Dover, who consider that Praxinoa is here describing an Adonis figure represented on the tapestries (A. S. F. Gow, "The *Adoniazusae* of Theocritus," *Journal of Hellenic Studies* 58 [1938], 198–99; idem, *Theocritus* 2:265, 288 n. 84f.; Dover, *Theocritus*, 206).

54. Cf. young Theseus who, dressed in a long tunic and with hair plaited, on his arrival in Athens was mocked by builders, who called him a girl ripe for marriage (Paus. 1.19.1).

55. Praxinoa is emphasizing a central aspect of Adonis's myth. See Ov. *Met.* 10.519–739 for a detailed version of the story of Adonis's disappointed manhood.

56. Later in this chapter, I discuss the issue of the homoerotic gaze implicit in Theocritus's representation of Praxinoa's response to Adonis. The main issue under consideration here is what a male bystander might find transgressive in Praxinoa's speech.

57. On the problematic issue of the bystander's use of Doric, see, e.g.: Hermann Fritzsche, *Theokrits Gedichte*, 3d ed., rev. by Eduard Hiller (Leipzig: B. G. Teubner, 1881), 187; W. C. Helmbold, "Theocritus 15.87–88," *Classical Philology* 46 (1951), 116; Gow, *Theocritus* 2:290 n. 88; Monteil, *Théocrite*, 160; Dover, *Theocritus*, 207; Gianfranco Fabiano, "Fluctuation in Theocritus' Style," *Greek, Roman, and Byzantine Studies* 12 (1971), 521–22; Horstmann, *Ironie und Humor*,

37; C. J. Ruijgh, "Le dorien de Théocrite: Dialecte cyrénien d'Alexandrie et d'Égypte," *Mnemosyne*, 4th ser., 37 (1984), 79; Zanker, *Realism in Alexandrian Poetry*, 164–65.

58. The exclamation μᾶ is used primarily by women: cf. Herodas 1.85 and 4.20. Melitodes may well be Persephone, a goddess associated with Syracusan women, according to the scholia to line 14 (Wendel, *Scholia*, 307).

59. Monteil, *Théocrite*, 160, instead suggests that the exclamation μᾶ serves to confirm the bystander's characterization of her speech: "Ce monosyllabe très ouvert fournit au reproche πλατειάσδοισαι une justification immédiate."

60. Gow, *Theocritus* 2:291 n. 95.

61. Dover, *Theocritus*, 208 n. 95.

62. Praxinoa's use of Bellerophon in this context seems to recall a memorable incident in Homer's *Iliad*, book 6 (144–211), when Glaucus, challenged by Diomedes for his identity on the battlefield, defiantly claims Bellerophon as heroic ancestor (for this suggestion, see also Horstmann, *Ironie und Humor*, 38 n. 94).

63. As Winkler explains, "To participate even passively in the public arena the minority must be bilingual; the majority feels no such need to learn the minority's language" (John J. Winkler, "Double Consciousness in Sappho's Lyrics," in *The Constraints of Desire: The Anthropology of Sex and Gender in Ancient Greece* [New York: Routledge, 1990], 174–76 [quote taken from 174–75]). See also Jean Baker Miller, *Toward a New Psychology of Women* (Boston: Beacon Press, 1976), esp. 10: "Subordinates . . . know much more about the dominants than vice versa."

64. For the tale of Proetus's wife and young Bellerophon, see, e.g., Hom. *Il.* 6.160–70.

65. On variation as a stylistic trait of Theocritus's poetry, see, e.g., Fabiano, "Fluctuation in Theocritus' Style," 517–37: "As for Theocritus, I am inclined to think that variation of the level of style, which appears not only in the pastoral but in almost every idyll, is one of the main agents of poetic unification" (537).

66. Cf. how Catullus puts down Egnatius in *Poem* 39.

67. Callim. *Hymn* 2.108–9.

68. On genre and style fluctuation, see, e.g., Fabiano, "Fluctuation in Theocritus' Style"; Legrand, *Étude sur Théocrite*, 413–20; Ludwig Deubner, "Ein Stilprinzip hellenistischer Dichtkunst," *Neue Jahrbücher für das klassische Altertum, Geschichte und deutsche Literatur und für Pädagogik* 47 (1921), 361–78.

69. See Pomeroy, "Technikai kai Mousikai," 52–53 and 64 n. 9; idem, *Women in Hellenistic Egypt*, esp. 60, 62 (plate 7), 71–72.

70. See, e.g., *P. Elephantine* 1 (an early Hellenistic marriage contract, dated to 311/310 B.C., available in translation in Pomeroy, *Goddesses*, 127–28; idem, *Women in Hellenistic Egypt*, 86–87).

71. This theme might have seemed uncomfortably familiar to audience members at the *Medea's* first performance (431) who had witnessed the passing of Pericles' citizenship law of 451/450, which required that a mother of Athenian citizens be an Athenian herself and thus encouraged Athenian men to discard alien wives (Arist. *Ath. Pol.* 26.4; for discussion of Pericles' law, see, e.g., A. R. W. Harrison, *The Law of Athens*, vol. 1, *The Family and Property* [Oxford: Clarendon Press, 1968], 25–29; Pomeroy, *Goddesses*, 66–70).

72. On the unusual placement of Hecate at Medea's hearth, see Denys L. Page, ed., *Euripides: Medea* (1938; reprint with corrections, Oxford: Clarendon Press, 1952), 102 n. 397.

73. For a discussion of Simaetha's spell as "therapeutic self-expression," see Hugh Parry, "Magic and the Songstress: Theocritus Idyll 2," *Illinois Classical Studies* 13 (1988), 43–55.

74. So, e.g., Anacreon fr. 356, 383, 409 *P.M.G.*; Ath. 11.475c–f. For other citations, in addition to Ath., see Gow, *Theocritus* 2:36 n. 2, who notes that Simaetha's κελέβα "is probably for the libation (43)."

75. On the identification of this bronze rhomb with the magic wheel of the refrain, see Heather White, "Spells and Enchantment in Theocritus' Idyll II," ch. 2 in *Studies in Theocritus and Other Hellenistic Poets* (Amsterdam: J. C. Gieben, 1979), 30–34.

76. *Idyll* 14 also highlights the theme of the clash between heterosexual love and the masculinized world of the gymnasium and the symposium: Aeschinas's obsession with Cynisca caused him to abandon the sympotic life.

77. Probably a love-potion (Gow, *Theocritus* 2:46 n. 58).

78. The association of the name Delphis with Delphi and hence Apollo also heightens the impression of class difference from Simaetha (whose name means snub-nosed; on Simaetha's name, see Dover, *Theocritus*, 95). Also, Simaetha saw Delphis on her way to Artemis's festival, and she compares his shine to that of the moon, with whom Artemis was often identified.

79. For this version of the Actaeon story, see Callim. *Hymn* 5.107–16; see also, e.g., Ov. *Met.* 3.138–252.

80. Simaetha was attracted by Delphis's gleaming athleticism, as shown by the full spectrum of "shiny, oily" words she uses in association with his athletic activities: λιπαρὰ παλαίστρα ("the palaestra shiny with oil," 51), στῆθος στίλβον ("his shining breast," 79), ὁ λιπαρόχρως Δέλφις ("shiny-skinned Delphis," 102), Δωρὶς ὄλπα ("his Doric oil-flask," 156). Delphis's invocation of Hephaestus Liparaios ("of [shiny] Lipara," 133) may also reinforce this association.

81. Frederick T. Griffiths, "Poetry as *Pharmakon* in Theocritus' *Idyll* 2," in *Arktouros: Hellenic Studies Presented to Bernard M. W. Knox*, ed. Glen W. Bowersock, Walter Burkert, and Michael C. J. Putnam (Berlin: Walter de Gruyter, 1979), 87–88. On Simaetha's subjective use of the adjective λιπαρός, see also Fabiano, "Fluctuations in Theocritus' Style," 523; Segal, "Space, Time, and Imagination," 110.

82. Artemis's identification with Selene, the Moon goddess (Dover, *Theocritus*, 101) may add another dimension to this reading, insofar as Simaetha invokes Selene and Hecate (also identified with Artemis, *Id.* 2.33) to help her resolve the crisis of identity she is experiencing because of Delphis. As shown above, the goddess Artemis seems central to Simaetha's recovery of herself.

83. On Egypt's tradition of magic, see, e.g., Siegfried Morenz, *Ägyptische Religion* (Stuttgart: W. Kohlhammer, 1960), esp. 27–28; John Baines, "Society, Morality, and Religious Practice," in *Religion in Ancient Egypt: Gods, Myths, and Personal Practice*, ed. Byron E. Shafer (Ithaca: Cornell University Press, 1991), 164–72 ("Magic and Divination"). On the influence of Egypt's magic on Greeks, see, e.g., Garth Fowden, *The Egyptian Hermes: A Historical Approach to the Late*

Pagan Mind (Cambridge and New York: Cambridge University Press, 1986), esp. 65–67.

84. For discussion (with references), see chapter 4, where I examine *Idyll* 15's representation of Arsinoe's Adonia.

85. E.g., Lysias's Euphiletus, in his self-defense for murdering Eratosthenes, traces Eratosthenes' passion for Euphiletus's wife to his seeing her attending a funeral (Lys. 1.8). Also, for an important reminder of the public nature of many of Greek women's religious roles, see Helene P. Foley, "The 'Female Intruder' Reconsidered: Women in Aristophanes' *Lysistrata* and *Ecclesiazusae*," *Classical Philology* 77 (1982), esp. 1–5.

86. The movement of *Idyll* 15's women from a private house through Alexandria's streets to an Adonis festival (traditionally a women's festival) enables Theocritus to explore an unusually full spectrum of female-male encounters and relations, both hostile and sympathetic: between husbands and wives, mothers and sons, men and women strangers, a king and subject women, a goddess and a youth.

87. On the significance of Mise's descent for *Mime* 1's plot, see Stern, "Herodas' *Mimiamb* 1," 161–65.

88. On the snake-burning as a scapegoat ritual, see Gow, *Theocritus* 2:430 n. 91; Jacob Stern, "Theocritus' *Idyll* 24," *American Journal of Philology* 95 (1974), 357.

89. Cf. Callim. *Hymn* 2, which represents a male ceremony of Apollo.

90. Although *Idyll* 26 ends with the poet-narrator ostensibly disassociating himself from Pentheus, the poem begins with a detailed description of the women's ritual activities (1–9), which puts both audience and poet-narrator in Pentheus's position as intruders. In Euripides' *Bacchae*, Pentheus spies on less ritually veiled activities than in *Idyll* 26, e.g., bacchantes singing bacchic songs and repairing their wands (1054–57; see too the messenger's report at 680–711). For a summary of scholarship comparing Euripides' *Bacchae* and Theocritus's *Idyll* 26, see K. J. McKay, "Theokritos' *Bacchantes* Re-examined," *Antichthon* 1 (1967), esp. 16–20.

91. The end of *Idyll* 26 absolves Agave and her sisters of blame (37–38). This is not a typical move: traditionally in Greek literature women who kill their children suffer retribution (see, e.g., Jeffrey Henderson, "Older Women in Attic Old Comedy," *Transactions and Proceedings of the American Philological Association* 117 [1987], 112). But in Theocritus's *Idyll* 26, Pentheus's mother and her sisters are absolved of his murder through Dionysus. A possible subtext here is that in a world of autocratic hegemonies, powerful and well-connected royal women (e.g., Olympias, herself a bacchant of Dionysus; Arsinoe II) could commit terrible (kinship) crimes with impunity: thus Olympias had Philip Arrhidaios (her stepson) executed and forced his wife Eurydice to commit suicide (Diod. 19.11; see Macurdy, *Hellenistic Queens*, 41–42; Elizabeth D. Carney, "Olympias," *Ancient Society* 18 [1987], 59).

92. Cf. Theocritus's representation of a public Adonia, sponsored by Arsinoe, and open to a public, mixed audience. In chapter 4, I discuss the poetic challenges involved in commemorating a public, official celebration of a traditionally private, countercultural festival.

93. By having the celebrant-narrator use the image of ἀελίῳ ἔνι πλαγγών ("a wax doll in the sun"; trans. A. W. Mair, "Callimachus" [1921], in *Callimachus: Hymns and Epigrams; Lycophron; Aratus*, trans. A. W. and G. R. Mair, 2d ed. [Cambridge: Harvard University Press, 1955], 131; 91) to describe Erysichthon as he wastes away, the poet highlights Erysichthon's feminized position in subjugation to Demeter: through hunger, Demeter transforms Erysichthon from a fierce leader of men to a subordinate. Also, the celebrant's use of the imagery of a lioness and a hunter repositions Erysichthon as fierce but hunted (hence feminized) when he replies to Demeter's warning: χαλεπώτερον ἠὲ κυναγόν / ὤρεσιν ἐν Τμαρίοισιν ὑποβλέπει ἄνδρα λέαινα / ὠμοτόκος ("with a look more fierce than that wherewith a lioness looks on the hunter on the hills of Tmarus—a lioness with new-born cubs"; trans. Mair, "Callimachus," 129; 50–52).

94. *Idyll* 17's inclusion of matrilineal identifications in a male-centered poem (an encomium of Ptolemy) underscores Theocritus's thematic emphasis on the importance of women in this poem (as elsewhere). On the prevalence of matrilineal identifications among women, see Marilyn Skinner, "Greek Women and the Metronymic: A Note on an Epigram by Nossis," *The Ancient History Bulletin* 1 (1987), 39–42.

95. Cf. Skinner's evaluation of Nossis *Ep.* 8 Gow and Page (= *A.P.* 6.353) which, by emphasizing the resemblance of a daughter to her mother, "implicitly repudiates the very structures of patriarchy by transforming the evidential basis for claims of paternity into a proof of the mother's vital role in the reproductive process" (Marilyn B. Skinner, "Nossis *Thēlyglōssos*: The Private Text and the Public Book," in Pomeroy, *Women's History*, 28, 30 [quote taken from 30]).

96. For pre-Callimachean literary passages, see, e.g., Eur. *Hipp.* 161–69, *Phoen.* 355. On the risks of childbirth, see, e.g., Pomeroy, *Goddesses*, 84–85; Robert Garland, *The Greek Way of Life: From Conception to Old Age* (Ithaca: Cornell University Press, 1990), 65–80. In Sparta, at least by *c.* 500 B.C., women who died in childbirth joined men who died in battle in being granted the exceptional honor of having their names inscribed on tombstones; the women either by Lycurgan law (Plut. *Lyc.* 27.2, if read with Latte's emendation) or by "*de facto* exemption by *c.* 500 . . . from the Spartan prohibition on named tombstones" (Paul Cartledge, "Spartan Wives: Liberation or Licence?" *Classical Quarterly*, n.s., 31 [1981], 95; see n. 72 on Latte's emendation).

97. See also Callim. *Hymn* 3.20–22; *Aetia* 3, fr. 79 (Diana Lucina); Eur. *Iph. Taur.* 1464–67 (an *aition* for the dedication to Artemis at Brauron of woven garments of women who died in childbirth). Cf. Callim. *Hymn* 3's *aition* for Artemis's role as goddess of childbirth: in contrast, she gave her own mother no pain either in childbirth or pregnancy (22–25).

98. In the fourth century and Hellenistic period, however, mothers seem to have taken more significant roles in arranging marriages: documents attest that mothers and fathers together, even mothers alone, were giving away brides (Xen. *Oec.* 7.11; *P. Elephantine* 1, dated 311/310 B.C.; for discussion of *P. Elephantine* 1 and other Hellenistic examples, see Pomeroy, *Goddesses*, 126–30; idem, *Women in Hellenistic Egypt*, 86–87, and esp. 90). For the suggestion that a seducer's mother might promote a seduction, see Lysias 1.20, where Euphiletus relates a

report that his wife, when attending a Thesmophoria, went off to the temple with the mother of Eratosthenes, his wife's seducer.

99. In the *Odyssey*'s typical cyclopean family, a mother is more subordinated: θεμιστεύει δὲ ἕκαστος / παίδων ἠδ' ἀλόχων ("Each male rules over his children and his wives," Hom. *Od.* 9.114–15 *O.C.T.*). For Hellenistic representations of the cyclopes as mature monsters, see, e.g., Callimachus's *Hymn* 3.46–86, esp. 51–56 (e.g., αἰνὰ πέλωρα / πρήσσιν Ὀσσαίοισιν ἐοικότα; "the terrible monsters like unto the crags of Ossa"; trans. Mair, "Callimachus," 65; 51–52). Cf. Theoc. *Id.* 7's mature Polyphemus, ὃς ὤρεσι νᾶας ἔβαλλε ("who pelted ships with mountains"; trans. Gow, *Theocritus* 1: 67; 152), whom Simichidas invokes in a wine appraisal as a drunken shepherd dancing among his pens (153).

100. The poet intensifies the horror of Pentheus's dismemberment by having Autonoa answer Pentheus's question and thus show that she recognizes him as human if not as her nephew (18–19).

101. For another Hellenistic example of a strong, independent mother, see Ap. Rhod. *Argon.* 4.866–79. By having Peleus recall, when the long-absent Thetis suddenly appears, how Thetis abandoned the family, how she threw a shrieking baby Achilles to the ground when Peleus interrupted her nightly routine of placing the baby in the fire, Apollonius draws attention to the theme of strong, independent (and volatile) mothers and the dangers they offer their families. (This theme is not without resonance in a story that features Medea.)

102. The exact situation in *Id.* 15.77 is uncertain (see Gow, *Theocritus* 2: 285–86 n. 77). For the meaning of νυός as "bride," cf. Theoc. *Id.* 18.15. But the male involved at *Id.* 15.77 need not be the bridegroom (although Praxinoa's use of the phrase might be more pointed in the context of an Adonia if a bridegroom and bride were intended).

103. Cf. Dover, *Theocritus*, 206, who suggests that Theocritus may just be "satirizing the unthinking use of clichés."

104. On how this identification offers a female take on heroism by suggesting its great cost to Hecabe (the loss of Hector), and on the Adonis hymn in general, see chapter 4.

105. J. C. Austin, "Significant Name in Herondas," 16, explains the name Lampriskos as emphasizing vigor: "λαμπρός, suggesting vigorous action with reference to the flogging scene." I would like to suggest another possibility: that the name Lampriskos could also signify "a dim light," thus indicating a dull schoolteacher.

106. See Xen. *Oec.* 7.12 (Ischomachus's advice to his wife that they will jointly plan how to train the children and thus be rewarded with good support in old age). Cf. Ar. *Nub.*, in which class differences between husband and wife lead to the father taking sole charge of their son's education.

107. On elderly Greek parents' dependency on their children, see, e.g., W. K. Lacey, *The Family in Classical Greece* (Ithaca: Cornell University Press, 1968), 25, 116–18; Garland, *Greek Way of Life*, 261–62. For evidence of Athenian legislation requiring children to care for parents, see, e.g., Dem. 24.107 and Diog. Laert. 1.55 (both cited in Lacey).

108. For useful discussions of Herodas's *Mime* 5, with attention to irony and

social issues, see David Konstan, "The Tyrant Goddess: Herodas's Fifth *Mime*," *Classical Antiquity* 8 (1989), 267–82; idem, *Sexual Symmetry*, 164–66.

109. Sparta differed from the Greek norm by including such practices as wife-sharing (for a convenient summary of the evidence, see D. M. MacDowell, *Spartan Law* [Edinburgh: Scottish Academic Press, 1986], 82–88; for an explanation of Spartan marriage practices, see Stephen Hodkinson, "Inheritance, Marriage, and Demography: Perspectives upon the Success and Decline of Classical Sparta," in *Classical Sparta: Techniques behind Her Success*, ed. Anton Powell [Norman: University of Oklahoma Press, 1989], esp. 90–93).

110. For evidence of this male attitude toward female slaves in the fifth and fourth centuries, with special attention to Athens, see Roger Just, *Women in Athenian Law and Life* (London and New York: Routledge, 1989), 138–43. For discussion of *Mime* 5's inversions of normative values, see Konstan, "Tyrant Goddess"; idem, *Sexual Symmetry*, esp. 165.

111. For speculation on possible divine identities for ἡ τύραννος, see Headlam and Knox, *Herodas*, 263–64 n. 77. The expression ἡ τύραννος can also refer to a queen or princess, however (thus, e.g., Eur. *Med.* 957), and the Hellenistic age was full of powerful queens (who were also often identified with goddesses) by whom one could swear. In any case, in the context of the poem, Bitinna's oath by an unnamed female tyrant has important thematic implications (on the role of the "tyrant goddess" in Herod. *Mime* 5, see Konstan, "Tyrant Goddess," 277, 280, 282).

112. On "the absence of male heads of household" in *Mime* 5, see Konstan, "Tyrant Goddess," 269; idem, *Sexual Symmetry*, 163, 165–66.

113. See, e.g., Pomeroy, *Women in Hellenistic Egypt*, 89–90.

114. On the thematic focus on human helplessness before the gods in Callimachus's *Hymns* 5 and 6, see Anthony W. Bulloch, "The Future of a Hellenistic Illusion: Some Observations on Callimachus and Religion," *Museum Helveticum* 41 (1984), esp. 225–28. As Bulloch remarks on the fate of Chariclo (and her son Teiresias) in *Hymn* 5, "now we find that they [the gods] can be randomly and unpredictably violent, even to the closest friends, and scarcely even acknowledge the friendship" (228).

115. On Callimachus's emphasis on "die Frau als Mutter" (especially sorrowing mother), see Konrat Ziegler's important article, "Kallimachos und die Frauen," in *Die Antike* 13 (1937), 23–24: "Dieser Dichter weiß etwas von Mutterliebe und Mutterleid" (24).

116. Ziegler, "Kallimachos und die Frauen," 24.

117. E.g., Polyphemus's mother in *Idyll* 11, whom he blames for not fostering his courtship of Galatea although she sees him wasting away for love (67–69). But note *Ep.* 20 Gow, attributed to Theocritus, which represents an inscription for a Thracian nurse's tomb monument set up by her male nursling (cf. Callimachus's *Ep.* 50). On the authenticity of the epigrams attributed to Theocritus, see Gow, *Theocritus* 2:527: "It can hardly be said that there is objective evidence against the authenticity of any of these 22 epigrams." See also Gow and Page, *Greek Anthology* 2:525–27. But cf. P. M. Fraser, *Ptolemaic Alexandria* 1:575 and 2:819 n. 175. On the manuscript tradition, see R. J. Smutny, *The Text History of*

the Epigrams of Theocritus, University of California Publications in Classical Philology, vol. 15, no. 2 (Berkeley, 1955).

118. E.g., *Idyll* 15's housewives' fantasy relationship with Adonis.

119. E.g., in *Idyll* 6, Damoetas's Polyphemus credits old Cotyttaris with showing him how to ward off the evil eye.

120. On a more prosaic level, in *Idyll* 11 Polyphemus claims that his mother will suffer when he tells her of his head- and footaches, but his report that she disregarded his earlier symptoms of lovesickness belies his expectations of her suffering now (67–71). Cf. *Idyll* 10, in which Milon mockingly suggests to lovesick Bucaeus to tell his mother his troubles.

121. Elaborations of Aphrodite's sorrow become dominant in later versions of the Adonis story: see, e.g., Bion 1 ("Lament for Adonis"), esp. 19–24, 40–62; Ov. *Met.* 10.722–27.

122. The only other gods to speak in Theocritus's poetry are Hermes (*Id.* 1.77–78) and Priapus (*Id.* 1.82–91). Note that all these gods with speaking parts appear in Thyrsis's song in *Idyll* 1. Also note that Aphrodite elicits a response from Daphnis while the others do not.

123. For discussion of Aphrodite's linkage with Arsinoe, in the context of Ptolemaic state ideology, see chapter 4.

124. Cf. Theoc. *Ep.* 4 (the statue of Priapus with a phallus dedicated to Aphrodite's works).

125. Segal aptly describes the water nymphs' feelings for Hylas as "maternal, enclosing love": "They treat him as a mother treats a child" (Charles Segal, "Death by Water: A Narrative Pattern in Theocritus," in Segal, *Poetry and Myth*, 58).

126. Griffiths characterizes *Idyll* 15's Aphrodite as "dignified, loving, almost maternal" (Griffiths, *Theocritus at Court*, 125).

127. Cypris is mentioned at *Hymn* 4.21 (an island patronized by Cypris), *Hymn* 4.308 (Cypris's statue), *Hymn* 5.21 (Cypris's constant combing of her hair in contrast to Athena's modesty). Two epigrams feature Aphrodite as recipient of offerings: *Ep.* 5 (a nautilus shell), *Ep.* 38 (a hetaira's dedication). Elsewhere Aphrodite receives mention as patron of Eryx (*Aet.* 2, fr. 43.53), creator of orators (*Aet.* 3, fr. 82.2–3), mistress of Adonis (*Iambus* 3, fr. 193.37); Lyricus 227 includes Aphrodite in an epiphany of gods (also Apollo and the Erotes) at a sympotic night-festival. *The Lock of Berenice* features Cypris and Aphrodite Zephyritis (*Aet.* 4, fr. 110.56–57, 64), and *Iambus* 10, fr. 200a (four lines) describes the cult of Aphrodite of Mount Castnion.

128. Apollonius Rhodius, like Theocritus and unlike Callimachus, privileges female erotic subjectivity, and the art of his psychological portraiture has received much well-deserved attention (see, e.g., Anthony W. Bulloch, "Hellenistic Poetry," ch. 18 in *Greek Literature*, vol. 1 of *The Cambridge History of Classical Literature*, ed. P. E. Easterling and B. M. W. Knox [Cambridge and New York: Cambridge University Press, 1985], esp. 591–93).

129. This theme, of course, corresponds to the relations of great goddesses and their consorts, e.g., Astarte and Tammuz, Cybele and Attis, Inanna and Dumuzi, Isis and Osiris. See Charles Segal, "Adonis and Aphrodite: Theocritus, *Idyll* 3.48," in Segal, *Poetry and Myth*, esp. 68–70. On links between Daphnis

and the male consorts Dumuzi, Tammuz, and Adonis (among others), see William Berg, *Early Virgil* (London: Athlone Press, University of London, 1974), 17–20, 197 n. 28; on Daphnis and Dumuzi in particular, see Halperin, *Before Pastoral*, esp. 112–14; Jasper Griffin, "Theocritus, the *Iliad*, and the East," *American Journal of Philology* 113 (1992), 203.

130. By having *Idyll* 3's goatherd cite among his role models Adonis and Endymion, Theocritus highlights the basic story pattern of love linked with death, and also draws attention to the amorous pretensions of a goatherd who aspires to the models of Adonis and Endymion.

131. Hera honors her for preferring the sea to Zeus (*Hymn* 4.247–48).

132. In Callimachus's poems, mothers can also be chaste: Teiresias's mother Chariclo belongs to Artemis's band (*Hymn* 5).

133. Whereas Theocritus typically domesticates and diminishes male monsters appearing in poems that feature their relations with women (e.g., *Idyll* 24's Heracles and *Idyll* 6's and 11's Polyphemus), Callimachus magnifies his cyclopes and thus emphasizes their frightening effects on females, e.g. *Hymn* 3.64–65: κείνους γε καὶ αἱ μάλα μηκέτι τυτθαί / οὐδέποτ' ἀφρικτὶ μακάρων ὁρόωσι θύγατρες ("On those [Cyclopes] not even the daughters of the Blessed look without shuddering, though long past childhood's years"; trans. Mair, "Callimachus," 65). In the context of *Hymn* 3, the cowardly, general female response contrasts with Artemis's precocious boldness: when just three, she sat on the cyclops Brontes' knees and tore hair from his breast for sport (72–79).

134. The maiden chorus suggest that Menelaus should have left Helen at her mother's side last night (13), praise Helen's potential for motherhood (21), promise they will think the next day of Helen as "tender lambs long for their mother's teat" (41–42), and pray that Helen and Menelaus will have sons (51).

135. The poem begins and ends with powerful, maternal women. The poem opens with Ino, Autonoa, and Agave (two of Pentheus's aunts and his mother, 1), then moves to Semele (Dionysus's mother and another of Pentheus's aunts) and Dionysus (6). The poem closes with a hymnic envoi that moves from Dionysus (through his father Zeus, included in a relative clause, 33–34) back to Semele and her sisters (35–38).

136. Mother and young similes: *Id.* 2.108–9, 3.15–16, 12.4, 13.12–13, 14.32–33, 14.39–40, 18.41–42, and 26.20–21. Father and young simile: *Id.* 13.8. It should be noted here that patrilineal descriptions are more common than matrilineal, but they appear with greatest frequency in epic narratives featuring male, heroic action and in court poetry emphasizing family dynasties: *Idylls* 15, 17, 18, 22, and 24.

137. Male seers appear in Theocritus's extant poems only twice, both times in heroic contexts: in *Idyll* 6, Damoetas assumes the voice of a cyclops, who rejects a seer's prophesy, a motif that enables Theocritus to allude ironically to the Homeric story of the cyclops's blinding (*Od.* 9.509). In *Idyll* 24, Alcmene, Heracles' mother, consults the seer Teiresias about the meaning of the snake incident.

138. A patriarchal world typically disregards its old women; Hellenistic art and literature was making them visible and part of the public discourse. Thus, for example, Callimachus's *Hecale* features an old woman who gives hospitality

to Theseus, a young hero on a quest, and in Herodas's *Mime* 1 an old bawd comes to visit (and solicit) a young married woman.

139. For discussion, see chapter 4.

140. Martin Robertson, *A History of Greek Art*, 2 vols. (London: Cambridge University Press, 1975), 1:388–89; R. R. R. Smith, *Hellenistic Sculpture*, 65. See, e.g., the beardless, effeminate Dionysus represented on an Attic red-figure pelike, *c.* 340, from the British Museum E 424 (illustration available in Thomas H. Carpenter, *Art and Myth in Ancient Greece: A Handbook* [London: Thames and Hudson, 1990], 52, no. 49) and the fourth-century representation of a fleshy, beardless adolescent Hermes on a carved column from the Temple of Artemis at Ephesus (illustration available in Brunilde Sismondo Ridgway, *Hellenistic Sculpture I: The Styles of ca. 331–200 B.C.* [Madison: University of Wisconsin Press, 1990], plate 5).

141. For important cautions concerning extrapolating dates and artists from Roman copies of fourth-century or Hellenistic art, such as the girlishly plump Apollo Sauroktonos (lizard-slayer), commonly attributed to Praxiteles, and the Pothos (the yearning one), commonly attributed to Skopas, see Ridgway, *Hellenistic Sculpture*, esp. 87, 91.

142. See, e.g., O. Murray, "Symposion und Männerbund," 50.

143. Dover, *Greek Homosexuality*, 69–73 (with illustrations from vase paintings); 79–80 (with several examples from fourth-century and Hellenistic literature, e.g., Rhianus's *Ep.* 3 Gow and Page [= *A.P.* 12.93], on the charms of various boys, starting with Theodorus's πίονα σαρκός / ἀκμὴν καὶ γυίων ἄνθος ἀκηράσιον ["plump ripeness of flesh and virgin bloom of limbs"; trans. W. R. Paton, *The Greek Anthology*, 5 vols. (Cambridge: Harvard University Press, 1916–18), 4:329, rev.; 3–4]).

144. On Hellenistic sculptures of hermaphrodites, see Robertson, *History of Greek Art*, esp. 1:551–52; Pollitt, *Art in the Hellenistic Age*, esp. 149; Ridgway, *Hellenistic Sculpture*, 328–30; R. R. R. Smith, *Hellenistic Sculpture*, esp. 133–34, 156. On hermaphrodites in Greek vase-paintings, see Dover, *Greek Homosexuality*, 72. On the hermaphrodite in general, see Marie Delcourt, *Hermaphrodite: Mythes et rites de la bisexualité dans l'antiquité classique* (Paris: Presses universitaires de France, 1958); idem, *Hermaphroditea: Recherches sur l'être double promoteur de la fertilité dans le monde classique* (Brussels: Latomus, 1966). All the above have plates showing hermaphrodites in Greek art.

145. See Dover, *Greek Homosexuality*, 54–55 (with references). See too, e.g., Ar. *Nub.* 964–66, 973–76.

146. Segal, "Death by Water," 60.

147. For Sappho, like Theocritus, Aphrodite is the major deity.

148. For Greek and Latin examples of the use of "down" imagery in descriptions of young males, see Headlam and Knox, *Herodas*, 38 n. 52. On youth as valued in *eromenoi*, see David M. Halperin, "The Democratic Body: Prostitution and Citizenship in Classical Athens," ch. 5 in *One Hundred Years of Homosexuality and Other Essays on Greek Love* (New York: Routledge, 1990), 90. For ancient references on "the sexual appeal of youthfulness to women," see 182 n. 21.

149. This is probably not Asclepiades of Samos. For discussion of authorship, see Gow and Page, *Greek Anthology* 2:150, who also note the ironic use of

down imagery here: "Adolescence is less admired by this lover than by other Greeks" (2:150 n. 46.1).

150. In attributing this fragment to Callim. *Hecale*, scholars often conjecture that the speaker is Hecale as she views young Theseus (see, e.g., A. S. Hollis, *Callimachus: Hecale* [Oxford: Clarendon Press, 1990], 184). Cf. Theocritus's presentation of Simaetha recalling her first view of Delphis and his companion, which, like Callim. *Hecale* fr. 274, includes a comparison to helichryse: τοῖς δ' ἧς ξανθοτέρα μὲν ἐλιχρύσοιο γενειάς ("Their beards were more golden than helichryse," *Id.* 2.78).

151. On the homoerotic appeal of youth, see Dover, *Greek Homosexuality*, 85–86.

152. Dover suggests that representations of Ganymede (and Tithonos) can serve as touch-stones for Greek male beauty (*Greek Homosexuality*, 6). Thus, e.g., Dioscorides *Ep.* 10 Gow and Page (= *A.P.* 12.37.3–4): τῶν Γανυμήδους / μηρῶν οἱ τούτου πουλὺ μελιχρότεροι ("His thighs were much more honey-sweet than Ganymede's," trans. Barbara Hughes Fowler, *Hellenistic Poetry: An Anthology* [Madison: University of Wisconsin Press, 1990], 289). On the motif of Ganymede in pederastic Greek epigrams, see Tarán, *Art of Variation*, 7–51. On Ganymede's appearances in the Middle Ages and Renaissance, see Leonard Barkan, *Transuming Passion: Ganymede and the Erotics of Humanism* (Stanford: Stanford University Press, 1991).

153. On the hermaphroditism of Erotes, see Delcourt, *Hermaphroditea*, 54–59 ("Éros androgyne"); Dover, *Greek Homosexuality*, 72 (and figures RS12 and RS20).

154. Although this Theocritus need not be the Hellenistic poet from Syracuse (on the uncertainty, see Gow and Page, *Greek Anthology* 2:161, on *Ep.* 6 = Callim. *Ep.* 52), Callimachus and Theocritus do seem to engage in poetic dialogue elsewhere; e.g., Callim. *Ep.* 46 may well be a witty response to Theoc. *Id.* 11 (for discussion, see Bulloch, "Hellenistic Poetry," 573).

155. For an example of a direct comparison of an *eromenos* to Ganymede, see Alcaeus of Messene *Ep.* 9 Gow and Page (= *A.P.* 12.64). This epigram, a prayer to Zeus for Peithenor to win an Olympic victory, refers to Peithenor as Aphrodite's second son and requests that Zeus not seize Peithenor instead of Ganymede. For references to other Hellenistic epigrams comparing *eromenoi* to Ganymede, see Gow and Page, *Greek Anthology* 2:14 (on Alcaeus *Ep.* 9).

156. *Idyll* 15's Adonia includes both men and women in its audience, as shown by the bystander's presence. Theocritus's *Idyll* 15 emphasizes how the celebration of Adonis's reunion with Aphrodite, the Adonia, can offer married women a safe fantasy of erotic autonomy. Several of Herodas's mimes also suggest the possibility of freedom from the sexual tyranny of husbands: through a slave-boy in *Mime* 5, dildoes in *Mime* 6, a lover (although rejected) in *Mime* 1. Cf. Mastromarco, *Public of Herondas*, 93–94.

157. Gow, *Theocritus* 2:301 n. 129, remarks that the adjective ῥοδόπαχυς (rosy-armed), used by the hymnist to describe Adonis at line 128, "is not used elsewhere of a male person." On Adonis's immaturity and effeminancy, see also Marcel Detienne, *The Gardens of Adonis: Spices in Greek Mythology*, trans. J. Lloyd (Atlantic Highlands, N.J.: Humanities Press, 1977), esp. 102, 122.

158. On Atalanta's nakedness, see William S. Anderson, *Ovid's* Metamorphoses: *Books 6–10* [Norman: University of Oklahoma Press, 1972], 523 n. 578–82: "Atalanta, like the usual athlete of ancient times, was running naked."

159. For discussion of Ovid's version of Adonis's story (and the linkage of Adonis and Atalanta), see Detienne, *Dionysos Slain*, 26–52.

160. On the hare as a love-gift for both men and women, see Schnapp, "Eros the Hunter," 71–87.

161. See Pl. *Leg.* 633b; Detienne, *Dionysos Slain*, 24–25; Schnapp, "Eros the Hunter," 72.

162. Ovid describes this flower as short lived (737–39). Interestingly, the anemone has both male and female parts (although perhaps not recognized as such in ancient times).

163. On the Greek eroticism of death, see, e.g., Emily Vermeule, "On the Wings of Morning: The Pornography of Death," in *Aspects of Death in Early Greek Art and Poetry* (Berkeley and Los Angeles: University of California Press, 1979), 145–77: "It was a formal principle of Greek myth and literature that love and death were two aspects of the same power, as in the myth of Persephone or Helen of Troy" (159). See too Jean-Pierre Vernant, "Feminine Figures of Death," in Vernant, *Mortals and Immortals*, 95–110. On the eroticism of death in Latin poetry, see Jasper Griffin, "Love and Death," ch. 7 in *Latin Poets*, 142–62. Cf. the fashion for representations of beautiful, dying women in art and literature of the late nineteenth century (see, e.g., Bram Dijkstra, "The Cult of Invalidism; Ophelia and Folly; Dead Ladies and the Fetish of Sleep," ch. 2 in *Idols of Perversity: Fantasies of Feminine Evil in Fin-de-Siècle Culture* [New York and Oxford: Oxford University Press, 1986], 25–63).

164. Similarly, Dioscorides *Ep.* 3 Gow and Page (= *A.P.* 5.53).

165. The *erastes* hopes that he and his *eromenos* might experience such a reciprocity of love that their memory too might transcend death (*Id.* 12.10–11).

166. For this point, see also Ziegler, "Kallimachos," 36.

167. Cf. Callim. *Iambus* 12, fr. 202.69, where the poet-narrator seems to be describing either Apollo (or himself) as still youthful and beardless: ἄχρι] σὸν γένειον ἀγνεύῃ τριχός[. For the suggestion that the description belongs to Apollo, see Rudolf Pfeiffer, *Callimachus*, 2 vols. (Oxford: Clarendon Press, 1949–53), 1:203–4 nn. 54ff.; to the poet-narrator, see Dawson, who translates "while my cheeks and chin are smooth and free of hair" (Christopher M. Dawson, "The Iambi of Callimachus: A Hellenistic Poet's Experimental Laboratory," *Yale Classical Studies* 11 [1950], 115). C. A. Trypanis, "Callimachus" in *Callimachus: Aetia, Iambi, Lyric Poems, Hecale, Minor Epic and Elegiac Poems, and Other Fragments; Musaeus: Hero and Leander* (Cambridge: Harvard University Press, 1975), follows Dawson.

168. R. R. R. Smith, *Hellenistic Sculpture*, 65, with illustrations 75, 76. For cautions on dating, see Ridgway, *Hellenistic Sculpture*, esp. 87 (as noted above).

169. On the homoerotic motif here, see Frederick Williams, *Callimachus: Hymn to Apollo: A Commentary* (Oxford: Clarendon Press; New York: Oxford University Press, 1978), 49–50 n. 49.

170. For the linkage between poetic and homoerotic amatory standards, see also Callim. *Ep.* 28. On the reference to homosexual courtship in *Iambus* 3, see,

e.g., C. M. Dawson, "Iambi of Callimachus," 38–39: since Euthydemus's defection, Callimachus "might as well live a eunuch's life" (quote taken from 39); P. M. Fraser, *Ptolemaic Alexandria* 1:739–40, 2:1040–41 n. 203. Callim. *Ep.* 32 (= *A.P.* 12.148) addresses a complaint of avarice to an *eromenos*. On the issue of payment for homosexual relations, see Dover, *Greek Homosexuality*, 106–9; on prices charged, see Halperin, "Democratic Body," 107–12.

171. On the representation of female figures according to male standards of beauty in the archaic and early classical age, see Dover, *Greek Homosexuality*, 70–73.

172. On the close similarities between Theoc. *Id.* 18.22–32 and Callim. *Hymn* 5.23–28, see Anthony W. Bulloch, *Callimachus: The Fifth Hymn* (Cambridge: Cambridge University Press, 1985), 131–40.

173. On the nuptial aspects of this simile, see J. M. Bremer, "Full Moon and Marriage in Apollonius' *Argonautica*," *Classical Quarterly*, n.s., 37 (1987), 423–26, who points out that the change in perceived application of the simile from Medea to Jason enables the reader to "experience the sentiments of the man and the woman very economically: in one and the same simile" (426).

Chapter 3. *Ekphrasis* and the Reception of Works of Art

1. Pliny *HN* 35.84–85: "vulgum diligentiorem iudicem quam se praeferens." According to Pliny, Apelles appraised the reliability of a viewer's response by occupation: when a shoemaker criticized painted sandals, Apelles repainted them, but Apelles disregarded that same shoemaker's remarks when he presumed to criticize more than just painted sandals. Another incident also shows Apelles' egalitarianism: when Alexander criticized Apelles' portrait, a horse was brought in, who neighed in response to the painted horse; Apelles thereupon declared the horse to have shown more artistic taste than Alexander (Ael. *VH* 2.3).

2. This red-figure krater is displayed in the New York Metropolitan Museum; a photograph is available in Robertson, *History of Greek Art* 2: plate 152a.

3. The painting is displayed in the Naples Museum; a photograph is available in Robertson, *History of Greek Art* 2: plate 187a. See too the Alexander mosaic, which shows a fallen Persian soldier whose frightened face is reflected in a shield (also in the Naples Museum, and in Robertson, *History of Greek Art* 2: plate 155). For Hellenistic descriptions of reflections, see, e.g., Ap. Rhod. *Argon.* 1.742–46 (Cytherea reflected in Ares' shield, as represented on Jason's purple cloak); Callim. *Aet.* 3, fr. 75.10–11 (the sacrificial knife reflected in the lustral water, as seen by the oxen).

4. Cf. W. H. Auden's poem "The Shield of Achilles," which highlights Thetis's subjective response as she gazes on the shield. The son never sees the shield; instead the mother views it in dismay. On Hellenistic representations of optical effects, see B. H. Fowler, *Hellenistic Aesthetic*, 17, 112–13.

5. See also Eva Keuls, "Plato on Painting," *American Journal of Philology* 95 (1974): 100–27.

6. E.g., Homer's description of Achilles' shield (*Il.* 18.478–608). For an excellent introduction to the ecphrastic tradition, see esp. Paul Friedländer, "Ein-

leitung: Über die Beschreibung von Kunstwerken in der antiken Literatur," in *Johannes von Gaza und Paulus Silentiarius: Kunstbeschreibungen Justinianischer Zeit* (Leipzig: B. G. Teubner, 1912), 1–103. On the linkage of visual art and poetry in the Hellenistic period, see Webster, *Hellenistic Poetry and Art*, 156–77; see also Zanker, *Realism in Alexandrian Poetry*, 39–112. For a recent and important introduction to Hellenistic *ekphrasis*, see Simon Goldhill, "The Naive and Knowing Eye: Ecphrasis and the Culture of Viewing in the Hellenistic World," in *Art and Text in Ancient Greek Culture*, ed. Goldhill and Robin Osborne (Cambridge and New York: Cambridge University Press, 1994), 197–223 (which includes a needed survey of ecphrastic Hellenistic epigrams, a brief and evocative discussion of *ekphrasis* in Theoc. *Id.* 15, a comparative glance at Herod. *Mime* 4, and much emphasis on "poetic self-reflexivity" and irony). On *ekphrasis* in the Renaissance, with attention to the reception of ancient *ekphrases*, see Svetlana Leontief Alpers, "*Ekphrasis* and Aesthetic Attitudes in Vasari's *Lives*," *Journal of the Warburg and Courtauld Institute* 23 (1960), 190–215. On the modern tradition of poetry on works of visual art, with emphasis on the importance of Auden's "Musée des Beaux Arts," see Alastair Fowler, *Kinds of Literature: An Introduction to the Theory of Genres and Modes* (Cambridge: Harvard University Press, 1982), 115–18; see also James A. W. Heffernan, *Museum of Words: The Poetics of Ekphrasis from Homer to Ashbery* (Chicago: University of Chicago Press, 1993), 135–89.

7. Zanker, *Realism in Alexandrian Poetry*, 10.

8. Motto and Clark, "Idyllic Slumming," 40. See also Griffiths, "Home before Lunch," 249: "the housewife's failure of imagination."

9. Griffiths, "Home before Lunch," 251. See also Motto and Clark, "Idyllic Slumming," 41: "[the women] ignorant alike of art and of life"; Walker, *Theocritus*, 94: "the vulgarity of their artistic tastes." So too Gow, "*Adoniazusae* of Theocritus," 202; Dover, *Theocritus*, 209.

10. Epigrams illustrate the ongoing interest in realism—e.g., thirty extant epigrams praise the realism of Myron's statue of a cow (Gow and Page, *Greek Anthology* 2 : 63–64). On the Hellenistic taste for realism, see, e.g., Pollitt, *Art in the Hellenistic Age*, esp. 141–47; Zanker, *Realism and Alexandrian Poetry*, esp. 42–46.

11. Useful articles on aesthetic issues raised in *Mime* 4 include Salomo Luria, "Herondas' Kampf für die Veristische Kunst," in *Miscellanea di Studi Alessandrini, in memoria di Augusto Rostagni* (Torino: Bottega d'Erasmo, 1963), 394–415; Thomas Gelzer, "Mimus und Kunsttheorie bei Herondas, Mimiambus 4," in *Catalepton: Festschrift für Bernhard Wyss zum 80. Geburtstag*, ed. Christoph Schäublin (Basel: Seminar für klassische Philologie der Universität Basel, 1985), 96–116.

12. E.g., Green, *Alexander to Actium*, 206, 246.

13. On Browning's "My Last Duchess," see, e.g., Robert Langbaum, *The Poetry of Experience: The Dramatic Monologue in Modern Literary Tradition*, 2d ed. (Chicago: University of Chicago Press, 1985), 79–86; see also Heffernan, *Museum of Words*, 139–45.

14. See Goldhill, "Naive and Knowing Eye," for an important "first step" toward a "rewriting of the history of ecphrasis not merely as the history of a rhetorical topos but as the history of the formations of a viewing subject" (223).

See also Gutzwiller, *Theocritus' Pastoral Analogies*, 90–94, who proposes a distinction between "epic-narrative" and "mimetic-dramatic" *ekphrases*. See too Skinner, "Nossis," 25–29, on Nossis's ekphrastic epigrams, their preoccupation "not so much with the painter's success in effecting a physical likeness as with his ability to capture distinctive traits of the sitter's personality" (26). For further studies on the subjective factor in *ekphrasis*, see, e.g., Gotthold Ephraim Lessing, *Laocoön: An Essay on the Limits of Painting and Poetry*, trans. Edward Allen McCormick (1766; New York: Bobbs-Merrill, 1962); Rudolf Arnheim, *Art and Visual Perception* (Berkeley and Los Angeles: University of California Press, 1954); Ernst Gombrich, *Art and Illusion: A Study in the Psychology of Pictorial Representation*, 2d ed., rev. (Princeton: Princeton University Press, 1961); Hagstrum, *Sister Arts*; Mary Ann Caws, *The Eye in the Text: Essays on Perception, Mannerist to Modern* (Princeton: Princeton University Press, 1981); and W. J. T. Mitchell, *Iconology: Image, Text, Ideology* (Chicago: University of Chicago Press, 1986).

15. On the function of descriptive passages in literature of the Second Sophistic, see Shadi Bartsch, *Decoding the Ancient Novel: The Reader and the Role of Description in Heliodorus and Achilles Tatius* (Princeton: Princeton University Press, 1989), esp. 3–39.

16. See, e.g., Hutchinson, *Hellenistic Poetry*, 13.

17. Psychological characterization is just one aspect of this choral ode's dramatic function in Euripides' *Electra*. For an important and wide-ranging discussion, see George B. Walsh, "The First *Stasimon* of Euripides' *Electra*," *Yale Classical Studies* 25 (1977), 277–89.

18. See, e.g., Simon Goldhill, *Reading Greek Tragedy* (Cambridge and New York: Cambridge University Press, 1986), 164–65.

19. Other sixth- and fifth-century works on this theme exist only as titles, summaries, or fragments—e.g., Aeschylus's *Theoroi e Isthmiastai*; Epicharmus's *Theoroi* (Epicharmus, frs. 79–80, in *Comicorum Graecorum Fragmenta*, ed. Georgius Kaibel, vol. 1.1, *Doriensium Comoedia Mimi Phlyaces*, 2d ed. [Berlin: Weidmann, 1958]; see also Epicharmus *ap.* Ath. 3.107a, 8.362b, 9.408d); Sophron's *Tai Thamenai ta Isthmia* (title taken from Kaibel, *Doriensium Comoedia*, 155).

20. On this *parodos*, see also G. Müller, "Beschreibung von Kunstwerken im Ion des Euripides," *Hermes: Zeitschrift für klassische Philologie* 103 (1975), 29–36; V. Rosivach, "Earthborns and Olympians: The Parodos of the *Ion*," *Classical Quarterly*, n.s., 27 (1977), 284–94; Froma I. Zeitlin, "The Artful Eye: Vision, Ecphrasis, and Spectacle in Euripidean Theatre," in Goldhill and Osborne, *Art and Text*, esp. 147–54.

21. The narrator comments on the subjectivity of Aeneas's aesthetic experience and the neutrality of art: he feeds his soul on an empty picture (Verg. *Aen.* 1.464). A work of art is neutral here insofar as it does not tell the viewer how to "read." The context of viewing and the viewer's preoccupations influence the process of "reading," but Aeneas's "misreading" of pictures of Troy's fall on the walls of Juno's temple shows that it is not necessary for the viewer to integrate visual art into its setting: art can transcend ideology. The irony of Aeneas's response to these pictures has been much discussed: see, e.g., Keith Stanley, "Irony and Foreshadowing in *Aeneid*, 1, 462," *American Journal of Philology* 86 (1965), 273–77; W. R. Johnson, *Darkness Visible: A Study of Vergil's* Aeneid (Berkeley and

Los Angeles: University of California Press, 1976), 103–5; Page duBois, *History, Rhetorical Description, and the Epic: From Homer to Spenser* (Cambridge: D. S. Brewer; Totowa, N.J.: Biblio, 1982), 32–35; R. O. A. M. Lyne, *Further Voices in Vergil's* Aeneid (Oxford: Clarendon Press, 1987), 209–10.

22. For a useful and clear introduction to cognitive factors in aesthetic response, see Michael J. Parsons, *How We Understand Art: A Cognitive Developmental Account of Aesthetic Experience* (Cambridge and New York: Cambridge University Press, 1987).

23. E.g., Giangrande, "Interpretation of Herodas," 93; White, "Theocritus' 'Adonis Song,'" 202; Green, *Alexander to Actium*, 246.

24. In Theoc. *Id.* 2, the Thracian nurse uses this verb to invite Simaetha to view a festival of Artemis (λιτάνευσε / τὰν πομπὰν θάσασθαι, "she entreated me / to see the ceremonial procession," 71–72). Callimachus uses the verb in *Hymn* 3 when Helios admires the nymphs dancing around Artemis (θεῆται, 181), and again in *Hymn* 6 when noninitiates are forbidden to look at the ceremonial basket of Demeter (θασεῖσθε, 3). So too in Eur. *Ion*, Ion uses the verb of viewing works of art in Apollo's sanctuary at Delphi (θεᾶσθ', 232). Also, in Men. *Sam.*, a young man describes himself viewing the Adonia as a θεατής ("spectator," 43). Further, the scholia to Theoc. *Id.* 15 use the verb in a title for one of Sophron's mimes to refer to viewers of the Isthmia (Ἴσθμια θεμένων; for the scholia, see Wendel, *Scholia*, 305; for discussion, see Gow, *Theocritus* 2: 265, with citation of Greek text of scholia).

25. This verbal adjective is also traditionally associated with rituals, ceremonial objects, and gods—e.g., in Hes. *Th.* the adjective θητόν (wondrous) is used of the wand Hesiod received from the Muses (31), and in Callim. *Hymn* 3 the adjective θητήν is used of Artemis (141). Pindar too repeatedly uses the adjective θαητός (wondrous): of a young man (θαητόν, *P.* 10.58), of the body (τὸ θαητὸν δέμας, *N.* 11.12), of a contest (θαητὸν ἀγῶνα, *O.* 3.36), of a girl's form (θαητὸν εἶδος, *P.* 9.108).

26. The motif of *ekphrasis* of woven materials was popular during the Hellenistic period (see, e.g., the *ekphrasis* of Jason's wondrous figured cloak at Ap. Rhod. *Argon.* 1.721–67). On the popularity of *ekphrasis*, see, e.g., Richard F. Thomas, "Callimachus, the *Victoria Berenices*, and Roman Poetry," *Classical Quarterly*, n.s., 33 (1983), 108–12 (109 n. 102 includes the Adonis figure on Theoc. *Id.* 15's figured tapestries). Also, on the popularity of finely woven and figured materials in the Hellenistic era, see Gow, *Theocritus* 2:286–87 n. 78; P. M. Fraser, *Ptolemaic Alexandria* 1:138; Thomas, "Callimachus," esp. III n. 108.

27. White argues that the Adonis figure described by Praxinoa is the same as the three-dimensional figure described by the hymnist (White, "Theocritus' 'Adonis Song,'" 199–203; so too Schwinge, *Künstlichkeit von Kunst*, 57 n. 27). For the purposes of this discussion, I follow Gow and Dover, who consider that the Adonis figure described by Praxinoa is represented on the tapestries (Gow, "*Adoniazusae* of Theocritus," 198–99; idem, *Theocritus* 2:265, 288 n. 84f.; Dover, *Theocritus*, 206). My argument is not materially affected by the number of Adonis figures in the display.

28. The word silver is emphasized by being the first substantive word after the verbal adjective θαητός (84) and by appearing in the line before its noun κλισμῶ (85).

29. Cunningham calls this speaker Phile (see discussion in "Herodas 4," esp. 119–20). For the purposes of this discussion, I have used the more traditional identification of the woman as Kokkale (for arguments in favor of the name Kokkale, see Mastromarco, *Public of Herondas*, 39–45).

30. In presenting this picture in pieces, Herodas anticipates a practice that becomes particularly popular in the Second Sophistic; for example, Lucian describes pictures first as puzzles and only afterward introduces interpreters (e.g., *Heracles*); for discussion, see Bartsch, *Decoding the Ancient Novel*, 15–30. By presenting a riddling *ekphrasis* through a fictive character, Herodas can involve and flatter readers (by allowing them to solve a puzzle that the fictive character does not), while also focusing on the psychology of aesthetic experience.

31. E.g., Headlam and Knox, *Herodas*, 200–1 n. 59–71; Webster, *Hellenistic Poetry and Art*, 159–60.

32. See passages given in Emma J. Edelstein and Ludwig Edelstein, *Asclepius: A Collection and Interpretation of the Testimonies*, 2 vols. (Baltimore: Johns Hopkins Press, 1945), 1: 303–15. Cf. Herod. *Mime* 4.14–16 and Polyb. *Hist.* 32.15.1–5, as cited in Edelstein and Edelstein, *Asclepius*, 306–7, no. 546.

33. On the Hellenistic taste for the grotesque, see Pollitt, *Art in the Hellenistic Age*, 134–35; B. H. Fowler, *Hellenistic Aesthetic*, 66–78.

34. On the artfulness of this representation, see, e.g., Arnott, "Herodas," 123–28.

35. The statue of an old man is barely mentioned (κεῖνον δέ, Κυννοῖ, τὸν γέροντ'; "and that old man, Kynno"; 30) when the attention shifts to a third statue (a boy strangling a goose, 30–31).

36. For discussion of the significance of the woman's name and stance, see Headlam and Knox, *Herodas*, 186–87; Cunningham, *Herodas*, 135.

37. On how Lucretius's vivid linkage of wounds and love in *De Rerum Natura* 4.1045–57, recalls the pervasive use of such imagery by Greek epigrammatists, see E. J. Kenney, "Doctus Lucretius," *Mnemosyne*, 4th ser., 23 (1970), 380–84.

38. An association of wounds and love can have shock value, particularly when placed in a woman's mouth—e.g., Clytemnestra horrifies the chorus of Argive elders when she describes how Agamemnon's and Cassandra's bloody deaths heighten her sexual pleasure (Aesch. *Ag.* 1388–92, 1444–47).

39. Gow, *Theocritus* 2: 287 n. 79.

40. Garson, "Aspect of Theocritean Humor," 296.

41. See also Griffiths, "Home before Lunch," 255; Goldhill, "Naive and Knowing Eye," 217.

42. Griffiths, *Theocritus at Court*, 122, notes: "Within the precincts of the palace both women feel the need to assume a more dignified tone."

43. See, e.g., Callim. *Ep.* 27.3–4: χαίρετε λεπταί / ῥήσιες ("hail, subtle / phrases"); and Callim. *Aet.* 1, fr. 1.11: κατὰ λεπτόν ("on a small scale"). On the use of λεπτός as a term representative of refined Hellenistic poetics, see Pfeiffer, *History of Classical Scholarship*, 137–38. See also Griffiths, *Theocritus at Court*, 7; Bulloch, "Hellenistic Poetry," 561. Of course Hellenistic literary terms had earlier roots, e.g., Ar. *Ra.* 1108: κἀποκινδυνεύετον λεπτόν τι καὶ σοφὸν λέγειν ("Venture to say something fine and clever"). On λεπτός, see esp. Erich Reitzenstein, "Zur Stiltheorie des Kallimachos," in *Festschrift Richard Reitzenstein*

(Leipzig: B. G. Teubner, 1931), 25–40 (but note Hutchinson's warning against overinterpretation; *Hellenistic Poetry*, 84 n. 116). See also Gelzer, "Mimus und Kunsttheorie," 105 n. 23.

44. Callimachus too seems to use the term λεπτός of woven materials at *Epica et Elegiaca Minora*, fr. 383.15: λεπταλέους ἔξυσαν (see Pfeiffer, *Callimachus* 1: 310 nn. 14, 15). Thomas notes that Callimachus's interest in weaving (here and elsewhere) "is doubtless connected with Callimachus' awareness of the metaphorical potential implied by this activity: elaborate weaving may stand for highly artistic poetic production" ("Callimachus," 107–8).

45. For a discussion of Hellenistic literary terms, see, e.g., Pfeiffer, *History of Classical Scholarship*, 135–38; see also Gelzer, "Mimus und Kunsttheorie" (on Theocritus's *Idyll* 15 and Herodas's *Mime* 4). For a handy table of literary terms used by Horace, Catullus, and Callimachus, see N. B. Crowther, "Horace, Catullus, and Alexandrianism," *Mnemosyne*, 4th ser., 31 (1978), 40.

46. See also Goldhill, "Naive and Knowing Eye," 218.

47. On the problems involved in evaluating depth of aesthetic experience, see B. H. Smith, *Contingencies of Value*, esp. 83–84.

48. Skinner, "Nossis," 32. On how the poet H. D. later challenges the hierarchical tradition that relegates women to small lyrical poems, see, e.g., Alicia Ostriker, "The Thieves of Language: Women Poets and Revisionist Mythmaking," in *The New Feminist Criticism: Essays on Women, Literature, and Theory*, ed. Elaine Showalter (New York: Pantheon Books, 1985), 314–38.

49. Horstmann, *Ironie und Humor*, 35.

50. If the hangings were meant to be garments on the Adonis and Aphrodite figures, the statement would not be expressed hypothetically (Gow, *Theocritus* 2: 287 n. 78; Atallah, *Adonis*, 110).

51. On the rarity of these terms and for descriptions of the garments so described, see Gow, "*Adoniazusae* of Theocritus," 184–87; and idem, *Theocritus* 2: 273 n. 21. Gow suggests that the compound ἐμπερονατρίς found in Hesychius's dictionary "if not a conflation of the two words in T., would seem to come from some other Doric writer" (*Theocritus* 2: 273 n. 21). So too Magnien, "Syracusain littéraire," 127: "Ces termes ne nous apparaissent pas, ou ne nous apparaissent que rarement dans le lexique grec, parce qu'ils appartiennent à une langue dont nous n'avons presque plus rien."

52. On Hellenistic ruler cults, see, e.g., Arthur Darby Nock, "Notes on Ruler-Cult, I–IV," *Journal of Hellenic Studies* 48 (1928), 21–48; idem, "ΣΥΝΝΑΟΣ ΘΕΟΣ," *Harvard Studies in Classical Philology* 41 (1930), 1–62; Julien L. Tondriau, "Princesses ptolémaïques comparées ou identifiées à des déesses (IIIe–Ier siècles avant J. C.)," *Bulletin de la Société royale d'archéologie d'Alexandrie* 37 (1948), 12–33; L. Cerfaux and J. Tondriau, *Le culte des souverains dans la civilisation gréco-romaine* (Tournai: Desclée and Co., 1957), esp. ch. 5, "L'Égypte ptolémaïque," 189–227; P. M. Fraser, *Ptolemaic Alexandria* 1: 213–46; S. R. F. Price, "Hellenistic Cities and Their Rulers," ch. 2 in *Rituals and Power: The Roman Imperial Cult in Asia Minor* (1984; reprint, Cambridge and New York: Cambridge University Press, 1986), 23–52.

53. Among the fourth-century philosophers, Plato and Aristotle examine moral issues involved in evaluating art. Later, Cicero, Quintilian, and Dio Chry-

sostum are among those who value works of art by their capacity to contribute to the religious and ethical life of the viewer. For example, Dio Chrysostom describes the benefits a spiritually troubled individual can obtain by beholding Phidias's statue of Zeus at Olympia: ἀνθρώπων δέ, ὃς ἂν ᾖ παντελῶς ἐπίπονος τὴν ψυχήν, πολλὰς ἀναντλήσας συμφορὰς καὶ λύπας ἐν τῷ βίῳ μηδὲ ὕπνον ἡδὺν ἐπιβαλλόμενος, καὶ ὃς δοκεῖ μοι κατ' ἐναντίον στὰς τῆσδε τῆς εἰκόνος ἐκλαθέσθαι ἂν πάντων ὅσα ἐν ἀνθρωπίνῳ βίῳ δεινὰ καὶ χαλεπὰ γίγνεται παθεῖν ("Whoever might be burdened with pain in his soul, having borne many misfortunes and pains in his life and never being able to attain sweet sleep, even that man, I believe, standing before this image, would forget all the terrible and harsh things which one must suffer in human life"; trans. Pollitt, *Art of Ancient Greece*, 62; *Or.* 12.51–52; Greek text taken from *Dio Chrysostom*, vol. 2 [Cambridge: Harvard University Press, 1977]).

54. Motto and Clark, "Idyllic Slumming," 41, and Griffiths, "Home before Lunch," 249, respectively. So too, e.g., Fritzsche, *Theokrits Gedichte*, 187: "τρυγόνες spricht ärgerlich der Mann, der im Königshofe neben den unermüdlich schwatzenden Weibern steht"; Monteil, *Théocrite*, 159: "invective d'un voisin aux deux bavardes"; Schwinge, *Künstlichkeit von Kunst*, who throughout his discussion of *Idyll* 15 refers to the women as "Klatschweiber," even when he applauds the liberty of their speech (57–59). The scholia, on the other hand, describe the bystander's irritation without endorsing it: τοῦτο δέ φησί τις παρεπόμενος καὶ ἀγανακτῶν ἐπὶ τῇ ἄγαν αὐτῶν ἀδολεσχίᾳ. διὸ καὶ ἐπιτιμᾷ αὐταῖς ὡς τὰ κατὰ μέρος τῶν εἰκόνων ἀνερευνώσαις ("Someone says this who is following alongside the women and feeling annoyed at their great volubility; wherefore he also censures them for examining the particularities of the images"; Greek text taken from Wendel, *Scholia*, 313).

55. Horstmann, *Ironie und Humor*, 36.

56. Although the poem may start for some readers with an apparent collusion between the poet and the reader against the women, the tone of the *ekphrasis* encourages the abandonment of an implied reader who holds conventional elitist views about women's incapacity for elevated aesthetic response and expects Theocritus's representations of fictive women responding to art to reflect such attitudes.

57. For a discussion of how Theocritus's poetry encourages this mode of self-recognition, see Simon Goldhill, *The Poet's Voice: Essays on Poetics and Greek Literature* (Cambridge and New York: Cambridge University Press, 1991), 246–72.

58. On similarities between *Idylls* 1 and 15, see Griffiths, *Theocritus at Court*, 124–28.

59. For a discussion of how *Id.* 1's rustic cup evokes earlier Homeric themes and *ekphrases* (e.g., Achilles' shield, *Il.* 18.478–608), see Halperin, *Before Pastoral*, 161–89. Cf. the similar exploitation of Achilles' shield in *A.P.* 11.48, a request to Hephaestus to make a decorated silver cup rather than a suit of armor, with the specific instruction that the decorations consist of vines, clusters, and Bacchus, not stars, chariots, and Orion (such decorations would recall Achilles' shield).

60. See Griffiths, *Theocritus at Court*, 124–28, esp. 126–27.

61. E.g., Lawall, *Theocritus' Coan Pastorals*, 27–30; Charles Segal, "'Since

Daphnis Dies': The Meaning of Theocritus' First Idyll," in *Poetry and Myth*, 29–33; Halperin, *Before Pastoral*, 161–89.

62. The goatherd animates the decorations within the cup as he describes them (cf. the description of Achilles' shield in Homer's *Iliad*, book 18).

63. Gow, *Theocritus* 2 : 110 n. 105.

64. On display in private homes in the fourth century, see Dem. 3.29; on floor mosaics in private homes from the fourth century, see Pollitt, *Art in the Hellenistic Age*, 210–29. In the fifth century, to commission works of art for the home was considered extravagant: the notoriously extravagant Alcibiades reportedly imprisoned an artist in his home to decorate it with paintings (Plut. *Alc.* 16).

65. Headlam and Knox, *Herodas*, lii and 362 n. 105, suggest that in *Mime* 7 the cobbler may also be marketing dildoes; I. C. Cunningham, "Herodas 6 and 7," *Classical Quarterly*, n.s., 14 (1964), 33–35, elaborates this suggestion. For arguments against, see Gilbert Lawall, "Herodas 6 and 7 Reconsidered," *Classical Philology* 71 (1976), 165–69.

66. On *Mime* 6's spoof of Orphic rituals and myths, see Jacob Stern, "Herodas' *Mimiamb* 6," *Greek, Roman, and Byzantine Studies* 20 (1979), 247–54 (Metro as Mother, Koritto as Kore, Euboule possibly as the Orphic myth's Eubouleus). One might also note the mention of an unchaste, sexually innovative "Artemeis" (*Mime* 6.87–90) and the suggestion of the goddess Athena as a maker of dildoes (65–67).

67. Frederic Will, *Herondas* (New York: Twayne Publishers, 1973), 100, notes "the strange beauty" of the image "soft as sleep" in reference to dildoes.

68. *Idyll* 15 and *Mime* 6 share other elements of language and shaping. Both poems start with a hostess bidding a guest sit and ordering a maid to fetch a chair (*Id.* 15.2–3: ὅρη δρίφον, Εὐνόα, αὐτᾷ . . . καθίζευ; *Mime* 6.1–2: κάθησο, Μητροῖ. τῆι γυναικὶ θὲς δίφρον / ἀναστᾶθεῖ͜οα). Both poems end with a similar declaration of the need to return home to feed the husband (*Id.* 15.146–48: ὥρα ὅμως κῆς οἶκον, 147; cf. 26; *Mime* 6.97–98: λαιμάτ[τε]ι̣ κὤρη / ἡμῖ[ν] ἀφ[......] ἐστί). Both poems include similarly worded abuse against a slave girl (*Id.* 15.30: μὴ δὴ πολύ, λᾳστρί; *Mime* 6.10: λῃστρί). Further, *Mime* 6's Koritto uses the word ἑορτή (holiday) in describing her slave as lazy: τὰ δ᾽ ἄλλ᾽ ἑορτή ("and the rest of you sheer idleness," 17); *Idyll* 15's Praxinoa precedes peremptory orders to her slave girl with a similar expression: ἀεργοῖς αἰὲν ἑορτά ("It's always holiday for those that have nothing to do," 26). Compare too the statement *Mime* 6's Koritto includes in her description of Kerdon's dildoes (οὐχὶ Κέρδωνος, / δόξεις; "you'll think [you see / the hands of Athena herself], not those of Kerdon"; 66–67) with the exclamation *Id.* 15's Gorgo makes on viewing the tapestries (θεῶν περονάματα φασεῖς, "you'll say they are gowns worthy of the gods," 79). Finally, just as in *Mime* 6, Kokkale addresses an audience of women with the vocative γυναῖκες ("women," 27) , so too in Theoc. *Id.* 15, the hymnist addresses an audience of women in her final farewell to Adonis (143). Less extensive similarities link Herodas's *Mime* 2 and Theocritus's *Idyll* 14: both poems feature violent sympotic behavior that involves the beating of a girl, and in both poems a speaker uses the phrase "a mouse caught in pitch" to describe himself (*Id.* 14.51 and *Mime* 2.62). But any discussion of influence between Herodas

and Theocritus is purely speculative, since we do not know the relative dates of Herodas's and Theocritus's poems.

69. For discussion of Sophron as a possible influence, see Ussher, "Mimiamboi of Herodas," 66–67. The scholia on Theoc. *Id.* 15 (Wendel, *Scholia*, 305) claim that *Id.* 15 was modeled after Sophron's mime on viewing the Isthmia. Thus some of the many linkages between Herodas's *Mimes* 4 and 6 and Theocritus's *Idyll* 15 may be due to common echoes of Sophron's mime on the Isthmia (and his mime on dildoes, fr. 24 Kaibel, *Doriensium Comoedia*). On Sophron as a source for Theoc. *Id.* 2, see the scholia (Wendel, *Scholia*, 269–70); Sophron, frs. 4–5 Kaibel, *Doriensium Comoedia*; for discussion, see Gow, *Theocritus* 2:33–35.

70. For a comparison of the thematic movements of *Idylls* 1 and 15, see Griffiths, *Theocritus at Court*, 124–28; see also Miles, "Characterization," 155–56.

71. For a recent discussion of Theocritus's use of frames, see Goldhill, *Poet's Voice*, 223–83. On framing techniques in narrative texts, see also, e.g., Mary Ann Caws, *Reading Frames in Modern Fiction* (Princeton: Princeton University Press, 1985).

72. On the topic of metapoetic passages, see Caws, *Metapoetics of the Passage*. On poetic closure in general, see the seminal book by Barbara Herrnstein Smith, *Poetic Closure: A Study of How Poems End* (Chicago: University of Chicago Press, 1968); see also Dan P. Fowler, "First Thoughts on Closure: Problems and Prospects," *Materiali e discussioni per l'analisi dei testi classici* 22 (1989), 75–122.

73. For a theoretical introduction to this subject, see Thomas G. Pavel's *Fictional Worlds* (Cambridge: Harvard University Press, 1986). Bulloch, "Hellenistic Poetry," 573, privileges fantasy in Theocritus's poetic project: "In fact the Idylls are essentially fantasy, and Theocritus' central concern in almost all of his poetry is with the art of illusion and the exploration of mood." On polarities in *Id.* 1, see Segal, "'Since Daphnis Dies.'" See also Lawall, *Theocritus' Coan Pastorals*, esp. 15–31.

74. *Pace* Miles, "Characterization," 155–56: "The effect of the goatherd's response to song [in *Idyll* 1] is not at all unlike that of Gorgo in *Idyll* 15 after she has heard a hymn. . . . The settings of the two *Idylls* may be quite different, but the mentality of the characters is the same."

75. The standard phraseology of hymnic endings includes the imperative farewell χαῖρε (farewell/rejoice) and a vocative. Χαῖρε occurs 28 times in the Homeric hymns, 16 times starting the line, as at *Id.* 15.149. In Hellenistic poetry, see also, e.g., Theoc. *Id.* 17.135 (χαῖρε, ἄναξ Πτολεμαῖε; "farewell, lord Ptolemy") and the close of Callim. *H. Apollo.*

76. Audience participation was traditionally integral to private celebrations of the Adonia. In *Idyll* 15, by including the audience's women in the next morning's ritual of grief and song, the hymnist maintains a mood of audience participation: ἀῶθεν δ' ἄμμες νιν ἅμα δρόσῳ ἀθρόαι ἔξω / οἰσεῦμες ποτὶ κύματ' ἐπ' ἀιόνι πτύοντα, / λύσασαι δὲ κόμαν καὶ ἐπὶ σφυρὰ κόλπον ἀνεῖσαι / στήθεσι φαινομένοις λιγυρᾶς ἀρξεύμεθ' ἀοιδᾶς ("At dawn we will gather with the dew and carry him [Adonis] outside / to the waves crashing on the shore, / and with hair unbound, robes in folds at our ankles, / breasts bare, we shall begin the funereal song"; 132–35).

77. Cf. the hymnic farewell of *Hom. H.* 26.12 (to Dionysus), where the par-

ticiple χαίροντας is also used to represent the recurring joy of the celebrants at what appears to be an annual festival: δὸς δ᾽ ἡμᾶς χαίροντας ἐς ὥρας αὖτις ἱκέσθαι ("Grant that we joyously reach this season again," trans. Apostolos N. Athanassakis, *The Homeric Hymns* [Baltimore and London: Johns Hopkins University Press, 1976], 65).

78. *Pace* Gow, *Theocritus* 2 : 303 n. 145: "I do not know ἡ θ. elsewhere so used, nor the adj. at all where there is so little perceptible emphasis on the sex."

79. Translations and interpretations commonly disregard the difference in gender of the artisans — e.g., Anthony Holden, *Greek Pastoral Poetry* (Harmondsworth: Penguin Books, 1974), 103: "What craftsmen they must have been / to make these, what artists to draw such lines." Cf. Griffiths, "Home before Lunch," 254, who overlooks the men who helped make the tapestries: "They [Gorgo and Praxinoa] see in the Adonis festival an affirmation of female power and self-sufficiency. . . . It was women who made the tapestries." Yet the anaphora of exclamatory pronouns (ποῖαι and ποῖοι) and the alliteration of πs (every other word through ποῖοι) highlight the artisans' difference in gender and their collaboration.

80. Miles, "Characterization," 156.

81. See, e.g., J. J. Pollitt, *The Ancient View of Greek Art: Criticism, History, and Terminology*, student ed. (New Haven: Yale University Press, 1974), 92–94 n. 28.

82. See discussion in Pfeiffer, *History of Classical Scholarship*, 138.

83. A conventional excuse for women's departures is to return home and feed a husband (in life, as in poetry, e.g., Herodas's *Mime* 6.97–98). But unlike *Mime* 6, *Idyll* 15 places this motif in a ritual context. On the importance of food within the family and in spiritual contexts, see, e.g., Dubisch, "Culture," esp. 207–8.

84. The two lines describing the singer's artistry balance the two lines describing Diocleides' hunger, a contrast underscored by the emphatic placement of ἁ θήλεια (referring to the woman singer) at the end of line 145 and of Διοκλείδας at the end of line 147.

85. But cf. Griffiths, *Theocritus at Court*, 118, for whom the definition of ὄλβιος remains economic in nature at the end of the poem, as earlier: "ὄλβος is shown in Egyptian society at large to derive ultimately from the royal house — surely a comforting notion for monarchy who kept so much of that ὄλβος for themselves." (So too Griffiths, "Home before Lunch," 255.)

86. On the novelist's concern about "the divergence of comfortable story and the non-narrative contingencies of modern reality," see Frank Kermode, *The Sense of an Ending* (1967; reprint, London and New York: Oxford University Press, 1968), 127–52 (quote taken from 128).

Chapter 4. Patronage

1. For a general survey of Greek patronage, see Gold, *Literary Patronage*, 15–37.

2. Strabo 17.793–94. On the institutionalized system of Ptolemaic patronage, see P. M. Fraser, *Ptolemaic Alexandria* 1 : 305–35 (with attention to the connection, through Demetrius of Phaleron, with the Lyceum's Mouseion, 314–15).

For a general discussion of royal patronage in the Hellenistic period, see Klaus Bringmann, "The King as Benefactor: Some Remarks on Ideal Kingship in the Age of Hellenism," in Bulloch et al., *Images and Ideologies*, 7–24.

3. P. M. Fraser, *Ptolemaic Alexandria* 1 : 307–8.

4. Ael. *VH* 3.17.

5. P. M. Fraser, *Ptolemaic Alexandria* 1 : 65, calls Theocritus (and his fellow countryman Archimedes) "Syracusan birds of passage."

6. On the availability of formal schooling for Greek females from the fourth century (and on the limited introduction of coeducation), see Pomeroy, "Technikai kai Mousikai," 51–68, and Cole, "Greek Women," esp. 227–33.

7. On the royal tutors, see, e.g., Pfeiffer, *History of Classical Scholarship*, 92, 154–55; P. M. Fraser, *Ptolemaic Alexandria* 1 : 309, 311, 322–23; Thomas Gelzer, "Transformations," in Bulloch et al., *Images and Ideologies*, 142.

8. The second generation of Ptolemies continued the tradition of cultivated tutors by appointing Apollonius Rhodius to teach Ptolemy III (P. M. Fraser, *Ptolemaic Alexandria* 1 : 309, 322–23).

9. See Macurdy, *Hellenistic Queens*, esp. 31–52; Pomeroy, *Women in Hellenistic Egypt*, 6–11; Carney, "Olympias," esp. 51–62; Elizabeth D. Carney, "The Career of Adea-Eurydice," *Historia: Zeitschrift für alte Geschichte* 36 (1987), 496–502.

10. See, e.g., Theoc. *Id*. 17.34–39, for praise of Berenice's intelligence and passion. See also Asclepiades 39 Gow and Page, which compares a Berenice with Aphrodite (although note uncertainties about its authorship and the identity of Berenice: Gow and Page, *Greek Anthology* 2 : 143).

11. Both Theoc. *Id*. 24 and Herod. *Mime* 3 represent women taking strong roles in their children's education: *Id*. 24's Alcmene selects Heracles' tutors and *Mime* 3's Metrotime tells the schoolmaster how to discipline her son.

12. For discussion (with references), see Stanley Mayer Burstein, *Outpost of Hellenism: The Emergence of Heraclea on the Black Sea* (Berkeley and Los Angeles: University of California Press, 1976), 86–87; idem, "Arsinoe II," 199.

13. On Arsinoe's rotunda, see James R. McCredie et al., *The Rotunda of Arsinoe*, vol. 7 of *Samothrace: Excavations Conducted by the Institute of Fine Arts of New York University*, ed. Karl Lehmann and Phyllis Williams Lehmann (Princeton: Princeton University Press, 1992). On the dedicatory inscription of Arsinoe's Rotunda, see also P. M. Fraser, *The Inscriptions on Stone*, vol. 2.1 of *Samothrace: Excavations Conducted by the Institute of Fine Arts of New York University*, ed. Karl Lehmann (New York: Pantheon Books, 1960), 48–50 (no. 10).

14. Frazer bases his proposal on similarities in style between Ptolemy's Propylon and Arsinoe's Rotunda (Alfred Frazer, *The Propylon of Ptolemy II*, vol. 10 of *Samothrace: Excavations Conducted by the Institute of Fine Arts of New York University*, ed. Karl Lehmann and Phyllis Williams Lehmann [Princeton: Princeton University Press, 1990], 225, 232). Georges Roux suggests that Arsinoe may have been Ptolemy's wife when she dedicated the Rotunda (McCredie et al., *Rotunda of Arsinoe*, esp. 231–39). On the dating of the Rotunda and Propylon, see also P. M. Fraser, *Inscriptions on Stone*, 5–6; Frazer, *Propylon of Ptolemy II*, 232–33 (with comment on Roux's suggestion).

15. Arsinoe helped sponsor worship at Samothrace, where Lysimachus was

granted divine honors, and she also sought refuge after Lysimachus's death in two places which granted Lysimachus divine honors while he was alive, Cassandreia and Samothrace. (Perhaps her familiarity with the notion of a deified king also led her later to encourage her brother's projects of self-deification.)

16. For the suggestion that Arsinoe's wealth enabled her to hire a mercenary force at Cassandreia, see Macurdy, *Hellenistic Queens*, 114-15.

17. See Rudolf Pfeiffer, "Arsinoe Philadelphos in der Dichtung," *Die Antike* 2 (1926), 161-74.

18. Theoc. *Id.* 15, esp. 23-24, 109-11.

19. P. M. Fraser, *Ptolemaic Alexandria* 1:207. See also Callim. *Lyrica* fr. 228 (with *dieg.*), in which the Dioskouroi carry off dead Arsinoe.

20. For translation of the Pithom stele, the evidence of this visit, see Édouard Naville, "La stèle de Pithom," *Zeitschrift für ägyptische Sprache und Altertumskunde* 40 (1902), 71-72, lines 12-16. See also, e.g., Macurdy, *Hellenistic Queens*, 119; Gow, *Theocritus* 2:339-40 nn. 86-90.

21. On the significance of the Decree of Chremonides, see Burstein, "Arsinoe II," 207-10 (a cautious approach, with useful summary of previous scholarship); Hauben, "Arsinoé II," 114-17; Christian Habicht, "Athens and the Ptolemies," *Classical Antiquity* 11 (1992), 72-73 (with attention to the redating of Arsinoe's death to 268).

22. The elite Alexandrian taste for the miniature shows a turning away not only from the spectacular displays of the Ptolemies (Schwinge, *Künstlichkeit von Kunst*, 40; Green, *Alexander to Actium*, 158, 183), but also from the monumental Egyptian world to which they had come, a world of, e.g., gigantic pyramids and temples and colossal statues. For a Greek perspective on Egypt's monumentality, see Hdt. 2.124-38, 148, 155, 175-76, etc. Thus Hdt. 2.148 (on a great Egyptian labyrinth): εἰ γάρ τις τὰ ἐξ Ἑλλήνων τείχεά τε καὶ ἔργων ἀπόδεξιν συλλογίσαιτο, ἐλάσσονος πόνου τε ἂν καὶ δαπάνης φανείη ἐόντα τοῦ λαβυρίνθου τούτου ("Were all that Greeks have builded and wrought added together the whole would be seen to be a matter of less labour and cost than was this labyrinth"; trans. A. D. Godley, *Herodotus*, vol. 1, *Books I–II*, rev. ed. [Cambridge: Harvard University Press, 1926], 455-57; Greek text *O.C.T.*).

23. On Alexandria's population to 215, see P. M. Fraser, *Ptolemaic Alexandria* 1:38-75.

24. See, e.g., Callim. *Iambus* 13, fr. 203, with *dieg.* (for discussion of variety in Callimachus's iambi, see D. L. Clayman, *Callimachus' Iambi* [Leiden: E. J. Brill, 1980], 48-51). On the Alexandrian fashion for mixing genres, see Kroll, "Kreuzung der Gattungen," 202-24; L. E. Rossi, "I generi letterari e le loro leggi scritte e non scritte nelle letterature classiche," *Bulletin of the Institute of Classical Studies* (University of London) 18 (1971), esp. 83-84. On Theocritus's mixing of genres and styles (e.g., bucolic poems written in hexameter verse and including Homeric diction), see Fabiano, "Fluctuation in Theocritus' Style," esp. 526-37. On mixing of genres in Hellenistic poetry (and on Theocritus's bucolic poetry as refashioned epic), see Halperin, *Before Pastoral*, esp. 193-266.

25. On streets named after Arsinoe, see P. M. Fraser, *Ptolemaic Alexandria* 1:35-36, 2:110 n. 276. On the joint temple of the Theoi Sotores (built by Ptolemy II), see Theoc. *Id.* 17.123-27. On the Alexandrian Arsinoeum (temple

of Arsinoe, left incomplete when Ptolemy II and the architect died) and its wondrous statuary and obelisk, see Pliny *HN* 34.148 (an iron statue of Arsinoe
planned for suspension from lodestone temple-vaulting), 36.69 (a 120-foot obelisk), 37.108 (a 6-foot topaz statue of Arsinoe); for discussion, see P. M. Fraser,
Ptolemaic Alexandria I : 25. On the royal palaces, see Strab. 17.793–94.

26. Ath. 5.197c–202a (for discussion, see E. E. Rice, *The Grand Procession of
Ptolemy Philadelphus* [London and New York: Oxford University Press, 1983]).

27. On Hellenistic ruler cults, see, e.g., Nock, "Notes on Ruler-Cult," 21–48;
idem, "ΣΥΝΝΑΟΣ ΘΕΟΣ," 1–62; Tondriau, "Princesses"; P. M. Fraser, *Ptolemaic Alexandria* I : 213–46; Price, "Hellenistic Cities," 23–52. For the suggestion
that redating Arsinoe's death to 268 makes it more possible that she helped set
up her own cult, see Gutzwiller, "Callimachus' *Lock*," 365 n. 22; see also D. B.
Thompson, *Ptolemaic Oinochoai*, 120 (cited by Gutzwiller, "Callimachus' *Lock*,"
366 n. 25). On redating Arsinoe's death to 268, see Grzybek, "Mort," 103–12.

28. On dedicatory plaques and oinochoai, see Louis Robert, "Sur un décret
d'Ilion et sur un papyrus concernant des cultes royaux," in *Essays in Honor
of C. Bradford Welles* (New Haven. American Society of Papyrologists, 1966),
202–10; P. M. Fraser, *Ptolemaic Alexandria* I : 190–91, 226–28, 240–43; D. B.
Thompson, *Ptolemaic Oinochoai*, esp. 16–17, 76, 96, 117.

29. On the advantages of mercenary service under the Ptolemies, see, for
example, E. G. Turner, "Ptolemaic Egypt," in Walbank et al., *Hellenistic World*,
124–25.

30. On the encomium as the purpose of the poem, see, e.g., Lawall, *Theocritus' Coan Pastorals*, 122; on the encomium as a digression, see, e.g., Legrand,
Étude sur Théocrite, 139. Schwinge, *Künstlichkeit von Kunst*, 64–65, also separates
the encomium from the fictive story. Stern, "Theocritus' *Idyll* 14," 58, and Griffiths, *Theocritus at Court*, 110–12, both approach the encomium from within the
fictive story, but with a focus on the "historical reality of Ptolemy" (phrase taken
from Griffiths, *Theocritus at Court*, 110).

31. Gow, *Theocritus* 2:259 n. 60. A person interested in enlisting (with the expectation of pay and land grants) could find more useful information in *Idyll* 17's
descriptions of Ptolemy's soldierly record, vast military force, surplus wealth,
and fertile and abundant lands.

32. Cf. *Id.* 16.27–28 (a poem directed toward Hieron II), where a value is set
on being a good host, even to a stranger.

33. Aeschinas's failure to investigate a rumor of Cynisca's unfaithfulness
(27–28) underscores his persistent obliviousness to signs of eros.

34. Cf. the contrast between Catullus's and Propertius's poetry's obsessive
fixation on a single love-object and Horace's poetry's less romanticized approach
to love.

35. The weight of the description (63–64, half the encomium) and the inclu-
sion of a prescriptive clause ($o\tilde{l}\alpha \chi\rho\dot{\eta} \beta\alpha\sigma\iota\lambda\tilde{\eta}$', "as befits a king," 64) place special
emphasis on the quality of generosity, critical to successful relationships between
patron and poet, paymaster and mercenary. Cf. *Id.* 17.106–16, 123–27. On Ptolemy II's sponsorship of Dionysiac artists, see *Id.* 17.112–16; P. M. Fraser, *Ptolemaic Alexandria*, I : 618–19, 2 : 870–71 n. 2 (on the exemption of Dionysiac artists
and other members of the cultural community from the salt tax).

36. Euergetes II, in his *Memoirs, FGrH* 234 F4 (= Ath. 13.576e–f), describes several of Ptolemy's mistresses (cf. Plut. *Mor.* 753e). Euergetes sums up Ptolemy's sexual character as ἐπιρρεπέστερος ὢν πρὸς ἀφροδίσια ("very inclined toward sexual pleasures"). On the deification of another mistress, Bilistiche, see Plut. *Mor.* 753e. See Cameron, "Two Mistresses," 287–304 (on Didyme and Bilistiche).

37. See Ath. 13.576f, 10.425e–f. So too Polyb. 14.11. At Theoc. *Id.* 4.31, Corydon mentions Glauce, a famous musician and possibly another of Ptolemy's favorites (for discussion, see Bulloch, "Hellenistic Poetry," 572).

38. Twice earlier, Thyonichus focuses attention on Aeschinas's immoderate desires (11, 57). These two passages are linked with Thyonichus's exhortation through the use of the vocative form of Aeschinas's name (only occurring at 10, 58, and 65), and lines 11 and 64 are further joined by the repetition of forms of the (immoderate) adjective πᾶς.

39. On how Ptolemy I and Ptolemy II exploited this appeal, see, e.g., Erich S. Gruen, *The Hellenistic World and the Coming of Rome*, 2 vols. (Berkeley and Los Angeles: University of California Press, 1984), 1:138 (with notes 37 and 38).

40. Cf. Herodas *Mime* 1.26–35, which places a description of Alexandria's glittery attractions in the mouth of a bawd. For an example of Ptolemy's playfulness, see Ath. 11.493e–494b.

41. Ptolemy himself blurred the boundary between private and public friendships and interests insofar as he treated Egypt as a royal possession and rewarded his designated friends by appointing them to high administrative offices (see, e.g., Green, *Alexander to Actium*, 192).

42. Euhemerus's travel novel offered opportune precedent for the Hellenistic practice of deifying mortal rulers: for instance, Zeus was originally a mortal king who, having set up cult worship for his grandfather Uranus, was also himself proclaimed a living god. On Euhemerus's work and its reception, see, e.g., P. M. Fraser, *Ptolemaic Alexandria*, 1: 289–95; see also Green, *Alexander to Actium*, esp. 55, 398–99.

43. I draw here on Kermode's useful distinction between myths and fictions: "Myths call for absolute, fictions for conditional assent" (*Sense of an Ending*, 39).

44. *Idyll* 14, which includes an encomium of Ptolemy, is Theocritus's only poem that does not refer to deities. By not referring here to gods, Theocritus also avoids the topic of the Ptolemies' possible deification.

45. Praxinoa justifies leaving her son at home by exclaiming δάκνει ἵππος ("the horse bites," 40); later she explains her fixation: ἵππον καὶ τὸν ψυχρὸν ὄφιν τὰ μάλιστα δεδοίκω / ἐκ παιδός ("From childhood on I've been most fearful of horses and cold snakes," 58). An underlying theme here is related to the Adonis story: if Praxinoa keeps her son away from horses and cold snakes, she can prevent him from becoming a man (and leaving her); Aphrodite has a similar thought about Adonis and wild beasts, esp. boars (see, e.g., Ov. *Met.* 10.539–52, cf. 708–16).

46. Gow, *Theocritus* 1:xxviii, points out that "some or all of the bucolic poems may well have been composed in Alexandria." On the dialogic possibilities available in presenting rural fictions to city folks, see, e.g., Leo Marx, *The Machine in the Garden: Technology and the Pastoral Ideal in America* (London and

New York: Oxford University Press, 1964); Raymond Williams, *The Country and the City* (New York: Oxford University Press, 1973); Annabel Patterson, *Pastoral and Ideology: Virgil to Valéry* (Berkeley and Los Angeles: University of California Press, 1987).

47. Cameron, "Two Mistresses," 287–95. For the connection between Ptolemy's and Asclepiades' Didyme, see also Pomeroy, *Women*, 55.

48. These lines, in conjunction with the two lines that follow, stress Bombyca's dark color: καὶ τὸ ἴον μέλαν ἐστί, καὶ ἀ γραπτὰ ὑάκινθος· / ἀλλ᾽ ἔμπας ἐν τοῖς στεφάνοις τὰ πρᾶτα λέγονται ("Dark is the violet and the lettered hyacinth, / yet in garlands these are accounted first"; trans. Gow, *Theocritus* 1 : 83; *Id.* 10.28–29). By having Bucaeus underscore society's inconsistency in mocking a woman's dark hues but not a flower's, the poet draws attention to the theme of ethnic prejudice. Also, through Bucaeus's oppositional fondness for the slender Bombyca, Theocritus can approach the issue of his own "unpopular" predilection for "slender," Callimachean values in art (e.g., small-scale poetic projects). Cf. Callim. fr. 398: Λύδη καὶ παχὺ γράμμα καὶ οὐ τορόν ("The *Lyde* is a fat and inelegant book," trans. Trypanis, "Callimachus," 247). On public partiality for grand Homeric epic, see Theoc. *Id.* 16.20. For a statement of Callimachean poetic values (through the fictive Lycidas), see Theoc. *Id.* 7.45–48.

49. Ath. 10.425e–f, 13.576f; Polyb. 14.11.

50. See, e.g., Theoc. *Id.* 17.95: ὄλβῳ μὲν πάντας κε καταβρίθοι βασιλῆας ("In riches he could outweigh all other kings"; trans. Gow, *Theocritus* 1 : 137).

51. *Id.* 17 praises Ptolemy's riches (95–97, 106–15), which enabled him to set golden and ivory representations of his mother and father in shrines (121–25). Ptolemy's *Pompe* also included statues and representations of gold, some sponsored by Ptolemy, e.g., a golden statue of Alexander (Ath. 5.202a); some financed by others, e.g., two golden portrait-statues of Ptolemy II on golden chariots (Ath. 5.203b). On Ptolemy's wealth, see also, e.g., Ath. 5.203b–c.

52. See discussion below.

53. Gow, *Theocritus* 2 : 199 n. 26.

54. On the indeterminacy of Bombyca's status and relation to Polybotas, see Gow, *Theocritus* 2 : 196–97 n. 15; Dover, *Theocritus*, 166–67. If Polybotas (man of many grazing animals) were wealthy, a flute girl's relation to him would probably be as slave or employee; but if not wealthy, she might be a daughter, whom he hires out.

55. Gow, *Theocritus* 2 : 196 n. 15; Strab. 10.489.

56. Callim. *Hymn* 1 is commonly dated early in Ptolemy's career. On the dating of *Hymn* 1 to a celebration of Ptolemy's accession to the throne (and birthday), see James J. Clauss, "Lies and Allusions: The Addressee and Date of Callimachus' *Hymn to Zeus*," *Classical Antiquity* 5 (1986), 155–70.

57. Cf. *Id.* 17.13–15 (on Ptolemy I).

58. For discussion of the panhellenic audience's effect on song, see G. Nagy, *Greek Mythology and Poetics* (Ithaca: Cornell University Press, 1990), esp. 37–47.

59. Their recruits included such outsiders as prostitutes, slaves, and freed persons. On the Epicureans' appeal to such persons, see Frischer, *Sculpted Word*, 206.

60. See Burkert, *Ancient Mystery Cults*, 40–41, 149 n. 67 (who cites Hdt.

2.171 for the claim that the Thesmophoria came to Greece from Egypt); Green, *Alexander to Actium*, 586–601. On the topic of religion in Alexandria, P. M. Fraser, *Ptolemaic Alexandria* 1:189–301 (ch. 5: "Religious Life") is fundamental (on the cult of Cybele and Attis in Alexandria, see 1:277–78). See too, e.g., Callim. *Ep.* 40, *Ep.* 47, *Ep.* 57, *Iambus* 3, fr. 193.34–38; Dioscorides *Ep.* 3 Gow and Page (= *A.P.* 5.53), *Ep.* 4 Gow and Page (= *A.P.* 5.193), *Ep.* 16 Gow and Page (= *A.P.* 6.220), *Ep.* 36 Gow and Page (= *A.P.* 11.195); Sotades fr. 3 Powell, *Coll. Alex.*

61. On the development of Hellenistic ruler cults, see, e.g., Green, *Alexander to Actium*, 396–406. On worship of the Olympian deities in Alexandria, see P. M. Fraser, *Ptolemaic Alexandria* 1:193–212.

62. On the Ptolemies' cultivation of a connection with Dionysus, see Walter Burkert, "Bacchic *Teletai* in the Hellenistic Age," in *Masks of Dionysus*, ed. Thomas H. Carpenter and Christopher A. Faraone (Ithaca: Cornell University Press, 1993), esp. 262–64. On how state support of Dionysus worship might heighten a Ptolemy's status and strengthen his genealogical claims, see P. M. Fraser, *Ptolemaic Alexandria*, esp. 1:202–3. On the connection of Alexander and Dionysus, see, e.g., Nock, "Notes on Ruler-Cult," 21–30. On how worship of Aphrodite began to coincide with Arsinoe's own, see Tondriau, "Princesses," 16–18; Fraser, *Ptolemaic Alexandria* 1:239–40; Pomeroy, *Women in Hellenistic Egypt*, esp. 30–38.

63. Rice, *Grand Procession*, 83–86. On Ptolemy II's extension of the empire, see also Theoc. 17.86–92 (with discussion in Gow, *Theocritus* 2:339–40 nn. 86–90); Polyb. 5.34.5–9 (with comment in Gruen, *Hellenistic World* 2:672).

64. See Theoc. *Id.* 17.112–14. For discussion of the Dionysiac guild in Ptolemaic Egypt, see P. M. Fraser, *Ptolemaic Alexandria* 1:203; Rice, *Grand Procession*, 52–58.

65. Thus P. M. Fraser, *Ptolemaic Alexandria* 1:197; Pomeroy, *Women in Hellenistic Egypt*, 30–31.

66. On Aphrodite as patroness of marriage (with references for cult titles such as Aphrodite Thalamon, "of the bridal chamber," Aphrodite Harma, "who yokes together," Aphrodite Nymphia, "the bridal Aphrodite"), see Lewis Richard Farnell, *The Cults of the Greek States*, vol. 2 (Oxford: Clarendon Press, 1896), 656–57. On Aphrodite as goddess of "passionate sex in marriage," see Paul Friedrich, *The Meaning of Aphrodite* (Chicago: University of Chicago Press, 1978), 142–43. See also Pomeroy, *Women in Hellenistic Egypt*, 31–38. For the important argument that the emergence of the Aphrodite cult in Alexandria and the emphasis in Alexandrian poetry on reciprocal passion in marriage reflected Ptolemaic policy to justify "the sharing of monarchic power by husband and wife," see Gutzwiller, "Callimachus' *Lock*," esp. 363–68 (quote taken from 364). On the importance of love in Ptolemaic ideology, see also Koenen, "Adaptation ägyptischer Königsideologie," esp. 157–68; idem, "Ptolemaic King," esp. 62. On the effect of powerful female patronage on courtly discourse during the Renaissance, see, e.g., Leonard Tennenhouse, "Sir Walter Raleigh and Clientage," in Lytle and Orgel, *Patronage in the Renaissance*, 246: "By encouraging her courtiers to make suit to her in the poetic language of love, Elizabeth had institutionalized her personal metaphor of rule."

67. Poetry identifying Arsinoe with Aphrodite includes the anonymous

hymn in Powell, *Coll. Alex.*, pp. 82–89. See also the epigrams connected with Arsinoe-Aphrodite's temple at Zephyrium: Callim. *Ep.* 5; Posidippus *Ep.* 12, 13 Gow and Page; Hedylus *Ep.* 4 Gow and Page (also available in Ath. 7.318b–d; 11.497d–e), with useful commentary in Gow and Page, *Greek Anthology*, vol. 2.

68. Gutzwiller, "Callimachus' *Lock*," 364–68. See also Pomeroy, *Women in Hellenistic Egypt*, 31–38.

69. Pomeroy, *Women in Hellenistic Egypt*, 36, suggests that "Theocritus has given the festival a domestic context and has described only the wedding night of Aphrodite and Adonis, because he is celebrating Aphrodite as goddess of marriage."

70. Strab. 17.789.

71. See, e.g., Paus. 1.6.8. Detienne, *Gardens of Adonis*, 66, emphasizes the Adonia's linkage with extramarital affairs: "The couple formed by Adonis and Aphrodite epitomized the type of relations that exist between a lover and his mistress."

72. On *Idyll* 15's reflection of cult practice, see Gow, "*Adoniazusae* of Theocritus," 180–204; Gow, *Theocritus* 2:262–304. See also Atallah, *Adonis*, 105–35; G. Glotz, "Les fêtes d'Adonis sous Ptolémée II," *Revue des études grecques* 33 (1920), 169–222.

73. E.g., Dioscorides *Ep.* 3 Gow and Page (= *A.P.* 5.53), *Ep.* 4 Gow and Page (= *A.P.* 5.193); Callim. *Iambus* 3, fr. 193.34–38. Sotades, a poet notorious for scurrilous verses against the Hellenistic courts, also wrote a poem called *Adonis* (fr. 3 Powell, *Coll. Alex.*). But cf. Nossis *Ep.* 5 Gow and Page (= *A.P.* 6.275), an epigram on the dedication of a perfumed headdress to Aphrodite (see discussion in Skinner, "Nossis," 24–25); and we also have evidence that Philicus, a member of Ptolemy II's tragic Pleiad, wrote a tragedy called *Adonis*, presumably elevated in tone (see P. M. Fraser, *Ptolemaic Alexandria* 1:198; 2:333 n. 62). For the observation that Callim. *Iambus* 3, fr. 193.34ff., which links Cybele and Adonis, treats contemptuously a cult sponsored by Arsinoe, see P. M. Fraser, *Ptolemaic Alexandria* 1:786.

74. E.g., Gow, "*Adoniazusae* of Theocritus," 202; Griffiths, "Home before Lunch," 256. W. C. Helmbold, "The Song of the Argive Woman's Daughter," *Classical Philology* 46 (1951), 17, asks "why is the song so long, so tedious, and so dull?" and suggests it may be a parody. Dover, *Theocritus*, 210, remarks: "I should have expected Theokritos to take the opportunity of showing how well he could write a hymn, not the opportunity of showing how badly most people wrote them; but this expectation founders on the hymn we have before us." Robert Wells, *Theocritus: The Idylls* (1988; reprint, London and New York: Penguin Books, 1989), 34, agrees that the hymn is probably a parody.

75. Dover, *Theocritus*, 209. See too Gow, "*Adoniazusae* of Theocritus," 202: "The extravagant commendations of 'the incorrigible Gorgo' are more amusing and more in keeping with her character if they are bestowed upon a work which, to a more cultivated taste, does not deserve them"; and Griffiths, "Home before Lunch," 249: "Yet this mawkish spectacle, gotten up for the consumption of the masses, parallels the Gothic novels and soap operas of our own day in symbolizing the housewife's failure of imagination."

76. Bulloch, "Hellenistic Poetry," 580: "A truly grand and rather exotic festi-

val hymn." So too Hutchinson, *Hellenistic Poetry*, 150 ("It is elevated and lavish in its language and feeling, and depicts the visual beauty and extravagance of the tableau created by the Queen"); Zanker, *Realism in Alexandrian Poetry*, 13 ("he has tried to invest the Adonis-rite at Alexandria with all the sensuousness, eroticism and pathos it will have held"). Before Bulloch, a favorable judgment of the hymn was rare. See, e.g., E. M. Forster, *Alexandria: A History and a Guide* (1922; reprint, with new introduction by Forster, Garden City, N.Y.: Anchor Books, 1961), 37: "a beautiful hymn."

77. Goldhill, *Poet's Voice*, 276–77; idem, "Naive and Knowing Eye," 219–21.

78. See Walter Burkert, *Structure and History in Greek Mythology and Ritual* (Berkeley and Los Angeles: University of California Press, 1979), 107, on the Adonia's "independence from and virtual antagonism to the established state cults." See also discussion in Detienne, *Gardens of Adonis*, esp. 79–82 and 99–131; and response by John J. Winkler, "The Laughter of the Oppressed: Demeter and the Gardens of Adonis," in *The Constraints of Desire: The Anthropology of Sex and Gender in Ancient Greece* (New York: Routledge, 1990), 188–209. Cf. Eva Stehle, "Sappho's Gaze: Fantasies of a Goddess and Young Man," *differences* 2 (1990), 103–7.

79. Men were probably used to a low level of involvement in celebrations of the Adonia: in literary representations of the Adonia of the fourth century B.C., men watch women celebrate and sometimes women invite them to private parties as "Adonis substitutes" (e.g., Men. *Sam.* 35–50; Ath. 13.579e–580a; Alciphron *Epist. Meret.* 14.8; cf. Lucian *Dial. Meret.* 17.297; Dioscorides *Epigrams* 3 and 4 Gow and Page = *A.P.* 5.53 and 5.193). For discussion of courtesans celebrating the Adonia, see Detienne, *Gardens of Adonis*, 64–66.

80. Ar. *Lys.* 378–98: a commissioner describes how private celebrations of the Adonia in 415 B.C. disturbed an assembly meeting (cf. scholia on Ar. *Lys.* 389). For discussion, see Detienne, *Gardens of Adonis*, esp. 65–66. For a linkage of the Adonia and the mutilation of Athens's herms, see Keuls, *Reign of the Phallus*, 23–32.

81. See T. W. Allen, W. R. Halliday, and E. E. Sikes, eds., *The Homeric Hymns*, 2d ed. (Oxford: Clarendon Press, 1936).

82. See Tondriau, "Princesses," 16–18; P. M. Fraser, *Ptolemaic Alexandria* 1: 197, 239–40; Pomeroy, *Women of Hellenistic Egypt*, 30–38.

83. For Ovid's version of Adonis's unhappy tale, see *Met.* 10.298–739.

84. Sotades was not known for his courtly tact. We have one line left of another poem, which addresses Ptolemy II (on his marriage to Arsinoe II): εἰς οὐχ ὁσίην τρυμαλιὴν τὸ κέντρον ὠθεῖς ("you are thrusting your prick into an unclean hole"; Sotades fr. 1 Powell, *Coll. Alex.* [Ath. 14.621a]). The one line we have left from a poem by Callimachus on the wedding of Arsinoe and Ptolemy, on the other hand, suggests a celebratory tone: Ἀρσινόης ὦ ξεῖνε γάμον καταβάλλομ' ἀείδειν ("I begin, stranger, my song of Arsinoe's wedding"; fr. 392, which Pfeiffer titles "In Arsinoes Nuptias?").

85. See Detienne, *Gardens of Adonis*, esp. 67–68.

86. For a fundamental discussion of strategies of praise in Theocritus's work, see Griffiths, *Theocritus at Court*, although he judges that "The Adonis hymn . . . conspicuously lacks the wit and evasiveness of the other courtly poems (apart from the *Ptolemy*)" (58).

87. See, e.g., Dover, *Theocritus*, 209–10; see also Goldhill, "Naive and Knowing Eye," 220–21.

88. On sexual ambiguity in Theocritus's representation of Adonis, see chapter 2.

89. Thus Forster, *Alexandria*, 37: "In this Hymn Theocritus displays the other side of his genius — the 'Alexandrian' side. He is no longer the amusing realist, but an erudite poet, whose chief theme is love." See also Zanker, *Realism in Alexandrian Poetry*, 14, who privileges love in Alexandrian poetry, but connects the emphasis on love with realism.

90. Although the verb φιλέω is traditional in descriptions of an immortal's relationship to a mortal (e.g., *Il*. 2.197, *Il*. 9.117; cf. *Od*. 15.245, *Il*. 16.94, *Il*. 7.204), still it is not typically used to describe a god's relation to cult sites. Instead the verbs ἔχω (e.g., *Hom. H*. 22.3), ἀνάσσω (e.g., *Il*. 1.38), and λαγχάνω (e.g., *Hom. H*. 6.2) customarily appear. For example, in Theocritus's *Id*. 17, the more typical verb ἔχω describes Aphrodite's connection with Cyprus: Κύπρον ἔχοισα Διώνας πότνια κούρα (36).

91. Although the gold has been variously interpreted (as jewelry, toys, money, etc.; for discussion, see, e.g., White, "Theocritus' 'Adonis Song,'" 192–94; W. Geoffrey Arnott, "The Stream and the Gold: Two Notes on Theocritus," in *Filologia e forme letterarie, Studi offerti a Francesco Della Corte*, vol. 1, *Letteratura greca*, ed. Sandro Boldrini et al. [Urbino: Università degli studi di Urbino, 1987], 343–46), scholars generally agree that a description of Aphrodite "playing" (particularly in the context of an Adonia) has an implicitly sensual resonance (see, e.g., Dover, *Theocritus*, 210 n. 101: "she also παίζει because the enjoyment of sex belongs to παιδιά"; White, "Theocritus' 'Adonis Song,'" 193; Arnott, "Stream and the Gold," 344–46).

92. As suggested earlier, a mother can fear that her *zopyrion* might one day develop into a *pyrros* like Adonis, and try to lock her boy away from danger (as Aphrodite tries to preserve Adonis): οὐκ ἀξῶ τυ, τέκνον. Μορμώ, δάκνει ἵππος. / δάκρυ' ὅσσα θέλεις, χωλὸν δ' οὐ δεῖ τυ γενέσθαι ("I will not take you, child. Mormo, the horse bites. / Cry however much you like, but I won't have you maimed"; 40–41).

93. Cf. a woman's derisive use of the term Adonis to refer to a weak, skinny boy, too short for his age (Ath. 13.580e–f: one of Machon's anecdotes of prostitutes).

94. Cf. *Idyll* 16's use of vulnerable young warriors (who die at Troy) to illustrate a poet's power to confer fame: especially the feminized Cycnus (θῆλυς ἀπὸ χροιᾶς, "maidenlike of skin"; trans. Gow, *Theocritus* 1:125; 49), but also Priam's long-haired sons (49), and Lycian princes (48; e.g., Glaucus and Sarpedon, doomed friends). Thus in *Idyll* 15, which represents a female festival sponsored by a female patron, Theocritus identifies a Trojan prince by his mother; but in *Idyll* 16, which asks for patronage from Hieron, king of Syracuse, the poet identifies the Trojan princes in the traditional (male) manner: by their father.

95. For Achilles' son as Neoptolemus, see, e.g., Hom. *Il*. and *Od*.; Soph. *Phil*.; Eur. *Andr*.

96. The hymnist's catalogue of warrior-heroes thus may suggest a feminine vantage on epics of war like the *Iliad*. Cf. *Idyll* 16, which, looking toward Hieron II, a commander who seized power in Syracuse through military force, also sug-

gests oppositional readings of Homer's epics (e.g., *Id.* 16.48–49, 54–56). Both *Idylls* 15 and 16 open a dialogue between culture's definition of masculinity as aggression and literature's capacity to redefine that ideal. *Idyll* 16 includes the famous pacifistic lines: ἀράχνια δ' εἰς ὅπλ' ἀράχναι / λεπτὰ διαστήσαιντο, βοᾶς δ' ἔτι μηδ' ὄνομ' εἴη ("May spiders spin their delicate webs over armour, and the cry of onset be no more even named"; trans. Gow, *Theocritus* 1 : 129; 96–97). On female reception of male-generated epics, see, e.g., John J. Winkler, "Public and Private in Sappho's Lyrics," in Foley, *Reflections of Women*, esp. 66–77; Lillian Eileen Doherty, "Gender and Internal Audiences in the *Odyssey*," *American Journal of Philology* 113 (1992), 161–77.

97. For the story of Hecuba's revenge on King Polymestor for murdering her son (Polydorus), see Euripides' *Hecuba*.

98. Just. *Epit.* 24.3.

99. Cf. Theoc. *Id.* 16.74, which offers Achilles and Ajax as models for Hieron. For the story of how later Alexandrians mocked Antoninus for imitating Alexander and Achilles, who were strong and tall whereas he was small (not unlike sickly Ptolemy II), see Herodian 4.9.3.

100. See Gow, *Theocritus* 2 : 335 nn. 53–57. A weak man physically (Strab. 17.789), Ptolemy II might have felt somewhat uneasy about meeting the expectations of leadership set by his father, a powerful general and shrewd politician. On the controversy concerning Ptolemy II's military prowess (and Arsinoe's influence), see, e.g., Burstein, "Arsinoe II," esp. 205 (who cites Ptolemy's accomplishments before marrying Arsinoe); Hauben, "Arsinoé II," 107–27 (who puts more emphasis on Arsinoe's political role).

101. On the political implications of Alexandrian poetry's rejection of epic, see Schwinge, *Künstlichkeit von Kunst*, esp. 40–43 (who cites Callim. *Aet.* 1, fr. 1.3–5 on 41: οὐχ ἓν ἄεισμα διηνεκὲς ἢ βασιλ[η / .....]ας ἐν πολλαῖς ἤνυσα χιλιάσιν / ἢ .....]. ους ἥρωας, ἔπος δ' ἐπὶ τυτθὸν ἐλ[ίσσω / παῖς ἄτ]ε; "[The Telchines blame me because] I did not accomplish one continuous poem of many thousands of lines on . . . kings or . . . heroes, but like a child I roll forth a short tale"; trans. Trypanis, "Callimachus," 5).

102. Pollock raises pertinent questions: "But what is the meaning of the equation of women's art with femininity and femininity with bad art? And, more significantly, why does the point have to be stressed so frequently?" (Griselda Pollock, *Vision and Difference: Femininity, Feminism, and the Histories of Art* [London and New York: Routledge, 1988], 24).

103. Griffiths, "Home before Lunch," 256.

104. For an interesting parallel, see Livy 41.20 (on the generosity of the Seleucid King Antiochus IV).

105. E.g., the reunion feast in Euripides' *Ion* includes gold bowls (1165–66), gold and silver cups (1175, 1181–82), abundant food (1169), and a tent (1129) shaded by embroidered tapestries (1132–66). In Latin literature, e.g., Peleus's wedding feast in Catullus's *Poem* 64 includes gold and silver (44), ivory thrones and bright cups (45), a couch of Indian tusk and a purple coverlet embroidered with figures (47–51), a doorway covered with soft green foliage (292–93; cf. the green bower laden with tender dill at *Id.* 15.119), and tables laden with food (304). So too Dido's banquet welcoming Aeneas in Vergil's *Aen.* 1 includes a

quantity of silver and golden embossed plates, a golden couch, golden tapestries (697–98), and purple coverlets, some embroidered. Both Peleus's and Dido's displays exemplify regal splendor, not "vulgarity": "tota domus gaudet regali splendida gaza" (Catull. *Poem* 64.46); "at domus interior regali splendida luxu" (Verg. *Aen.* 1.637). Further, poets customarily praise the generosity of rulers and patrons and thereby encourage "appropriate" expenditures (e.g., Bacchyl. *Ode* 3.11–22, 63–66; Pind. *Nem.* 1.19–33; Pind. *Isthm.* 1.60–68). Thus Theocritus's *Idyll* 17 praises Ptolemy for using his wealth to honor gods (106–9) and also describes the system of benefactions in regard to poets (115–17).

106. On the Ptolemies' wealth, see, e.g., M. Rostovtzeff, *The Social and Economic History of the Hellenistic World*, 3 vols. (Oxford: Clarendon Press, 1941), 1: 407–11; Préaux, *Monde hellénistique*, esp. 1:208–9. Ath. 5.197c–202a provides a detailed account of a lavish ceremonial procession sponsored by Ptolemy II (for discussion, see Rice, *Grand Procession*).

107. The Petrie papyrus, dated not later than 250 B.C., indicates that private individuals (this one probably a man since the expenditures include bath and barber) continued to contribute to celebrations of the Adonia in Ptolemaic Egypt (J. P. Mahaffy and J. G. Smyly, eds., *The Flinders Petrie Papyri*, vol. 3, [Dublin: Academy House, 1905], no. 142). For discussion, see Glotz, "Fêtes," 169–222 (for a summary of Glotz's commentary, see Gow, "*Adoniazusae* of Theocritus," 180–83 [available again in Gow, *Theocritus* 2:262–63]). See also Atallah, *Adonis*, 136–40.

108. Gow, *Theocritus* 2:296 n. 118, footnote 1: "Shaped cakes as offerings were sometimes at any rate merely cheap substitutes for the animals they represented (Hdt. 2.47, Suid. *s.v.* Βοῦς ἕβδομος), and these would find no place in Arsinoe's celebrations." Yet shaped cakes need not be cheap; see, e.g., the pastry eggs (33.6), cake piglets (40.4), and pastry thrushes (69.6) featured at Trimalchio's luxurious dinner in Petronius's *Satyricon*. In the *Satyricon*, food allusions are part of the iconography representing the crossing of boundaries and instability of categories and meaning. In *Idyll* 15, in which the crossing of boundaries (life and death, mortal and immortal, male and female, royalty and commoner, house and palace) is also an important theme, food allusions would not be out of place. The poetic structure and grammar of the passage in *Idyll* 15 that lists offerings strengthen an identification of the creatures of line 118 as shaped cakes. If line 118 is taken in association with the cakes, a single sentence encompasses all the offerings, a sentence gracefully structured in a chiastic ring (location, offering, offering, location), with the πάρεστι of line 118 recalling the κεῖται of line 112. The heavy alliteration of τs in lines 117 and 118, compared with the previous five lines, further encourages the reader to associate line 118 (the creatures) with line 117 (the cakes).

109. E.g., Barriss Mills, *The Idylls of Theocritus* (West Lafayette: Purdue University Press, 1963), 59; Daryl Hine, *Theocritus: Idylls and Epigrams* (New York: Atheneum, 1982), 58; Anna Rist, *The Poems of Theocritus* (Chapel Hill: University of North Carolina Press, 1978), 141; Thelma Sargent, *The Idylls of Theocritus: A Verse Translation* (New York: W. W. Norton, 1982), 61; Wells, *Theocritus*, 105; Zanker, *Realism in Alexandrian Poetry*, 13. But while most of the British and Americans require "meat" (e.g., Dover, *Theocritus*, 118: "If this line referred to

cakes of different shapes, there would be no reference to meat"), the French prefer "cake" (see Atallah, *Adonis*, 123, followed by Monteil, *Théocrite*, 164). See also White, "Theocritus' 'Adonis Song,'" 197–98, who posits both shaped cakes and wax fruits among the offerings.

110. Gow, *Theocritus* 1:118, transfers the strong stop from line 118 to line 117, which supports his interpretation of 118 as referring to "meats" not "shaped cakes" (for discussion, see 2:296 n. 118).

111. Griffiths, "Home before Lunch," 256.

112. I have followed Ahrens's reading of ἁμά in 127 (so too Monteil, *Théocrite*, 165 n. 127: "une couche qui est nôtre"). Gow, *Theocritus* 2:300–1 nn. 126f., prefers ἄμμιν to Ahrens's ἁμά. Dover, *Theocritus*, 213 n. 127, reads ἄλλα (with the mss., except *K*) (so too R. J. Cholmeley, *The Idylls of Theocritus* [London: George Bell and Sons, 1906], 301), but also approves ἁμά: "Confusion between ΛΛ and M was easy in ancient texts, since the midpoint of M was lower than in a modern M." White, "Theocritus' 'Adonis Song,'" 203–5, reads ἀλλὰ (with *K*) and so does not place a full stop afterwards.

113. A repetition of the verb πονέω links the creative activity of making cakes with weaving tapestries (ποῖαί σφ' ἐπόνασαν ἔριθοι, 80; cf. εἴδατά θ' ὅσσα γυναῖκες ἐπὶ πλαθάνω πονέονται, 115), and among the modern Hellenistic writers, the verb πονέω can represent poetic craftsmanship. Rosenmeyer, *Green Cabinet*, 22, defines Callimachean πόνος as "the careful and self-denying labor that goes into the making of the good poem." In Theocritus's *Idyll* 7, the verb ἐκπονέω describes making poetry (51) and the noun πόνος is associated with the cicadas' song (139); for discussion, see Harry Berger Jr., "The Origins of Bucolic Representation: Disenchantment and Revision in Theocritus' Seventh *Idyll*," *Classical Antiquity* 3 (1984), 16–20.

114. On Ptolemy II's acquisition of Samos, see M. Cary, *A History of the Greek World: 323 to 146 BC*, 2d ed., rev. (1951; reprint, London: Methuen, 1978), 104; Graham Shipley, *A History of Samos: 800–188 BC* (Oxford: Clarendon; New York: Oxford University Press, 1987), 182–83; on Ptolemy II's acquisition of Miletus, see, e.g., Cary, *History*, 104 (with app. 5, 387–89).

115. *Idyll* 15's spatial and temporal movement highlights the issue of how a public Adonia might attract marginal viewers by moving outlanders — Syracusan, Doric-speaking women — from Alexandria's suburbs through crowded streets to the palace grounds to view an Adonia, a celebration of an exotic marginal god (who has himself been moved from the cultish margins to the ideological center of the state).

116. The implied audience of *Id.* 15's Adonia, for a brief moment, includes a hypothetical Samian shepherd. The actual audience could have included Samians as well. On the presence of Samians in Egypt, especially Alexandria, during the Hellenistic period, see Shipley, *History of Samos*, 225–26. See also Callim. *Ep.* 37 Gow and Page (*A.P.* 7.459), an epitaph for Crethis, a working-class Samian girl (for discussion, see Gow and Page, *Greek Anthology* 2:194; P. M. Fraser, *Ptolemaic Alexandria* 1:577).

117. So Bulloch, "Hellenistic Poetry," 541: "The new regime determined to build for themselves in Africa a way of life which was powerfully and essentially Greek." See also Zanker, *Realism in Alexandrian Poetry*, 19–22.

118. See, e.g., W. W. Tarn, *Hellenistic Civilisation*, rev. author and G. T. Griffith, 3d ed. (1952; reprint, Cleveland: World Publishing, 1961), 196–97; P. M. Fraser, *Ptolemaic Alexandria* 1:106–15; Préaux, *Monde hellénistique* 2:587–601; Koenen, "Ptolemaic King," 40 (on possible influences between the Greek and Egyptian legal systems, see ibid., esp. 40–43, with references).

119. By bringing a private ritual into the public arena, Arsinoe's Adonia blurred the boundaries between public and private life. That this was part of the program is suggested by how the Arsinoe cult also emphasized the association of public and private rites of worship, as shown by an Alexandrian decree regulating the festival of Arsinoe, which approved private sacrifices along the public procession route (on this decree, see Robert, "Sur un décret," esp. 192–210; P. M. Fraser, *Ptolemaic Alexandria* 1:229–30, 2:378 n. 315; D. B. Thompson, *Ptolemaic Oinochoai*, 71–73).

120. Examples of local pride in *Idyll* 15: Syracusans vaunting their ethnic origin (90–93) and hypothetical islanders praising their own work (126–27).

121. See discussion in Burkert, *Structure and History*, esp. 102–11. See also Griffin, "Theocritus," 203. The name Adonis recalls *adon*, a Semitic word meaning Lord (Burkert, *Structure and History*, 105). Gow, *Theocritus* 2:264, suggests that the Adonia in the Fayyûm, as analyzed by Glotz, "Fêtes," has an Egyptian flavor that makes it differ from worship in Alexandria (as represented by Theocritus). So too the cult of Sarapis, also supported by the Ptolemies, seems to have eventually transcended cultural difference (see, e.g., P. M. Fraser, "Two Studies on the Cult of Sarapis in the Hellenistic World," *Opuscula Atheniensia* 3 [1960], 8–9, 15–17). On the cult of Sarapis, see also, e.g., P. M. Fraser, *Ptolemaic Alexandria* 1:246–76; John E. Stambaugh, *Sarapis under the Early Ptolemies* (Leiden: E. J. Brill, 1972).

122. See, e.g., A. Rosalie David, *The Ancient Egyptians: Religious Beliefs and Practices* (London: Routledge and Kegan Paul, 1982), 107–8.

123. P. M. Fraser, *Ptolemaic Alexandria* 1:206, 255; Dorothy J. Thompson, *Memphis under the Ptolemies* (Princeton: Princeton University Press, 1988), 28–29, 212–13. See also Hdt. 2.48's description of Egyptian "Dionysus-processions" featuring women carrying puppets with immense phalluses made erect by pulling strings (for discussion of the link between the Egyptian ithyphallic Osiris, Herodotus's Egyptian "Dionysus," and the Greek Dionysus [with refs.], see Alan B. Lloyd, *Herodotus: Book II: Commentary 1–98* [Leiden: E. J. Brill, 1976], 220–24 [on Hdt. 2.48]; cf. the 180-foot golden phallus displayed in Ptolemy's Procession of Dionysus, Ath. 5.201e).

124. D. J. Thompson, *Memphis under the Ptolemies*, 202–3.

125. See, e.g., Hdt. 2.112; D. J. Thompson, *Memphis under the Ptolemies*, 88–90.

126. On how the Egyptianization of *oinochoai* (wine jugs) made for the Ptolemaic ruler-cult helped draw in non-Greeks as well as Greeks, see D. B. Thompson, *Ptolemaic Oinochoai*, esp. 119–21. See also Callim. fr. 383.14 for a possible representation of a collaboration between Egyptian and Colchian women in weaving a celebratory cloth for Berenice (for discussion, see Thomas, "Callimachus," esp. 106–8). For a discussion of how the Ptolemies contrived to appeal to both Greeks and Egyptians, see Koenen, "Ptolemaic King."

127. J. B. Miller, *New Psychology*, 113.

128. On the importance of Argos in Ptolemaic propaganda and the political suggestiveness of references to Argos in Alexandrian poetry, see Bulloch, *Callimachus*, 12–13 (with attention to Callim. *Hymn 5*'s setting in Argos), who accounts for the link between the Macedonian and Peloponnesian towns called Argos: "Although the town of Argos with which the Argeads were connected was actually situated in northern Macedonia, it was the practice even in the fifth century to give them a more romantic and flattering origin by making Peloponnesian Argos their homeland and thus giving them an ancient and impeccable Dorian descent, through Temenus, from Heracles and Dionysus." On the Ptolemies' interest in publicizing their connection with the Argead dynasty, see also W. S. Greenwalt, "Argaeus, Ptolemy II, and Alexander's Corpse," *The Ancient History Bulletin* 2 (1988), 39–41.

129. See discussion in chapter 2.

130. *Pace* Gow, "*Adoniazusae* of Theocritus," 202: "The extravagant commendations of 'the incorrigible Gorgo' are more amusing and more in keeping with her character if they are bestowed upon a work which, to a more cultivated taste, does not deserve them." So too Griffiths, "Home before Lunch," 249: "the housewife's failure of imagination." See also Miles, "Characterization," 156; Motto and Clark, "Idyllic Slumming," 41; Walker, *Theocritus*, 94.

131. For evidence, see Gow, *Theocritus* 2:83 (on *Id.* 4.31). On the possible impact at court of a reference to Glauce, see Bulloch, "Helenistic Poetry," 572.

132. Bakhtin and Lyotard both emphasize the oppositional value of little voices/stories to monologic or grand narratives (on correspondences between Bakhtin's and Lyotard's theories, see David Carroll, "Narrative, Heterogeneity, and the Question of the Political: Bakhtin and Lyotard," in *The Aims of Representation: Subject/Text/History*, ed. Murray Krieger [New York: Columbia University Press, 1987], 69–106; see also Bruce Henricksen's summary in *Nomadic Voices: Conrad and the Subject of Narrative* [Urbana: University of Illinois Press, 1992], esp. 11–14).

133. On the Samothracian gods as saviors at sea, see Burkert, *Greek Religion*, 284. Although the Samothracian gods are unknown, the central deities may well be a female (probably a Cybele-type) attended by two males comparable to the Dioskouroi (Susan Guettel Cole, *Theoi Megaloi: The Cult of the Great Gods at Samothrace* [Leiden: E. J. Brill, 1984], 3). Burkert, *Greek Religion*, 283–84, includes among the deities featured at Samothrace the Cybele-type deity prominent in Samothracian coinage and a young, subordinated male god (who acts as a servant), which would correspond to the gender dynamics of Aphrodite and Adonis. Cf. also Theoc. *Id.* 1's cup decoration of a woman flanked by two males, and the triad composed of Helen and the Dioskouroi, important figures in Ptolemaic propaganda and Theocritus's poetry as well (e.g., *Idylls* 18 and 22).

134. P. M. Fraser, *Ptolemaic Alexandria* 1:207. On the Dioskouroi as saviors at sea, see Burkert, *Greek Religion*, 213. Thus Theoc. *Id.* 22 (on the Dioskouroi), with its emphasis on the Dioskouroi's status as saviors at sea (6–22), may look toward Arsinoe. On Arsinoe's connection with Helen and the Dioskouroi, see Giuseppina Basta Donzelli, "Arsinoe simile ad Elena (Theocritus Id. 15.110)," *Hermes: Zeitschrift für klassische Philologie* 112 (1984), 306–16. The Dioskouroi

also offered attractions to royals moving toward self-deification, as Burkert's description suggests: "The Dioskouroi, like Heracles [also favored at Alexandria], . . . were seen as guiding lights for those hoping to break out of the mortal sphere into the realm of the gods" (Burkert, *Greek Religion*, 213). Callim. *Lyrica* fr. 228 (see *dieg.*) has the Dioskouroi carry dead Arsinoe to the sky.

135. On Arsinoe's assimilation with Aphrodite as protector of the maritime empire, see, e.g., Robert, "Sur un décret," 198–202; Hauben, "Arsinoé II," 111–14. See too the epigrams on the temple of Aphrodite at Cape Zephyrium, dedicated by an admiral: Callim. *Ep.* 5; Posidippus *Ep.* 12, 13 Gow and Page; Hedylus *Ep.* 4 Gow and Page (also available in Ath. 7.318b–d; 11.497d–e).

136. On the connection of savior gods with Alexandria's lighthouse, see Sostratus's dedicatory inscription as reported in Lucian *Hist. Conscr.* 62: these gods have been understood to refer to Berenice and Ptolemy I or to the Dioskouroi. See Gow and Page, *Greek Anthology* 2:490 (on Posidippus *Ep.* 11): "It is difficult to believe that such a dedication at Alexandria [Sostratus's] was not intended at least to include them [Ptolemy I and Berenice]." See too P. M. Fraser, *Ptolemaic Alexandria* 1:19, who remarks in a discussion on the uncertainties of the inscription's authenticity (and the savior gods' identity) that perhaps the inscription's "savior gods" refer to "all those deities who protect seafarers" (for discussion, see 1:18–19).

137. On temples and shrines of Bilistiche-Aphrodite, see, e.g., P. M. Fraser, *Ptolemaic Alexandria* 1:239–40. Harpalus, a Macedonian who embezzled Alexander's funds, also set up a temple and altar of Pythionice-Aphrodite when his Athenian courtesan Pythionice died (Ath. 13.595c). On the shrine of Arsinoe-Aphrodite at Zephyrium, see P. M. Fraser, *Ptolemaic Alexandria* 1:239–40; Posidippus's *Epigrams* 12 and 13 Gow and Page; Strab. 17.800.

138. A. Bouché-Leclercq, *Histoire des Lagides*, vol. 1, *Les cinq premiers Ptolémées (323–181 avant J.-C.)* (1903; reprint, Brussels: Culture et civilisation, 1963), 185 n. 1 (cited by Macurdy, *Hellenistic Queens*, 124; Tondriau, "Princesses," 31). On public honors for Ptolemy's mistresses, see too Edwyn R. Bevan, *The House of Ptolemy: A History of Egypt under the Ptolemaic Dynasty* (1927; rev. reissue, Chicago: Argonaut, 1968), 77–78.

139. See chapter 2.

140. Gow, *Theocritus* 2:346 n. 130 (on *Id.* 17); followed by Schwinge, *Künstlichkeit von Kunst*, 61.

141. Griffiths, *Theocritus at Court*, 61. Greek text taken from F. H. Sandbach's Loeb edition (*Plutarch's Moralia*, vol. 9, trans. Edwin L. Minar Jr., F. H. Sandbach, and W. C. Helmbold [Cambridge: Harvard University Press, 1969]).

142. Griffiths, *Theocritus at Court*, 61. On the association of Arsinoe with Hera, see, e.g., P. M. Fraser, *Ptolemaic Alexandria* 1:35, 237–38; McCredie et al., *Rotunda of Arsinoe*, 238 n. 26 (Georges Roux). On the association of Ptolemy II with Zeus, see, e.g., P. M. Fraser, *Ptolemaic Alexandria* 1:666–67, 194–95.

143. Callimachus's hymns do not feature Aphrodite and Dionysus (the Ptolemies' most favored deities), but they do feature Zeus and Hera. Aphrodite only briefly enters *Hymn* 5 (to Athena) in a contrast between her intensive beauty ritual and Athena's simpler self-care (21–22).

144. See, e.g., P. M. Fraser, *Ptolemaic Alexandria* 2:915 n. 284; Griffiths, *The-*

ocritus at Court, 62–63; Clauss, "Lies and Allusions." See also Green, *Alexander to Actium*, 172. But cf. Thomas Gelzer, "Kallimachos und das Zeremoniell des Ptolemäischen Königshauses," in *Aspekte der Kultursoziologie: Aufsätze zur Soziologie, Philosophie, Anthropologie und Geschichte der Kultur: Zum 60. Geburtstag von Mohammed Rassem*, ed. Justin Stagl (Berlin: Dietrich Reimer, 1982), 22. For a judicious warning against over-imaginative historical references, see F. Williams, *Callimachus*, 1 (on Callim. *Hymn* 2 [to Apollo]).

145. See, e.g., P. M. Fraser, *Ptolemaic Alexandria* 1:652, 2:915 n. 284 (who dates *Hymn* 1 between 280 and 275); Clauss, "Lies and Allusions," esp. 158–59 (who suggests the date of Ptolemy II's accession to the throne in 285/284 or its anniversary in 284/283).

146. See, e.g., P. M. Fraser, *Ptolemaic Alexandria* 1:652, 657–58 (who suggests 271/270 as a probable date for *Hymn* 4); W. H. Mineur, *Callimachus: Hymn to Delos* (Leiden: E. J. Brill, 1984), 16–18 (who suggests the date 274).

147. See P. M. Fraser, *Ptolemaic Alexandria* 1:652, 2:915 n. 287.

148. On Greek reactions to the incestuous Ptolemaic marriage, see, e.g., P. M. Fraser, *Ptolemaic Alexandria* 1:117–18. See also Carney, "Reappearance of Sibling Marriage," 420–21, 428–29, who cautions against "overestimat[ing] Hellenic disapproval" and cites Sotades' remark, which "rather than manifesting moral outrage, seems intended to make fun" (428).

149. Scholia Theoc. *Id.* 17.128 (Wendel, *Scholia*, 325). See also Macurdy, *Hellenistic Queens*, 120–21; Burstein, "Arsinoe II," 205–7.

150. Mineur also suggests a possible reference to Ptolemy II in Callim. *Hymn* 4.240–43 (*Callimachus*, 203 n. 240f: "The Alexandrian audience may have thought here of Philadelphus, who πλείστας ἔσχεν ἐρωμένας (Athen. *Deipn.* 13.576e, f.)." On Ptolemy's mistresses, see also Plut. *Mor.* 753e; Cameron, "Two Mistresses," 287–304.

151. Because Asteria refused the amorous Zeus, Hera forgives her here for helping Leto, Zeus's pregnant mistress. Cf. Ap. Rhod. *Argon.* 4.790–94, where Hera reminds Thetis that she earned her favor by refusing Zeus's lovemaking.

152. See, e.g., Paus. 1.10.3–5; Burstein, "Arsinoe II," 199–200 (with references in n. 11).

153. Gercke also suggests this allusion in Callim. *Hymn* 3.134–35 to Arsinoes I and II (Alfred Gercke, "Alexandrinische Studien," *Rheinisches Museum für Philologie*, n.s., 42 [1887], 273–75).

154. Any reservations about court ideology that Callimachus's references to Zeus and Hera's marriage may suggest, however, are indirect, available for cynical (and informed) audience members, but not necessary for enjoyment of the poems. Callimachus also wrote more directly (and in a more courtly manner) of Arsinoe and other Ptolemaic women. See, e.g., Callim. fr. 392, which Pfeiffer titles "In Arsinoes Nuptias?" (we have only one line left); fr. 228, on Arsinoe's death (the least fragmentary section, 40–75, approaches the death from her sister Philotera's vantage); *Lock of Berenice* (to Berenice II, wife of Ptolemy III). See Schwinge, "Gedichte auf Frauen des Königshauses," in *Künstlichkeit von Kunst*, 67–72. On Callim. *Lock of Berenice*, see Gutzwiller, "Callimachus' *Lock*,"; Koenen, "Ptolemaic King," 89–113.

155. *Idyll* 18 ironizes the theme of mutual passion by having its maiden's cho-

rus sing a wedding song mocking Menelaus's early slumber on his wedding night and exalting Helen's beauty and talents. On the disparity between "the divine stature of Helen" and "the rather hapless figure which Menelaus cuts," see David Konstan, "A Note on Theocritus *Idyll* 18," *Classical Philology* 74 [1979], 233–34.

156. Theoc. *Id.* 12.10–11 includes a wish for mutuality in a homoerotic context. See also Alcaeus of Messene *Ep.* 9 Gow and Page (= *A.P.* 12.64), which presents a prayer to Zeus for ὁμοφροσύνη (like-mindedness) between *erastes* and *eromenos* (6). On the rarity of "erotic reciprocity" between ancient Greek males (outside Plato), due to the problematic nature of the passive sexual role for males, see David M. Halperin, "Why is Diotima a Woman," ch. 6 in *One Hundred Years of Homosexuality and Other Essays on Greek Love* (New York: Routledge, 1990), 129–37 (but see also 225, addendum). See too Dover, *Greek Homosexuality*, 52.

157. On Hellenistic poetry's emphasis on passion without reciprocity and marriage without passion, see Vatin, *Recherches sur le mariage*, esp. 46, 53–54, 56.

158. See also Mastromarco, *Public of Herondas*, 93.

159. On the importance of imagery of mutual married love in the Ptolemies' project of self-legitimation, see Gutzwiller, "Callimachus' *Lock*," esp. 363–68. See too Koenen, "Adaptation ägyptischer Königsideologie," 157–68; Mary Ann Rossi, *Theocritus' Idyll XVII: A Stylistic Commentary* (Amsterdam: Adolf M. Hakkert, 1989), esp. 188–89; Koenen, "Ptolemaic King," 62. On the theme of reciprocal love in Hellenistic poetry, see M. A. Rossi, *Theocritus' Idyll XVII*, 79, with references.

160. This term comes from Sir John Vanbrugh's *The Provok'd Wife* (1697), 1.1 (cited by Spacks, *Gossip*, 122). On the later Alexandrian fashion for defamatory jokes against authority, see Herodian 4.9.2–3: πεφύκασι δέ πως εἶναι φιλο-σκώμμονες καὶ λέγειν εὐστόχους ὑπογραφὰς ἢ παιδιάς, ἀπορριπτοῦντες ἐς τοὺς ὑπερέχοντας πολλὰ χαρίεντα μὲν αὐτοῖς δοκοῦντα ("To a certain extent it was a natural feature of the people to indulge in lampoons and repetition of many pungent caricatures and jokes belittling the authorities, since they are considered very witty by the Alexandrians"; trans. C. R. Whittaker, *Herodian*, vol. 1, *Books I–IV* [Cambridge: Harvard University Press, 1969], 423). Thus later Alexandrians reportedly considered such jokes as calling Antoninus's mother Jocasta (and thus hinting at incest) παίζειν (playing), although Antoninus did not (Herodian 4.9.3).

161. Griffiths, *Theocritus at Court.*

162. See Schwinge, *Künstlichkeit von Kunst*, 66.

163. Gow, *Theocritus* 2 : 331 n. 26.

164. Cunningham, *Herodas*, 66 n. 30, reads line 30's "good king" as Ptolemy Philadelphus: "θεῶν ἀδελφῶν [of the brother-sister gods] is an attribute to distinguish this τέμενος [shrine] from all others, and does not necessitate understanding βασιλεύς of a different king" (see also idem, "Herodas 1.26ff.," 7–9). On the possibility that line 30's "good king" might also refer to Ptolemy III, see, e.g., P. M. Fraser, *Ptolemaic Alexandria* 2 : 878 n. 30; Sherwin-White, *Ancient Cos*, 95 n. 60. For a brief history of scholarly opinion, see Mastromarco, *Public of Herondas*, 3–4 (who supports the identification with Ptolemy Philadelphus).

165. The self-proclaimed brother-sister gods are Ptolemy II and Arsinoe II.

166. Headlam and Knox, *Herodas*, 23–24 n. 26; followed by Cunningham, *Herodas*, 65 n. 26. On the title θεά for Arsinoe, see P. M. Fraser, *Ptolemaic Alexandria* 2 : 367 n. 228.

167. See Griffiths, *Theocritus at Court*.

168. Marylin B. Arthur, "Early Greece: The Origins of the Western Attitude toward Women," in Peradotto and Sullivan, *Women*, 50.

Conclusion

1. As Hutcheon emphasizes, "there is no directly and naturally accessible past 'real' for us today: we can only know—and construct—the past through its traces, its representations" (Linda Hutcheon, *The Politics of Postmodernism* [London and New York: Routledge, 1989], 113).

2. The series of framing devices distancing his story underscores Comatas's isolation: Lycidas performs a song describing a celebration at which Tityrus shall perform a song describing how a king imprisons Comatas in a coffer. On the thematic significance of Comatas's imprisonment, see also Berger, "Origins of Bucolic Representation," 35–39. Cf. the iconoclastic poet Timon's mockery of the cloistered environment available in Alexandria as a "birdcage of the Muses."

3. On the importance of friendship as a factor in audience reception, see Wayne C. Booth, *The Company We Keep: An Ethics of Fiction* (Berkeley and Los Angeles: University of California Press, 1988).

Appendix 1. Translations of Theocritus' Urban Mimes

1. On *Idyll* 2's line numeration, see Gow, *Theocritus* 2 : 40; followed by Dover, *Theocritus*, 103 n. 23; but cf. White, "Spells," 22–30.

Appendix 2. Circe Allusion (*Id.* 15.79)

1. Christopher Wordsworth, *Theocritus*, 2d ed. (Cambridge: Deighton Bell and Associates, 1877), 126; Fritzsche, *Theokrits Gedichte*, 186; Cholmeley, *Idylls of Theocritus*, 299.

2. Praxinoa, in describing the tapestries, shows how the woven figures can present an illusion of reality to the viewer.

3. On entering the ceremonial grounds through crowded doors, Gorgo and Praxinoa view tapestries that elicit their admiration. A courtly encounter with a polite stranger (69–75) brings the women into the elevated atmosphere of the palace grounds; fear for clothing is transformed into pleasure at viewing woven art. In an environment where everyone is turning into pigs, as Praxinoa claims, what saves the women and the stranger who looks after them? In the *Odyssey*, Hermes provides Odysseus with an herb to protect him from Circe's powers. Perhaps polite behavior is a moly in *Idyll* 15: a means to transcend the squalidness of the street.

4. For an important discussion of Callimachus's use of allusion, see An-

thony W. Bulloch, "Callimachus' *Erysichthon,* Homer, and Apollonius Rhodius," *American Journal of Philology* 98 (1977), 97–123: "irony, wit and allusion are also the *means* by which Callimachus revivifies the traditional material and makes it pointedly real for his contemporaries" (114). See also Herter's and Giangrande's fundamental articles: Hans Herter, "Kallimachos und Homer: Ein Beitrag zur Interpretation des Hymnos auf Artemis," in *Xenia Bonnensia; Festschrift zum Fünfundsiebzigjährigen Bestehen des Philologischen Vereins und Bonner Kreises* (Bonn: F. Cohen, 1929), 50–105; Giuseppe Giangrande, "'Arte Allusiva' and Alexandrian Epic Poetry," *Classical Quarterly,* n.s., 17 (1967), 85–97; idem, "Hellenistic Poetry and Homer," *L'antiquité classique* 39 (1970), 46–77. On the function of allusion in Alexandrian poetry, see too Bing, *Well-Read Muse,* esp. 73–75.

5. Horstmann, *Ironie und Humor,* 35.

References

Ahmed, Leila. *Women and Gender in Islam: Historical Roots of a Modern Debate.* New Haven: Yale University Press, 1992.

Albert, Winfried. *Das mimetische Gedicht in der Antike: Geschichte und Typologie von den Anfängen bis in die augusteische Zeit.* Frankfurt am Main: Athenäum, 1988.

Allen, T. W., W. R. Halliday, and E. E. Sikes, eds. *The Homeric Hymns.* 2d ed. Oxford: Clarendon Press, 1936.

Alpers, Svetlana L. "*Ekphrasis* and Aesthetic Attitudes in Vasari's *Lives*." *Journal of the Warburg and Courtauld Institute* 23 (1960) : 190–215.

Anderson, William S. *Ovid's* Metamorphoses: *Books 6–10.* American Philological Association Series of Classical Texts. Norman: University of Oklahoma Press, 1972.

Archer, Léonie J., Susan Fischler, and Maria Wyke, eds. *Women in Ancient Societies: "An Illusion of the Night."* New York: Routledge, 1994.

Arend, Walter. *Die typischen Scenen bei Homer.* Problemata, Forschungen zur klassischen Philologie, no. 7. Berlin: Weidmann, 1933.

Arnheim, Rudolf. *Art and Visual Perception.* Berkeley and Los Angeles: University of California Press, 1954.

Arnold, Matthew. "Pagan and Mediaeval Religious Sentiment." In *Essays in Criticism*, 174–99. Boston: Ticknor and Fields, 1865.

Arnott, W. Geoffrey. "Herodas and the Kitchen Sink." *Greece and Rome*, 2d ser., 18 (1971) : 121–32.

———. "The Stream and the Gold: Two Notes on Theocritus." In *Filologia e forme letterarie, Studi offerti a Francesco Della Corte.* Vol. 1, *Letteratura greca*, ed. Sandro Boldrini et al., 335–46. Urbino: Università degli studi di Urbino, 1987.

Arthur, Marylin B. "Early Greece: The Origins of the Western Attitude toward Women." In Peradotto and Sullivan, *Women*, 7–58. Albany: State University of New York Press, 1984.

Ashcroft, Bill, Gareth Griffiths, and Helen Tiffin. *The Empire Writes Back: Theory and Practice in Post-Colonial Literatures*. New Accents. London and New York: Routledge, 1989.

Atallah, Wahib. *Adonis dans la littérature et l'art grecs*. Études et commentaires, no. 62. Paris: C. Klincksieck, 1966.

Athanassakis, Apostolos N., trans. *The Homeric Hymns*. Baltimore and London: Johns Hopkins University Press, 1976.

Austin, J. C. "The Significant Name in Herondas." *Transactions and Proceedings of the American Philological Association* 53 (1922): 16–17.

Austin, Norman. "Name Magic in the Odyssey." *California Studies in Classical Antiquity* 5 (1972): 1–19.

Bagnall, Roger S. "Greeks and Egyptians: Ethnicity, Status, and Culture." In *Cleopatra's Egypt: Age of the Ptolemies*, 21–27. Catalog of an exhibition held at the Brooklyn Museum. New York: Brooklyn Museum, 1988.

Baines, John. "Society, Morality, and Religious Practice." In *Religion in Ancient Egypt: Gods, Myths, and Personal Practice*, ed. Byron E. Shafer, 123–200. Ithaca: Cornell University Press, 1991.

Bakhtin, Mikhail M. *The Dialogic Imagination: Four Essays*. Edited by Michael Holquist. Translated by Caryl Emerson and Michael Holquist. Slavic Series, no. 1. Austin: University of Texas Press, 1981. Originally published as *Voprosy literatury i estetiki* (Moscow: Khudozhestvennia literatura, 1975).

———. *Rabelais and His World*. Translated by Hélène Iswolsky. Bloomington: Indiana University Press, 1984. Originally published as *Tvorchestvo Fransua Rable i narodnaja kul'tura srednevekov'ja i Renessansa* (Moscow: Khudozhestvennia literatura, 1965).

Barkan, Leonard. *Transuming Passion: Ganymede and the Erotics of Humanism*. Stanford: Stanford University Press, 1991.

Bartsch, Shadi. *Decoding the Ancient Novel: The Reader and the Role of Description in Heliodorus and Achilles Tatius*. Princeton: Princeton University Press, 1989.

Baslez, Marie-Françoise. *L'étranger dans la Grèce antique*. Realia. Paris: Société d'édition «Les belles lettres,» 1984.

Bérard, Claude, Christiane Bron, Jean-Louis Durand, Françoise Frontisi-Ducroux, François Lissarrague, Alain Schnapp, and Jean-Pierre Vernant. *A City of Images: Iconography and Society in Ancient Greece*. Translated by Deborah Lyons. Princeton: Princeton University Press, 1989.

Berg, William. *Early Virgil*. London: Athlone Press, University of London, 1974.

Berger, Harry, Jr. "The Origins of Bucolic Representation: Disenchantment and Revision in Theocritus' Seventh *Idyll*." *Classical Antiquity* 3 (1984): 1–39.

Bernard, Paul. "An Ancient Greek City in Central Asia." *Scientific American* 247 (Jan. 1982): 148–59.

Bevan, Edwyn. *The House of Ptolemy: A History of Egypt under the Ptolemaic Dynasty*. Revised reissue. Chicago: Argonaut, 1968. First published as *A History of Egypt under the Ptolemaic Dynasty* (London: Methuen, 1927).

Bilde, Per, Troels Engberg-Pedersen, Lise Hannestad, and Jan Zahle, eds. *Eth-

nicity in Hellenistic Egypt. Studies in Hellenistic Civilization, no. 3. Aarhus: Aarhus University Press, 1992.

Bing, Peter. *The Well-Read Muse: Present and Past in Callimachus and the Hellenistic Poets*. Hypomnemata, no. 90. Göttingen: Vandenhoeck and Ruprecht, 1988.

Boardman, John. *The Greeks Overseas: Their Early Colonies and Trade*. Rev. and enl. ed. New York: Thames and Hudson, 1980.

Booth, Wayne C. *The Company We Keep: An Ethics of Fiction*. Berkeley and Los Angeles: University of California Press, 1988.

Borza, Eugene N. "The Symposium at Alexander's Court." In *Archaia Makedonia, III*, Anakoinoseis kata to Trito Diethnes Symposio, Thessalonike, 21–25 septemvriou 1977, 45–55. Hidryma Meleton Chersonesou tou Haimou, no. 193. Thessaloniki, 1983.

Bouché-Leclercq, A. *Histoire des Lagides*. Vol. 1, *Les cinq premiers Ptolémées (323–181 avant J.-C.)*. Reprint. Brussels: Culture et civilisation, 1963. Originally published in 1903 (Paris: E. Leroux).

Bourdieu, Pierre. *La distinction: Critique sociale du jugement*. Paris: Les éditions de minuit, 1979. Published in English as *Distinction: A Social Critique of the Judgement of Taste*, trans. Richard Nice (Cambridge: Harvard University Press, 1984).

Bowie, Ewen. "*Miles Ludens*? The Problem of Martial Exhortation in Early Greek Elegy." In O. Murray, *Sympotica*, 221–29.

Bowman, Alan K. *Egypt after the Pharaohs: 332 BC–AD 642: From Alexander to the Arab Conquest*. Berkeley and Los Angeles: University of California Press, 1986.

Bremen, Riet Van. "Woman and Wealth." In Cameron and Kuhrt, *Images of Women*, 223–42.

Bremer, J. M. "Full Moon and Marriage in Apollonius' *Argonautica*." *Classical Quarterly*, n.s., 37 (1987): 423–26.

Bringmann, Klaus. "The King as Benefactor: Some Remarks on Ideal Kingship in the Age of Hellenism." In Bulloch et al., *Images and Ideologies*, 7–24.

Brink, C. O. "Ennius and the Hellenistic Worship of Homer." *American Journal of Philology* 93 (1972): 547–67.

Bulloch, Anthony W. "Callimachus' *Erysichthon*, Homer, and Apollonius Rhodius." *American Journal of Philology* 98 (1977): 97–123.

———. *Callimachus: The Fifth Hymn*. Cambridge: Cambridge University Press, 1985.

———. "The Future of a Hellenistic Illusion: Some Observations on Callimachus and Religion." *Museum Helveticum* 41 (1984): 209–30.

———. "Hellenistic Poetry." Chapter 18 in *Greek Literature*. Vol. 1 of *The Cambridge History of Classical Literature*, ed. P. E. Easterling and B. M. W. Knox, 541–621. Cambridge and New York: Cambridge University Press, 1985.

Bulloch, Anthony W., Erich S. Gruen, A. A. Long, and Andrew Stewart, eds. *Images and Ideologies: Self-Definition in the Hellenistic World*. Hellenistic Culture and Society, no. 12. Berkeley and Los Angeles: University of California Press, 1993.

Burkert, Walter. *Ancient Mystery Cults*. Carl Newell Jackson Lectures, 1982. Cambridge: Harvard University Press, 1987.

———. "Bacchic *Teletai* in the Hellenistic Age." Chapter 11 in *Masks of Dionysus*, ed. Thomas H. Carpenter and Christopher A. Faraone, 259–75. Myth and Poetics. Ithaca: Cornell University Press, 1993.

———. *Greek Religion*. Translated by John Raffan. Cambridge: Harvard University Press, 1985. Originally published as *Griechische Religion der archaischen und klassischen Epoche* (Stuttgart: W. Kohlhammer, 1977).

———. *Structure and History in Greek Mythology and Ritual*. Sather Classical Lectures, vol. 47. Berkeley and Los Angeles: University of California Press, 1979.

Burn, Andrew Robert. *The Lyric Age of Greece*. London: E. Arnold, 1960.

Burstein, Stanley Mayer. "Arsinoe II Philadelphos: A Revisionist View." In *Philip II, Alexander the Great, and the Macedonian Heritage*, ed. W. Lindsay Adams and Eugene N. Borza, 197–212. Washington, D.C.: University Press of America, 1982.

———. *Outpost of Hellenism: The Emergence of Heraclea on the Black Sea*. University of California Publications, Classical Studies, vol. 14. Berkeley and Los Angeles: University of California Press, 1976.

Burton, Joan B. "The Function of the Symposium Theme in Theocritus' *Idyll* 14." *Greek, Roman, and Byzantine Studies* 33 (1992): 227–45.

Bury, J. B., and Russell Meiggs. *A History of Greece: To the Death of Alexander the Great*. 4th ed. New York: St. Martin's, 1975.

Cairns, Francis. *Generic Composition in Greek and Roman Poetry*. Edinburgh: Edinburgh University Press, 1972.

Cameron, Alan. "Asclepiades' Girl Friends." In Foley, *Reflections of Women*, 275–302.

———. "Two Mistresses of Ptolemy Philadelphus." *Greek, Roman, and Byzantine Studies* 30 (1989): 287–311.

Cameron, Averil, and Amélie Kuhrt, eds. *Images of Women in Antiquity*. Detroit: Wayne State University Press, 1983.

Carney, Elizabeth D. "The Career of Adea-Eurydice." *Historia: Zeitschrift für alte Geschichte* 36 (1987): 496–502.

———. "Olympias." *Ancient Society* 18 (1987): 35–62.

———. "The Reappearance of Royal Sibling Marriage in Ptolemaic Egypt." *La parola del passato* 42 (1987): 420–39.

Carpenter, Thomas H. *Art and Myth in Ancient Greece: A Handbook*. World of Art. London: Thames and Hudson, 1990.

Carroll, David. "Narrative, Heterogeneity, and the Question of the Political: Bakhtin and Lyotard." In *The Aims of Representation: Subject/Text/History*, ed. Murray Krieger, 69–106. New York: Columbia University Press, 1987.

Carter, L. B. *The Quiet Athenian*. Oxford: Clarendon Press; New York: Oxford University Press, 1986.

Cartledge, Paul. "Spartan Wives: Liberation or Licence?" *Classical Quarterly*, n.s., 31 (1981): 84–105.

Cary, M. *A History of the Greek World: 323 to 146 BC*. 2d ed., rev. 1951. Reprint, London: Methuen, 1978.

Caws, Mary Ann. *The Eye in the Text: Essays on Perception, Mannerist to Modern*. Princeton: Princeton University Press, 1981.

———. *A Metapoetics of the Passage: Architextures in Surrealism and After*. Hanover, N.H.: University Press of New England, 1981.

———. *Reading Frames in Modern Fiction*. Princeton: Princeton University Press, 1985.

Cerfaux, L., and J. Tondriau. *Le culte des souverains dans la civilisation gréco-romaine*. Bibliothèque de théologie, 3d series, vol. 5. Tournai: Desclée and Co., 1957.

Cholmeley, R. J. *The Idylls of Theocritus*. London: George Bell and Sons, 1906.

Clauss, James J. "Lies and Allusions: The Addressee and Date of Callimachus' *Hymn to Zeus*." *Classical Antiquity* 5 (1986) : 155–70.

Clayman, D. L. *Callimachus' Iambi*. Mnemosyne, supplement no. 59. Leiden: E. J. Brill, 1980.

Cole, Susan Guettel. "Could Greek Women Read and Write?" In Foley, *Reflections of Women*, 219–45.

———. *Theoi Megaloi: The Cult of the Great Gods at Samothrace*. Études préliminaires aux religions orientales dans l'Empire romain, vol. 96. Leiden: E. J. Brill, 1984.

Copley, Frank O. *Exclusus Amator: A Study in Latin Love Poetry*. American Philological Association Monograph Series, no. 17. Baltimore, 1956.

Cornford, Francis Macdonald, trans. *The Theaetetus*. In *Plato's Theory of Knowledge: The* Theaetetus *and the* Sophist *of Plato, Translated with a Running Commentary,* 15–163. London: Routledge and Kegan Paul, 1935.

Crow, Thomas E. *Painters and Public Life in Eighteenth-Century Paris*. New Haven: Yale University Press, 1985.

Crowther, N. B. "Horace, Catullus, and Alexandrianism." *Mnemosyne*, 4th ser., 31 (1978) : 33–44.

Cunningham, I. C. *Herodae Mimiambi cum Appendice Fragmentorum Mimorum Papyraceorum*. Bibliotheca Scriptorum Graecorum et Romanorum Teubneriana. Leipzig: B. G. Teubner, 1987.

———. "Herodas 4." *Classical Quarterly*, n.s., 16 (1966) : 113–25.

———. *Herodas: Mimiambi*. Oxford: Clarendon Press, 1971.

———. "Herodas 1.26ff." *Classical Review* 15 (1965) : 7–9.

———. "Herodas 6 and 7." *Classical Quarterly*, n.s., 14 (1964) : 32–35.

David, A. Rosalie. *The Ancient Egyptians: Religious Beliefs and Practices*. Library of Religious Beliefs and Practices. London: Routledge and Kegan Paul, 1982.

Davies, J. K. "Cultural, Social, and Economic Features of the Hellenistic World." Chapter 8 in Walbank et al., *Hellenistic World*, 257–320.

Davis, Gregson. "Modes of Consolation: *Convivium* and *carpe diem*." Chapter 3 in *Polyhymnia: The Rhetoric of Horatian Lyric Discourse*, 145–88. Berkeley and Los Angeles: University of California Press, 1991.

Dawson, Christopher M. "The Iambi of Callimachus: A Hellenistic Poet's Experimental Laboratory." *Yale Classical Studies* 11 (1950) : 1–168.

Dawson, David. *Allegorical Readers and Cultural Revision in Ancient Alexandria*. Berkeley and Los Angeles: University of California Press, 1992.

Delcourt, Marie. *Hermaphrodite: Mythes et rites de la bisexualité dans l'antiquité classique*. Paris: Presses universitaires de France, 1958.

―――. *Hermaphroditea: Recherches sur l'être double promoteur de la fertilité dans le monde classique*. Brussels: Latomus, 1966.

Demand, Nancy H. *Urban Relocation in Archaic and Classical Greece: Flight and Consolidation*. Oklahoma Series in Classical Culture, vol. 6. Norman: University of Oklahoma Press, 1990.

Desroches-Noblecourt, Christiane. *La femme au temps des pharaons*. Paris: Stock/Laurence Pernoud, 1986.

Detienne, Marcel. *Dionysos Slain*. Translated by Mireille Muellner and Leonard Muellner. Baltimore: Johns Hopkins University Press, 1979. Originally published as *Dionysos mis à mort* (Paris: Editions Gallimard, 1977).

―――. *The Gardens of Adonis: Spices in Greek Mythology*. Translated by J. Lloyd. European Philosophy and the Human Sciences. Atlantic Highlands, N. J.: Humanities Press, 1977. Originally published as *Les jardins d'Adonis* (Paris: Editions Gallimard, 1972).

Deubner, Ludwig. "Ein Stilprinzip hellenistischer Dichtkunst." *Neue Jahrbücher für das klassische Altertum, Geschichte und deutsche Literatur und für Pädagogik* 47 (1921) : 361–78.

de Vries, G. J. "Theocritea." *Mnemosyne*, 4th ser., 20 (1967) : 435–39.

Dihle, Albrecht. "Response." In Bulloch et al., *Images and Ideologies*, 287–95.

Dijkstra, Bram. "The Cult of Invalidism; Ophelia and Folly; Dead Ladies and the Fetish of Sleep." Chapter 2 in *Idols of Perversity: Fantasies of Feminine Evil in Fin-de-Siècle Culture*, 25–63. New York and Oxford: Oxford University Press, 1986.

Doherty, Lillian Eileen. "Gender and Internal Audiences in the *Odyssey*." *American Journal of Philology* 113 (1992) : 161–77.

Donzelli, Giuseppina Basta. "Arsinoe simile ad Elena (Theocritus Id. 15,110)." *Hermes: Zeitschrift für klassische Philologie* 112 (1984) : 306–16.

Dougherty, Carol. "Linguistic Colonialism in Aeschylus' *Aetnaeae*." *Greek, Roman, and Byzantine Studies* 32 (1991) : 119–32.

―――. *The Poetics of Colonization: From City to Text in Archaic Greece*. New York and Oxford: Oxford University Press, 1993.

Dover, Kenneth J. *Greek Homosexuality*. Cambridge: Harvard University Press, 1978.

―――. *Theocritus: Select Poems*. Basingstoke and London: MacMillan Education, 1971.

Dubisch, Jill. "Culture Enters through the Kitchen: Women, Food, and Social Boundaries in Rural Greece." In *Gender and Power in Rural Greece*, ed. Dubisch, 195–214. Princeton: Princeton University Press, 1986.

duBois, Page. *History, Rhetorical Description, and the Epic: From Homer to Spenser*. Cambridge: D. S. Brewer; Totowa, N.J.: Biblio, 1982.

Dunbabin, T. J. *The Western Greeks: The History of Sicily and South Italy from the Foundation of the Greek Colonies to 480 B.C.* Oxford: Clarendon Press, 1948. Reprint, Chicago: Ares Publishers, 1979.

Edelstein, Emma J., and Ludwig Edelstein. *Asclepius: A Collection and Interpretation of the Testimonies*. 2 vols. Johns Hopkins University, Publications of the Institute of the History of Medicine, 2d series, Texts and Documents, vol. 2. Baltimore: Johns Hopkins Press, 1945. Reprint, Ancient Religion and Mythology, 2 vols. in 1 (Salem: Ayer Company).

Fabiano, Gianfranco. "Fluctuation in Theocritus' Style." *Greek, Roman, and Byzantine Studies* 12 (1971) : 517–37.

Fantham, R. Elaine. "Mime: The Missing Link in Roman Literary History." *Classical World* 82 (1989) : 153–63.

Farnell, Lewis Richard. *The Cults of the Greek States*. Vol. 2. Oxford: Clarendon Press, 1896.

Finley, Moses I. *Ancient Sicily*. Rev. ed. London: Book Club Associates, by arrangement with Chatto and Windus, 1979.

Foley, Helene P. "The 'Female Intruder' Reconsidered: Women in Aristophanes' *Lysistrata* and *Ecclesiazusae*." *Classical Philology* 77 (1982) : 1–21.

———, ed. *Reflections of Women in Antiquity*. New York: Gordon and Breach Science Publishers, 1981.

Forbes Irving, P. M. C. *Metamorphosis in Greek Myths*. Oxford: Clarendon Press; New York: Oxford University Press, 1990.

Forster, E. M. *Alexandria: A History and a Guide*. Reprint, with a new introduction by E. M. Forster. Garden City, N.Y.: Anchor Books, 1961. Originally published in 1922 (Alexandria: W. Morris).

Fowden, Garth. *The Egyptian Hermes: A Historical Approach to the Late Pagan Mind*. Cambridge and New York: Cambridge University Press, 1986.

Fowler, Alastair. *Kinds of Literature: An Introduction to the Theory of Genres and Modes*. Cambridge: Harvard University Press, 1982.

Fowler, Barbara Hughes. *The Hellenistic Aesthetic*. Wisconsin Studies in Classics. Madison: University of Wisconsin Press, 1989.

———, trans. *Hellenistic Poetry: An Anthology*. Wisconsin Studies in Classics. Madison: University of Wisconsin Press, 1990.

Fowler, Dan P. "First Thoughts on Closure: Problems and Prospects." *Materiali e discussioni per l'analisi dei testi classici* 22 (1989) : 75–122.

Fraisse, Jean-Claude. *Philia: La notion d'amitié dans la philosophie antique: Essai sur un problème perdu et retrouvé*. Bibliothèque d'histoire de la philosophie. Paris: Philosophique J. Vrin, 1974.

Fraser, Nancy. *Unruly Practices: Power, Discourse, and Gender in Contemporary Social Theory*. Minneapolis: University of Minnesota Press, 1989.

Fraser, P. M. *The Inscriptions on Stone*. Vol. 2.1 of *Samothrace: Excavations Conducted by the Institute of Fine Arts of New York University*, ed. Karl Lehmann. Bollingen Series, no. 60. New York: Pantheon Books, 1960.

———. *Ptolemaic Alexandria*. 3 vols. Oxford: Clarendon Press, 1972.

———. "Two Studies on the Cult of Sarapis in the Hellenistic World." *Opuscula Atheniensia* 3 (1960) : 1–54.

Frazer, Alfred. *The Propylon of Ptolemy II*. Vol. 10 of *Samothrace: Excavations Conducted by the Institute of Fine Arts of New York University*, ed. Karl Lehmann and Phyllis Williams Lehmann. Bollingen Series, no. 60. Princeton: Princeton University Press, 1990.

Freeman, Kathleen, trans. "On the Killing of Eratosthenes the Seducer." Chapter 4 in *The Murder of Herodes and Other Trials from the Athenian Law Courts,* 43–53. London: MacDonald, 1946.

Friedländer, Paul. "Einleitung: Über die Beschreibung von Kunstwerken in der antiken Literatur." In *Johannes von Gaza und Paulus Silentiarius: Kunst-beschreibungen Justinianischer Zeit*, 1–103. Leipzig: B. G. Teubner, 1912.

Friedrich, Paul. *The Meaning of Aphrodite*. Chicago: University of Chicago Press, 1978.

Frischer, Bernard. *The Sculpted Word: Epicureanism and Philosophical Recruitment in Ancient Greece*. Berkeley and Los Angeles: University of California Press, 1982.

Fritzsche, Hermann. *Theokrits Gedichte*. 3d ed. Revised by Eduard Hiller. Leipzig: B. G. Teubner, 1881.

Garland, Robert. *The Greek Way of Life: From Conception to Old Age*. Ithaca: Cornell University Press, 1990.

Garson, R. W. "An Aspect of Theocritean Humor." *Classical Philology* 68 (1973): 296–97.

Gelzer, Thomas. "Kallimachos und das Zeremoniell des Ptolemäischen Königshauses." In *Aspekte der Kultursoziologie: Aufsätze zur Soziologie, Philosophie, Anthropologie und Geschichte der Kultur: Zum 60. Geburtstag von Mohammed Rassem*, ed. Justin Stagl, 13–30. Berlin: Dietrich Reimer, 1982.

———. "Mimus und Kunsttheorie bei Herondas, Mimiambus 4." In *Catalepton: Festschrift für Bernhard Wyss zum 80. Geburtstag*, ed. Christoph Schäublin. Basel: Seminar für klassische Philologie der Universität Basel, 1985.

———. "Transformations." In Bulloch et al., *Images and Ideologies*, 130–51.

Gercke, Alfred. "Alexandrinische Studien." *Rheinisches Museum für Philologie*, n.s., 42 (1887): 262–75.

Giangrande, Giuseppe. "'Arte Allusiva' and Alexandrian Epic Poetry." *Classical Quarterly*, n.s., 17 (1967): 85–97.

———. "Hellenistic Poetry and Homer." *L'antiquité classique* 39 (1970): 46–77.

———. "Interpretation of Herodas." *Quaderni urbinati di cultura classica* 15 (1973): 82–98.

———. "Sympotic Literature and Epigram." In *L'épigramme grecque*, 91–177. Entretiens sur l'antiquité classique, vol. 14. Geneva: Fondation Hardt, 1968.

Giovannini, Adalberto. "Greek Cities and Greek Commonwealth." In Bulloch et al., *Images and Ideologies*, 265–86.

Glotz, Gustave. "Les fêtes d'Adonis sous Ptolémée II." *Revue des études grecques* 33 (1920): 169–222.

Godley, A. D. *Herodotus*. Vol. 1, *Books I–II*. Rev. ed. Loeb Classical Library. Cambridge: Harvard University Press, 1926.

Gold, Barbara K. *Literary Patronage in Greece and Rome*. Chapel Hill: University of North Carolina Press, 1987.

Goldhill, Simon. "The Naive and Knowing Eye: Ecphrasis and the Culture of Viewing in the Hellenistic World." In Goldhill and Osborne, *Art and Text*, 197–223.

———. *The Poet's Voice: Essays on Poetics and Greek Literature*. Cambridge and New York: Cambridge University Press, 1991.

———. *Reading Greek Tragedy*. Cambridge and New York: Cambridge University Press, 1986.

Goldhill, Simon, and Robin Osborne, eds. *Art and Text in Ancient Greek Culture*. Cambridge Studies in New Art History and Criticism. Cambridge and New York: Cambridge University Press, 1994.

Gombrich, E. H. *Art and Illusion: A Study in the Psychology of Pictorial Represen-tation.* 2d ed., rev. The A. W. Mellon Lectures in the Fine Arts, 1956. Bollin-gen Series, no. 35. Princeton: Princeton University Press, 1961.

Gomme, A. W., A. Andrewes, and K. J. Dover. *A Historical Commentary on Thucydides.* Vol. 4. Oxford: Clarendon Press, 1970.

Goudriaan, Koen. "Ethnical Strategies in Graeco-Roman Egypt." In Bilde et al., *Ethnicity in Hellenistic Egypt,* 74–99.

———. *Ethnicity in Ptolemaic Egypt.* Dutch Monographs on Ancient History and Archaeology, vol. 5. Amsterdam: J. C. Gieben, 1988.

Gow, A. S. F. "The *Adoniazusae* of Theocritus." *Journal of Hellenic Studies* 58 (1938):180–204.

———. *Theocritus.* 2d ed. 2 vols. Cambridge: Cambridge University Press, 1952.

Gow, A. S. F., and D. L. Page. *The Greek Anthology: Hellenistic Epigrams.* 2 vols. Cambridge: Cambridge University Press, 1965.

Green, Peter. *Alexander to Actium: The Historical Evolution of the Hellenistic Age.* Hellenistic Culture and Society, no. 1. Berkeley and Los Angeles: University of California Press, 1990.

———, ed. *Hellenistic History and Culture.* Hellenistic Culture and Society, no. 9. Berkeley and Los Angeles: University of California Press, 1993.

Greenwalt, W. S. "Argaeus, Ptolemy II, and Alexander's Corpse." *The Ancient History Bulletin* 2 (1988):39–41.

Griffin, Jasper. "Decadence Revisited." *New York Review of Books* 38. 9 (1990): 57–62.

———. *Latin Poets and Roman Life.* Chapel Hill: University of North Carolina Press, 1986. Originally published in 1985 (London: Gerald Duckworth).

———. "Theocritus, the *Iliad,* and the East." *American Journal of Philology* 113 (1992):189–211.

Griffiths, Frederick T. "Home before Lunch: The Emancipated Woman in The-ocritus." In Foley, *Reflections of Women,* 247–73.

———. "Poetry as *Pharmakon* in Theocritus' *Idyll* 2." In *Arktouros: Hellenic Studies Presented to Bernard M. W. Knox,* ed. Glen W. Bowersock, Walter Burkert, and Michael C. J. Putnam, 81–88. Berlin: Walter de Gruyter, 1979.

———. *Theocritus at Court.* Mnemosyne, supplement no. 55. Leiden: E. J. Brill, 1979.

Gruen, Erich S. *The Hellenistic World and the Coming of Rome.* 2 vols. Berkeley and Los Angeles: University of California Press, 1984.

Grzybek, Erhard. "La mort d'Arsinoé II Philadelphe." In *Du calendrier macé-donien au calendrier ptolémaïque: Problèmes de chronologie hellénistique,* 103–12. Schweizerische Beiträge zur Altertumswissenschaft, no. 20. Basel: Friedrich Reinhardt, 1990.

Gutzwiller, Kathryn J. "Callimachus' *Lock of Berenice*: Fantasy, Romance, and Propaganda." *American Journal of Philology* 113 (1992):359–85.

———. *Theocritus' Pastoral Analogies: The Formation of a Genre.* Wisconsin Studies in Classics. Madison: University of Wisconsin Press, 1991.

Gutzwiller, Kathryn J., and Ann Norris Michelini. "Women and Other Strangers: Feminist Perspectives in Classical Literature." In *(En) Gendering Knowledge: Feminists in Academe,* ed. Joan E. Hartman and Ellen Messer-Davidow, 66–84. Knoxville: University of Tennessee Press, 1991.

Habicht, Christian. "Athens and the Ptolemies." *Classical Antiquity* 11 (1992): 68–90.

Hagstrum, Jean H. *The Sister Arts: The Tradition of Literary Pictorialism and English Poetry from Dryden to Gray*. Chicago: University of Chicago Press, 1958.

Halperin, David M. *Before Pastoral: Theocritus and the Ancient Tradition of Bucolic Poetry*. New Haven: Yale University Press, 1983.

———. "The Democratic Body: Prostitution and Citizenship in Classical Athens." Chapter 5 in *One Hundred Years of Homosexuality and Other Essays on Greek Love*, 88–112. New Ancient World. New York: Routledge, 1990.

———. "Why Is Diotima a Woman?" Chapter 6 in *One Hundred Years of Homosexuality and Other Essays on Greek Love*, 113–51. New Ancient World. New York: Routledge, 1990.

Halperin, David M., John J. Winkler, and Froma I. Zeitlin, eds. *Before Sexuality: The Construction of Erotic Experience in the Ancient Greek World*. Princeton: Princeton University Press, 1990.

Harrison, A. R. W. *The Law of Athens*. Vol. 1, *The Family and Property*. Oxford: Clarendon Press, 1968.

Hauben, Hans. "Arsinoé II et la politique extérieure de l'Égypte." In van't Dack, van Dessel, and van Gucht, *Egypt*, 99–127.

Havelock, Christine Mitchell. *Hellenistic Art: The Art of the Classical World from the Death of Alexander the Great to the Battle of Actium*. 2d ed. New York and London: W. W. Norton, 1981.

Hawley, Richard. "The Problem of Women Philosophers in Ancient Greece." Chapter 4 in Archer, Fischler, and Wyke, *Women in Ancient Societies*, 70–87.

Headlam, Walter, and A. D. Knox, eds. *Herodas: The Mimes and Fragments*. Cambridge: Cambridge University Press, 1922. Reprint, Greek Texts and Commentaries (Salem: Ayer Company, 1988).

Heffernan, James A. W. *Museum of Words: The Poetics of Ekphrasis from Homer to Ashbery*. Chicago: University of Chicago Press, 1993.

Helmbold, W. C. "The Song of the Argive Woman's Daughter." *Classical Philology* 46 (1951): 17–24.

———. "Theocritus 15.87–88." *Classical Philology* 46 (1951): 116.

Henderson, Jeffrey. "Older Women in Attic Old Comedy." *Transactions and Proceedings of the American Philological Association* 117 (1987): 105–29.

Henricksen, Bruce. *Nomadic Voices: Conrad and the Subject of Narrative*. Urbana: University of Illinois Press, 1992.

Herter, Hans. "Kallimachos und Homer: Ein Beitrag zur Interpretation des Hymnos auf Artemis." In *Xenia Bonnensia; Festschrift zum Fünfundsiebzigjährigen Bestehen des Philologischen Vereins und Bonner Kreises*, 50–105. Bonn: F. Cohen, 1929.

Hine, Daryl, trans. *Theocritus: Idylls and Epigrams*. New York: Atheneum, 1982.

Hodkinson, Stephen. "Inheritance, Marriage, and Demography: Perspectives upon the Success and Decline of Classical Sparta." In *Classical Sparta: Techniques behind Her Success*, ed. Anton Powell, 79–121. Oklahoma Series in Classical Culture, vol. 1. Norman: University of Oklahoma Press, 1989.

Holden, Anthony. *Greek Pastoral Poetry*. Penguin Classics. Harmondsworth: Penguin Books, 1974.

Hollis, A. S. *Callimachus: Hecale*. Oxford: Clarendon Press; New York: Oxford University Press, 1990.

Hopkinson, Neil, ed. *A Hellenistic Anthology*. Cambridge Greek and Latin Classics. Cambridge and New York: Cambridge University Press, 1988.

Hornblower, Simon. *The Greek World, 479–323 BC*. Classical Civilizations. Reprint, with corrections. London and New York: Methuen, 1985.

Horstmann, Axel E.-A. *Ironie und Humor bei Theokrit*. Beiträge zur klassischen Philologie, no. 67. Meisenheim am Glan: Anton Hain, 1976.

Humphreys, Sally C. *Anthropology and the Greeks*. International Library of Anthropology. London and Boston: Routledge and Kegan Paul, 1978.

Hutcheon, Linda. *The Politics of Postmodernism*. New Accents. London and New York: Routledge, 1989.

Hutchinson, G. O. *Hellenistic Poetry*. Oxford: Clarendon Press; New York: Oxford University Press, 1988.

Isenberg, Charles, and David Konstan. "Pastoral Desire: The Third Idyll of Theocritus." *Dalhousie Review* 64 (1984) : 302–15.

Johnson, W. R. *Darkness Visible: A Study of Vergil's Aeneid*. Berkeley and Los Angeles: University of California Press, 1976.

Joyce, James. *Ulysses*. Revised edition, corrected and reset, New York: Random House, 1961. Originally published in 1922 (Paris: Shakespeare and Company).

Just, Roger. *Women in Athenian Law and Life*. London and New York: Routledge, 1989.

Kahrstedt, Ulrich. "Frauen auf antiken Münzen." *Klio* 10 (1910) : 261–314.

Kaibel, Georgius, ed. *Comicorum Graecorum Fragmenta*. Vol. 1.1, *Doriensium Comoedia Mimi Phlyaces*. 2d ed. Berlin: Weidmann, 1958.

Kennedy, Robinette. "Women's Friendships on Crete: A Psychological Perspective." In *Gender and Power in Rural Greece*, ed. Jill Dubisch, 121–38. Princeton: Princeton University Press, 1986.

Kenney, E. J. "Doctus Lucretius." *Mnemosyne*, 4th ser., 23 (1970) : 366–92.

Kermode, Frank. *The Sense of an Ending: Studies in the Theory of Fiction*. Bryn Mawr: The Mary Flexner Lectures, 1965. 1967. Reprint, London and New York: Oxford University Press, 1968.

Keuls, Eva C. "Plato on Painting." *American Journal of Philology* 95 (1974) : 100–27.

———. *The Reign of the Phallus: Sexual Politics in Ancient Athens*. New York: Harper and Row, 1985.

Kilmer, Martin F. *Greek Erotica: On Attic Red-Figure Vases*. London: Duckworth, 1993.

Koenen, Ludwig. "Die Adaptation ägyptischer Königsideologie am Ptolemäerhof." In van't Dack, van Dessel, and van Gucht, *Egypt*, 143–90.

———. "The Ptolemaic King as a Religious Figure." In Bulloch et al., *Images and Ideologies*, 25–115.

Konstan, David. "A Note on Theocritus *Idyll* 18." *Classical Philology* 74 (1979) : 233–34.

———. *Sexual Symmetry: Love in the Ancient Novel and Related Genres*. Princeton: Princeton University Press, 1994.

————. "The Tyrant Goddess: Herodas's Fifth *Mime.*" *Classical Antiquity* 8 (1989) : 267–82.

Kraemer, Ross Shepard. *Her Share of the Blessings: Women's Religions among Pagans, Jews, and Christians in the Greco-Roman World.* New York and Oxford: Oxford University Press, 1992.

Kristeva, Julia. *Strangers to Ourselves.* Translated by Leon S. Roudiez. European Perspectives. New York: Columbia University Press, 1991. Originally published as *Étrangers à nous-mêmes* (Paris: Arthème Fayard, 1988).

Kroll, W. "Die Kreuzung der Gattungen." In *Studien zum Verständnis der römischen Literatur,* 202–24. Stuttgart: J. B. Metzler, 1924.

Lacey, W. K. *The Family in Classical Greece.* Ithaca: Cornell University Press, 1968.

Langbaum, Robert. *The Poetry of Experience: The Dramatic Monologue in Modern Literary Tradition.* 2d ed. Chicago: University of Chicago Press, 1985.

Lattimore, Richmond, trans. *The Iliad of Homer.* Chicago: University of Chicago Press, 1951.

Launey, Marcel. "L'exécution de Sotadès et l'expédition de Patroklos dans la mer Égée (266 av. J.C.)." *Revue des études anciennes* 47 (1945) : 33–45.

Lawall, Gilbert. "Herodas 6 and 7 Reconsidered." *Classical Philology* 71 (1976) : 165–69.

————. *Theocritus' Coan Pastorals: A Poetry Book.* Publications of the Center for Hellenic Studies. Washington, D.C.: Center for Hellenic Studies, 1967.

Leach, Edmund. *Culture and Communication: The Logic by Which Symbols Are Connected: An Introduction to the Use of Structuralist Analysis in Social Anthropology.* Themes in the Social Sciences. Cambridge and New York: Cambridge University Press, 1976.

Legrand, Ph.-E. *Étude sur Théocrite.* Bibliothèque des Écoles françaises d'Athènes et de Rome, no. 79. Paris, 1898.

Lessing, Gotthold Ephraim. *Laocoön: An Essay on the Limits of Painting and Poetry.* 1962. Translated by Edward Allen McCormick. New York: Bobbs-Merrill. Reprint, Baltimore: Johns Hopkins University Press, 1984. Originally published in 1766 as *Laokoon, oder über die Grenzen der Malerei und Poesie.*

Levi, Peter. "People in a Landscape: Theokritos." In *Hellenistic History and Culture,* ed. Peter Green, 111–37. Berkeley and Los Angeles: University of California Press, 1993.

Lewis, Naphtali. *Greeks in Ptolemaic Egypt: Case Studies in the Social History of the Hellenistic World.* Oxford: Clarendon Press; New York: Oxford University Press, 1986.

Liddell, Henry George, and Robert Scott. *A Greek-English Lexicon.* 9th ed., with supplement. Oxford: Clarendon Press, 1968.

Lloyd, Alan B. *Herodotus: Book II: Commentary 1–98.* Études préliminaires aux religions orientales dans l'Empire romain, vol. 43. Leiden: E. J. Brill, 1976.

Lloyd, G. E. R., ed. *Hippocratic Writings.* Translated by J. Chadwick, W. N. Mann, I. M. Lonie, and E. T. Withington. Enl. ed. Harmondsworth: Penguin Books, 1978.

Long, A. A. "Post-Aristotelian Philosophy." Chapter 19 in *Greek Literature.*

Vol. 1 of *The Cambridge History of Classical Literature*, ed. P. E. Easterling and B. M. W. Knox, 622–41. Cambridge and New York: Cambridge University Press, 1985.

Long, A. A, and D. N. Sedley. *The Hellenistic Philosophers*. Vol. 2, *Greek and Latin Texts: With Notes and Bibliography*. 1987. Reprint, Cambridge and New York: Cambridge University Press, 1989.

Longega, Gabriella. *Arsinoë II*. Università degli studi di Padova, pubblicazioni dell'Istituto di storia antica, vol. 6. Rome: «L'Erma» di Bretschneider, 1968.

Lord, A. B. *The Singer of Tales*. Cambridge: Harvard University Press, 1960.

Luria, Salomo. "Herondas' Kampf für die veristische Kunst." In *Miscellanea di studi Alessandrini, in memoria di Augusto Rostagni*, 394–415. Torino: Bottega d'Erasmo, 1963.

Lyne, R. O. A. M. *Further Voices in Vergil's* Aeneid. Oxford: Clarendon Press; New York: Oxford University Press, 1987.

————. *The Latin Love Poets: From Catullus to Horace*. Oxford: Clarendon Press; New York: Oxford University Press, 1980.

Lytle, Guy Fitch, and Stephen Orgel, eds. *Patronage in the Renaissance*. Folger Institute Essays. Princeton: Princeton University Press, 1981.

MacDowell, D. M. *Spartan Law*. Scottish Classical Studies, no. 1. Edinburgh: Scottish Academic Press, 1986.

Macurdy, Grace Harriet. *Hellenistic Queens: A Study of Woman-Power in Macedonia, Seleucid Syria, and Ptolemaic Egypt*. Studies in Archaeology, no. 14. Baltimore: Johns Hopkins Press, 1932.

Magnien, Victor. "Le Syracusain littéraire et l'Idylle XV de Théocrite." *Mémoires de la Société de linguistique de Paris* 21 (1920) : 49–85, 112–38.

Mahaffy, J. P., and J. G. Smyly, eds. *The Flinders Petrie Papyri*. Vol. 3. Dublin: Academy House, 1905.

Mair, A. W., trans. "Callimachus." In *Callimachus: Hymns and Epigrams; Lycophron; Aratus*, trans. A. W. and G. R. Mair. 2d ed. Loeb Classical Library. Cambridge: Harvard University Press, 1955. Mair's translation was first published in 1921 (Loeb Classical Library).

Marx, Leo. *The Machine in the Garden: Technology and the Pastoral Ideal in America*. London and New York: Oxford University Press, 1964.

Mastromarco, Giuseppe. *The Public of Herondas*. London Studies in Classical Philology, vol. 11. Amsterdam: J. C. Gieben, 1984.

McCredie, James R., Georges Roux, Stuart M. Shaw, and John Kurtich, with contributions by Phyllis Williams Lehmann, Phyllis Pray Bober, and Günter Kopcke; Laura M. Gadbery, Elsbeth B. Dusenbery, and Elizabeth Oustinoff. *The Rotunda of Arsinoe*. Vol. 7 of *Samothrace: Excavations Conducted by the Institute of Fine Arts of New York University*, ed. Karl Lehmann and Phyllis Williams Lehmann. Bollingen Series, no. 60. Princeton: Princeton University Press, 1992.

McKay, K. J. "Theokritos' *Bacchantes* Re-examined." *Antichthon* 1 (1967):16–28.

McKechnie, Paul. *Outsiders in the Greek Cities in the Fourth Century BC*. London and New York: Routledge, 1989.

Meister, K. "Agathocles." Chapter 10 in Walbank et al., *Hellenistic World*, 384–411.

Miles, Gary B. "Characterization and the Ideal of Innocence in Theocritus' Idylls." *Ramus* 6 (1977): 139–64.

Miller, J. Hillis. *The Linguistic Moment: From Wordsworth to Stevens*. Princeton: Princeton University Press, 1985.

Miller, Jean Baker. *Toward a New Psychology of Women*. Boston: Beacon Press, 1976.

Mills, Barriss, trans. *The Idylls of Theocritus*. West Lafayette: Purdue University Press, 1963.

Mineur, W. H. *Callimachus: Hymn to Delos*. Mnemosyne, supplement no. 83. Leiden: E. J. Brill, 1984.

Mitchell, W. J. T. *Iconology: Image, Text, Ideology*. Chicago: University of Chicago Press, 1986.

Monteil, Pierre. *Théocrite: Idylles (II, V, VII, XI, XV)*. «Érasme», Collection de textes grecs commentés. Paris: Presses universitaires de France, 1968.

Morenz, Siegfried. *Ägyptische Religion*. Stuttgart: W. Kohlhammer, 1960.

Motto, Anna Lydia, and John R. Clark. "Idyllic Slumming 'Midst Urban Hordes: The Satiric Epos in Theocritus and Swift." *The Classical Bulletin* 47 (1971): 39–44.

Müller, G. "Beschreibung von Kunstwerken im Ion des Euripides." *Hermes: Zeitschrift für klassische Philologie* 103 (1975): 29–36.

Murray, A. T. *Demosthenes: Private Orations*. Vol. 3, *Orations L-LIX*. Loeb Classical Library. Cambridge: Harvard University Press, 1939.

———. *Homer: The Odyssey*. 2 vols. Loeb Classical Library. Cambridge: Harvard University Press, 1919.

Murray, Oswyn. "The Affair of the Mysteries: Democracy and the Drinking Group." In Murray, *Sympotica*, 149–61.

———. "Aristeas and Ptolemaic Kingship." *Journal of Theological Studies*, n.s., 18 (1967): 337–71.

———. *Early Greece*. 2d ed. Cambridge: Harvard University Press, 1993.

———. "The Greek Symposion in History." In *Tria corda: Scritti in onore di Arnaldo Momigliano*, ed. E. Gabba, 257–72. Biblioteca di Athenaeum, no. 1. Como: Edizioni New Press, 1983.

———. "Symposion and Männerbund." In *Concilium Eirene* 16, ed. P. Oliva and A. Frolíková, 47–52. Prague, 1982.

———. "Symposium and Genre in the Poetry of Horace." *Journal of Roman Studies* 75 (1985): 39–50.

———. "War and the Symposium." In Slater, *Dining*, 83–103.

———, ed. *Sympotica: A Symposium on the* Symposion. Oxford: Clarendon Press, 1990.

Nagy, G. *Greek Mythology and Poetics*. Myth and Poetics. Ithaca: Cornell University Press, 1990.

Naville, Édouard. "La stèle de Pithom." *Zeitschrift für ägyptische Sprache und Altertumskunde* 40 (1902): 66–75.

Niles, John D. "Patterning in the Wandering of Odysseus." *Ramus* 7 (1978): 46–60.

Nock, Arthur Darby. "Notes on Ruler-Cult, I–IV." *Journal of Hellenic Studies* 48 (1928): 21–43.

————. "ΣΥΝΝΑΟΣ ΘΕΟΣ." *Harvard Studies in Classical Philology* 41 (1930) : 1–62.

O'Connor, David K. "The Invulnerable Pleasures of Epicurean Friendship." *Greek, Roman, and Byzantine Studies* 31 (1990) : 165–86.

Onians, John. *Art and Thought in the Hellenistic Age: The Greek World View, 350–50 BC.* London: Thames and Hudson, 1979.

Osborne, Robin. *Demos: The Discovery of Classical Attika.* Cambridge Classical Studies. Cambridge and New York: Cambridge University Press, 1985.

Ostriker, Alicia. "The Thieves of Language: Women Poets and Revisionist Mythmaking." In *The New Feminist Criticism: Essays on Women, Literature, and Theory,* ed. Elaine Showalter, 314–38. New York: Pantheon Books, 1985.

Page, Denys L., ed. *Euripides: Medea.* 1938. Reprint, with corrections. Oxford: Clarendon Press, 1952.

Parry, Hugh. "Magic and the Songstress: Theocritus Idyll 2." *Illinois Classical Studies* 13 (1988) : 43–55.

Parsons, Michael J. *How We Understand Art: A Cognitive Developmental Account of Aesthetic Experience.* Cambridge and New York: Cambridge University Press, 1987.

Paton, W. R., trans. *The Greek Anthology.* 5 vols. Loeb Classical Library. Cambridge: Harvard University Press, 1916–18.

Patterson, Annabel. *Pastoral and Ideology: Virgil to Valéry.* Berkeley and Los Angeles: University of California Press, 1987.

Pavel, Thomas G. *Fictional Worlds.* Cambridge: Harvard University Press, 1986.

Pellizer, Ezio. "Outlines of a Morphology of Sympotic Entertainment." Translated by Catherine McLaughlin. In O. Murray, *Sympotica,* 177–84.

Peradotto, John, and J. P. Sullivan, eds. *Women in the Ancient World: The Arethusa Papers.* SUNY Series in Classical Studies. Albany: State University of New York Press, 1984.

Peremans, Willy. "Les Lagides, les élites indigènes et la monarchie bicéphale." In *Le système palatial en Orient, en Grèce et à Rome.* Actes du Colloque de Strasbourg, 19–22 juin 1985, ed. E. Lévy, 327–43. Université des sciences humaines de Strasbourg, Travaux du Centre de recherche sur le Proche-Orient et la Grèce antiques, no. 9. Leiden: E. J. Brill, 1987.

Pfeiffer, Rudolf. "Arsinoe Philadelphos in der Dichtung." *Die Antike* 2 (1926) : 161–74.

————. *Callimachus.* 2 vols. Oxford: Clarendon Press, 1949–53. Reprint, Greek Texts and Commentaries, 2 vols. in 1 (New York: Arno Press, 1979).

————. *History of Classical Scholarship.* Vol. 1, *From the Beginnings to the End of the Hellenistic Age.* Oxford: Clarendon Press, 1968.

Pickard-Cambridge, Arthur. "The Artists of Dionysus." Chapter 7 in *The Dramatic Festivals of Athens.* 1968. 2d ed. Revised by John Gould and D. M. Lewis. Reissue, with supplement and corrections, 279–323. Oxford: Clarendon Press; New York: Oxford University Press, 1988.

Pollitt, J. J. *The Ancient View of Greek Art: Criticism, History, and Terminology.* Student edition. Yale Publications in the History of Art, no. 26. New Haven: Yale University Press, 1974.

———. *Art in the Hellenistic Age*. Cambridge and New York: Cambridge University Press, 1986.

———. *The Art of Ancient Greece: Sources and Documents*. 2d ed. Cambridge and New York: Cambridge University Press, 1990.

Pollock, Griselda. *Vision and Difference: Femininity, Feminism, and the Histories of Art*. London and New York: Routledge, 1988.

Pomeroy, Sarah B. *Goddesses, Whores, Wives, and Slaves: Women in Classical Antiquity*. New York: Schocken Books, 1975.

———. "Technikai kai Mousikai: The Education of Women in the Fourth Century and in the Hellenistic Age." *American Journal of Ancient History* 2 (1977): 51–68.

———. *Women in Hellenistic Egypt: From Alexander to Cleopatra*. New York: Schocken Books, 1984.

———, ed. *Women's History and Ancient History*. Chapel Hill: University of North Carolina Press, 1991.

Powell, J. U. *Collectanea Alexandrina: Reliquiae minores poetarum Graecorum aetatis Ptolemaicae 323–146 A.C.* (= *Coll. Alex.*). Oxford: Clarendon Press, 1925.

Préaux, Claire. *Le monde hellénistique: La Grèce et l'Orient de la mort d'Alexandre à la conquête romaine de la Grèce (323–146 av. J.-C.)*. 2d ed. 2 vols. Nouvelle Clio, L'histoire et ses problèmes. Paris: Presses universitaires de France, 1987–88.

———. "Le statut de la femme à l'époque hellénistique, principalement en Égypte." In *La femme*. Recueils de la Société Jean Bodin pour l'histoire comparative des institutions, vol. 11, 1: 127–75. Brussels: Éditions de la Librairie encyclopédique, 1959.

Price, Simon R. F. "Hellenistic Cities and Their Rulers." Chapter 2 in *Rituals and Power: The Roman Imperial Cult in Asia Minor*, 23–52. 1984. Reprint, Cambridge and New York: Cambridge University Press, 1986.

———. "The History of the Hellenistic Period." Chapter 13 in *The Oxford History of the Classical World*, ed. John Boardman, Jasper Griffin, and Oswyn Murray, 315–37. Oxford: Oxford University Press, 1986.

Propp, Vladímir. *Morphology of the Folktale*. Translated by Lawrence Scott. 2d ed. Rev. Louis A. Wagner. American Folklore Society Bibliographical and Special Services, vol. 9. Indiana University Research Center in Anthropology, Folklore, and Linguistics, no. 10. Austin: University of Texas Press, 1968. Originally published as *Morfologija skazki* (Leningrad, 1928).

Rabinowitz, Nancy Sorkin, and Amy Richlin, eds. *Feminist Theory and the Classics*. New York: Routledge, 1993.

Reich, Hermann. *Der Mimus: Ein litterar-entwickelungsgeschichtlicher Versuch*. Berlin: Weidmann, 1903.

Reitzenstein, Erich. "Zur Stiltheorie des Kallimachos." In *Festschrift Richard Reitzenstein*, 23–69. Leipzig: B. G. Teubner, 1931.

Rice, E. E. *The Grand Procession of Ptolemy Philadelphus*. Oxford Classical and Philosophical Monographs. London and New York: Oxford University Press, 1983.

Richlin, Amy, ed. *Pornography and Representation in Greece and Rome*. New York and Oxford: Oxford University Press, 1992.

Ricoeur, Paul. *Oneself as Another*. Translated by Kathleen Blamey. Chicago: University of Chicago Press, 1992. Originally published as *Soi-même comme un autre* (Paris: Seuil, 1990).

Ridgway, Brunilde Sismondo. "Ancient Greek Women and Art: The Material Evidence." *American Journal of Archaeology*, 2d ser., 91 (1987) : 399–409.

———. *Hellenistic Sculpture I: The Styles of ca. 331–200 B.C.* Wisconsin Studies in Classics. Madison: University of Wisconsin Press, 1990.

Rieu, Emile Victor, trans. *Apollonius of Rhodes: The Voyage of Argo: Argonautica*. 2d ed. London: Penguin Books, 1971.

Rist, Anna. *The Poems of Theocritus*. Chapel Hill: University of North Carolina Press, 1978.

Robert, Louis. "Sur un décret d'Ilion et sur un papyrus concernant des cultes royaux." In *Essays in Honor of C. Bradford Welles*, 175–211. American Studies in Papyrology, vol. 1. New Haven: American Society of Papyrologists, 1966.

Roberts, Colin H. "Literature and Society in the Papyri." *Museum Helveticum* 10 (1953) : 267–68.

Robertson, Martin. *A History of Greek Art*. 2 vols. London: Cambridge University Press, 1975.

Rogers, Benjamin Bickley. *Aristophanes*. Vol. 1, *The Acharnians, the Knights, the Clouds, the Wasps*. Loeb Classical Library. Cambridge: Harvard University Press, 1924.

Rosenmeyer, T. G. *The Green Cabinet: Theocritus and the European Pastoral Lyric*. Berkeley and Los Angeles: University of California Press, 1969.

Rosivach, V. "Earthborns and Olympians: The Parodos of the *Ion*." *Classical Quarterly*, n.s., 27 (1977) : 284–94.

Rossi, L. E. "I generi letterari e le loro leggi scritte e non scritte nelle letterature classiche." *Bulletin of the Institute of Classical Studies* (University of London) 18 (1971) : 69–94.

Rossi, Mary Ann. *Theocritus' Idyll XVII: A Stylistic Commentary*. Classical and Byzantine Monographs, vol. 15. Amsterdam: Adolf M. Hakkert, 1989.

Rostovtzeff, M. *The Social and Economic History of the Hellenistic World*. 3 vols. Oxford: Clarendon Press, 1941.

Rudd, Niall. *Juvenal: The Satires*. The World's Classics Paperback. Oxford and New York: Oxford University Press, 1992.

Ruijgh, C. J. "Le dorien de Théocrite: Dialecte cyrénien d'Alexandrie et d'Égypte." *Mnemosyne*, 4th ser., 37 (1984) : 56–88.

Samuel, Alan E. *The Shifting Sands of History: Interpretations of Ptolemaic Egypt*. Publications of the Association of Ancient Historians, no. 2. Lanham, Md.: University Press of America, 1989.

Sargent, Thelma, trans. *The Idylls of Theocritus: A Verse Translation*. New York: W. W. Norton, 1982.

Schaps, David M. *Economic Rights of Women in Ancient Greece*. 1979. Reprint, Edinburgh: Edinburgh University Press, 1981.

Schnapp, Alain. "Eros the Hunter." In Bérard et al., *City of Images*, 71–87.

Schneider, Carl. *Kulturgeschichte des Hellenismus*. 2 vols. Munich: C. H. Beck, 1967.

Schwinge, Ernst-Richard. *Künstlichkeit von Kunst: Zur Geschichtlichkeit der alexandrinischen Poesie*. Zetemata, no. 84. Munich: C. H. Beck, 1986.

Scodel, R. "Wine, Water, and the Anthesteria in Callimachus Fr. 178 Pf." *Zeitschrift für Papyrologie und Epigraphik* 39 (1980) : 37–40.

Seaton, R. C., trans. *Apollonius Rhodius: The Argonautica*. Loeb Classical Library. Cambridge: Harvard University Press, 1912.

Segal, Charles. "Adonis and Aphrodite: Theocritus, *Idyll* 3.48." In Segal, *Poetry and Myth*, 66–72. First published in *L'antiquité classique* 37 (1969): 82–88.

———. "Death by Water: A Narrative Pattern in Theocritus." In Segal, *Poetry and Myth*, 47–65. First published in *Hermes: Zeitschrift für klassische Philologie* 102 (1974): 20–38.

———. *Poetry and Myth in Ancient Pastoral: Essays on Theocritus and Virgil*. Princeton Series of Collected Essays. Princeton: Princeton University Press, 1981.

———. "Running after Philinus (Theocritus, *Idyll* 2.114ff.)." *Estudios clásicos* 26 (1984) : 347–50.

———. "'Since Daphnis Dies': The Meaning of Theocritus' First Idyll." In Segal, *Poetry and Myth*, 25–46. First published in *Museum Helveticum* 31 (1974): 1–22.

———. "Space, Time, and Imagination in Theocritus' Second *Idyll*." *Classical Antiquity* 4 (1985) : 103–19.

———. "Underreading and Intertextuality: Sappho, Simaetha, and Odysseus in Theocritus' Second Idyll." *Arethusa* 17 (1984) : 201–9.

Seltman, Charles. *Women in Antiquity*. London and New York: Thames and Hudson, 1956.

Shepherd, W. G., trans. *Horace: The Complete Odes and Epodes: With the Centennial Hymn*. Penguin Classics. Harmondsworth: Penguin Books, 1983.

Sherwin-White, Susan M. *Ancient Cos: An Historical Study from the Dorian Settlement to the Imperial Period*. Hypomnemata, no. 51. Göttingen: Vandenhoeck and Ruprecht, 1978.

Sherwin-White, Susan, and Amélie Kuhrt. *From Samarkhand to Sardis: A New Approach to the Seleucid Empire*. Hellenistic Culture and Society, no. 13. Berkeley and Los Angeles: University of California Press, 1993.

Shipley, Graham. *A History of Samos: 800–188 BC*. Oxford: Clarendon; New York: Oxford University Press, 1987.

Skinner, Marilyn B. "Greek Women and the Metronymic: A Note on an Epigram by Nossis." *The Ancient History Bulletin* 1 (1987) : 39–42.

———. "Nossis *Thēlyglōssos*: The Private Text and the Public Book." In Pomeroy, *Women's History*, 20–47.

Slater, William J., ed. *Dining in a Classical Context*. Symposium at McMaster University, September 1989. Ann Arbor: University of Michigan Press, 1991.

Smith, Barbara Herrnstein. *Contingencies of Value: Alternative Perspectives for Critical Theory*. Cambridge: Harvard University Press, 1988.

———. *Poetic Closure: A Study of How Poems End*. Chicago: University of Chicago Press, 1968.

Smith, R. R. R. *Hellenistic Sculpture: A Handbook*. World of Art. London: Thames and Hudson, 1991.

Smutny, R. J. *The Text History of the Epigrams of Theocritus*. University of California Publications in Classical Philology, vol. 15, no. 2. Berkeley, 1955.

Snyder, Jane McIntosh. *The Woman and the Lyre: Women Writers in Classical Greece and Rome*. Ad Feminam: Women and Literature. Carbondale: Southern Illinois University Press, 1989.

Sowa, Cora Angier. *Traditional Themes and the Homeric Hymns*. Chicago: Bolchazy-Carducci Publishers, 1984.

Spacks, Patricia M. *Gossip*. Chicago: University of Chicago Press, 1986. Originally published in 1985 (New York: A. A. Knopf).

Spivak, Gayatri Chakravorty. *In Other Worlds: Essays in Cultural Politics*. New York: Methuen, 1987.

Stambaugh, John E. *Sarapis under the Early Ptolemies*. Études préliminaires aux religions orientales dans l'Empire romain, vol. 25. Leiden: E. J. Brill, 1972.

Stanley, Keith. "Irony and Foreshadowing in *Aeneid*, I, 462." *American Journal of Philology* 86 (1965) : 267–77.

Stehle, Eva. "Sappho's Gaze: Fantasies of a Goddess and Young Man." *differences* 2 (1990) . 88–125.

Stern, Jacob. "Herodas' *Mimiamb* 1." *Greek, Roman, and Byzantine Studies* 22 (1981) : 161–65.

———. "Herodas' *Mimiamb* 6." *Greek, Roman, and Byzantine Studies* 20 (1979) : 247–54.

———. "Theocritus' *Idyll* 14." *Greek, Roman, and Byzantine Studies* 16 (1975) : 51–58.

———. "Theocritus' *Idyll* 24." *American Journal of Philology* 95 (1974) : 348–61.

Sutton, Robert F., Jr. "Pornography and Persuasion on Attic Pottery." In Richlin, *Pornography and Representation*, 3–35.

Syme, Ronald. *The Roman Revolution*. Reprint, London and New York: Oxford University Press, 1960. Originally published in 1939 (Oxford: Clarendon Press).

Talbert, R. J. A. *Timoleon and the Revival of Greek Sicily: 344–317 B.C.* Cambridge Classical Studies. Cambridge: Cambridge University Press, 1974.

Tarán, Sonya Lida. *The Art of Variation in the Hellenistic Epigram*. Columbia Studies in the Classical Tradition, vol. 9. Leiden: E. J. Brill, 1979.

Tarn, W. W. *Hellenistic Civilisation*. 3d ed. Revised by the author and G. T. Griffith. Reprint. Meridian Books. Cleveland: World Publishing, 1961. The third edition was originally published in 1952 (London: E. Arnold).

Tennenhouse, Leonard. "Sir Walter Raleigh and Clientage." In Lytle and Orgel, *Patronage*, 235–58.

Thomas, Richard F. "Callimachus, the *Victoria Berenices*, and Roman Poetry." *Classical Quarterly*, n.s., 33 (1983) : 92–113.

Thompson, Dorothy Burr. *Ptolemaic Oinochoai and Portraits in Faience: Aspects of the Ruler-Cult*. Oxford Monographs on Classical Archaeology. Oxford: Clarendon Press, 1973.

Thompson, Dorothy J. *Memphis under the Ptolemies*. Princeton: Princeton University Press, 1988.

Thompson, Stith. *Motif-Index of Folk-Literature: A Classification of Narrative Elements in Folktales, Ballads, Myths, Fables, Mediaeval Romances, Exempla, Fabli-*

aux, Jest-Books, and Local Legends. Rev. and enl. ed. 6 vols. Bloomington: Indiana University Press, 1955–58.

Tondriau, Julien L. "Princesses ptolémaïques comparées ou identifiées à des déesses (IIIe–Ier siècles avant J. C.)." *Bulletin de la Société royale d'archéologie d'Alexandrie* 37 (1948) : 12–33.

Trypanis, C. A., trans. "Callimachus." In *Callimachus: Aetia, Iambi, Lyric Poems, Hecale, Minor Epic and Elegiac Poems, and Other Fragments; Musaeus: Hero and Leander.* Loeb Classical Library. Cambridge: Harvard University Press, 1975. Trypanis's translation was first published in 1958 (Loeb Classical Library).

Turner, E. G. "Ptolemaic Egypt." Chapter 5 in Walbank et al., *Hellenistic World,* 118–74.

Turner, Victor. *The Anthropology of Performance.* New York: Performing Arts Journal Publications, 1986.

———. *Dramas, Fields, and Metaphors: Symbolic Action in Human Society.* Symbol, Myth, and Ritual. Ithaca: Cornell University Press, 1974.

———. *From Ritual to Theatre: The Human Seriousness of Play.* Performance Studies, vol. 1. New York: Performing Arts Journal Publications, 1982.

Ussher, R. G. "The Mimiamboi of Herodas." *Hermathena* 129 (1980) : 65–76.

van Gennep, Arnold. *The Rites of Passage.* Translated by Monika B. Vizedom and Gabrielle L. Caffee. Chicago: University of Chicago Press, 1960.

Van Sickle, J. "Epic and Bucolic (Theocritus, *Id.* VII; Virgil, *Ecl.* I)." *Quaderni urbinati di cultura classica* 19 (1975) : 45–72.

van't Dack, E., P. van Dessel, and W. van Gucht, eds. *Egypt and the Hellenistic World.* Proceedings of the International Colloquium, Leuven, 24–26 May 1982. Studia Hellenistica, no. 27. Louvain, 1983.

Vatin, Claude. *Citoyens et non-citoyens dans le monde grec.* Regards sur l'histoire. Paris: Société d'édition d'enseignement supérieur, 1984.

———. *Recherches sur le mariage et la condition de la femme mariée à l'époque hellénistique.* Bibliothèque des Écoles françaises d'Athènes et de Rome, no. 216. Paris: Éditions E. de Boccard, 1970.

Vercoutter, Jean. "La femme en Egypte ancienne." In *Préhistoire et antiquité.* Vol. 1 of *Histoire mondiale de la femme,* ed. Pierre Grimal, 61–152. Paris: Nouvelle librairie de France, 1965.

Vermeule, Emily. "On the Wings of Morning: The Pornography of Death." Chapter 5 in *Aspects of Death in Early Greek Art and Poetry,* 145–77. Sather Classical Lectures, vol. 46. Berkeley and Los Angeles: University of California Press, 1979.

Vernant, Jean-Pierre. *Mortals and Immortals: Collected Essays.* Edited by Froma I. Zeitlin. Princeton: Princeton University Press, 1991.

Walbank, F. W. *The Hellenistic World.* Rev. ed. Cambridge: Harvard University Press, 1993. This edition was originally published in 1992 (London: Fontana).

Walbank, F. W., A. E. Astin, M. W. Frederiksen, and R. M. Ogilvie, eds. *The Hellenistic World.* Vol. 7.1 of *The Cambridge Ancient History.* 2d ed. London and New York: Cambridge University Press, 1984.

Walker, Steven F. *Theocritus.* Twayne's World Authors, no. 609. Boston: Twayne Publishers, 1980.

Walsh, George B. "The First *Stasimon* of Euripides' *Electra*." *Yale Classical Studies* 25 (1977): 277–89.

Warner, Rex, trans. *The Medea*. In *Euripides I*. The Complete Greek Tragedies, ed. David Grene and Richmond Lattimore. Chicago: University of Chicago Press, 1955. Warner's translation was originally published in 1944.

Webster, T. B. L. *Hellenistic Poetry and Art*. London: Methuen, 1964.

Wells, Robert, trans. *Theocritus: The Idylls*. Reprint. Penguin Classics. London and New York: Penguin Books, 1989. Originally published in 1988 (Manchester: Carcanet).

Wendel, Carol. *Scholia in Theocritum Vetera; Scholia in Technopaegnia Scripta*. Leipzig: B. G. Teubner, 1914.

West, M. L., ed. *Delectus ex Iambis et Elegis Graecis*. Oxford Classical Texts. Oxford: Clarendon Press; New York: Oxford University Press, 1980.

White, Heather. "Spells and Enchantment in Theocritus' Idyll II." Chapter 2 in *Studies in Theocritus and Other Hellenistic Poets*, 17–35. London Studies in Classical Philology, vol. 3. Amsterdam: J. C. Gieben, 1979.

———. "Theocritus' 'Adonis Song'." *Museum Philologum Londiniense* 4 (1981): 191–206.

———. "Two Textual Problems in Theocritus' Idyll XV." Chapter 8 in *Essays in Hellenistic Poetry*, 61–67. London Studies in Classical Philology, vol. 5. Amsterdam: J. C. Gieben, 1980.

Whittaker, C. R. *Herodian*. Vol. 1, *Books I-IV*. Loeb Classical Library. Cambridge: Harvard University Press, 1969.

Wilamowitz-Moellendorff, Ulrich von. "Aratos von Kos." *Nachrichten von der k. Gesellschaft der Wissenschaften zu Göttingen, Philologisch-historische Klasse* (1894): 182–99. Also available in idem, *Kleine Schriften*, vol. 2, *Hellenistische, spätgriechische und lateinische Poesie*, ed. Rudolf Pfeiffer, Rudolf Keydell, and Harald Fuchs, 71–89. Reprint, Berlin: Akademie, 1971.

Will, Édouard. *Histoire politique du monde hellénistique (323–30 av. J.-C.)*. 2d ed. 2 vols. Annales de l'Est, Mémoires nos. 30, 32. Nancy: Presses universitaires de Nancy, 1979–82.

———. "The Succession to Alexander." Chapter 2 in Walbank et al., *Hellenistic World*, 23–61.

Will, Frederic. *Herondas*. Twayne's World Authors, no. 227. New York: Twayne Publishers, 1973.

Williams, Frederick. *Callimachus: Hymn to Apollo: A Commentary*. Oxford: Clarendon Press; New York: Oxford University Press, 1978.

Williams, Raymond. *The Country and the City*. New York: Oxford University Press, 1973.

Winkler, John J. "The Constraints of Eros." In *Magika Hiera: Ancient Greek Magic and Religion*, ed. Christopher A. Faraone and Dirk Obbink, 214–43. New York: Oxford University Press, 1991.

———. "Double Consciousness in Sappho's Lyrics." In *The Constraints of Desire: The Anthropology of Sex and Gender in Ancient Greece*, 162–87. New Ancient World. New York: Routledge, 1990.

———. "The Laughter of the Oppressed: Demeter and the Gardens of Adonis." In *The Constraints of Desire: The Anthropology of Sex and Gender in Ancient Greece*, 188–209. New Ancient World. New York: Routledge, 1990.

———. "Public and Private in Sappho's Lyrics." In Foley, *Reflections of Women*, 63–89.

Wood, Ellen Meiksins. *Peasant-Citizen and Slave: The Foundations of Athenian Democracy*. 1988. Reprint, with corrections, London and New York: Verso, 1989.

Wordsworth, Christopher. *Theocritus*. 2d ed. Cambridge: Deighton Bell and Associates, 1877.

Zanker, Graham. "Current Trends in the Study of Hellenic Myth in Early Third-Century Alexandrian Poetry: The Case of Theocritus." *Antike und Abendland* 35 (1989): 83–103.

———. *Realism in Alexandrian Poetry: A Literature and Its Audience*. London and Wolfeboro, N. H.: Croom Helm, 1987.

Zeitlin, Froma I. "The Artful Eye: Vision, Ecphrasis, and Spectacle in Euripidean Theatre." In Goldhill and Osborne, *Art and Text*, 138–96.

Ziegler, Konrat. "Kallimachos und die Frauen." *Die Antike* 13 (1937): 20–42.

Index

Passages Cited

Aelianus
Varia Historia
  2.3: 213 n. 1
  3.17: 223 n. 4
  13.22: 185 n. 24
Aeschylus
Agamemnon
  1388–92: 217 n. 38
  1444–47: 217 n. 38
Alcaeus of Messene
Epigrams
  9.6 Gow and Page (= *A.P.* 12.64): 239
  n. 156
  9 Gow and Page (= *A.P.* 12.64): 211
  n. 155
Alciphron
Epistulae Meretriciae
  14.8: 230 n. 79
Anacreon
  fr. 356 *P.M.G.*: 203 n. 74
  fr. 383 *P.M.G.*: 203 n. 74
  fr. 409 *P.M.G.*: 203 n. 74
Anthologia Palatina
  7.413: 105
  11.48: 219 n. 59
  13.16: 200 n. 39
Antipater Sidonius
Epigrams
  16 Gow and Page: 193 n. 94
  17 Gow and Page: 193 n. 94
Apollodorus
  1.5.1: 201 n. 51

Apollonius Rhodius
Argonautica
  1.721–67: 216 n. 26
  1.742–46: 213 n. 3
  3.47–54: 188 n. 47
  4.90–91: 64
  4.167–73: 91–92
  4.790–94: 238 n. 151
  4.866–79: 206 n. 101
  4.1726: 201 n. 51
Appian
Syriaca
  63: 3
Archilochus
  114.4 West: 193 n. 92
Aristophanes
Acharnenses
  524–29: 193 n. 85
  960: 194–95 n. 108
Lysistrata
  378–98: 230 n. 80
  387–98: 146
  781–96: 198 n. 28
Nubes
  964–66: 210 n. 145
  973–76: 210 n. 145
Ranae
  1108: 217 n. 43
Vespae
  1253–55: 26
Aristotle
apud Cicero *Brutus*
  46: 184 n. 11

Composition: G & S Typesetters, Inc.
Text: 10/13 Galliard
Display: Galliard
Printing and binding: Thomson-Shore, Inc.

Date Due